The SAGE Dictionary of
Sports Studies

Dominic Malcolm

SAGE Publications
Los Angeles · London · New Delhi · Singapore

First published 2008

SAGE Publications Ltd
1 Oliver's Yard
55 City Road
London EC1Y 1SP

SAGE Publications Inc.
2455 Teller Road
Thousand Oaks, California 91320

SAGE Publications India Pvt Ltd
B 1/I 1 Mohan Cooperative Industrial Area
Mathura Road, New Delhi 110 044

SAGE Publications Asia-Pacific Pte Ltd
33 Pekin Street #02-01
Far East Square
Singapore 048763

Library of Congress Control Number: 2007922934

British Library Cataloguing in Publication data

A catalogue record for this book is available
from the British Library

ISBN 978-1-4129-0734-7
ISBN 978-1-4129-0735-4 (pbk)

Typeset by C&M Digitals (P) Ltd., Chennai, India
Printed on paper from sustainable resources
Printed in India at Replika Press Pvt. Ltd.

Contents

CONTENTS

List of Contributors

Alan Bairner, Loughborough University, UK

John Bale, Aarhus Universitet, Denmark; Keele University, Staffordshire, UK

Celia Brackenridge, Brunel University, Uxbridge, UK

Susan Capel, Brunel University, Uxbridge, UK

Ben Carrington, University of Texas at Austin, US

Jay Coakley, University of Colorado at Colorado Springs, US

Tim Crabbe, Sheffield Hallam University, UK

Garry Crawford, University of Salford, UK

Mike Cronin, Boston College, Dublin, Republic of Ireland

Paul Darby, University of Ulster at Jordanstown, Northern Ireland

Peter Donnelly, University of Toronto, Canada

Simon Eassom, Victoria University, Melbourne, Australia

Chris Gratton, Sheffield Hallam University, UK

Ken Green, University of Chester, UK

Patricia Griffin, University of Massachusetts, Amherst, US

Allen Guttmann, Amherst College, Massachusetts, US

John D. Horne, Edinburgh University, Scotland, UK

Barrie Houlihan, Loughborough University, UK

P. David Howe, Loughborough University, UK

Martin Johnes, University of Wales, Swansea, Wales, UK

Tara Magdalinski, University of Queensland, Australia

Louise Mansfield, Canterbury Christ Church University, Canterbury, UK

Andrew Parker, University of Warwick, UK

Dawn Penney, University of Tasmania, Tasmania, Australia

Emma Rich, Loughborough University, UK

David Rowe, University of Western Sydney, Australia

Kimberly S. Schimmel, Kent State University, Ohio, US

Andy Smith, University of Chester, UK

Jennifer Smith Maguire, University of Leicester, UK

Nigel Thomas, Staffordshire University, UK

Ivan Waddington, Norwegian School of Sport Sciences, Oslo, Norway; University College Dublin, Republic of Ireland; University of Chester, UK

Mike Weed, Canterbury Christ Church University, Canterbury, UK

Belinda Wheaton, University of Brighton, UK

List of Abbreviations

AGIL	adaption, goal attainment, integration and latency (or pattern maintenance)
ATP	Association of Tennis Professionals
BASEM	British Association of Sport and Exercise Medicine
BMI	body-mass index
CARE	Charlton Athletic Race Equality
CCCS	Centre for Contemporary Cultural Studies
CCPR	Central Council of Physical Recreation
CCT	compulsory competitive tendering
CCTV	closed-circuit television
CPSU	Child Protection in Sport Unit
CSA	child sexual abuse
DSO	Direct Service Provider
EPO	erythropoietin
FA	Football Association
FARE	Football Against Racism in Europe
FIFA	Fédération Internationale de Football Association
FSA	Football Supporters' Association
GAA	Gaelic Athletic Association
GCSE	General Certificate of Education
HRE	Health Related Exercise
HRPE	Health-Related Physical Education
ICF	International Classification of Functioning, Disability and Health
ICIDH	International Classification of Impairment, Disability and Handicap
IGB	international governing body
IMUSA	Independent Manchester United Supporters' Association
IOC	International Olympic Committee
ISA	independent supporters' association
ITE	Initial Teacher Education

LGBT	lesbian, gay, bisexual and transsexual
MCC	Marylebone Cricket Club
MMSL	multidimensional model of sports leadership
NBA	National Basketball Association
NCAA	National Collegiate Athletic Association
NCPE	National Curriculum for Physical Education
NFL	National Football League
NHL	National Hockey League
NOC	national olympic committee
NSPCC	National Society for the Prevention of Cruelty to Children
PE	physical education
PESSCL	Physical Education and School Sport Club Links
PFA	Professional Footballers Association
POMS	profile of mood states
RFU	Rugby Football Union
SANROC	South African Non-Racial Olympic Committee
SEN	special educational needs
SSC	Specialist Sports College
TOP	The Olympic Partner Programme
UCI	Union Cycliste International
UEFA	Union of European Football Associations
UPIAS	Union of the Physically Impaired Against Segregation
WADA	World Anti-Doping Agency
WHO	World Health Organization
WTA	Women's Tennis Association
YMCA	Young Men's Christian Association

Introduction

Sports studies is an emerging academic discipline, reputed to be the fastest growing subject area in the UK. The impetus for this growth appears to be market driven. In part this is a consequence of the expansion of employment opportunities in the sport and leisure fields. Gratton and Taylor (2000: 19) note that employment in sport in the UK rose by 28 per cent between 1985 and 1995, and that by the end of that period sport accounted for 1.61 per cent of the total UK workforce. By 2003 the figure for sports-related employment had risen to 2 per cent (or approximately 515,000 jobs). The leisure industry (much of which is sporting or sports-related) is even larger, employing 13.5 per cent of UK workers (Prospects.ac.uk).

But this growth in employment is itself partly a consequence of the increasing cultural centrality of sport in Western cultures in recent years. Once a peripheral or playful aspect of social life, sport is now centre stage. Almost a third of the UK population tuned in to watch Portugal knock England out of the 2006 FIFA World Cup Finals. But sport is more properly a global phenomenon. An incredible 1.5 billion television viewers worldwide are estimated to have watched the tournament's opening match and FIFA estimated that over 30 billion people would watch some television coverage of the tournament.

This dictionary is another consequence of the growing recognition in recent years of sport's social significance. A number of the entries contained herein describe this growth in more detail. Some bring these modern phenomena into sharper relief by providing comparisons with the sports forms of previous eras and some highlight the social issues that have arisen in conjunction with these changes. Other entries look at the psychological techniques and the social policies used to make sport 'work' more effectively for us as participants and citizens, while others detail the methods by which researchers have attempted to understand more about the social world of sport. And some entries introduce the reader to the theoretical concepts that are being used to make sense of these developments. Sports studies is an emerging discipline, and thus much of the clarification, definition and consolidation that other subjects take for granted, still needs to be achieved. This dictionary is intended as a tool to be used for this end; an educational resource for all those interested in the study of the social aspects of sport.

As with all emerging disciplines subject to relatively rapid change, it is difficult to define clearly where the boundaries lie; to pin down exactly what sports studies is. The one thing that is clear about sports studies is that it is, fundamentally, a multidisciplinary subject; however, from this consensus there are many points of departure. Indeed, like the folk games played in England during medieval times, the same name may be given to degree courses (or games) with radically different structures and contents, and a range of different names can be given to courses (or games) that are essentially the same. For instance, some courses labelled 'sports studies' retain significant elements of the natural scientific study of sport; what I will refer to here as 'sports science'. Others labelled 'sports studies' have a not dissimilar content to those labelled 'sport, leisure and culture' or 'sport, culture and the media'. Such variation makes the decision over what (sub-)disciplines to include far from easy. For better or worse the main categories used when drawing up the list of entries have been: sociology; history; psychology; economics, management and business; politics and policy; physical education and health; and research methods. There is also a passing mention of sports geography and sports anthropology.

However, the challenge for students of sports studies is not to see these areas as compartmentalized, but to embrace the interdisciplinary nature of the subject. Many entries contained in the dictionary cut across these disciplinary boundaries. Only once was it necessary to include entries from different disciplines for a single subject – for both psychologists and sociologists emotion was too significant a topic to be covered adequately in one entry. More commonly, it has been possible to include a number of different disciplinary perspectives in the same entry (e.g. the entry for broadcasting rights contains a discussion of both economic and sociological approaches). My hope is that such an approach will help students to reflect more critically on sporting phenomena.

Once the general areas of study were decided upon, the next challenge was to draw up a list of entries which was broadly representative of these different approaches, and to write entries which were inclusive of the range of views on, and approaches to, particular subjects. In this respect a dictionary entails different challenges to many other forms of academic writing. For most researchers, their discipline and particular theoretical orientation exerts a significant influence upon which research path they forge. My training as a sociologist, and in particular a sociologist who is largely known for his work within the figurational sociological tradition, is both constraining and enabling in this respect. Regardless of the subject matter, it is impossible to put one's 'sociological imagination' to one side; thus, whilst this dictionary is multidisciplinary, inevitably there is a bias towards sociology. To some degree this is a constraint but if any discipline should dominate it is probably appropriate that it should be sociology. As Coakley and Dunning argue, sociology was the first sport-related sub-discipline to emerge in an institutionalized form and is now the best established (2000: xxi).

But my particular sociological approach also lends itself to the multidisciplinary nature of sports studies and the production of the kind of publication attempted here. Elias, upon whose work figurational sociology is largely founded, considered himself not simply as a sociologist, but as 'a human scientist ... (who) concerned himself with studying humans "in the round"; that is, in their bio-, psycho, socio-historical aspects and with the complex ... ways in which these aspects are interconnected' (Dunning, 2002: 215).

The dictionary, however, is not solely the product of my labours. I am very grateful to the 33 guest authors who have provided 41 different entries. This has been invaluable in helping me to bridge those areas where my understanding was not so thorough. Whilst they largely determined the content of and deserve the credit for those entries, the overall selection, and the breadth and comprehensive nature of the coverage of the dictionary as a whole, have been my responsibility. The degree to which I have been successful in this endeavour can be judged only by the degree to which students who use this text find it useful, and by the extent to which other teachers of sports studies recommend the dictionary to their students because they feel that subjects have been presented in a fair and even-handed way.

What can readers expect from the dictionary and how should it be used? It should be reiterated that the focus of this dictionary is the social aspects of sport: on the whole it does not report on particular sporting feats or contests. The exceptions to this – such as entries for Heysel and Hillsborough – concern events that had a broader social impact, that evoked changes in policy or altered perceptions about sport, its participants and spectators. Similar criteria were applied to the selection of individuals. Again, the remit of this dictionary was not to include the biographies of the great and the good of sport. However, a few individuals – notably David Beckham and Michael Jordan – have been included. These people have been included not because they have been particularly successful in their fields (though, of course, this is often the case) but because their broader social impact has subsequently become the focus of academic research in sports studies. Finally, while it has not been my intention to provide a comprehensive coverage of key texts in sports studies, some classic works have been included as entries. My reason for doing this was that some texts have become so seminal that often writers refer to them without fully describing to the reader what ideas that text conveyed. This, my teaching experience has shown me, can sometimes cause problems for those who are relatively new to the area.

Particular texts, events and individuals, however, rarely form the focus of academic curricula or modules of study. My intention in compiling this dictionary has been to provide something which will be directly relevant to students' programmes of study. To this end, I hope that the dictionary will be used in a number of ways: as an essential tool for students of sports studies to turn to when, in the process of reading and researching, concepts and ideas are raised, about which they wish to know more or simply clarify meaning; as a reference source, providing a quick source of factual information; and as a means to obtain a baseline of knowledge, a grasp of the essential points related to a particular area. But the dictionary is also intended to be used at the start of the research process and consequently most entries not only provide a concise definition, but highlight the key debates and the main research topics on a particular theme. In this respect the dictionary also provides an entry point into the field and this is the rationale behind providing a short list of key readings for all, or almost all, entries. In addition to this, most entries include links to other entries in the dictionary (signalled by the use of bold type). These links are designed to encourage 'joined up' thinking and enable the dictionary to be a research resource in itself. By consulting a range of different entries the reader will be able to gain a broader appreciation of a topic and its many related facets.

However this dictionary is used, I hope that the reader finds it informative and enlightening. Most of all, however, I hope that students of sports studies who use the dictionary find it a stimulating experience, and are encouraged to continue their engagement with the field. Sports studies is not only an area that I myself have enjoyed studying, but one which is increasingly gaining recognition for its importance, and its ability to help us understand the social world in which we live.

References

Coakley, J. and Dunning, E. (2000) *Handbook of Sports Studies*. London: Sage.

Dunning, E. (2002) 'Figurational contributions to the sociological study of sport', in J. Maguire and K. Young (eds), *Theory, Sport & Society*. London: Jai. pp. 211–38.

Gratton, C. and Taylor, P. (2000) *Economics of Sport and Recreation*. London: Routledge.

A

ABORIGINE

The term aborigine (or aboriginal) refers to any of the indigenous populations that existed before the arrival of colonial settlers. Most commonly we use the term aborigine to refer to the indigenous populations of Australia (usually Aborigine) and North America (usually Native American). However, continuing the legacy of the colonial settlers, this labelling tends to have the effect of falsely homogenizing what are, in fact, very diverse and culturally distinct populations.

What aborigine populations do tend to have in common is their displacement and persecution at the hands of colonial settlers. Many aspects of traditional aboriginal culture (including what appears to have been a very rich sport/leisure tradition) have been wiped out as native populations have been forced to conform to the ways of European colonizers (**imperialism**). Sport has, historically, played a central role in the attempts of colonizers to assimilate and 'civilize' aborigine communities. Throughout the process of colonization, integration has been characterized by persistent persecution, racism and continuing disadvantage. Such has been the scale of suffering that aborigines now tend to constitute only very small minority populations (e.g. accounting for just 1 per cent of Australia's and 2 per cent of Canada's total population. There are about 2.1 million Native Americans among the 300 million citizens of the United States).

Research on aboriginal sport centres on two separate processes: the representation of aborigine athletes in mainstream sport and the attempt to sustain aborigine cultures and identities via sports events specifically designed for, and restricted to, indigenous populations. With regard to the former, despite the relative absence of mainstream sporting opportunities for aborigine men and women, a few internationally significant aborigine athletes have emerged; most notably Billy Mills, a Native American athlete who won the 10,000 metres at the 1964 Olympics, Australian tennis star Evonne Goolagong, Canadian athlete Angela Chalmers, and Cathy Freeman, Australian winner of the women's 400 metres at the Sydney Olympics of 2000. The press have largely portrayed these athletes as 'success stories', overcoming adversity to achieve sporting success. However, such athletes have had to tread a delicate path between conforming to 'white' or mainstream expectations (and thus being allowed to participate, receive government funding, etc.) and not appearing so integrated as to invoke the anger of, and perhaps be rejected by, their aborigine communities (Freeman, for instance, held both an Australian and an Aboriginal flag during her victory lap in Sydney).

Participation in major sports events has provided the opportunity to make poignant political and social statements. While Cathy Freeman's actions and media portrayal bolstered the image of Australian national unity and harmony, the staging of the Olympics in Sydney allowed others to make more radical and critical statements. There were complaints about the marginalization of Aborigines in the Sydney organizing and bidding committees, complaints over the portrayal of Aborigines in the Sydney bid, and a campaign which argued that state-perpetrated human rights abuses against Aborigines should effectively disqualify Australia from hosting the games. While few tangible concessions were won, the Games did provide the opportunity to raise awareness and make issues such as inequality and ingrained racism increasingly prominent.

Outside the mainstream, Eurocentric, sports system, the establishment of 'all-aboriginal' sports and festivals (e.g. the Yuendumu Games or 'Black Olympics' in Australia, and the 'Northern Games' in Canada) are attempts to reverse the decline of indigenous cultures and redefine ethnic identities. Moreover, there are increasing movements towards 'international' sporting forums and events for indigenous populations (the International Aboriginal Cup between indigenous Australians and Canadians, for instance). However, those athletes integrated into, and successful within, 'mainstream' sport often feel alienated from these all-aboriginal events because their assimilation has entailed a degree of distancing from their own culture. Ironically, at the same time they tend to feel alienated within mainstream sport due to the persistence of racism (**race**).

Finally, a number of authors have noted that American team sports tend to draw on Native American names and/or symbols, e.g. the Washington Redskins. Rather than being respectful of these cultures, the use of such symbols tends to perpetuate a stereotype that unsympathetically evokes the history of violent persecution which aborigine communities have faced. Such insensitivity is clearly likely to contribute to the social exclusion of aborigines in sport in particular, and in society more generally.

Key Reading

Hargreaves, J.A. (2000) *Heroines of Sport: The Politics of Difference and Identity*. London: Routledge. esp. Ch. 4.

Oxendine, J. (1988) *American Indian Sports Heritage*. Champaign, IL: Human Kinetics.
Tatz, C. (1987) *Aborigines in Sport*. Adelaide, South Australia; Australian Society for Sports History.

AEROBICS

Aerobics and similar kinds of 'exercise to music' physical activities emerged in the 1970s, popularized particularly through the Jane Fonda 'workout' video. The vast majority of aerobics participants are female and while competitive and sport-like aerobics events exist (**sport, definition of**), it is largely as part of the development of a broader fitness industry that sociologists of sport have analysed aerobics. Sociological focus has centred on the relevance of aerobics in terms of **gender** relations and the sociology of the **body**. For instance, though it is claimed that this group of activities served to promote more active images of femininity, through the use of lycra and 'figure hugging' clothing, it also fuelled the **sexualization** of the sporting female body.

Margaret MacNeil (1988) was perhaps the first social scientist to examine this type of physical activity, noting that the television production of aerobics (e.g. the camera angles, lighting, etc.) portrayed women's physical activities as something close to soft pornography. Moreover, exercise classes, clothing and videos represented a **commodification** of feminine style. Females are 'sold' these narcissistic commodities via sexuality and glamour and through this process, which associates women more with appearance than performance, the view that sport is a male-appropriate and female-inappropriate activity is perpetuated.

Similarly Maguire and Mansfield (1998) argue that women take part in aerobics largely because they are persuaded that participation will enable them to achieve what Markula (1995) has called the 'firm but shapely, fit but sexy, strong but thin' body. Women seek to lose fat, and tone and shape their muscles to produce a slender, tight body in accordance with idealized images of the female figure. However, theorists largely agree that while women's increased participation in sport (and sport-like activities such as aerobics) is a positive development, there are considerable negative consequences of their increasing popularity. Markula (1995), for instance, argues that women wish to conform to the 'feminine ideal' but perceive its actualization to be impossible. The typical aerobics setting, in highly mirrored rooms, acts as a form of **surveillance** and control. Aerobics thus becomes disciplinary (**discipline**) and restrictive. Consequently, aerobicizing women come to hate those very parts of their body which define them as women. The logical outcome of this, Markula argues, is that women come to hate looking like women. However, it is also important to note that research has increasingly shown that there is a clear contradiction between the dominant images associated with aerobics and the personal experiences of many women. Rather than being oppressive, participating in aerobics classes provides a safe and sociable environment that is both pleasurable in itself, but may also enhance self-esteem.

Key Reading

MacNeil, M. (1988) 'Active women, media representations, and ideology', in J. Harvey and H. Cantelon (eds), *Not Just a Game: Essays in Canadian Sport Sociology*. Ottawa: Ottawa University Press, pp. 195–211.

Maguire, J. and Mansfield, L. (1998) 'Nobody's perfect: women, aerobics and the body beautiful', *Sociology of Sport Journal*, 15 (2): 109–37.

Markula, P. (1995) 'Firm but shapely, fit but sexy, strong but thin: the postmodern aerobicizing female bodies', *Sociology of Sport Journal*, 12 (4): 424–53.

AGE

(lifestyle sports; retirement; youth sport participation)

AGENCY AND STRUCTURE

Sociologists widely agree that social phenomena are mainly determined by a combination of two main factors: agency and structure. However, they are divided over the relative significance of agency and structure, and the relationship between the two. Some (e.g. advocates of structural **functionalism** and more traditional froms of **Marxism**) argue that social life is largely determined by social structure, and that human actions are a product of that structure (these might be termed macro-sociological approaches). Others (e.g. advocates of **symbolic interactionism**) emphasize the capacity of individuals to shape the social world (these might be termed micro-sociological approaches. See **macro- and micro-sociology**). For instance, whilst the former might explain the deviant behaviour of elite athletes (drug taking, violence, etc.) as a product of the organization of professional sport, the latter might explain such behaviour as a product of a more 'individual' choice relating to how people see themselves and/or would like others to see them; in other words, identity.

A third group of sociological theories (e.g. **figurational sociology**; **structuration theory**) takes as their starting point the 'dilemma' that sociologists have traditionally had in understanding, and speaking about, the relationship between agency and structure (also referred to as the individual and society); the so-called 'agency–structure dilemma'. Linguistically, just by referring to agency and structure (e.g. 'the athlete' and 'the sports system') we necessarily separate out that which is, in reality, one and the same. The humans that sociologists study are social beings, against which asocial humans would provide a sharp contrast, i.e. there would be no language, no regular, patterned or consistent ways of behaving, and no social norms. However, it also makes little sense to conceptualize society as somehow distinct, or existing separately, from human beings. Society is nothing more and nothing less than the networks of relationships formed by human beings.

The dilemma for sociologists is to avoid both the reductionism inherent in focusing too closely upon the individual/agency, and the tendency towards **reification**, which accompanies a strong emphasis on the determinant nature of society/structure. In attempts to overcome such problems, terms such as figuration and structuration have been introduced. Followers of Bourdieu have also argued that his concept of **habitus** has successfully overcome this dilemma.

Key Reading

Dunning, E. (1992) 'Figurational sociology and the sociology of sport: some concluding remarks', in E. Dunning and C. Rojek (eds), *Sport and Leisure in the Civilizing Process: Critique and Counter-Critique*. Basingstoke: Macmillan. pp. 221–84.

AGGRESSION

An everyday term used to encapsulate a broad range of behaviours, from a rather forward approach (e.g. to driving a car) to physical attack. Consequently, for use as an analytic term, sports researchers define it rather more narrowly. Aggression is generally defined as intended behaviour that results in physical or psychological harm or injury to another living thing. Aggressive acts may be verbal or physical. They should be distinguished from **violence** (which is generally deemed to be more extreme) and assertive behaviour (where there is no intent to harm). However, aggression can be further subdivided into: (1) hostile (or reactive) aggression, where

the intent to harm is primary; and (2) instrumental aggression, where the intent to harm may be a secondary goal, e.g. to winning a game, scoring a goal, etc.

In defining aggression, and distinguishing aggression from similar behaviours, a number of factors tend to be considered. In addition to the intent to do harm, acts are normally labelled aggressive only if they violate social norms. The perceived degree of injury or harm inflicted is also likely to be influential. Beyond this it is known that one's direct involvement and one's relationship to the perpetrator and victim influence the categorization of behaviour as aggression (e.g. a parent is more likely to define behaviour towards their child as aggressive, than might a more neutral observer), as does the perception of the social context (behaviour in a place of worship is likely to be defined differently to behaviour on a football pitch).

One of the main difficulties aggression poses for social scientists is that it is particularly difficult to measure. External measures may include crime statistics or, for sport, penalty and foul counts. However, these measures are problematic as not all fouls are aggressive, and not all aggressive acts result in fouls. Moreover, external measures necessarily focus more on the outcome (i.e. injury, harm) than the intention. However, external measures may have more validity when assessing what forms of aggression should be/are deemed legitimate, and what contextual factors (e.g. crowd noise) are likely to increase aggression (**aggression, causes of**).

Internal measures of aggression involve investigating the individual's desire to aggress, and individual perceptions of aggression. Measures such as asking athletes how often they feel aggressive are, however, problematic due to the incongruity between aggressive feelings and aggressive acts, the tendency for a time delay between the aggressive acts and the perpetrator's assessment, and the disinclination of research subjects to discuss openly what might be deemed deviant acts (**deviance**).

Key Reading

Gill, D. (2000) *Psychological Dynamics of Sport and Exercise.* Champaign, IL: Human Kinetics.

Kerr, J.H (2004) *Rethinking Aggression and Violence in Sport.* London: Routledge.

Widmeyer, W.N., Dorsch, K. D., Bray, S.R. and McGuire, E.J. (2002) 'The nature, prevalence and consequences of aggression in sport', in J.M. Silva and D.E. Stevens (eds), *Psychological Foundations of Sport.* Boston: Allyn and Bacon. pp. 328–51.

AGGRESSION, CAUSES OF

There are three general approaches to the causes of **aggression**. While these encompass a far wider range of theories and more explicit explanations, generally speaking, aggression is viewed as something that is: (1) biologically determined; (2) learned; or (3) stimulated/triggered by specific events.

The first explanations of aggression were largely biologically based. Instinct theory, for instance, suggests that people have an innate instinct for aggression; it may build up and then need to be expressed, leading to **catharsis**. There is, however, little empirical evidence to support the existence of an innate and/or pent up body of aggression, and thus there is a tendency for this argument to be circular (people are aggressive because they have an aggressive instinct; we know that people have this aggressive instinct because they are aggressive). Related to this is the theory that aggression is related to testosterone and while some evidence suggests that higher testosterone levels may lead individuals to be more aggressive, people with relatively low testosterone levels (e.g. females) can also be aggressive.

The second general approach encompasses **social learning theory**. This essentially suggests that aggression is learned as a result of direct and indirect experience, and direct and indirect reinforcement (e.g. through reward for, or the non punishment of, aggressive behaviour).

The third approach is epitomized by the Frustration-Aggression Theory. This states that aggression is the consequence of frustration (such as an inability to achieve a particular goal), and hence losing teams commit more fouls than winning teams, impeded players may strike opponents, etc. (this too may lead to **catharsis**). The problem for this theory is that it is either circular (frustration causes aggression, but we only know that people are frustrated because they become aggressive) or that there is clear counter-evidence (examples where frustration does not manifest itself as aggression). Berkowitz's reformulation (1993) – that frustration may not lead to aggression, but increases **arousal** and anger and therefore the *propensity* to be aggressive – combines elements of frustration-aggression and social learning theories and is currently one of the most popular explanations of the causes of aggression.

Research in sports psychology has centred around these three general approaches. Researchers have looked at those situations that might increase frustration, such as particular rivalries, losing at home as opposed to losing away from home, losing late in the game, losing by large margins or to opponents one considers inferior/as a consequence of underperforming. Aggression may also be the product of retaliation but this, of course, begs the question what caused the aggressive act that sparked the retaliation. Researchers have also examined how aggressive behaviour may be learnt (e.g. from interaction with parents and coaches) as well as what, more specifically, has been learnt. Athletes therefore might be aggressive because they perceive such actions to have been beneficial to them in the past. Athletes may engage in aggressive behaviour because they see themselves as fulfilling a particular role (**group dynamics**), because they wish to present themselves to others in a certain way (e.g. to demonstrate commitment to team mates and coaches and augment their place in the team), or because aggressive behaviour is seen as an important part of group norms and team **cohesion**. Finally, it has been suggested that aggression stems from **motivation**; more specifically, that those who are highly ego-oriented are more likely to be aggressive than those who are task-oriented or who are disengaged or express indifference.

In addition to these theories it should be remembered that aggression is contoured by broader social factors. More specifically, it is clear that **gender**, social **class** and age influence aggression (most aggressive acts are perpetrated by young, working-class males; see e.g. **football hooliganism**) and that the definition of an act as aggressive is culturally and temporally specific (i.e. in different societies, at different times, people tend to tolerate different levels of violence; see e.g. **civilizing process**).

Key Reading

Berkowitz, L. (1993) *Aggression: Its Causes, Consequences and Control*. New York: Atherton Press.

Kerr, J.H. (2004) *Rethinking Aggression and Violence in Sport*. London: Routledge.

Widmeyer, W.N., Bray, S.R., Dorsch, K.D. and McGuire, E.J. (2002) 'Explanations for the occurrence of aggression', in J.M. Silva and D. E. Stevens (eds), *Psychological Foundations of Sport*. Boston: Allyn and Bacon. pp. 352–79.

ALCOHOL

Collins and Vamplew (2002) describe the link between alcohol and sport as symbiotic; that is to say, it is difficult to conceive of one without the other. In their book, *Mud, Sweat and Beers*, they trace this relationship through four angles: the role of the public house as the initial basis of many sports teams (**commercialization**), but now as the venue for the consumption of televised sports coverage (**post-fandom**); the ways in which the brewing industry has used sport to sell alcohol (**sponsorship** and advertising); the relationship between alcohol and the behaviour of sports crowds (**puritans**' objections to sport, and more recent concerns about **football hooliganism**); and changing attitudes towards alcohol's relationship with sports performance, used as a performance enhancing drug in the early twentieth century (**drugs**), now viewed as highly detrimental to **health**. In addition to this, sociologists have been concerned to examine the role of alcohol in (predominantly) male sports such as rugby, and in initiation, or 'hazing', rituals in university and college sports. Drinking alcohol (especially in large quantities) is often closely linked to **masculinity** and should thus be seen as a gendered social practice (**gender**).

Key Reading

Collins, T. and Vamplew, W. (2002) *Mud, Sweat and Beers: A Cultural History of Sport and Alcohol*. Oxford: Berg.

Sheard, K. and Dunning, E. (1973) 'The rugby club as a type of male preserve: some sociological notes', *International Review of Sport Sociology*, 8 (1): 5–24.

Vamplew, W. (2005) 'Drink and the sportsperson: an anomolous alliance', *Sport in History*, 25 (3): 390–411.

ALIENATION

In its broadest sense alienation refers simply to estrangement or a lack of involvement in a situation, social group or community. In its more sociologically rigorous sense, alienation is a concept used by Marxists (**Marxism**) to describe the social relations of production within capitalist societies. For Marx, human potential and creativity develop out of social relations. However, in the exploitative framework of capitalist production (where wages are kept low and maximum profit extracted from the workers' labour) human development is stifled. Workers are subject to the demands and interests of the owners of capital, work has no intrinsic satisfaction, and thus human creativity cannot develop. The social relations of capitalism, Marxists claim, are played out in sport just as they are in any other capitalist industry. Athletes sell their labour power and lose control of their product (the sporting contest) and are thus alienated just as workers are in more conventional forms of industrial production.

Marxists also stress the importance of the relationship between the producer and the product in generating alienation. When the object (commodity) that the worker produces does not belong to him/her, but to their employer (**commodification**), and when, as in modern highly specialized industries, the worker is confined to a small part of the broader production process (seeing little of the end-product or its consumption), feelings of alienation are generated. In the sporting context, athletes may come to see themselves as interchangeable pieces in a broader production machine (i.e. a substitute in a team sport). Training, which breaks down sporting practices to their smallest parts, is akin to work on a factory production line, where the final product is obscured from the producer. Thus the relationship between the producer and the product in sport under capitalism leads to the athlete's alienation.

The sporting use of alienation, however, is taken slightly further by Jean-Marie Brohm (1978) who argues that participation in sport in capitalist societies leads the athlete to become alienated not just from the practice of sport, but from his/her own **body**. The body becomes just a means to an end, an instrument or tool within the production process. Modern **sports medicine** practices may lead athletes to have little or no control over their body, and **drugs** may reduce one's capacity to even 'feel' one's body.

Key Reading

Beamish, R. (1982) 'The political economy of professional sport', in J. Harvey and H. Cantelon (eds), *Not Just a Game: Essays in Canadian Sport Sociology*. Ottawa: University of Ottawa Press. pp. 141–57.

Brohm, J.-M. (1978) *Sport – A Prison of Measured Time*. London: Ink Links.

ALTERNATIVE SPORTS

(**lifestyle sports**)

AMATEURISM

The creed of not being paid to play can be understood only in relation to people actually being paid to play; amateurism was a response to professionalism. Indeed, conflicts between ideals of amateurism and professionalism were central to the culture and governance of British sport from the late nineteenth century. Yet amateurism was about more than money: it was an ideology, a code of conduct, an outlook on sport and life. Combining nineteenth-century middle-class ideas and older upper-class sporting ideals, amateurism involved playing the game for its own sake rather than winning, an adherence to **fair play** and disciplinary codes, a disdain for **gambling**, and winning with grace but losing without candour.

Above all, amateurism was about social position. To be an amateur in late Victorian and Edwardian Britain was to not need paying in order to play. Thus enforcing amateur regulations was about displaying status (**class**; **social stratification**), avoiding too much mixing with the masses and preventing the challenges to the older hierarchies that were beginning to emerge in the realms of work and politics. In cricket, for example, where amateurs and professionals often played in the same team, social distinction was preserved through the use of different changing rooms and different ways of writing names and, initially, by requiring professionals to labour with bowling and even menial tasks such as cleaning the kit. Yet, despite the snobbery that underpinned amateurism, there was a general reluctance in most sports to impose explicit class-based restrictions on participation, though rowing and athletics were nineteenth-century exceptions. In most amateur sports, exclusion was enforced more subtly, through relying on economic realities to ensure working men could not afford time off work to play with their social betters.

The impact of controversies over amateurism can be clearly seen in rugby. The growth of socially mixed northern teams in the late nineteenth century led to **broken-time payments**, where working men were compensated for missing work in order to play. Such payments, however, not only offended the amateur principles of some of the elite, but also threatened to take power away from the middle classes, both on and off the playing field. These tensions, fuelled by north–south rivalries, were so profound that they led rugby to split into two codes, later known as league and union, in 1895.

Of course, the rhetoric of amateurism did not always match reality. Nowhere was this clearer than in the case of cricketer W. G. Grace (1848–1915). Undoubtedly the most famous sportsman of the Victorian era, Grace was a doctor and a gentleman but he was also supremely competitive and certainly not above gamesmanship and demanding excessively generous expenses. Definitions of amateurism and regulations over what expenses and payments were permissible varied from sport to sport and diversified as the twentieth century progressed. Amateurism thus evolved into a code defined as much by the circumstances and prejudices of an individual sport's administrators as by its historic origins. 'Shamateurism' was as common as amateurism.

Although amateurism was tied up with notions of Britain's social and moral superiority, it did spread across the globe with the diffusion of British sports (**globalization**; **imperialism**) and was championed as much for the link it created with British sporting ideals as its own perceived worth. Thus while British soccer sanctioned professionalism in 1885, professionalism did not become common in Continental Europe until the 1920s. Even then amateurism remained influential and West German football did not become professional on a full time basis until 1963.

Television was to prove the undoing of amateurism in elite sport. Extensive **media** coverage opened up opportunities to exploit sport commercially and enrich its heroes (**commercialization**). This created tensions between the amateur traditions of the administrators and the commercial demands of sport's star performers. Distinctions between amateurs and professionals were also becoming increasingly anachronistic in post-1945 Britain, when the rigid and snobbish class system, which had given birth to the classifications, was crumbling. Furthermore, amid the rhetoric of national decline that was so common in early post-war Britain, professionalizing industry and administration was deemed important to modernizing the nation. Amateurism was thus increasingly outdated in sport and beyond.

The amateur ideal was nonetheless resilient. Cricket abolished the professional–amateur distinction in 1963 but athletics did not permit payment for performance until 1981. Other sports responded to tensions by slowly becoming explicitly commercial (as in the case of professional golf), by turning a blind eye to transgressions of the amateur code (as in the case of parts of rugby union), or by essentially allowing paid amateurs (as in tennis). Ultimately, money ruled and amateurism gave way to commercial pressures across senior sport. Rugby union was one of the last to embrace professionalism, but when it did so in 1995 the change was sudden and profound, revolutionizing the character and foundations of the game overnight. The sport's traditions and history were cast aside, as its administrators feared being left behind in a marketplace dominated by television.

The ideology of modern Olympism (**IOC**) was also influenced profoundly by the ideals of British amateurism; fair play and the valuing of taking part over winning were key components of the Olympic philosophy. But the growing television coverage of the Olympics, and the commercialization that coverage brought, undermined the stance taken by the International Olympic Committee (**IOC**) on amateurism. Suspicions over the extent to which state-sponsored athletes of the communist bloc were actually unpaid also helped undermine the amateur status of the Games in the West, where there was an unwillingness to uphold the ethos if it meant losing to Cold War rivals (**propaganda**). There was also something hypocritical about the accusations of professionalism levelled at the communist states from Western athletes who drew income from **athletic scholarships** in US colleges. The huge commercial success of the 1984 Los Angeles Games opened the floodgates for change and the Olympics became overtly professionalized. Olympic boxing remains amateur but this situation stems from the unwillingness of professional promoters to cede their own influence to the Olympic movement. Other Olympic events, especially those played by women, also remained amateur, but this was more rooted in a lack of commercial interest in the sports than any ideological stance.

By the end of the twentieth century amateurism had come to mean unprofessional, not in the sense of not being paid but rather in not performing competently. An ideology that had dominated the origins of **modern sport** and influenced its course across the globe had died at the hands of the very pressures that had given it a *raison d'être*. Commercialism and the influence of money undermined amateurism but perhaps this was inevitable in the capitalist global market (**globalization**).

Key Reading

Allison, L. (2001) *Amateurism in Sport: An Analysis and a Defence*. London: Frank Cass.

Holt, R. (1990) *Sport and the British: A Modern History*. Oxford: Oxford University Press.

Smith, A. and Porter, D. (eds) (2000) *Amateurs and Professionals in Post-War British Sport*. London: Frank Cass.

Martin Johnes

AMBUSH MARKETING

Developed in the 1990s, ambush marketing in sport emerged out of the broader growth in the **sponsorship** of sport. In contrast to conventional sponsors who pay the sports team/event/individual for the right to be associated with an activity, ambush marketers seek to give consumers the impression of association, without actually paying a fee to the team/event/individual. Sometimes this is done to weaken the impact of a competitor's official sponsorship of an activity, and serves thus to confuse the consumer and misrepresent the official sponsorship of the event.

Ambush marketing may take the form of: (1) sponsoring the *broadcasting* of an event (which is normally cheaper) rather than sponsoring the event itself; (2) aggressively placing commercials during the televising of an event; (3) sponsoring a team or individual involved in the event; and (4) promotion and marketing that draw on the broader cultural themes generated by an event (e.g. launching a football-linked promotional campaign in the run up to a major tournament), thus giving the impression of an official association with that tournament.

The growth of ambush marketing has had significant implications for sport. First, ambush marketing poses a danger to sports bodies because often none of the income spent filters through to the sport itself. Second, it has had a negative impact on sponsorship revenues as sponsors fear that, if successfully 'ambushed' by a competitor, they might not reap the full benefits of sponsorship. Third, ambush marketing has led to conflict between event organizers and athletes. Event organizers have sought to limit the potential ambushing of official sponsors by exerting greater control over the sponsorship rights and contracts of athletes, while athletes have increasingly sought to secure the legal ownership of their image rights.

Key Reading

Battacharjee, S. and Rao, G. (2006) 'Tackling ambush marketing: the need for regulation and analysing the present legislative and contractual efforts', *Sport in Society*, 9 (1): 128–49.

Gratton, C. and Taylor, P. (2000) *Economics of Sport and Recreation*. London: Routledge.

AMERICAN EXCEPTIONALISM

(sports space)

ANABOLIC STEROIDS

(drugs, classes of)

ANCIENT OLYMPIC GAMES

Many have idolized the sports of ancient Greece as representing the pinnacle of civilized sporting achievement, but empirical data increasingly show this to be largely a myth. Among the sporting festivals of ancient Greece, the Olympic Games held at Olympia were the most significant. The origins of the ancient Olympic Games are unknown, but the earliest remaining record of a victor's name comes from 776 BC. It is highly likely that the competitive games grew out of religious ceremonies designed to celebrate and appease the Gods (religion).

The Games continued for approximately 1000 years, but they changed considerably over this time and so one must be wary of making overly generalized comments. However, by 472 BC the form of the Games had become relatively stable. Zeus became the primary God honoured through the Games. Working in the four-yearly cycle that

we see for the modern Olympic Games (IOC), the festival became fixed as a five-day combination of prayers, oaths, sacrifices and 12 game contests: 2 equestrian events; 6 track and field events; a foot race for athletes dressed in armour; and the 3 physical contact contests, wrestling, boxing and Pancration (note that the ancient Greek Olympics did not include the marathon, which is a modern glorification of the exertions of a young Athenian named Pheidippides). Participants in the Games were freeborn males only. Slaves and foreigners were permitted to watch, but women were entirely excluded. Women participated in a parallel but separate athletic festival, in honour of Zeus's sister/wife, Hera.

Compared to modern sport these events had less-detailed and less-differentiated rules, which were customary rather than written. While umpires and judges were in attendance, in all likelihood, rules were enforced less strictly and less consistently than we would expect in today's sporting contests. While modern sports are largely organized along the principles of fair play, the game contests of ancient Greece were governed by a warrior ethos that primarily rewarded bravery and valour.

Contests tended to be far more violent than today's sports, with the Pancration the most violent event. Running races involved jostling and physical contact. Chariot races invariably included collisions. In one chariot race it was reported that only one of the original 40 entrants finished. The organizers of the ancient Greek Olympics employed whip-bearers and truncheon-bearers to keep both spectators and competitors under control. Drunken rowdiness was such a problem at the Pythian Games at Delphi that spectators were forbidden from bringing wine into the stadium (Guttmann, 1986). Elias (1971) usefully links the relatively high level of violence in these game contests to the violent tenor of life in ancient Greek society more generally (e.g. he notes that if murder was committed in Greek society, it was the duty of the victim's kin rather than the state to exact revenge, that genocide was not uncommon, and that some city-states, notably Sparta, were organized on the basis of the perception of the constant threat of war). The notion of the Olympic truce is a reflection of this, based as it was on the assumption that travel between different regions was normally a hazardous and physically dangerous affair.

Though being an athlete was an expensive pastime, the only prizes to be won at Olympia were honorary olive crowns. Athletes paid for specialized diets, full-time training and the services of a coach, and had extensive travel commitments (to Olympia and the similar, though less prestigious, Pythian, Isthmian and Nemean Games). Initially, this meant that participants were largely the sons of the wealthy, but wealthy patrons and public figures increasingly realized the gains that could be reaped from association with a successful athlete and started to provide financial assistance to lower-class athletes of promise. Baker (1982) has consequently argued that despite the lack of direct material reward, the ancient Olympic Games were a 'maze of commercial enterprise' (**commercialization**). A clear sign of this was the development of athletic guilds in the second century BC that bargained for athletes' rights.

We know so much about the ancient Greek Games because the sporting activities were closely recorded in art, poetry and the writings of philosophers. Though some athletes were criticized as 'all brawn and no brain', the Greek ideal twinned the athletic and the cerebral. Due to the relative frequency of violence in ancient Greek society, the weak held a low social status. Conversely Plato is thought to have competed in the Isthmian Games. Plato and Aristotle gave lectures and taught in gymnasiums. It is the closeness between physical activities and what in modern societies tend to be thought of as 'higher' cultural practices that led many to mistakenly think that the game contests of ancient Greece were a pinnacle of civilized sporting achievement. Such a reading, however, obscures the generally violent tenor of the society in general, and the violent nature of the sports of ancient Greece in particular.

Key Reading

Baker, W.J. (1982) *Sports in the Western World.* Otowa, NJ: Rowan and Littlefield. esp. Ch. 2.
Elias, N. (1971) 'The genesis of sport as a sociological problem', in E. Dunning (ed.), *The Sociology of Sport: A Selection of Readings.* London: Frank Cass, pp. 88–115.
Finley, M. and Pleket, H. (1976) *The Olympic Games.* London: Chatto and Windus.
Guttmann, A. (1986) *Sports Spectators.* New York: Columbia University Press.

ANIMAL SPORTS

A significant feature of the festive culture of England up until the Victorian era. Although initially animal sports were largely rural-based activities, they survived initial urbanization processes (**city**). As a form of **folk games**, animal sports tended to be locally specific, with rules and customs that were orally transmitted, and characterized by **gambling**, eating, revelry, the consumption of **alcohol** and relatively high levels of **violence**.

Holt (1989) highlights four animal sports in particular (1) throwing at cocks – a bird would be tethered and participants paid to throw stones etc., with the person throwing the object that eventually killed the bird taking the cock as a prize; (2) cock-fighting – owners would pit their cock against an opponent's, sometimes in specially constructed 'cockpits' to contain the birds and aid viewing (see also **deep play**); (3) bull baiting (and less commonly bear baiting) – owners would set their dogs (and bulldogs in particular) on the bull in the belief that such 'baiting' improved the meat; and (4) bull running – bulls would be chased through streets and beaten with sticks prior to slaughter. That the bulldog became an English emblem reveals the popularity and social significance of such events. Many public houses in England retain a name (e.g. The Cock Inn, The Bull) that demonstrates and preserves the link between animal sports and the festive nature of these events (Collins and Vamplew, 2002).

Animal sports died out for a number of reasons. First, there were objections from **Puritans** whose religious sensitivities were offended by the sports and their accompanying revelry. However, the anti-animal sport movement strengthened as Puritanism waned, and Methodists assumed the mantle of the main critics of animal sports on religious grounds. Second, new attitudes to man's relationship with the 'natural' world became influential, whereby there was a loss of confidence in man's supremacy and a recognition that animals, as God's creatures, had certain rights. Third, the new urban professional classes became increasingly influential inside and outside Parliament, establishing the Society for the Prevention of Cruelty to Animals in 1824, the campaigns of which were instrumental in producing the Cruelty to Animals Act of 1835.

That **fox-hunting** survived indicates that the attacks on animal sports were as much about social control (there was a persistent concern that such festivities generated unruly and uncontrollable mobs and thus posed a threat to property and social stability) as they were about cruelty. Holt (1989) cites three other broader social processes that were influential in the decline of animal sports. First, he notes that the history of animal sports provides supporting evidence for Elias's theory of the **civilizing process**. Second, Holt notes the role of the development of a skilled and literate working-class elite in actively rejecting animal sports (possibly seeking to enhance their social status by aligning themselves with the middle classes and so distancing themselves from the lower working classes). Third, he cites the changing power relations in rural communities, and especially the gentry's lost confidence in their social status, partly following the French Revolution, and partly due to their declining financial power. Customary

bonds and duties were weakened, and the gentry withdrew (both physically and in terms of their support) from the activities of the masses. Thus animal sports lost the powerful allies who had previously protected them from abolition.

Key Reading

Collins, T. and Vamplew, W. (2002) *Mud, Sweat and Beers: A Cultural History of Sport and Alcohol.* Oxford: Berg.

Holt, R. (1989) *Sport and the British: A Modern History.* Oxford: Oxford University Press.

For a French comparison, see also Holt, R. (1981) *Sport and Society in Modern France.* Basingstoke: Macmillan.

ANOMIE

'Founding father' of sociology Émile Durkheim (1858–1917) originally described anomie as a state of moral de-regulation. Durkheim saw anomie as developing out of rapid social change (e.g. from an agrarian-based to an industrial society), which led to a situation whereby previously accepted norms and values became outmoded and, crucially, were not replaced by another broadly accepted, more adequate and contemporaneously relevant set of values.

Robert Merton subsequently refined Durkheim's concept of anomie to be more akin to 'normlessness' (**functionalism; 'soft' functionalism**). For Merton, anomie arose where social systems were relatively poorly integrated and where different individuals reacted in different ways to the pursuit of institutional goals. Merton suggests five different responses to institutionalized goals: conformity, innovation, ritualism, retreatism and rebellion. Where individuals adopt different responses to institutionalized goals we see anomie and deviant behaviour (**deviance**).

Sociologists of sport have thus largely used the concept of anomie when investigating deviance such as cheating and the use of **drugs** in sport. In the case of drug use, for instance, Lüschen (2000), following Merton, has argued that athletes' behaviour can best be understood as innovation; that is to say the acceptance of the general goal of achievement and performance in sport, but the rejection of conventional means for attaining that outcome, and thus their replacement with new or 'illegal' means.

Key Reading

Blackshaw, T. and Crabbe, T. (2004) *New Perspective on Sport and 'Deviance': Consumption, Performativity and Social Control*. London: Routledge.

Loy, J.W. and Booth, D. (2000) 'Functionalism, sport and society', in J. Coakley and E. Dunning (eds), *Handbook of Sports Studies*. London: Sage, pp. 8–27.

Lüschen, G. (2000) 'Doping in sport as deviant behaviour and its social control', in J. Coakley and E. Dunning (eds), *Handbook of Sports Studies*. London: Sage, pp. 461–76.

ANTI-RACISM

Because of the game's popularity, social significance, and the multi-ethnic composition of professional football players, anti-racism in British sport has largely focused on football (**race**). Launched by the Commission for Racial Equality and the Professional Footballers Association in 1993, Let's Kick Racism out of Football was the first national anti-racism in sport campaign. It was designed to combat racist chanting and practices (e.g. the throwing of bananas at black players on the pitch) but was initially supported by just 40 of the 92 Football League clubs. The remainder largely denied either that a problem existed, or that the problem was one which they, as football clubs, should or could address.

Since 1997 Kick it Out has taken responsibility for running Let's Kick Racism out of Football and has widened its campaign to address grassroots football, conduct outreach work with local minority ethnic communities, develop educational materials for schools, and coordinate the annual national anti-racism week. A number of regional anti-racist organizations have also emerged, including Show Racism the Red Card in the north-east of England, which utilizes a variety of media to dissipate players' and managers' views on racism, and Football Unites, Racism Divides, which is a partnership of fan groups, Sheffield United FC, local police and council officers. In addition to these, many clubs have their own initiatives, the most notable of which are Charlton Athletic Race Equality (CARE) and Leicester City's Foxes Against Racism.

These campaigns have been successful in making sports organizations more proactive in dealing with racism in sport and, with legislative help in the form of the 1991 Football Offences Act, many of the more overt forms of racism have been suppressed. However, these successes have now been tarnished by the dominance of the perception of what critics have termed the **racist–hooligan couplet**. Key 'race' problems seemingly unaffected by anti-racist movements also remain in football. These include the following: (1) the lack of participation in elite sport among British-Asians; (2) the lack of minority ethnic managers and administrators; and (3) broader issues of institutional racism within the game, e.g. in terms of local league rules that may effectively bar minority ethnic groups from participation.

Finally it should be noted that these campaigns have led to a number of imitators in various countries across Continental Europe, coordinated by FARE (Football Against Racism in Europe), and in other British sports. In 1995, following *Wisden Cricket Monthly*'s publication of an article called 'Is it in the Blood?' (in which Robert Henderson argued that the poor record of the England cricket team was connected to the prevalence of players who had been born overseas and/or had spent much of their childhood living in other countries), a cricket anti-racism pressure group, Hit Racism for Six, was formed. Similarly in 1996, the magazine *Open Rugby* announced that rugby league had launched its own version, Let's Tackle Racism. These movements, however, have attracted rather less **media** attention, government funding or academic interest.

Key Reading

Carrington, B. and McDonald, I. (2003) 'The politics of "race" and sports policy', in B. Houlihan (ed.), *Sport and Society: A Student Introduction*. London: Sage, pp. 125–42.

Garland, J. and Rowe, M. (2001) *Racism and Anti-Racism in British Football*. Basingstoke: Palgrave.

http://en.farenet.org/ Home page of Football Against Racism in Europe.

Malcolm, D. (2002) '"Clean bowled"? Cricket, racism and equal opportunities', *Journal of Ethnic and Migration Studies*, 28 (2): 307–25.

ANTI-TRUST LAWS

Laws that operate in the United States and delineate the legal boundaries within which corporations may act to preserve their interests. For the purposes of sports law there are two key sections of the 1890 Sherman Act: Section 1, focusing on 'restraint of trade', and Section 2, relating to monopolization and monopoly practices.

By decree of Congress, however, American professional sports leagues are largely exempt from anti-trust laws. The rationale for this is that, compared to other businesses, there is a mutual interdependence of competitors or teams in sport and thus all teams benefit from the equalization of sporting competition. Certain monopolistic practices, for instance **player reservation systems**, the sale of television **broadcasting rights** as a **cartel** rather than as individual teams, etc., are justified on the basis that they will improve the **competitive balance** of a league, while anything less equitable may lead to economic inequalities and, therefore, negatively affect uncertainty of outcome. However, allowing leagues to act as cartels ultimately impinges upon the employment rights of workers and forces **media** companies to pay higher fees for broadcasting rights. This, together with the ability to restrict the supply of team **franchises**, inflates the price at which franchises are sold and has allowed certain individuals to make considerable profits. In recent years, however, the European Commission has also been seen to accept similar arguments to those used by American sports leagues to justify the exemption of European sporting bodies from laws regarding anti-competitive practices.

Key Reading

Gardiner, S., with James, M., O'Leary, J. and Welch, R. (2001) *Sports Law*, 2nd edn. London: Cavendish Publishing. esp. Ch. 9.

Roberts, G.R. (1991) 'Professional sports and the antitrust laws', in P.D. Staudohar and J.A. Mangan (eds), *The Business of Professional Sports*. Urbana and Chicago: University of Illinois Press. pp. 135–51.

ANXIETY

A negative emotional state that refers to both mental processes, such as worrying (cognitive anxiety), and automatic physiological responses, such as increased heart rate (somatic anxiety). Anxiety is a form of, but should be analysed distinctly from, **arousal** (which refers to a more general state of activity measured on a continuum from comatose to highly excited. See also **stress**).

Psychologists further distinguish between trait and state anxiety. *Trait anxiety* refers to anxiety as a component of **personality**, and to the degree to which one is predisposed to experience anxiety, while *state anxiety* refers to the moment-to-moment experiences of anxiety. While to some degree cognitive and somatic anxiety are linked, and to some degree a strong relationship exists between trait and state anxiety, these relationships are far from perfect and psychologists, in attempting to unpack these different forms of anxiety, refer to the *multidimensional nature of anxiety*. For instance, even athletes with high trait anxiety can learn to control the cognitive and somatic effects of anxiety with practice and regular exposure to particular environments. Similarly, trait and state anxiety may be present in different proportions at different moments of sporting performance and build-up (e.g. one is likely to experience more cognitive anxiety in the days prior to a significant sporting event, but more somatic anxiety in the minutes leading up to the start of the event).

While there is very little consensus over the exact nature of the link between arousal, anxiety and performance, most research indicates that a link does indeed exist. The most widely used theory in this regard is the inverted-U hypothesis, which states that increased arousal will positively affect performance up to an optimal point (the peak of the inverted-U) after which increased levels of arousal will reduce performance. Moreover, the optimal arousal level will vary according to the complexity of the task to be performed. Complex tasks that require high levels of decision making and thought (e.g. a snooker shot) have a lower optimal level of arousal than do relatively simplistic and/or physical tasks such as tackling (where higher levels of arousal may be optimal).

Despite the fact that the validity of the inverted-U hypothesis as a general theoretical model is widely accepted, a number of criticisms have been made: (1) the model falsely conflates arousal with anxiety, and overlooks the distinction between cognitive and somatic anxiety; (2) there is no evidence to suggest that optimal arousal for performance should be in the middle of the curve; and (3) the inverted-U hypothesis is solely descriptive and offers no *explanation* as to why sports performance may vary from context to context.

Key Reading

Jones, J.G. (1995) 'More than just a game: research developments and issues in competitive anxiety in sport', *British Journal of Psychology*, 86: 449–78.

APARTHEID

A term derived from the Afrikaans word meaning 'apartness'; it was a system of racial segregation and discrimination enforced by successive South African governments from 1948 to 1991. Apartheid affected every facet of South African life during this period, creating townships, separate education systems and, of course, separate sport systems. Apartheid was brutally and violently enforced by the legal, political and military bodies in South Africa and enabled a privileged white minority to retain control of the country and repress the overwhelming black majority's call for democratic rights.

In 1962 SANROC (South African Non-Racial Olympic Committee) was launched. SANROC's aim was to replace the existing, whites-only Olympic Association as the recognized representative of the **IOC** in South Africa. SANROC was rapidly banned by the South African state. However, the IOC (the charter of which forbids racial discrimination) stipulated that South Africa would have to make a number of changes to its sporting system if it wished to participate in the 1964 Tokyo Olympic Games. South Africa's insistence that sport in the country must comply with South African 'customs' (i.e. apartheid) meant that the IOC's conditions could not be met and the IOC withdrew South Africa's invitation.

Sport had traditionally held a central place in South African culture and the Olympic ban clearly caused annoyance to South African politicians. However, when cricket and rugby, the sports holding the greatest significance for white male South African identity (**sport, social significance of**), became subject to protests and boycotts, it became apparent that sporting isolation would have a significant effect (given that most nations continued to trade and have economic links with South Africa). Up to this point the cricket and rugby authorities in countries that made regular tours to South Africa to play test matches (and where whites were in the majority) had been prepared to send all-white teams to enable sporting links to continue, despite the fact that it meant compromising their selection process (e.g. the New Zealand Rugby Union, which regularly selected Maori players to play both home and away). However, in 1968 the issue finally came to a head, when the MCC (Marylebone Cricket Club) and the English press deliberated over the inclusion of Basil D'Oliveira (a 'cape-coloured' batsman/all-rounder from South Africa who had settled in England eight years earlier) in the England team to tour South Africa. Being black, D'Oliveira would have had no legal right to share facilities with white players and would thus publicly expose the inequalities of apartheid. When D'Oliveira wasn't selected in the initial tour party, protestors argued that the MCC had bowed to political pressure, but a subsequent injury to the England bowler Tom Cartwright opened the way for D'Oliveira's inclusion. The South African premier, John Vorster, complained that the MCC had allowed political activists, and SANROC in particular, to select the side and refused to allow D'Oliveira to enter South Africa (noting for instance that D'Oliveira – primarily a batsman – had been picked as a replacement for a bowler). The MCC cancelled the tour.

The D'Oliveira issue accelerated the process of sport playing a key role in the international opposition to apartheid. The 'Stop the Seventy Tour' campaign successfully halted the proposed South African cricket team's tour to England two years later, and protests further disrupted a South African rugby union tour to Britain. In 1971, Prime Minister Vorster announced that a 'multinational' sports programme would be implemented in South Africa, allowing the different 'races' to compete against each other as separate 'nations'. Few felt that this marked a significant change as whites continued to monopolize sports facilities and receive the majority of funding.

The South Africans remained excluded from the Olympic movement. Building on earlier successes, the anti-apartheid movement, in the form of the Supreme Council for Sport in Africa, objected to New Zealand's participation in the Montreal Olympics (on account of New Zealand rugby union's continued links with South Africa) and a **boycott** by African nations ensued. A year later, governments from the nations making up the British Commonwealth signed the **Gleneagles Agreement**, condemning apartheid and pledging to take measures to increase South Africa's sporting isolation.

Many individuals (and some sports organizations) continued their sporting links with South Africa. Some simply argued that 'sport and politics shouldn't mix', others (e.g. English cricketers who took part in 'rebel' tours to South Africa) that any restriction on their activities would be an unreasonable 'restraint of trade'. Some claimed that by playing against multiracial teams, or by coaching non-whites, their activities were effectively challenging apartheid and that therefore such sporting contact should be permitted. Many (e.g. rebel 'England' cricket teams, golfers, black American boxing champion, Mike Weaver, etc.) were clearly attracted mainly by the large amounts of money South African authorities offered.

In 1981, the United Nations issued a 'blacklist' of sports performers who continued ties with South Africa. As well as shaming, this blacklist had the effect of jeopardizing England cricket tours to the West Indies in 1981 (with Robin Jackman, for instance, being refused permission to enter Guyana) and India in 1982. Notable South African cricketers (Allan Lamb, Robin Smith) and athletes (Zola Budd and Sidney Maree) 'defected' to Britain and America amid much protest. This, however, was a further sign that sporting isolation was having a significant impact.

As a consequence of international pressure (how much of it is attributable to sport-related activities we will never know) apartheid eventually collapsed. Long-term prisoner Nelson Mandela was released from custody on Robben Island in 1991 and, at the ensuing elections, became South African president. The sports world welcomed South Africa back with open arms and when South Africa hosted and won the 1995 Rugby World Cup, Mandela very deliberately aligned himself with the South African rugby captain, François Pienaar, in an attempt to unify the nation and offer hope for the future.

Key Reading

Archer, R. and Bouillon, A. (1982) *The South Africa Game*. London: Zed Press.

Jarvie, G. (1985) *Class, Race and Sport in South Africa's Political Economy*. London: Routledge.

Lapchick, R. (1975) *The Politics of Race and International Sport*. Westport, CT: Greenwood Press.

Williams, J. (2001) *Cricket and Race*. Oxford: Berg. esp. Chs 3 and 4.

ARCHERY

Still practised today as an Olympic sport, archery is of particular historical and socio-logical significance as a **medieval sport** form. In England during this period, archery was a distinctly middle-class or bourgeois sport, in contrast to the **tournament** and the **folk games** that were the preserve of knights and the masses respectively.

In 1252, Henry III pronounced that all subjects with property worth between 40 and 100 shillings should own a bow and arrows, and some of the most famous English mili-tary victories in the fourteenth century (e.g. Bannockburn in 1314 and Crecy in 1346) were attributed to the extensive and skilled use of longbows. These military victories led to further state proclamations that gradually spread compulsory bow ownership and

statutory regular practice down the social and economic order. This, in turn, resulted in the suppression of other pastimes and games. While the growing military role of archery had much to do with the decline of the **tour-nament** as a form of training for war, the rise of the gun (significant in the defeat of Richard III at the Battle of Bosworth in 1485) eventu-ally led to a decline in the military signifi-cance of archery.

By the early fourteenth century the first guilds of crossbowmen had been founded. Though clearly these guilds had a military and/or law enforcement purpose, it seems that a primary motivation for founding guilds was the enjoyment derived from participation and the sociability such guilds provided. Shooting guilds became a manifestation of the emerging bourgeois life and restricted membership enabled a degree of status exclusivity and dis-tinction. Subtle **class** gradations were intro-duced: crossbowmen were wealthy merchants or nobility; longbowmen were less affluent, often rural-based merchants.

Guilds often became the means by which towns were represented and competed against each other. Like the tournaments, increasingly elaborate ceremonies and festiv-ities grew up around the central, sporting, event. Unlike tournaments, archery contests occurred at fixed points in the calendar (e.g. on the day of the guild's patron saint), which was probably a legacy of the earlier royal proclamations that insisted on regular Sunday and holiday practice. Thus, as the early military roots of archery gave way to a growing, and more economically based, class consciousness, archery became a means by which local identities and status hierarchies could be maintained and reproduced.

Key Reading

Guttmann, A. (1986) *Sports Spectators*. New York: Columbia University Press.

Henricks, T. (1991) 'Sport in the later Middle Ages', in *Disputed Pleasures: Sport and Society in Pre-Industrial England*. Westport, CT: Greenwood Press. pp. 41–68.

Mandell, R. (1984) *Sport: A Cultural History.*
New York: Columbia University Press.
esp. Ch. 6.

AROUSAL

Refers to the intensity of behaviour, ranging on a continuum from deep sleep/coma state to high levels of excitation. Arousal is a multidimensional state with both physiological and cognitive components. However, research has indicated a very poor correlation between different types of physiological response to arousal (e.g. increased heart rate may not be linked to perspiration) and a poor correlation between cognitive and physiological responses to arousal (e.g. self-reported measures of nervousness may not correspond to changes in heart rate). Strictly speaking, the term arousal involves no negative or positive evaluation of the state; however, within the psychology of sport one will often find the terms arousal and **anxiety** used interchangeably (see also **stress**).

ATHLETIC SCHOLARSHIPS

Prior to 1953, US college students were eligible for financial assistance only on the basis of academic performance and financial need. By widening the funding criteria to include athletic performance the relationship between colleges and athletes was irrevocably altered. Athletic scholarships now underpin the US college sports system. Such scholarships effectively provide a mechanism by which higher education institutions can financially recompense formally amateur 'student-athletes' (**amateurism**). Such a mechanism has grown in importance in recent years as college sports have experienced considerable **commercialization**, with the fees that **media** companies pay for **broadcasting**

rights being a particularly significant source of income. The National Collegiate Athletic Association (NCAA) has, however, remained resolute in its desire to retain the image of its sports as amateur. From this, tensions arise.

Critics of the athletic scholarship system argue that it enables colleges to exploit students. The term 'student-athlete' effectively denies college sports stars the right to be officially recognized as workers and thus reduces their legal rights (e.g. to pensions, compensation on the termination of contract, etc.). The NCAA argues that this exception is warranted because: (1) 'student-athletes' get a free education; and (2) 'student-athletes' are members of, and represent, the student body. However, critics point out that most athletic scholarships are terminated by coaches rather than professors, on the basis of sports performance not academic attainment. These conditions mean not only that athletic scholarships do not necessarily entail a free education, but also that 'student-athletes' are not normal members of the student body; they are in fact 'paid for play'. Moreover, graduation rates for those on athletic scholarships are relatively low (a 1999 survey found that just 58 per cent graduated within six years of starting a degree). Tellingly, there appears to be an inverse relationship between graduation rates and the revenue generated by a sports programme; that is to say, athletic scholarships to the most commercially successful sports are least likely to result in educational qualifications.

Athletic scholarships are also the mechanism by which US colleges recruit athletic talent from other countries. In this respect they also contribute to the increasing trend of **sport labour migration**.

Key Reading

Bale, J. (1991) *The Brawn Drain: Foreign Student-Athletes in American Universities.* Illinois: University of Illinois Press.
Sack, A.L. and Staurowsky, E.J. (1998) *College Athletes for Hire: The Evolution and*

Legacy of the NCAA Amateur Myth. Westport, CT: Praeger.

Smith, R.A. (1988) *Sports and Freedom: The Rise of Big-Time College Athletics.* Oxford: Oxford University Press.

Staurowsky, E.J. (2004) 'Piercing the veil of amateurism: commercialisation, corruption and US college sports', in T. Slack (ed.), *The Commercialisation of Sport.* London: Routledge. pp. 143–63.

ATTENTIONAL FOCUS

(concentration)

AUTO-ETHNOGRAPHY

(ethnography)

B

BALINESE COCK-FIGHTING

(deep play)

BARBARIANS, GENTLEMEN AND PLAYERS

Originally published in 1979, Dunning and Sheard's *Barbarians, Gentlemen and Players* is a sociological study of the development of rugby football. *Barbarians* represents a significant marker in the development of not only the sociology of sport, but also sport's historical study. As a critical case study, the value of *Barbarians* goes beyond the specificities of rugby football, and provides a theoretical framework for the understanding of how **modern sport** came to take the shape that we know today.

Dunning and Sheard divide the development of rugby and association football into five main, overlapping stages (as signalled by the use of the word 'about' with reference to dates): (1) from at least the fourteenth into the twentieth century when football typically exhibited the characteristics of a **folk game**; (2) from about 1750 to 1840 when these folk games were taken into and adapted to suit the particular environment of the English public schools; (3) from about 1830 to 1860 when the games were relatively rapidly transformed into rule-bound, and more formally structured, activities with specific codes governing behaviour (**public school status rivalry**); (4) from about 1850 to 1900 when the different forms of football spread into society at large, entailing the establishment of national governing bodies, and emergent forms of professionalism (**amateurism**); and (5) from about 1900 onwards, when the various rugby and football codes matured, refined their rule codes and organizational forms and developed career structures for players. The second edition of *Barbarians*, published in 2005, includes an afterword in which subsequent commercialization and professionalization developments are discussed, and critiques of the original version of *Barbarians* are addressed.

Building on this classification of sport into the different stages of modernization, *Barbarians* attempts to be of broader sociological value, throwing light on: (1) the development of the British **class** structure (and particularly the public schools); (2) the reasons why Britain was the first country to develop **modern sport** forms; (3) Elias's theory of the **civilizing process**; and (4) the trend towards increasing seriousness and competitiveness in sport (**commercialization**) as well as its increasing centrality in contemporary culture (**sport, social significance of**). Dunning and Sheard argue that, with respect to the first point, the nineteenth-century process of **embourgeoisement** (which they define as the growing power of the industrial middle classes) was of critical importance, having a significant impact on then contemporary institutions and values. Modern sport forms first emerged in England because of the specificity of these class relations, and the relative independence of the ruling classes from the monarchy. A process of mutual accommodation between the former and emerging ruling classes led to the persistence of amateur values and institutions in British sport, and a 'less pure' form of capitalism than in, say, the United States. With regard to the theory of the civilizing process, Dunning and Sheard argue that rugby underwent two main spurts in which the standards of **violence** control advanced in the sense that the exercise of stricter and more even self-control was demanded of players (e.g. the introduction of referees, rule-making bodies and the abolition of practices such as **hacking**). Finally, the increasing seriousness of modern sport Dunning and Sheard attribute to 'functional democratization'; the trend towards increasing levels of interdependency and an equalizing of power balances (e.g. between social classes, the sexes) in society entailed by such things as a complex division of labour in industrial production.

Sport has also become culturally more central due to: (1) the changing balance between work and leisure; (2) the growing secularization of society; (3) the role of sport in generating mimetic excitement (**quest for excitement**); (4) the importance of sport as a site for the generation of masculine identity (**male preserve**; and **masculinity**); and (5) sport's role in promoting social integration. Dunning and Sheard argue that the increasing levels of violence evident in sport in the 1970s – including **football hooliganism** – can be attributed to this set of interdependent factors. In conclusion, they suggest therefore that the civilizing process may be curvilinear, with functional democratization producing consequences that in the longer term are 'civilizing', but which in their early stages may be 'de-civilizing'.

Key Reading

Collins, T. (2005) 'History, theory and the "civilizing process"', *Sport in History*, 25 (2): 289–306.
Curry, G., Dunning, E. and Sheard, K. (2006) 'Sociological versus empicirist history: some comments on Tony Collins's "History, theory and the 'civilizing process'"', *Sport in History*, 26 (1): 110–23.
Dunning, E. and Sheard, K. (2005) *Barbarians, Gentlemen and Players: A Sociological Study of the Development of Rugby Football*, 2nd edn. London; Routledge.

BARMY ARMY

A name bestowed on a group of England cricket supporters by the Australian press in 1994/5. Largely male and middle class, Barmy Army members drew attention to themselves because of their vociferous, partisan, and **carnival**-esque supporting style, which ran directly counter to the idealized English tradition of reserved, polite and genteel cricket spectatorship.

Parry and Malcolm (2004) have argued that the Barmy Army emerged, and assumed considerable social significance, due to society-wide processes (time–space compression, the development of **new laddism**), sports-wide processes (changes in supporter cultures and football supporter cultures in particular (fans)) and cricket-specific processes (cricket's **commercialization** and internationalization). Moreover, the Barmy Army represents a new form of English national identity that is at odds with, and defined in opposition to, traditional notions of Englishness, especially as expressed through cricket (**nationalism**).

Key Reading

Parry, M. and Malcolm, D. (2004) 'England's Barmy Army: commercialization, masculinity and nationalism', *International Review for the Sociology of Sport*, 39 (1): 73–92.

BAUDRILLARD

(**hyperreal**)

BECKHAM, DAVID (1975–)

Born in Leytonstone, east London, David Beckham overcame early concerns that he was too small to be a professional footballer to make his debut as a Manchester United player in 1995. Signed to the club at the age of 13, Beckham played a key role in United's successful English Football Premiership campaign of 1995–6, and scored a 'wondergoal' against Wimbledon at the start of the following season, evoking comparisons with Brazilian football legend Pele with a shot from the halfway line. Vilified by the English **media** and public following his sending off in a World Cup game against Argentina in 1998 (a game England subsequently lost to exit the tournament), Beckham won back supporters by playing a key role in United's 1998–9 treble winning season. Following stories of acrimony between himself and manager Alex Ferguson, Beckham left United for Real Madrid in 2003.

Though by no means the world's most talented footballer, Beckham, like **Michael Jordan** and **Tiger Woods**, can only be understood in light of the broader **celebrity** process in sport. As for Jordan and Woods, a number of social scientists have tried to make sense of the Beckham phenomenon. Beckham, it has been noted, appeals to a very diverse audience: traditional football fans (both at club and national level), who admire his skill and work ethic; conservatives, who admire his monogamy and commitment to family values; young males (both heterosexual and gay), for whom he is a fashion icon; young females, who see him as a sex symbol and/or admire him for his 'New man' image; and older women, in whom he evokes maternal feelings. Some have accused him of being superficial, artificial and lacking in substance and comedians have portrayed him as unintelligent. However, without doubt Beckham has a carefully crafted, multifaceted and complex image to which people from multiple market segments can relate, and feel at ease. This both maximizes his commercial value and his prominence as a celebrity.

Beckham's rise to celebrity status owes much to the specific time and space in which he arose. Relevant factors often cited include the following: (1) the weakening of restrictive labour practices in football which increased the power of players relative to clubs (see also the **Bosman ruling**); (2) the growing prominence of players' agents in sport; (3) the increasing assertion of the interests of the biggest English football clubs which led to the formation of the Premier League; (4) the coincidence of this with the development of satellite television in England and the increased competition for the **broadcasting rights** for football; (5) the increased competition between newspapers (and tabloids in particular) which led to the increased coverage of sport; and (6) broader processes relating to **consumer culture** and the **commercialization** and **commodification** of sport. These factors combined to increase the cultural centrality and financial significance of football in England in the late 1990s, and thus predicated Beckham's rise to celebrity. In addition to this, football is the global game par excellence, and England is at the hub of world football (**globalization**). Perhaps unlike any other sport, football evokes emotions akin to those more normally associated with **religion** (see also **fans**). Cashmore (2004) also points to the timing of Beckham's marriage coinciding as it did with the national grief over the death of Princess Diana and leading at the time to considerable media debate about whether the Beckhams, in the wake of Diana's death and growing disillusionment with the royal family more generally, could supersede the monarchy as cultural icons.

But, analysts ask, why, as opposed to football contemporaries such as Michael Owen or Jamie Redknapp, has Beckham achieved this level of celebrity status? Cashmore (2004) argues that Beckham has been turned into a commodity, to be bought and sold like any other, but highlights three key aspects of this process. First, Beckham started his career with Manchester United, the biggest team in England and dominant in English football in the mid- to late 1990s. United also have a global following unmatched by any other club (with a reputed 17 million fans in Asia) and were proactive in nurturing their own international brand image for economic gain at this time. Thus the rise of United and of Beckham were highly interdependent (Beckham was the first sportsperson to include discussions about image rights in contractual negotiations with his club, attempting to place a monetary value on the relative enhancement value of his image and his club's brand).

Second, Cashmore points to the role of Victoria Adams, Beckham's wife, who prior to meeting Beckham was a member of the pop band the Spice Girls. Having personally experienced the benefits that a highly sculptured, well-publicized, branded image could reap, Victoria Beckham has been influential in bringing in advisers and actively moulding and developing Beckham's image in a style, and to an extent, not seen before among sports celebrities.

Third, Cashmore points to the role of adidas, the sports good manufacturer and one of Beckham's major sponsors. In particular, the influence of adidas can be seen in Beckham's 2003 move to Real Madrid. In 2002 Manchester United signed a 13-year £300 million shirt **sponsorship** deal with adidas's arch rival **Nike**, providing the sports manufacturer with control of the club's global replica kit and merchandising business. This caused a clash of interests for Beckham through his links with adidas. In contrast, Real Madrid and leading Real Madrid players such as Zinedine Zidane were signed to adidas and thus Cashmore argues that the sponsor had a clear vested interest in facilitating the deal. Indeed, global sales of Real Madrid replica shirts increased by 350 per cent during Beckham's first year with the club.

In addition to this, Whannel (2001) and Cashmore and Parker (2003) have placed greater emphasis on Beckham's role as a 'gender pioneer', and in part filling a role created by a more general crisis in **masculinity**. Beckham, they note, has subverted many football conventions about masculinity and sexuality. Though his playing style accords

with conventional styles of (football) masculinity (he is renowned for his 'work rate', competitiveness, and fondness of training), he is in part a product of and an agent of change in turn of the century masculinity, with men increasingly being seen as caring nurturers, family-centred, and narcissistic and style conscious. While allegations in 2004 of extra-marital affairs threatened to tarnish this image, Beckham remained popular with sponsors, signing a £40 million deal with Gillette later that year.

Key Reading

Cashmore, E. (2004) *Beckham*. Cambridge: Polity.

Cashmore, E. and Parker, A. (2003) 'One David Beckham? Celebrity, masculinity and the soccerati', *Sociology of Sport Journal*, 20 (3): 214–31.

Smart, B. (2005) *The Sports Star: Modern Sport and the Cultural Economy of Sporting Celebrity*. London: Sage.

Whannel, G. (2001) 'Punishment, redemption and celebration in the popular press: the case of David Beckham', in D.L. Andrews and S.J. Jackson (eds), *Sport Stars: The cultural politics of sporting celebrity*. London: Routledge. pp. 138–50.

BEDOUIN SYNDROME

Identified by anthropologists, the Bedouin syndrome rests on the following principles: (1) the friend of a friend is a friend; (2) the enemy of a friend is an enemy; (3) the enemy of an enemy is a friend; and (4) the friend of an enemy is an enemy. In relation to sport, the Bedouin syndrome has been used to explain the seemingly temporary and ad-hoc allegiances formed by football supporters and football hooligans in particular. Thus gangs from different estates or areas of a city, between whom there might in other contexts be antipathy, cooperate with each other when supporting the team that represents their city, and in the face of football hooligans from other cities. Similarly Balinese villagers will set aside their local differences and bet on their enemies' cocks during inter-village cock fights (**deep play**). The Bedouin syndrome can also be used to understand why the hooligans of various football clubs stand together when following a national side, and in the face of a common (i.e. international) enemy. Moreover, this fluid pattern of unity and disunity, claim Dunning et al. (1988), is characteristic of the 'ordered segmentation' of, and social bonding within, the communities which they argue provide the overwhelming majority of football hooligans (**football hooliganism**).

Key Reading

Dunning, E., Murphy, P. and Williams, J. (1988) *The Roots of Football Hooliganism: An Historical and Sociological Study.* London: Routledge and Kegan Paul.

BEST, GEORGE (1946–2005)

Born in Belfast on 22 May 1946 and buried in the same city on 3 December 2005. For a time between these two dates, in a life punctuated by numerous highs and lows, he arguably became the greatest soccer player in the world. But Best was also an alcoholic whose long struggle with his illness came to an end with his death on 25 November 2005.

Best's relevance for sports studies lies in the claim that he became British football's first **media** sport star. Commonly described in the tabloid press as 'the Fifth Beatle', he was strongly identified with the 'Swinging Sixties' phenomenon and he quickly became as well known for his lifestyle away from football as for his exploits with Manchester United, the club he joined in 1961 (**Munich air disaster**). It is widely, but mistakenly, believed that Best's career in football was relatively short as a consequence of his drift into alcoholism. In fact, he played professionally from 1961 until 1983 in a career that included

361 games for Manchester United, with whom he won the European Cup in 1968, and 37 international matches for Northern Ireland. As his health and form began to decline, he also represented the Jewish Guild, Stockport County, Cork Celtic, Fulham, Hibernian and AFC Bournemouth and had spells in Australia, with Brisbane Lions, and in the USA, with Los Angeles Aztecs, Fort Lauderdale Strikers and San Jose Earthquakes.

Although largely ignored by sociologists of sport at the height of his powers, interest in Best has grown as part of a more general growth of concern with **celebrity** and sport stardom. Ellis Cashmore has suggested that Best was never subjected to the same degree of scrutiny that has been reserved more recently for players such as **David Beckham**. In the case of Best, however, Garry Whannel (2002) is correct to point out that there has been a tendency to present his entire life, both as a player and, thereafter, as a celebrity, as 'a moral homily – a warning like a nineteenth-century moral tract, concerning the dangers of giving way to emotion, desire, hedonism and **alcohol**'. Whannel is also right to note the value of Chas Critcher's notion of 'dislocation' for an understanding of George Best's life and early death. Like many players before him, and an even larger number since, Best was dislocated from his working-**class** origins. He was also dislocated from his native Northern Ireland. Less often mentioned but arguably no less important, he was dislocated from his Ulster Protestant parental culture when he joined Manchester United (**religion**), a club with long-standing links to Catholic Ireland and to the Irish diaspora in Manchester and Salford. Indeed, throughout much of Best's Old Trafford career, the dominant figure at the club was Sir Matt Busby, the manager, who was himself a devout Catholic.

It is, of course, wrong to argue that Best's later difficulties can be wholly attributed to this triple dislocation. For example, it should also be acknowledged that his mother died at an early age, another victim of alcoholism. Despite evidence of **violence**, particularly towards wives and girlfriends, Best remained popular in his native Northern Ireland. Indeed, more than most sports stars from that divided society, he was able to unite people across the sectarian divide (**sectarianism**), a fact that was highlighted by the diverse range of mourners who attended his funeral and by the renaming of Belfast's City Airport in his honour.

Key Reading

Andrews, D.L. and Jackson, S.J. (eds) (2001) *Sport Stars. The Cultural Politics of Sporting Celebrity*. London: Routledge.

Bairner, A. (2004) 'Where did it all go right? George Best, Manchester United and Northern Ireland', in D.L. Andrews (ed.), *Manchester United. A Thematic Study*. London: Routledge. pp. 133–46.

Lovejoy, J. (1999) *Bestie*. London: Pan Books.

Whannel, G. (2002) *Media Sport Stars. Masculinities and Moralities*. London: Routledge.

Alan Bairner

BEST VALUE

(compulsory competitive tendering)

BEYOND A BOUNDARY

Marxist philosopher and political activist CLR James's (1901–89) part autobiographical analysis of cricket in the Caribbean. Originally published in 1963, James argued that cricket shaped Caribbean society in much the same way as did political movements, economic forces, and educational systems, and that it did so with equal significance. Cricket, according to James, is a sphere of social life where broader social hierarchies and **class** and **race** tensions are writ large.

Cricket, like Caribbean societies more generally, was shaped by the historical legacies of **imperialism** and slavery. Though slavery had long since been abolished in the Caribbean (in 1838), clubs remained strictly demarcated according to colour, class, status and **religion**. Cricket thus replicated and reproduced the pattern of social relations that had evolved under slavery, in some way contrary to the more radical changes occurring elsewhere in Caribbean society. That everyone knew his place (and in James's time cricket was an all-male institution) revealed how deeply internalized and how universally accepted social inequalities were. White players and administrators continued to dominate the game. Black players were excluded from representative sides due to social rather than playing considerations. The campaign to have Frank Worrell appointed as captain of the West Indies cricket team (a campaign in which James was an active contributor) marked a watershed, but Worrell's university education and English experience were clearly as important to the selectors as his playing ability and leadership qualities.

James's work has been so influential that subsequent writing on cricket in the Caribbean has developed a somewhat homogeneous character, focusing almost solely on **nationalism**. However, there are two valuable lessons to be learnt from James. First, rather than just breaking down social barriers, sport is also important in constructing or producing social inequality. Second, and this lesson is summed up in James's now classic question which prefaces *Beyond a Boundary* – 'What do they know of cricket who only cricket know?' – is that to understand the social impact and importance of a sport, it is necessary to understand the broader social context in which the sport is played.

Key Reading

Beckles, H.McD. and Stoddart, B. (eds) (1995) *Liberation Cricket: West Indies Cricket Culture*. Manchester: Manchester University Press.

James, C.L.R. (1963) *Beyond a Boundary*. London: Hutchinson.

Stoddart, B. (2004), 'Sport, colonialism and struggle: C.L.R. James and cricket', in R. Giulianotti (ed.), *Sport and Modern Social Theorists*. Basingstoke: Palgrave Macmillan. pp. 111–28.

BINARIES

Particularly important in the post-structuralist sociology of Jacques Derrida (**post-structuralism**), and consequently work in the sociology of sport influenced by his ideas. Derrida argues that Western philosophical ideas (**modernity**) are based on the binary opposition of reality and myth but that it is false to portray reality, or some kind of objective truth, as existing outside of human consciousness. Rather, 'reality' is a highly subjective notion, personal to the individual, and shaped by broader power struggles. The reality/myth binary (and others such as nature/nurture, presence/absence, masculine/feminine (**queer theory**) is based on a 'violent heirarchy' in which the first term is prioritized and seen as superior, and the second term subordinated. But Derrida argues that binaries depend on each other for meaning and that, singly, no element of a binary opposition can ever be said to exist in its own right, or be fully present (or absent). In short, they are both present and absent at the same time; we can only, for instance, understand **masculinity** in comparison to, and in contrast with, femininity.

Cheryl Cole has been particularly influential in applying Derrida's notion of binaries, and indeed Derrida's work more broadly, to the study of sport. Cole (1998) has questioned the nature/nurture binary in sport, arguing that the notion of the 'natural' **body** is always contaminated by the presence of the notion of the 'unnatural body', and that consequently the natural/unnatural binary is always in flux. Similarly, Cole and Andrews (1996) argue that the mediated images of basketball stars Earvin 'Magic' Johnson and **Michael Jordan** were never self-contained but always dependent on the absent other.

Key Reading

Andrews, D. (2000) 'Posting up: French post-structuralism and the critical analysis of contemporary sporting culture', in J. Coakley and E. Dunning (eds), *Handbook of Sports Studies*. London: Sage. pp. 106–37.

Cole, C.L. (1998) 'Addiction, exercise and cyborgs: technologies of deviant bodies', in G. Rail (ed.), *Sport and Postmodern Times*. New York: State University of New York Press. pp. 261–76.

Cole, C.L. and Andrews, D. (1996) '"Look – it's NBA *Showtime!*": visions of race in the popular imaginary', in N.K. Denzin (ed.), *Cultural Studies: A Research Volume*, Vol. 1. pp. 141–81.

BLOOD-DOPING

Involves the removal of blood from an athlete, and its subsequent re-infusion. When the blood is removed, bone marrow is stimulated to produce replacement red blood cells; when, nearer to competition, it is reintroduced into the body, the oxygen-carrying capacity of the blood is increased, enabling muscles to work more efficiently. While blood-doping does not involve the administration of drugs, it is clearly a performance-enhancing technique (**drugs, classes of**).

The Finnish distance runner Lasse Viren was accused of blood-doping during the 1970s (an allegation that he strongly denied), but the use of this doping practice really came to the attention of sports administrators and the public following the revelation that a number of members of the highly successful US cycling team at the 1984 Olympics had been blood-doped. Partly on the grounds that this gave athletes an unfair advantage, and partly on the grounds that blood removal and re-infusion were potentially hazardous to athletes' health, the **IOC** banned the practice prior to the 1988 Olympic Games (**drugs, prohibition of**).

Blood-doping is of particular sociological interest, however, in that an analysis of the development of this technique shows the close link between **sports medicine** and **drug** use in sport. Waddington (2000) has shown that blood-doping was developed very much in the mainstream of sports medicine. Initially, few doctors were concerned about the ethical considerations of the practice; by the late 1980s, however, a 'new moral orthodoxy' was established, with sports physicians acting not only as technical experts, but as 'moral policemen', whose role it was to educate athletes and to catch drug cheats. The repositioning of sports medicine in this way led athletes to be portrayed as having almost sole responsibility for drug use in sport. This obscured the integral role of sports medicine in developing drug use in sport. The analysis of blood-doping, therefore, highlights the increasingly close relationship between athletes and sports physicians as a central cause of the increase in the use of performance-enhancing drugs in sport during the twentieth century.

Key Reading

Voy, R. (1991) *Drugs, Sport and Politics.* Champaign, IL: Leisure Press.

Waddington, I. (2000) *Sport, Health and Drugs: A Critical Sociological Perspective.* London: E. & F.N. Spon. esp. Ch. 8.

BLOOD SPORTS

(**animal sports; fox-hunting**)

BODY

Given that the body is clearly so central to sport, it is perhaps odd that sport and the body only became established as a sociological research area in the 1990s (and hence the charge that prior to this sociology was 'disembodied'). The reason for this initial absence has been attributed to the Western tradition of assigning priority to the mind over the body (also referred to as Descartean Dualism). The subsequent growth of this area seems to stem partly from an increasing engagement with theorists such as **Bourdieu, Elias**, and **Foucault** in the sociology of sport, as well as the impact of **feminism** and the increasing importance of consumption (as opposed to production) in society (**consumer culture**). A central premise underlying research in this area is the belief that to truly understand social aspects of sport, we must look at the role of the body in sport, and the effects of sport on the body.

Loy et al. (1993), drawing on the work of Frank, suggest that research on the body can be organized around four areas: (1) the communicative body; (2) the disciplined body; (3) the dominating body; and (4) the mirroring body. Research, they suggest, has shown that in sport the body is an important *communicative*, or impression management, tool used to show an athlete's commitment to an activity, or membership of a subculture or group. Sports participation also serves to *discipline* and control the body either directly (e.g. **aerobics**, bodybuilding) or indirectly (e.g. through associated dietary control prevalent in sports such as gymnastics and boxing (**eating disorders**). Such discipline might be a consequence of the relatively free choices made by individuals or of the work of powerful groups or institutions such as the state. Thus bodily control might serve different functions, such as preparing people for work or for war, or the fostering of national identity through sport. Related to this, bodies can also be *dominating* in that the body is implicated in **gender**, **race** and **class** power relationships (following Elias and Bourdieu respectively, for expressing one's conjunction with the **civilizing process** and demarcating the distinction between different social groups (see also **habitus**). Finally, bodies have been analysed as *mirroring* our social relations, mediated particularly through consumption. For instance, others will seek to judge us (our class, race, gender) according to the way we look, and, increasingly, the things that we purchase to 'adorn' our bodies (clothing, lean muscular bodies developed in gyms, cosmetic surgery, etc.) reveal our social location.

Cole (2000) contests the notion that the body has been absent from the sociology of sport (arguing rather that the body is inherent to the work of Elias, Bourdieu, etc. but that theorists merely didn't recognize its significance). Cole also proposes a different typology of sociological research on sport and the body, highlighting three interdependent streams: (1) the relationship between sport and the body in **modernity**; (2) sport's role in creating or resolving 'deviant' bodies (**deviance**); and (3) the effects of **commercialization** on the sport–body interrelationship.

In this first stream, researchers have sought to illustrate that the development of modern sport, to varying degrees, served the bodily/corporeal needs that arose in modernity. It is argued, for instance, that if the state required fit and healthy bodies for warfare it thus encouraged (sometimes legalized) participation in sports (**Turnen**). Alternatively sport aided production in emergent capitalist economies by providing a workforce with fit, healthy and disciplined bodies (**discipline; rational recreation**). The team sports pursued and fostered in the English public schools developed not only bodies that could be sent out into the Empire (**imperialism**), but also a specific kind of bourgeois sporting body that served as a marker of status and thus distinction from other social groups. Sport in this era has also been identified as challenging an American crisis in **masculinity**, which is thought to have developed as a consequence of urbanization and work becoming less physically demanding (**city, the**). In connection with these processes, **sports medicine** and sports science can be seen to have contributed to the modernist project through its emphasis not only on calibrating and recording sporting achievements of the body, but also on developing the body

and enabling it to perform more efficiently (i.e. coaching sciences, performance-enhancing **drugs**). Sports science becomes part of the broader structures of social power, used, for instance, to impose a strict male–female separation through sex tests (which the existence of transsexuals such as ex-tennis professional Renee Richards challenges), and as part of the Cold War ideological conflict (e.g. the West's questioning of the sporting practices of communist Eastern European countries in the 1970s and 1980s, particularly in relation to gender (**propaganda**)).

In the second stream, researchers have examined the way **deviance** becomes *embodied*, focusing on **violence** (both directed at others and to one's own body pain and injury), bodybuilding (which alerts us to the blurred border of the natural and unnatural) and **celebrity** (e.g. Magic Johnson's announcement that he was HIV positive). Finally, more closely overlapping with the Loy et al. typology, Cole discusses the role of the body in consumer culture, the preoccupation with **health** and self-improvement, the use of sporting and healthy bodies (and specific sporting personnel) to sell a range of products, and the interaction of celebrity bodies and the fitness industry (e.g. through workout videos).

Between them, these two typologies give a fairly comprehensive overview of the area, but the existence of two such divergent typologies is also indicative of a key issue for students of sport and the body. Twenty years ago, research in the sociology of sport rarely made explicit reference to the body: to some extent this omission has now been corrected. However, it is difficult to clearly delineate sport and the body as a research area, for taken to its logical extreme, the body is always present and therefore the body must necessarily form the focus of all the sociology of sport research. This, however, would be no more desirable than the situation in which the body is totally absent.

The increased focus on the body in both the sociology of sport and sociology more generally holds the promise that the former will become more central to the sociological discipline. The sociology of sport is in a unique position to demonstrate to the parent discipline the importance of the body in producing cultural and economic **capital**, and the attainment and maintenance of social status. Indeed, to some extent the rise of the sociology of the body has occurred in parallel with a rise in the sociology of sport.

Key Reading

Cole, C.L. (2000) 'Body studies in the sociology of sport', in J. Coakley and E. Dunning (eds), *Handbook of Sports Studies*. London: Sage. pp. 439–60.

Loy, J., Andrews, D. and Rinehart, R. (1993) 'The body in culture and sport', *Sport Science Review*, 2: 69–91.

Maguire, J. (1993) 'Bodies, sportscultures and societies: a critical review of some theories in the sociology of the body', *International Review for the Sociology of Sport*, 28: 33–52.

BODYLINE

The debate over the England cricket team's use of 'bodyline' (initially termed 'fast leg theory') dominated the 1932/3 test series against Australia, but was to have longer-lasting implications for relations between these two Empire nations (**imperialism**). Bodyline involved the persistent use of short-pitched fast bowling at the body of the batsman, and the positioning of a relatively large number of fielders on one side of the field (the 'leg' side). It was a tactic designed primarily to combat the success of Australian batsman Donald Bradman. That fast bowlers use of short-pitched deliveries ('bouncers') in order to disconcert the batsman was not a particularly new technique. However, bodyline was different in terms of: (1) the sustained nature of the attack, which therefore restricted the batsman's scoring opportunities; (2) the number of leg side fielders regularly deployed; (3) the lack of compassion with which the tactic was used (e.g. persisting to bowl bodyline at batsmen who had been hit and were visibly

shaken); and, perhaps most importantly of all, (4) because of the social context in which the matches took place.

The main 'English' protagonists were the captain, Douglas Jardine (a Scot), and his fast bowlers, Voce, Bowes, Allen and, most famously, Harold Larwood. When Australian wicketkeeper Bertie Oldfield was hit by a Larwood bouncer, the Australian Board of Control sent a telegram to the MCC claiming that bodyline had led to injuries and an 'intensely bitter feeling' between the players. Crucially they labelled it 'unsportsmanlike' (**fair play**). The MCC defended their team but offered the Australians the option of cancelling the tour. Jardine insisted that the accusation 'unsportsmanlike' be retracted, which (reluctantly) it was. On his return to England, however, Jardine was shunned by the cricketing authorities. Larwood never played for England again and emigrated to Australia where he was seen as a victim of the English **class** system.

Australian accounts of bodyline tend to be based on a theory of 'innocent professionals manipulated by wicked amateurs' (Birley, 1999: 103). More accurately, however, it should be conceived of in terms of the development of the importance of winning (relative to taking part (**amateurism**)), the changing balance of power in Anglo-Australian relations (according to Stoddart the Australians challenged the imperial tradition that Britain set the standards for 'civilized' behaviour), and the changing levels of **violence** in cricket, related to the **commercialization** and **globalization** of the sport.

Key Reading

Birley, D. (1999) *A Social History of English Cricket*. London: Aurum Press.

Malcolm, D. (2004) 'Cricket: civilizing and de-civilizing processes in the imperial game', in E. Dunning, D. Malcolm and I. Waddington (eds), *Sport Histories: Figurational Studies of the Development of Modern Sports*. London: Routledge. pp. 71–87.

Sissons, R. and Stoddart, B. (1984) *Cricket and Empire: The 1932 Bodyline Tour of Australia*. London: Allen and Unwin.

BOSMAN RULING

In July 1990, Jean-Marc Bosman, a relatively unknown Belgian footballer, took legal action against his club, RC Liege, for restraint of trade (**player reservation systems; retain and transfer system**). Liege had blocked Bosman's proposed move to French club US Dunkerque. The Belgian civil courts backed Bosman, and UEFA (Union of European Football Associations) – acting on behalf of the Belgian Football Association – took the case to the European Court of Justice. Citing Article 48 of the Treaty of Rome, the court ruled that restrictions on football players' free movement at the end of their contracts (e.g. the charging of transfer fees) were illegal.

The Bosman ruling had two key effects on football. First, footballers were granted the same rights as other workers in the European Union (EU). Leading players subsequently became increasingly powerful relative to clubs, commanding higher incomes and/or longer contracts. As a consequence of this ruling it also became clear that domestic leagues within the EU could not restrict the number of 'foreign' players which individual clubs could play in any one game, for EU citizens have equal legal status throughout the Union and discrimination on the basis of nationality is illegal. This increased the movement of players not just between clubs domestically, but also between EU countries (**sport labour migration**).

Second, the Bosman ruling ended an age of innocence when football authorities acted outside the parameters of normal legislation. A flood of legal complaints followed the ruling, including: (1) the right of clubs (as businesses) to trade anywhere in the EU (hence Wimbledon FC's proposed move to Dublin); (2) the potential abuse of power by the monopolies formed by national leagues and UEFA (**cartel**), which effectively restricts the trade of competitor organizations (i.e. rival leagues); and, related to this, (3) the collective sale of **broadcasting rights** by football leagues.

EU-wide regulations were subsequently applied to countries that make up the European Economic Area (those countries with which the EU has agreements over rights of free movement and trade, but which are not EU members). However, a more measured and less confrontational approach by the EU towards the regulation of football (and sport more generally) appeared at the 1997 Amsterdam Treaty. This recognized that there where instances when sport should *not* be treated as a 'normal' business. A number of legitimate exemptions were recognized, including: (1) where sporting objectives such as equality of sporting competition can only be reached by otherwise uncompetitive practice (e.g. where individual clubs' earnings or outgoings such as salaries are restricted to promote more even sporting contests (**competitive balance**)); (2) where practices can be seen to contribute towards the generation of national identity (which the EU recognizes as both a desirable and inherent feature of sport (**nationalism**)); and (3) where governing bodies can be seen to be acting 'for the greater good' of the professional and amateur game (thus in such circumstances it may be permissible to restrict the economic interests of professional clubs in favour of the grassroots of the game).

Key Reading

Foster, K. (2000) 'European law and football: who's in charge?', in J. Garland, D. Malcolm and M. Rowe (eds), *The Future of Football: Challenges for the Twenty-First Century*. London: Frank Cass. pp. 39–51.
Gardiner, S., with James, M., O'Leary, J. and Welch, R. (2001) *Sports Law*, 2nd edn. London: Cavendish Publishing.
Parrish, R. (2002) 'Football's place in the single European market', *Soccer and Society*, 3 (1): 1–21.

BOURDIEU

(**capital; field; habitus**)

BOYCOTTS

A boycott involves the refusal of one team/nation to compete with or alongside another in a sporting event, invariably with the intention of altering the political policies of the boycotted state. Boycotts have been identified as one of two primary ways in which political interests can use sport for their own ends (the other being the **propaganda** use a host nation can make while staging an event – e.g. the Nazi's use of the 1936 Berlin Olympics). There have been two main types of boycott in sport: (1) the boycott of sporting links with particular countries, most notably South Africa under the **apartheid** regime (see also **Gleneagles Agreement**); and (2) the boycott of particular events, most notably the Olympic Games (**IOC**). Boycotts exploit the popularity and mass appeal of sports to make a highly public statement about the acceptability or otherwise of another state's actions, policies or philosophies.

The 1936 Berlin Olympics witnessed the first attempted boycott, but during the Cold War period, sports boycotts became more frequently used in international conflict and propaganda wars. Between 1968 and 1996 boycotts on a greater or lesser scale occurred at each summer Olympic Games. The three most significant boycotts occurred in 1976, 1980 and 1984. In 1976, 28 African national Olympic committees withdrew their athletes from the Montreal Games. The Supreme Council for Sport in Africa had requested that New Zealand be barred from the Games on account of their rugby union team's continued links with South Africa (the IOC countered that they could not ban New Zealand, as rugby union was not, and still is not, an Olympic sport). In this instance, the threat of boycott failed to invoke a policy change, and the relatively low power and prestige of the African nations involved meant that many judged that the Games were only minimally impaired by their absence.

In 1980, the United States led a 62-nation boycott of the Moscow Olympic Games in protest against the Soviet invasion of Afghanistan. Other notable absentees included Canada, Israel, West Germany and Japan. However, the British team competed, ignoring Prime Minister Margaret Thatcher's instructions to boycott the Games. While not invoking a change in political policy either, this boycott (weakened by British non-compliance) was more effective in that American television broadcaster NBC and a number of other wealthy Western broadcasters cancelled their contracts to cover the Games, thus reducing revenue for the Games Organizing Committee.

The Russian-led boycott of the 1984 Los Angeles Olympic Games, though formally based on security issues and the infringement of their athletes' rights, is widely believed to have effectively been in retaliation for the American boycott of the Moscow Games four years earlier. While 16 nations joined the boycott, the Romanian team, part funded by the IOC and the Los Angeles Organizing Committee, broke the boycott and harmed its effectiveness. The Games were marked by their spectacular showbiz-style presentation, audiences whose displays of **nationalism** were fuelled by the broader political conflict, and tremendous commercial success (**commercialization**). Though clearly part of the propaganda war, many felt that the Russians (who at that time were the most successful nation in terms of winning Olympic medals) would have gained more political leverage had they participated.

Houlihan (1994) argues that in order for a boycott to be successful the following factors are essential: (1) the issue must be, and must remain, clear-cut; (2) there must be an expectation that the boycott will have an effect on policy; (3) states must appear to boycott voluntarily (i.e. are not compelled by superpower nations); and (4) the event must be deemed to have been diminished by the withdrawal. Because these factors so rarely all came together, boycotts have now largely gone out of fashion. Boycotts are unsubtle actions and history shows that often the boycotters, or intermediaries such as the IOC, became more embarrassed than the intended victim. Moreover, for many the propaganda opportunity of attending may be more useful than blanket withdrawal. Participation allows smaller-scale demonstrations to take place during the event, and these may be viewed more sympathetically than withdrawal, thus having a more significant impact.

Key Reading

Guttmann, A. (1992) *The Olympics: A History of the Modern Games*. Urbana and Chicago: University of Illinois Press. esp. Ch. 10.

Houlihan, B. (1994) *Sport and International Politics*. London: Harvester Wheatsheaf.

BREAD AND CIRCUSES

(Roman Games)

BROADCASTING RIGHTS

Sports teams own the intellectual copyright to their performances. Moreover, the marginal cost to a sports team of broadcasting one of its matches is very low (compared, say, to wages, building a **stadium**). These factors combine to make the sale of broadcasting rights to **media** companies an attractive proposition for sports teams (see also **Internet**).

Sport, however, is a 'perishable good'. Moreover, its highest value occurs when it is live and thus when sports teams are exploiting another key income source – revenue from ticket sales. Consequently, owners of sports teams and leagues were initially reluctant to allow events to be broadcast on television through fear that such access would reduce spectatorship. In the US, clubs operated 'blackouts' that prevented live coverage being shown within particular geographical areas. In the UK, the rights to a limited number of mainly football matches were sold.

The degree to which exposure on television reduces ticket sales (and associated revenues such as merchandise sales) remains debated. Baimbridge et al. (1996) found evidence of a negative impact on Premiership football and rugby league in England in the 1990s, though a longer-term perspective suggests that the growth in the broadcasting of football in England during the 1990s has increased interest in football in general, and attendance at live games across the sport.

However, such has been the increase in revenues accruing from the sale of broadcasting rights in recent years that the effect on live attendance has become less relevant. The cost of broadcasting rights for each English Premiership football match increased from £0.64 million in 1992 to £4.76 million in 2007. Broadcasting rights now account for 56 per cent of American football's total revenue in the US (Sandy et al., 2004) and up to 42 per cent of the total revenue of some Premiership football clubs (Gratton and Taylor, 2000). Worldwide broadcasting rights for the 2006 FIFA World Cup were sold for $2.5 billion (though the company that bought them subsequently went bankrupt when advertising revenues and the willingness of **fans** to subscribe to pay-per-view access were lower than expected). Such income shifts are indicative of a change in the balance of power between sports governing bodies and **media** companies, and between sports governing bodies and their different types of consumer.

In Europe the sale of broadcasting rights for football dwarfs those of other sports. BSkyB devotes three-quarters of its expenditure on UK sports broadcasting rights to Premiership football. But the sale of European broadcasting rights raises much less than in the US; in 1998 the sale of broadcasting rights raised $2.2 billion for American football, $0.53 billion for the NBA (National Basketball Association) and $0.6 billion for baseball. In part this difference is a consequence of government legislation in Europe (notably the UK, but also Germany, Italy and Denmark) which defines certain events as 'listed', meaning that the sale of broadcasting rights is restricted so that public access is guaranteed (**listed events**). However, it must also be recognized that the US is a wealthier nation, that the **franchise**-based, **cartel** sports leagues in North America effectively create scarcity value, and that American sports tend to be structured in ways more favourable to broadcasting (e.g. with more regular and predictable breaks in play that facilitate higher advertising revenues).

The key political issues regarding broadcasting rights are: (1) whether certain groups in the population are effectively excluded through cost (the rationale for the 'listed' status of certain sports events); (2) whether the structuring of sports events for television audiences (either in scheduling or in format) discriminates against those who attend the live event (**fans** who might be seen as more 'committed' or more 'traditional'); and (3) whether broadcasters have become too powerful relative to sports bodies (**media**; and **vertical integration**).

Economically, the central issues revolve around the effect of the sale of broadcasting rights on the **competitive balance** of a sports league. Some leagues, such as the NFL (American football), mainly sell broadcasting rights as a single entity (there are limited amounts teams can make through the sale of local broadcasting rights) and distribute income evenly between teams (there are relatively small bonus payments for teams that reach the play-offs). In the European Champions League for football, revenue is distributed according to participation in the tournament and playing success, but most significantly according to the fees that a team's domestic broadcaster has paid (see Solberg and Gratton, 2004). In English football, Premiership revenues are allocated according to the number of appearances in televised matches and final placement in the league.

A further related issue stemming particularly from the Premiership has been the degree to which the income from the sale of broadcasting rights effectively separates some sports leagues from the rest. The financial gulf between the Premiership and the football leagues below it has meant that the contest to get into the Premiership is extremely competitive. The play-off match to get into the Premiership has been dubbed the richest match on the planet, worth an estimated £60 million to the 2007 winner. These pressures have led clubs to take extreme financial risks and have also led some into bankruptcy.

Key Reading

Baimbridge, M., Cameron, S. and Dawson, P. (1996) 'Satellite television and the demand for football: a whole new ball game', *Scottish Journal of Political Economy*, 43 (3): 317–33.

Gratton, C. and Taylor, P. (2000) *Economics and Sport and Recreation*. London: Routledge. esp. Chs 9–12.

Sandy, R., Sloane, P.J. and Rosentraub, M. (2004) *The Economics of Sport: An International Perspective*. Basingstoke: Palgrave Macmillan. esp. Ch. 6.

Solberg, H.-A. and Gratton, C. (2004) 'Would European soccer clubs benefit from playing in a super league?', *Soccer and Society*, 5 (1): 61–81.

BROKEN-TIME PAYMENTS

One of the two initial forms of financial recompense in rugby, signalling the monetarization and professionalization of the game (**amateurism**). Broken-time payments were justified as compensation for the loss of earnings players incurred as a consequence of playing the game. It was the debate over broken-time payments that led to the 1895 split between the RFU and the Northern Union, which later (in 1922) became the Rugby League.

The rugby establishment resisted professionalization on the grounds that it led to idleness and would degrade the game. Broken-time payments were resisted on the more specific grounds that they discriminated against the middle class (in that compensation for loss of earnings was greater for those in higher earning occupations and thus clubs would be less able to pay, and less likely to play, middle-class players) and that this would lead to the exclusion of this **class** from the sport (and the exclusion of amateurs more generally). Conversely, rugby administrators in Yorkshire and Lancashire saw broken-time payments as the only way of inhibiting the rising trend of professionalism in the game, and keeping a semblance of amateur control.

The Northern Union was established with the sole aim of securing the legitimacy of recompensing players for their 'broken-time'. It insisted that the loss of time be bona fide and, importantly, it established a clause which stated that broken-time payments could only be paid to those in 'legitimate' occupations. Players had their registrations suspended for working in public houses, or simply for moving jobs without informing the rugby authorities. These paternalistic employment regulations were partly an attempt to keep the game respectable (by discouraging 'idleness', drinking and **gambling**) but partly an exercise in social control of the lower classes.

Key Reading

Collins, T. (1998) *Rugby's Great Split: Class, Culture and the Origins of Rugby League Football*. London: Frank Cass.

Dunning, E. and Sheard, K. (2005) *Barbarians, Gentlemen and Players: A Sociological Study of the Development of Rugby Football*, 2nd edn. London: Routledge.

BROUGHTON, JACK (1703–89)

A prizefighter and early boxing entrepreneur. Formerly a pupil at **Figg**'s 'School of Arms', Broughton opened the Haymarket (boxing) Amphitheatre in London. However, more significant in the long term were Broughton's rules, devised in 1743 following the death of a boxer in Broughton's ampitheatre, and his introduction of 'mufflers' (an early form of glove) in 1747. These rules governed boxing for over a century when they were superseded by the rules drawn up by the Marquess of Queensberry (widely adopted by 1865).

Sheard (2004) notes that almost all of Broughton's rules were introduced to protect **gambling** interests, rather than in an attempt to protect boxers' **health**. Boxing, like other eighteenth-century sports such as cricket and horse racing, was characterized by the regular and heavy gambling of aristocrats and gentry (in 1750 the Duke of Cumberland placed a £10,000 bet on Broughton to win a contest). In connection with this, 'mufflers' were only used in training, not in actual contests. Their introduction, Sheard (2004) argues, was linked to growing sensitivity over appearances and the need of the upper classes not to take on the (rough) appearance of those deemed their social inferiors (**civilizing process**).

Concerns over the brutality of boxing (and perhaps also stemming from the Duke of Cumberland's anger at losing the £10,000 bet) led to the closure of Broughton's Ampitheatre in 1750, but there is some debate over the significance of this. Brailsford (1988) argues that closure stunted boxing's development. Sheard, however, argues that in addition to this, it should be noted that closure effectively drove boxing underground (and into rural areas) and this had the unintended consequence of reducing the theatricality and exhibition that early **commercialization** processes had spawned in boxing at this time. Sheard argues that the closure, therefore, enabled boxing to develop into a 'true' sport, unhindered by a theatrical rival (**play and dis-play**; **quest for excitement**), which was beneficial to boxing's longer-term survival.

Key Reading

Brailsford, D. (1988) *Bareknuckles: A Social History of Prizefighting*. Cambridge: Lutterworth Press.

Sheard, K. (2004) 'Boxing in the western civilizing process', in E. Dunning, D. Malcolm and I. Waddington (eds), *Sport Histories: Figurational Studies of the Development of Modern Sports*. London: Routledge. pp. 15–30.

BURNOUT

Can be defined as physical or emotional exhaustion, depression or disillusionment. In sport, burnout is a term commonly used to explain the premature ending, or the lack of fulfilment, of a promising athletic career. Jennifer Capriati is perhaps the most famous example of burnout, reaching the semi-finals of the French Open Tennis tournament in 1990 at the age of 14, and winning a gold medal at the Barcelona Olympics in 1992. However, in the next two years she was arrested for shoplifting and for the possession of marijuana. She withdrew from competitive tennis for a while before making a successful comeback by winning the Australian Open in 2001. There are, of course, many other cases where promising athletes have failed to fulfil their early potential, but few of these receive such publicity.

Within sport studies both psychologists and sociologists have attempted to develop frameworks to understand burnout. Smith (1986), a psychologist, argues that there is a four-stage progression to athletic burnout: (1) coaches and parents place pressure on a child to train and be competitive; (2) the child athlete perceives these pressures as either acceptable or threatening; (3) if the child athlete feels threatened by such pressures, he/she reacts with a 'negative' psychological response, such as fatigue, declining **motivation**, etc.; (4) a psychological coping strategy is developed manifesting itself, for instance, in decreased levels of performance, exploration of alternative lifestyles and, in the extreme, complete withdrawal from sport.

Coakley's sociological analysis of burnout, (1992), however, focuses on the organization of high performance sport. Burnout, Coakley suggests, is likely to occur when being a young athlete interferes or clashes with other stages of social development normally associated with adolescence. Interviewees who had experienced burnout felt that they had lost control over their sporting lives, felt unable to develop other, non-sporting, aspects of their lives and identities (e.g. developing sexual relations), and came to associate sport with high levels of **stress** and low levels of fun. Thus Coakley argued that while the management of stress helped prevent burnout, it was also important to empower young athletes, providing them with a greater input into the social organization of training and competition.

Key Reading

Coakley, J. (1992) 'Burnout among adolescent athletes: a personal failure or social problem?', *Sociology of Sport Journal*, 9 (3): 271–85.

Gould, D. (1996) 'Personal motivation gone awry: burnout in competitive athletics', *Quest*, 48 (3): 275–89.

Smith, R.E. (1986) 'Toward a cognitive-affective model of athletic burnout', *Journal of Sport Psychology*, 8 (1): 36–50.

BUSBY BABES

(**Munich air disaster**)

C

CAPITAL

For Marx, capital is often used interchangeably with the means of production within capitalist economies. Under the economic system known as capitalism, the private ownership and control of capital distinguishes the proletariat and bourgeoisie **class**es, and thus forms the central dynamic of historical change (**Marxism**). In this respect, Marxist sociologists of sport may talk about commercial sports teams as capital (i.e. the means of production to which athletes devote their labour). Reference may also be made to the way sport serves 'the needs of capital' (e.g. through creating a fit and healthy workforce (**rational recreation**)), but, responding to the criticism that they are guilty of **reification**, such phrases are increasingly rare in sociology.

The notion of capital, however, has been expanded by Pierre Bourdieu, and it constitutes one of the three central concepts in his work (see also **field** and **habitus**). For Bourdieu, as for Marx, capital is a form of power; however, unlike Marx, he sees power as derived from a variety of sources. Consequently, Bourdieu speaks not only of 'economic capital' (wealth), but also of 'cultural capital' (the consumption of cultural goods, such as sport). To a lesser extent terms such as 'social capital' (prestige), 'educational capital' (qualifications) and 'symbolic capital' (reputation and image) are also used. Thus access to a prestigious golf club may require both economic capital (through high membership fees) and cultural capital (through the need to be nominated by existing members).

Educational capital (such as the school that one attended) may also be helpful. Once achieved, however, membership of a prestigious golf club is likely to lead to heightened cultural, social and symbolic capital. Advocates of Bourdieu's work argue that by embracing an expanded concept of capital (or capitals), he successfully distances himself from the criticism traditionally levelled at Marxism; that is to say, that the perspective is economically deterministic. Critics of Bourdieu argue that the very use of the term capital, however, illustrates a residual reliance on economic power, if only in the last instance.

Key Reading

Laberge, S. and Kay, J. (2002) 'Pierre Bourdieu's sociocultural theory and sport practice', in J. Maguire and K. Young (eds), *Theory, Sport & Society*. Oxford: Jai, pp. 239–66.

Tomlinson, A. (2004) 'Pierre Bourdieu and the sociological study of sport: habitus, capital and field', in R. Giulianotti (ed.), *Sport and Modern Social Theorists*. London: Palgrave Macmillan. pp. 161–72.

CARNIVAL

The central characteristic of carnival is the temporary negation or subversion of the structures and hierarchies that generally dominate a society. The Caribbean roots of carnival involve the temporary (and perhaps only theoretical) suppression of social and political tensions combined with a stylized and ritualized conflict expressed through satire, parody and mimicry of their colonial masters by the lower-class blacks (**imperialism**). More broadly speaking, carnival involves colourful, loud, irreverent, gregarious and ostentatious displays (i.e. a release from traditional social constraints).

The first analysis of the carnivalesque character of sport was provided by Richard Burton (1985). Cricket in the West Indies, he argued, provided a context for carnivalesque social resistance, where leading cricketers became the equivalent of carnival kings, 'princes of the people, symbolic subverters and destroyers of a world where white is might'. Richard Guiliannotti (1999) has been prominent in expanding these ideas to football spectatorship, citing Scotland's **Tartan Army** as perhaps the most renowned example of carnivalesque fans, alongside Danish 'Roligans', Norwegian 'Drillos' and Dutch 'Oranji'.

A central debate over the interpretation of the carnivalesque character of sports **fans** concerns the degree to which such groups have been manufactured and manipulated by the **media** and sports governing bodies for the positive, media friendly, images they present (in contrast, for instance, with coverage of **football hooliganism**). However, Guiliannotti's work, and work on the **Barmy Army**, indicate that fans are far more active in constructing their own image and thus the scope for social resistance by sports fans is a tangible phenomenon.

Key Reading

Burton, R.D.E. (1985) 'Cricket, carnival and street culture in the Caribbean', *British Journal of Sports History*, 2 (2): 179–97.
Guiliannotti, R. (1999) *Football: A Sociology of the Global Game*. Cambridge: Polity.

CARTEL

A collusive association (e.g. a sports league) of individual enterprises (e.g. sports teams or clubs) in order to monopolize the production and distribution of a product or service (e.g. football matches) and/or control prices, etc. for members' economic gain. Cartels are generally illegal or are subject to state regulation, for they tend to limit competition between producers and this tends to be to the disadvantage of consumers and employees. However, most sports leagues either act as, or contain features of, a cartel. These might include: (1) the redistribution of income between parties (e.g. sharing gate receipts, money from **sponsorship** and the sale of **broadcasting rights**); (2) the distribution of playing talent through **player reservation systems**; (3) salary caps that prevent too much inequality in playing strength; and (4) the restriction of output through the control on the number of teams in a league, or the number of competitions sanctioned by the cartel.

Regulators have traditionally shown considerable tolerance towards sports which operate as cartels, swayed by the argument that such equalizing measures are required to ensure uncertainty of outcome (**competitive balance**), which itself is argued to be vital to the continued appeal of sports. Thus, while the cartel effectively limits the earnings of the leading members of the league, this restriction is seen as a necessary evil that ensures the longer-term viability (and profit maximization) of the group as a whole.

Key Reading

Slack, T. (2004) *The Commercialisation of Sport*. London: Routledge.
Grattan, C. and Taylor, P. (2000) *Economics of Sport and Recreation*. London: E. & F.N. Spon.

CATHARSIS

Originally an Aristotelian concept referring to the purging of **emotions** through the evocation of anger, pity, etc. while watching drama or reading literature. In the context of sport, the catharsis hypothesis suggests that as a consequence of vicariously experiencing the **aggression** and **violence** of others, one's own feelings of aggression are purged. Thus, the argument proceeds, by witnessing violent sports events (either live or on television), spectators are able to release their aggression/frustration and thus are less inclined to be violent. However, though difficult to test with any great accuracy, the majority of experiments by social psychologists have failed to support the catharsis theory, and indeed many point to the phenomenon of sports crowd violence as providing contrary evidence; that is to say, watching violent sporting encounters *leads* to greater levels of violence and aggression.

The notion of catharsis in sport has largely been associated with the sociological theory of **functionalism**. Catharsis, it has been argued, has been identified as one of the socio-emotional **functions of sport**. Catharsis, however, is also evident in Elias and Dunning's early work on sport, emotions and the **quest for excitement**, which has led to the twin claims that: (1) figurational sociology is essentially a form of functionalism; and (2) that the theory of the quest for excitement can be empirically falsified (i.e. that sport can lead to increased violence and aggression). Dunning (1999), however, refutes both these claims, stating that figurational sociology does not contain the 'harmonistic bias' of which functionalists have been criticized, and that his and Elias's original use of catharsis centrally involved the *generation* of high levels of emotion and excitement in leisure, rather than the *purging* thereof.

Key Reading

Dunning, E. (1999) *Sport Matters: Sociological Studies of Sport, Violence and Civilization*. London: Routledge. esp. Ch. 1.

Guttmann, A. (1986) *Sport Spectators*. New York: Columbia University Press.

Smith, M. (1983) *Violence and Sport*. Toronto: Butterworths.

CELEBRITY

A celebrity can be defined as someone who is known for being well known, someone whose name was first made by the news, but whose name itself now makes news. In recent times, sports celebrities have moved to the vanguard of popular culture and have become as big as celebrities from popular music and film.

While societies have always had their famous leaders, heroes or stars, many social scientists argue that the contemporary notion of celebrity should be seen as analytically separate. Whereas sports heroes like W.G. Grace (**amateurism**) and 'Babe' Ruth were both revered within and members of their local communities, and famous largely on account of their sporting achievements, today's celebrities have a global impact. Increasingly, image (as opposed to heroic sporting feats) is the key to an individual's celebrity status and, in contrast to celebrities of the past, there is now a lifestyle chasm between celebrities and **fans** and a perception that they inhabit separate social worlds.

Two questions are central to this area of study: What features of contemporary society account for the growth in the distinction and recognition of celebrity? And why, within this trend, have sports celebrities become so prominent? In answer to the first question, Rojek (2001) argues that the rise of celebrity can be linked to three interconnected historical processes: (1) the democratization of society (and the decline of traditional establishment figures such as monarchs); (2) the decline of organized **religion** and the secularization of society, which enable the quality of the 'sacred' to become more widely dispersed; and (3) the **commodification** of everyday life whereby celebrities become commodities to which consumers are attracted. In contemporary society it is only through the process of consumption that celebrity status becomes concrete (**consumer culture**).

In answer to this second question, it should be noted that during the twentieth century there was a noticeable shift away from the celebration of political, business and professional personnel, towards the fields of entertainment in general, and sport in particular. This, in many ways, was symptomatic of the shift in importance away from production and towards consumption during the latter part of the twentieth century. With regard to sport, however, four main factors should be considered: (1) the growth of satellite television, the expansion of sports broadcasting and the place of sport in TV culture and the **media** more broadly; (2) the increased social cachet of sport through increased emphasis on **health**, fitness and the **body**; (3) the role of sports stars as a countervailing presence to the crisis in **masculinity**; and (4) the **commercialization** and growing economic power of the sports industry. In addition to this, Smart (2005) argues, modern celebrities have a distinct (unique even) aura of authenticity (compared, say, to film or rock stars), demonstrated through their regular live and unmediated performance of rare and valued skills.

Increasingly, social scientists have examined individual sports celebrities, the most notable of which have been **David Beckham**, **George Best**, **Michael Jordan**, **Anna Kournikova**, and **Tiger Woods**. These case studies have revealed a number of pertinent trends. First, they have highlighted the role of advertising and merchandise, both in making money for the celebrity and thus elevating their lifestyle beyond the reach of 'normal' people, and in creating the image of the sports celebrity, who may now be seen as relatively proactive in his/her self-promotion. Companies such as **Nike** not only use celebrities to sell their products, but become central in the process that sees a skilled athlete develop into a celebrity. Second, case studies have highlighted the importance of the celebrity's links to corporations (epitomized in Beckham's negotiations with Manchester United over the relative enhancement values of his 'image' and their 'brand'). Third, the role of intermediaries (e.g. agents) has been revealed. Celebrities have entourages that protect the celebrity's financial interests, handle publicity and seek to establish a

monopoly position over (and thus control of) the celebrity's image. Fourth, the centrality of image has been highlighted. Though clearly manufactured, image must be grounded and believable. However, an open-ended or ambiguous image may enable a greater number of people to 'buy into' it, and allow the celebrity to develop over time and thus have a longer 'shelf-life'. Finally, the longevity of sporting celebrity is linked to lasting playing success. Though Kournikova represents something of an exception, authenticity has been described as a 'vulnerable quality', such that dips in form or too close an association with corporations (e.g. the suspicion that an athlete cares more about money than performance or that the sponsor 'pulls the strings') can lead to a fall from grace and a decline in status.

Key Reading

Andrews, D. and Jackson, S. (eds) (2001) *Sports Stars: The Cultural Politics of Sporting Celebrity*. London: Routledge.

Rojek, C. (2001) *Celebrity*. London: Reaktion Books.

Smart, B. (2005) *The Sports Star: Modern Sport and the Cultural Economy of Sporting Celebrity*. London: Sage.

CENTRAL COUNCIL OF PHYSICAL RECREATION (CCPR)

Established in 1935 and up until 1972 (and the formation of the **Sports Council**) the CCPR was the main sports administration body in the UK, owning and running the five national sports centres (Crystal Palace, Bisham Abbey, Lilleshall, Plas y Brenin and Holme Pierrepont). However, with the establishment of the Sports Council, an agreement was reached that saw these facilities transferred to government ownership in exchange for continued government funding of the CCPR. The CCPR became an umbrella organization for national governing and representative bodies of sport and recreation in the UK, but in contrast to the Sports Council this agreement enables the CCPR to retain a high degree of independence.

The CCPR now represents 270 separate bodies with sporting interests, and around 150,000 voluntary sports clubs. It claims to speak, and act, to 'promote, protect and develop the interests of sport and physical recreation at all levels'. While the stated policy goals of the two organizations show considerable overlap, the CCPR is distinct from the Sports Council in that: (1) it is not a government agency (and thus has greater independence from government); (2) it does not allocate grants; and (3) its leadership is democratically elected by the membership.

By emphasizing its independence from government, the CCPR claims to represent the 'real' voice of sport (though in reality it is an amalgam of diverse and at times competing interest groups). Thus the CCPR attempts to influence government policy through lobbying and submitting views to parliamentary committees on relevant legislation. The CCPR is also active internationally, as a member of the European Parliament Sports Inter Group, and with similar European organizations through ENGSO (European Non-Governmental Sports Organization).

Key Reading

Houlihan, B. (1991) *The Government and Politics of British Sport*. London: Routledge.
www.ccpr.org.uk Home page of the Central Council of Physical Recreation.
www.engso.com Home page of the European Non-Governmental Sports Organisation.

CHARIOT RACES

Of all the **Roman Games**, chariot races were held most frequently, and attracted the greatest number of spectators. While the Colosseum in which the **gladiators** performed held 50,000, the Circus Maximus in which chariot races were staged could hold up to 250,000.

Many of the charioteers were initially slaves, but a great deal of them subsequently bought their freedom with their prize money. Some free men chose to enter the profession, accepting the substantial prize money and public adulation available as compensation for the low status generally and officially accorded. Chariots were normally pulled by two or four horses, but sometimes by up to seven. Races were either individual or team events consisting of two, three or four chariots. In team events, team mates colluded to block or foul the opposition's best racer. This, and the physical demands of being pulled around sharp turns, made events highly dangerous. Charioteers carried knives to enable them to cut themselves loose from the reins (which they wrapped around their waists and wrists) should their chariot overturn. Nevertheless, many charioteers died young.

The chariot races were controlled by wealthy owners who developed great stables of horses (much like modern horse racing and for many of the same reasons). These stables formed the basis of the *circus factions* (Cameron, 1976), or teams which were referred to by their colour. Four existed initially: the Reds, the Whites, the Blues and the Greens. Eventually, however, the Reds and the Whites became absorbed into the Blues and the Greens respectively, leaving just two factions. There is evidence of regular and large-scale rioting stemming from chariot races (in Constantinople in particular), with wooden stands burned to the ground and troops called upon to restore order. It remains debated whether such factions and riots were essentially politically motivated or even divided into different social **class** groupings, for while intuitively this seems likely, documentary evidence is sparse.

Key Reading

Cameron, A. (1976) *Circus Factions: Blues and Greens in Rome and Byzantium*. Oxford: Clarendon Press.

Guttmann, A. (1986) *Sports Spectators*. New York: Columbia University Press.

Harris, H.A. (1972) *Sport in Greece and Rome*. London: Thames and Hudson.

CHILD SEXUAL ABUSE (CSA)

A relatively recent addition to the sociology of sport literature; the first conceptual and empirical studies on CSA appeared in the late 1980s and early 1990s (Brackenridge, 2001). Early studies arose from wider literatures on harassment and discrimination in sport, notably from work on women and **gender** politics since abuse, harassment and discrimination are conceptually linked. CSA is thus cast as one form of sexual **violence** in sport.

Evidence for CSA in sport has been accumulated as much through the case files of governing bodies of sport as by primary research, with awareness of the issue having been raised through child protection policy, advocacy and training work since the early 1990s. Indeed, the evidence base for CSA is still much smaller than that for adult sexual harassment in sport. This is partly due to the complexity of ethics protocols in such a sensitive research area, and partly due to the historic focus on intra-familial abuse in the general sociology literature which thus ignores sport and leisure as potential sites for CSA.

In order to make sense of the prominence of CSA in contemporary sport it is important to problematize the concept. The notion of a 'child', for example, is itself a contested concept, drawing on both legal and developmental interpretations. The legal age of consent varies widely from country to country, from as young as 12 to as old as 21. In sport, junior/senior distinctions also vary, meaning that there is no simple correspondence between chronological, developmental and 'sport' age. It has also been hypothesized that early-peaking sports may pose greater risks for sexual abuse than those where elite athletes tend to be much older (Brackenridge, 2001). Concern for children's safety from sexual exploitation in sport has led to a number of significant policy responses, led by the Sport England/NSPCC coalition that funds the Child Protection in Sport Unit (CPSU) (www.thecpsu.org.uk).

'Abuse' is also variously interpreted. According to the NSPCC, sexual abuse is just one form of child abuse, the others being emotional abuse, physical abuse, neglect and bullying (www.thecpsu.org.uk). Of these, research suggests that sexual abuse may be the least *prevalent* yet most *prominent* form. Why? The emergence of CSA as an issue in sport has been linked to wider social trends and **moral panics** associated with threats to the family, for example following the Cleveland sex abuse scandal in the early 1980s. These moral panics have been explained by both preoccupations with **risk** in late **modernity** and attempts to defend traditional sexual boundaries in the face of the liberalization of sex and gender relations.

Within sport, several high-profile cases of sexual abuse came to the courts in the early 1990s and drew significant **media** attention since they involved national and Olympic coaches such as Paul Hickson from British swimming and Graham James from Canadian ice hockey (Kirby et al., 2000). What constitutes abuse in sport is also contested since, in some sports, sexual relationships between coaches and athletes, or between athletes, are normative despite often crossing legal thresholds. The physical and erotic content of sport has also been used to explain what are objectively defined as sexually abusive relationships yet subjectively appear to be consensual. Feminist sociologists (**feminism**) and child welfare specialists argue that the notion of consent in a sexual relationship is rendered invalid by the structural power differential between the coach (dominant), who is in a position of trust, and the athlete (subservient), or between a senior and more junior athlete. Indeed, such is the concern in the UK about coaches engaging in sexual relationships with athletes age 16 or 17, i.e. *above* the legal age of consent, that the Home Office is even considering extending the law to make such relationships illegal. The issue of what constitutes sexual abuse is further complicated in same-sex relationships between team members, which may be strictly legal but culturally sanctioned. Indeed, homophobic harassment in sport often acts as a form of socio-sexual regulatory control.

Another important form of sexual abuse in sport occurs through 'hazing', whereby new players or 'rookies' are induced into the **subculture** of a sport through sexually degrading or illegal initiation rituals, often **alcohol-fuelled**. This phenomenon has been more widely acknowledged and researched in North American sport than elsewhere (Johnson and Holman, 2003) but is evident in many other global sport cultures.

As yet, there are limited data available on the prevalence of CSA in sport but it is clear that both male and female athletes can be victims. Perpetrators of CSA are usually in positions of authority, most frequently but not exclusively male coaches, but athlete-generated abuse also occurs, usually through hazing or bullying. The status and power of the coach/abuser act effectively as an alibi for him/her, making it difficult for victims to report what has happened to them. Because of this, CSA is frequently kept secret and continues over long periods of time.

Sport is also an important site for recognizing young athletes who have been abused outside sport, usually in the family, and for referring them to experts for advice, support and redress. This can only be done where comprehensive policies and education on CSA are in place.

Policy responses to CSA vary widely from country to country, with some – notably former Eastern bloc countries and many developing countries – still being in denial about the possibility that such a phenomenon exists in sport. Others, however, have put in place extensive procedures, codes of conduct and training programmes.

Key Reading

Brackenridge, C.H. (2001) *Spoilsports: Understanding and Preventing Sexual Exploitation in Sport*. London: Routledge.

Brackenridge, C.H. and Fasting, K. (eds) (2002) *Sexual Harassment and Abuse in Sport – International Research and Policy Perspectives*. London: Whiting and Birch.

Johnson, J. and Holman, M. (eds) (2003) *Making the Team: Inside the World of Sports Hazing and Initiations*. Toronto: Canadian Scholars' Press.

Kirby, S., Greaves, L. and Kankivsky, O. (2000) *The Dome of Silence: Sexual Abuse and Harassment in Sport*. London: Zed Books.

www.thecpsu.org.uk Home page of the Sport England/NSPCC Child Protection in Sport Unit.

Celia Brackenridge

CHOKING

While different sports may have their own name for this phenomenon (the 'yips' in golf, 'dartitis' in darts), choking refers to the inability of an athlete to regain control over his/her performance as it progressively deteriorates. Choking therefore should be conceived of as a process rather than an event. It can happen to participants at all levels of sport and depends upon the emotional significance of the event for the individual (e.g. the competition is seen as important, the competition reaches a critical stage, or the competitor perceives themselves being evaluated by coaches, peers, etc.). The process of choking normally entails certain physiological changes (perspiration, increased muscle tension, breathing and pulse rate) and attentional changes (an increasingly internal and narrow focus, and reduced flexibility of approach (**concentration**)). The consequences for performance are commonly a breakdown in timing and coordination, fatigue, a propensity to rush, and the inability to attend to task relevant cues, often characterized by self-doubt and negative **self-talk**.

Key Reading

Weinberg, R. and Gould, D. (2003) *Foundations of Sport and Exercise Psychology*. Champaign, IL: Human Kinetics.

CITY, THE

The urbanizing landscapes and expanding capitalist economic system that transformed the societies of Europe and North America fueled the evolution of contemporary sport. Stimulating and sustaining urban growth necessitated the mass production of agricultural and material goods, disrupting traditional patterns of work, leisure and land use. In large cites, such as London and New York, immigrants with widely diverse sporting backgrounds adjusted to the routine of congested urban-industrial culture, which created both the demand and the means for the development and growth of sports. As a result, as Steven Reiss has documented, most current major sports evolved, or were invented, in the city.

Cities were the sites of dense populations, transportation networks, technological innovations, discretionary incomes and the entrepreneurial spirit necessary for the success of commercial sports (**commercialization**). Additionally, cities were the focus of concerns for **health**, morality and community, which continually served as rationales for promoting sports to urbanites. Through numerous case studies, sport historians have documented how the development of both sport and cities was intertwined and how early sport was promoted as a means both to escape urban problems and for building urban (sub)communities. David Nasaw (1993), for example, shows how it would be wrong to simply view cities as the causes of social problems which sports helped solve; rather cities need to be seen as providing the conditions necessary for the rapid growth of sports. Other scholars, including Melvin Adelman and Steven Hardy, considered sports as both cause and effect in the development of physical structures, social organizations and ideologies in Boston and New York between 1820 and 1915 (for a review of historical literature on sport and the city, see Hardy, 1997; Schimmel, 2006).

A further dominant theme in the sport studies literature on the contemporary city is the examination of the ways in which sport has come to be valued not for its own sake, but as a means to other desirable ends, both intangible and tangible. For example, sport is often utilized to promote a city and in an attempt to foster a sense of urban identity and enhance the quality of life of urban residents. The connection of sports with cities for the purposes of 'place advertising' is often forged by city governments, local-level business elites and/or city 'boosters'. Even in small towns, local chambers of commerce place road signs that announce to visitors that the town is 'Home of the Champions' in some type of sport. Government subsidies of high school and college sports in the United States are anchored, in part, in the belief that success in sport brings recognition to host cities and creates solidarity among local citizens. This rationale extends to elite-level sport. One of the reasons state and local tax monies are invested in professional team **franchises** in North America is the belief that these franchises are catalysts for civic community building and that they express to the rest of the continent that the city deserves 'big time' status. Sports mega-events serve similar functions at a global level (**mega-events, hosting of**). Cities spend enormous amounts of money to bid on and host large, high-profile sports events as a means to promote a city 'image' to the rest of the world. For example, local boosters in Atlanta used the 1996 Olympic Games to promote the city as a racially integrated community symbolic of the 'new south', and boosters in Sydney promoted the city during the 2000 Games as a friendly and environmentally conscious community (Lenskyj, 2000).

Closely related to these issues of image and community, city boosters promote the idea that sport has tangible benefits for city residents. City governments, for example, support inner-city 'midnight basketball' leagues in an effort to reduce crime rates. In addition, in cities around the globe, sport **stadiums** and infrastructure construction are connected to urban regeneration schemes through the belief that elite sports teams and events stimulate the local economy and create jobs. Scholars who study sport-related urban development, however, refute the claim that this type of civic investment provides real benefits for the city as a whole. Empirical evidence shows that while some groups in a city may profit, others are actually burdened (Schimmel, 2002).

Sports studies scholars view with deep caution any notion that sports can act as a solution to general urban problems. In spite of the fact that sport may create a sense of attachment that is important at an interpersonal level, sport does not significantly change the economic, social, and political realities of everyday urban life (**social inclusion**). While acknowledging that sport is meaningful at interpersonal levels and can contribute positively to civic initiatives, it is important to consider whose interests are served by the images, traditions and identities associated with sport. As has been the case since the rise of sport in urban-industrial contexts, ethnic assimilation, **class** conflict, control of urban space, and ethnic/**race** and **gender** relations are inseparable from the promotion of contemporary sports (Schimmel, 2006).

Key Reading

Hardy, S. (1997) 'Sport in urbanizing America: a historical review', *Journal of Urban History*, 23 (6): 675–708.

Lenskyj, H.J. (2000) *Inside the Olympic Industry: Power, Politics, and Activism*. Albany, NY: State University of New York Press.

Nasaw, D. (1993) *Going Out: The Rise and Fall of Public Amusements*. New York: Basic Books.

Schimmel, K.S. (2002) 'The political economy of place: urban and sport studies perspectives', in J. Maguire and K. Young (eds), *Theory, Sport & Society*. London: Elsevier Science. pp. 335–51.

Schimmel, K.S. (2006) 'Sports and the city', in G. Ritzer (ed.), *The Encyclopedia of Sociology*. Malden, MA: Blackwell.

Kimberly S. Schimmel

CIVILIZING PROCESS

Norbert Elias describes the theory of civilizing processes as a 'central theory' which underpins and informs his broader theoretical approach, **figurational sociology**. Elias argued that in Western Europe since the Middle Ages (**medieval sport**) there has taken place an empirically observable decline in people's propensity for obtaining pleasure from participating in, and witnessing acts of, physical **violence**. Occurring simultaneously with processes of state formation (especially the monopolization of the means of violence and the means of taxation), there have been, argues Elias, unplanned, long-term changes in patterns of human behaviour, whereby there is increased social pressure on people to exercise stricter and more continuous self-control. More particularly, there has been a 'dampening of *Angriffslust*'; literally translated, a decline in the lust for attacking. This socially generated change in personality structure, or **habitus**, has primarily entailed two features: (1) a lowering of the 'threshold of repugnance', such that, for instance, people in modern societies would be likely to express disgust at forms of behaviour which were more readily acceptable in the Middle Ages; and (2) a socially generated, psychologically internalized, stricter taboo on violence, which is characterized by the generation of feelings of guilt and anxiety on the breaking or infringement of such taboos. At the same time, the tendency to push violence 'behind the scenes' of social life, and to stigmatize, imprison or hospitalize those who openly derive pleasure from violence has increased.

Conversely, the significance of sport in modern societies is partly due to the 'controlled de-controlling' of these processes of emotional control that players and spectators experience, what Elias and Dunning termed a **quest for excitement (emotion)**. In sporting contexts, relatively high degrees of emotional expression and violence are afforded relatively high degrees of public tolerance.

Elias's works on the sports-like activities of ancient Greece (**ancient Olympic Games**) and the **Roman Games**, and the development of **fox-hunting** into a **modern sport (sportization and parliamentarization)**, focused explicitly on the control, and tolerance, of **violence** in sport. Civilizing processes also take the role of a 'central theory' in a number of figurational sociological studies of sport including: Dunning and Sheard's work on the development of football and rugby (**Barbarians, Gentlemen and Players**); Sheard's work on the development of boxing and birdwatching (more properly 'twitching'); and Malcolm's work (2002) on the development of cricket. These authors demonstrate that modern sports have developed from relatively violent **folk games**, and that debates about tolerable levels of violence and injury have been influential in shaping the specific rule codes in accordance with which these sports are played. To a lesser extent, the role of civilizing processes is discussed in the 'Leicester School' work on **football hooliganism**, Maguire's work on globalization (1999) and Malcolm and Sheard's work on the management of pain and injury in rugby union.

Key Reading

Dunning, E. (1999) *Sport Matters: Sociological Studies of Sport, Violence and Civilization*. London: Routledge.

Dunning, E., Malcolm, D. and Waddington, I. (eds) (2004) *Sport Histories: Figurational Studies in the Development of Modern Sports*. London: Routledge.

Maguire, J. (1999) *Global Sport: Identities, Societies, Civilizations*. Oxford: Polity Press.

Malcolm, D. (2002) 'Cricket and civilizing processes: a response to Stokvis', *International Review for the Sociology of Sport*, 37 (1): 37–57.

CLASS

Social class is one of the three main forms of **social stratification** traditionally used by sociologists (see also **gender** and **race**/ethnicity). Despite its longevity as a concept, there is no consensus over how class should be defined. Most commonly, governments and the **media** define social class in terms of occupation. Occupations are split between manual (working-class) and non-manual (middle-class) occupations (more accurately this is a definition of occupational, or socio-economic class). Within **Marxism**, class is defined according to a person's ownership/ control of the means of production (the bourgeoisie do and the proletariat don't). Others use a broader definition. Coakley (2006), for instance, defines social class as 'the categories of people who share an economic position in society based on a combination of their income, wealth, education, occupation and social connections'.

In societies dominated by ideas about democracy, equal opportunity, etc., public discussions of social class are becoming increasingly rare. Moreover, certain significant changes to class in recent years have fuelled the perception that we now live in a 'classless society'. These include: (1) the demise of traditional manual labour; (2) increasing unemployment; (3) increasing numbers of women in the workforce; (4) the reduction in the number of 'jobs for life'; (5) the decline of communities structured around industries such as coal mining, and thus a decline in 'class consciousness'; and (6) the rise of new social movements and interest groups that cut across traditional class boundaries (e.g. environmentalism).

Despite such changes, class has not gone away; rather, it has changed form, meaning and influence in contemporary societies (**social inclusion**). Membership of a social class still influences access to wealth, education, healthcare, etc. In relation to sport: (1) higher social classes are more likely to participate in sport than lower social classes; (2) different social classes are likely to take part in *different types* of sport (a disproportionate number of rugby union participants are middle class, while a disproportionate number of football participants are working class); and (3) the middle classes are more likely to spectate at all sports events, including sports traditionally viewed as working class (e.g. football (**embourgeoisement**)).

Explaining class differences in sports participation and spectatorship in terms of economic factors is both common and problematic. Wealth clearly enables participation/spectatorship in certain sports (e.g. yachting, polo), but cannot be used as a blanket explanation. For instance, despite being essentially the same game, rugby union and rugby league have very different class profiles (**broken-time payments**). Similarly cross-cultural comparison shows that sports have different class compositions, and different class connotations, in different societies (e.g. compare cricket in Australia and England, or golf in England and America with golf in Scotland or Norway where the game is more 'open' and less elitist). Finally, sports clubs often operate self-recruiting mechanisms, which means that wealth does not guarantee access (e.g. requiring new members to be nominated by existing ones, 'playing in rules' to ensure that new members attain a desired playing standard, and enforcing etiquette and dress codes).

In opposition to economic explanations, sociologists have proposed a number of ways in which class, and its influence, can be understood. For instance **functionalism** sees inequality (e.g. class) as permanent, necessary and inevitable. For functionalists, inequality is a *functional prerequisite*, a way of allocating scarce resources to roles that need filling. Class inequalities (expressed by wealth and lifestyle) provide the motivation, and act as the reward, for people to fill important positions. High rates of social mobility ensure the best distribution of talent. Critics of this approach question: (1) whether the most important roles are rewarded with the highest incomes (are professional footballers more 'important' to the social system than police officers?); and (2) why class positions are so enduring and why social mobility is so rare (**socialization**).

Marxist-based explanations of social class view the relationship between classes as inherently exploitative. The common division of society into middle and working classes obscures the 'real' societal division (between the bourgeoisie and proletariat). The potential for social mobility provides an *illusion* of an escape route and promotes the notion that society is meritocratic. This ideology distracts the proletariat from their 'real' interests, their 'class consciousness' (i.e. the recognition of economic exploitation), and thus staves off revolution. Critics of this approach question whether: (1) the distinction between the bourgeoisie and proletariat is the only, or most significant, category of class; and (2) economic position so directly determines values, attitudes and 'class interests'.

Those sociologists who see class as more multifaceted and complex, determined not solely by occupation but also by wealth, education, social contacts, etc., may, in addition, see class as partly self-defined (influenced by the way we see ourselves and the groups to which we would like to belong). This approach draws upon the tradition of **symbolic interactionism** but also correlates with the theoretical traditions of **figurational sociology** and the work of Pierre Bourdieu. In this respect it is useful to see class in terms of the *construction*, the *organization* and the *consumption* of sport.

Sport, it can be argued, has been *constructed* as a function of social class. Many sports came into being as a consequence of social elites competing with each other and to the exclusion of other social groups. For instance, Dunning and Sheard (2005) argue that rugby and association football emerged as a consequence of Rugby and Eton's **public school status rivalry**. Sports developed out of the social conflict either between or within social classes. Conflict is based on both economics and social status.

Sport, furthermore, has been *organized* according to social class and historically, **amateurism** has been the most prevalent manifestation of this. However, the system of **franchises** in American major league sports acts as a vehicle for the transference of public money into the hands of a few wealthy individuals, as civic leaders provide financial incentives to attract sports teams to their cities (see also **city** and **stadium**). The cost of admission to sports events also effectively organizes sport on a class basis (**independent supporters' associations**).

Finally, the way in which individuals *consume* sport can construct and reinforce class boundaries. For Bourdieu, sport acts as a kind of badge of social exclusivity and cultural distinctiveness for the dominant classes, and as a means of control or containment of the working classes. Furthermore, for him, sports participation is not a matter of personal choice or individual preference; a person's disposition towards particular sports stems from their **socialization** into, and learning of, a particular position in the social order. Sports are also part of the lifestyles that distinguish social classes, and act as class signifiers (**habitus**).

Importantly, Bourdieu noted that the working and professional classes were characterized by different views of the **body**. While the working classes view their bodies as a 'means to an end', professional classes view their bodies as an 'end in itself'. Thus, the working classes favour sports such as boxing (where the body is used as a tool), while higher ranked social groups are more likely to embrace sports such as **aerobics** (where motivation stems from the desire to alter body shape). Different social groups also expect to accrue different 'social' profits (i.e. through the status exclusivity of particular activities, and heightened or consolidated prestige) and this leads to distinct lifestyle patterns for different social classes (see also *Theory of the Leisure Class, The*).

In a variety of ways, therefore, sports help to generate class-based identities and provide social status. In this respect, class remains a key area for research within sports studies.

Key Reading

Armour, K. (2000) '"We're all middle class now." Sport and social class in contemporary Britain', in K. Armour and R. Jones (eds), *Sociology of Sport: Theory and Practice*. Harlow: Longman. pp. 68–82.

Bourdieu, P. (1978) 'Sport and social class', *Social Science Information*, 17 (6): 819–40.

Coakley, J. (2006) *Sport in Society: Issues and Controversies*, 9th edn. Boston: McGraw-Hill.

Dunning, E. and Sheard, K. (2005) *Barbarians, Gentlemen and Players: A Sociological Study of the Development of Rugby Football*, 2nd edn. London: Routledge.

Horne, J., Tomlinson, A. and Whannel, G. (1999) *Understanding Sport: An Introduction to the Sociological and Cultural Analysis of Sport*. London: E. & F.N. Spon. esp. Ch. 5.

COHESION

Can be defined as the tendency of a group to stick together. Cohesion is: (1) multidimensional (groups cohere for multiple reasons); (2) dynamic (reasons for cohesion may change over time); (3) instrumental (groups must have a purpose); and (4) affective (group membership evokes emotional responses). Psychologists typically refer to *task cohesion* (working towards a particular goal, such as winning matches) and *social cohesion* (the attractiveness of interpersonal relations, or attractiveness of belonging to the group per se). Cohesive groups and sports teams may have one or both of these characteristics.

In order to understand cohesion in sports groups Carron (1982) has developed a framework focusing on four factors: environmental, personal, leadership and team. *Environmental* factors that have been investigated include things like proximity (e.g. the effect on college athletes of living together in dorms), the degree to which athletes see themselves as a distinct and separate group (augmented, e.g. through initiation rites), contractual bonds and group size (i.e. the larger the group the harder it is likely to be to sustain cohesion). *Personal* factors can be classified into three categories: (1) demographic characteristics such as **gender** and social **class**; (2) cognitions and motives (e.g. satisfaction); and (3) behaviour (such as sacrifices made for the group, adherence to schedules, the absence of **social loafing**). In general it is believed that the more similar the personal characteristics, the more cohesive the group. *Leadership* refers to the decision-making processes (including devolvement) and communication within the group and the compatibility between coaches and players. Finally, *team* factors that have been identified as significant include the stage of development of a group (**group development**), the stability of the group (how long it has been together) and the establishment of shared experiences, the existence of norms (e.g. relating to performance or training), and the status of individuals within the group (star players are more likely to perceive cohesion to exist than 'bit part' players, a feature exacerbated in 'losing' teams where playing success is elusive).

Key Reading

Carron, A.V. (1982) 'Cohesiveness in sport groups: interpretations and considerations', *Journal of Sport Psychology*, 4: 123–38.
Carron, A.V. and Hausenblas, H.A. (1998) *Group Dynamics in Sport*. Morgantown, WV: Fitness Information Technology.

COLD WAR

(boycotts; propaganda)

COLLEGE SPORTS

(athletic scholarships)

COLONIALISM

(imperialism)

COMMERCIALIZATION

Refers to the process whereby something (e.g. sport) becomes increasingly organized as an exchange of goods and services (see also **commodification**). Often this exchange is driven by the desire to make a financial profit. In short, the commercialization of sport is the process whereby team games, in particular, increasingly come to be organized as a business or economic enterprise.

Aspects of commercialism can be seen in the 'sports-like' activities of ancient Rome (**ancient Olympic Games**; **sport, definition of**), but it is more useful to trace the development of commercial sports back to eighteenth-century Europe, and England in particular. Sport emerged as a commercial activity at the point at which events (matches, races, bouts) ceased to be oriented solely towards participants (producers), and became largely organized for the consumption of spectators. Public House owners both started to exploit existing sports events by setting up temporary stalls, and provided facilities where sports such as cricket, quoits, horse racing, cock-fighting, etc. could be staged. As the eighteenth century progressed, tavern owners began to charge admission fees to supplement the profits made through the sale of refreshments and lodgings (**alcohol**). Subsequently, the emergent ruling bodies of sport (e.g. the Jockey Club, the MCC) established their own, permanent, facilities (i.e. Newmarket racecourse, Lord's cricket ground) to contain the 10,000-plus spectators that could be attracted to the major sporting events of eighteenth-century England.

Historically, therefore, the preconditions for the commercialization of sport have been identified as urbanization (**city, the**), industrialization, a political and economic system facilitating the private accumulation of wealth, and the availability of a relatively large amount of leisure time for the masses. In one of the earliest sociological analyses of this process, Gregory P. Stone (1955) argued that commercialization led 'play' (unscripted, spontaneous) to become overshadowed by '*dis*-play' (pre-arranged, staged, spectacular); that is to say, in some respects commercialization is the very antithesis of sport (**'play and dis-play'**). However, most agree that perhaps the most dramatic commercial transformations to sport postdate Stone, and have resulted from the growing influence of the mass **media**. More recent research has sought to describe in more detail the effects of the commercialization of sport, and to propose various explanations for these processes.

A most commonly cited effect of commercialization is the alteration of the rules and structure of sports to speed up action, increase scoring opportunities, increase the **competitive balance** of fixtures, and provide time for advertisement breaks (**sponsorship**). The development of one-day cricket, the introduction of tie-breaks in tennis, the change from 15 to 12 rounds in boxing, and the reduction of the number of free throws in basketball, are all examples of the way in which sports have been shaped by commercial considerations. Furthermore, the timing of events may be influenced by commercial considerations. The introduction of *Monday Night Football* in the US and the regular staging of Premiership football fixtures on Sunday afternoons in England are examples of the way in which media companies persuade sports organizations to schedule events to maximize television audiences. In order to cater for a more diverse audience, sports may be organized along more 'spectacular' lines, such that they appeal to non-experts as much as traditional fans. Music and cheerleaders may be used to generate 'atmosphere'. Style and marketing are thought to replace substance and skill. Such changes may lead to forms of resistance from more 'traditional' **fan** groups (**independent supporters' associations; supporters direct**).

Others have identified changes to the way in which players, coaches, etc. approach sport as a consequence of its increasing commercialization. Some claim that the increase in potential financial gains leads to a 'win at all costs' mentality. This may lead to **violence** against opponents and self (through the use of **drugs** and the long-term consequences of playing through **pain and injury**), 'negative', or defensive tactics, and the harnessing of individualism into rigid team systems. An extension of this is the notion that sports organizations also orientate themselves towards maximizing income and, consequently, they quickly replace players and coaches if results are not favourable, and they seek to appeal to wealthier types of fan (e.g. middle class, families) and corporate sponsors in particular. Common in the US, though not in Europe, is the related trend of relocating sports teams (**franchises**) to cities that offer the promise of larger audiences and greater financial return. As this implies, while athletes may become increasingly wealthy as a consequence of the commercialization of sport, they are also likely to be less influential in the running of the sport.

Explanations of why sport has commercialized differ according to different theoretical positions. An explanation derived from **functionalism**, for instance, would argue that commercial sport demonstrates that desirable characteristics will be rewarded (competition, commitment, etc.) and that mass spectacles provide a means of social integration and cohesion (while 'negative' aspects such as drug use and violence are dysfunctions). From the viewpoint of **Marxism**, we might argue that the commercialization of sport is a clear example of the tendency of capitalist interests to seek out and exploit new markets, that sport promotes behavioural characteristics which are beneficial to capitalist production (routinization, subjugation of the individual to the team), and that athletes are proletarianized, alienated and exploited like other workers (**alienation**). In contrast, **figurational sociology** eschews economic determinism, and argues that the commercialization of sport (in the UK at least) stems from the changing power balances among the principal groups involved. They point towards the respective roles of the aristocracy and gentry (as opposed to the primacy of the bourgeoisie) in the development of sport in the eighteenth and nineteenth centuries, and to the shift in the balance of power between spectators, players, administrators, sponsors and the media during the twentieth century (e.g. what Dunning (1999) calls the 'football figuration').

Finally, one should be cautious not to overestimate the extent of the commercialization of sport. Despite rapid changes in recent years, one of the peculiar aspects of sport is its *relative autonomy* from commercial processes, for in sport the ideal of **amateurism** is, to some degree, still cherished and a distrust of all things commercial continues. Commercialization is an issue in sport because it remains contested in ways that are simply accepted in other entertainment industries (e.g. music, cinema). Students of sport need to be wary of the often highly value-laden character of debates about commercialization (e.g. arguments that commercial interests debase or ruin sports, that 'real' fans are being displaced by 'new fans' (**essentialism; fans**)). More helpfully, we should conceive of these changes as shifts in the balance of power so that, historically, we can see a shift in the balance of power between players and spectators, and later from 'live' spectators to media companies catering for the spectator at home.

Key Reading

Dunning, E. (1999) *Sport Matters: Sociological Studies of Sport, Violence and Civilization.* London: Routledge. esp. Ch. 5.
Sewart, J. (1987) 'The commodification of sport', *International Review of the Sociology of Sport*, 22 (2): 171–91.
Slack, T. (ed.) (2004) *The Commercialisation of Sport.* London: Frank Cass.
Stone, G. (1955) 'American sports: play and dis-play, *Chicago Review*, ix.

COMMODIFICATION

A commodity is an economic good, bought and sold in the marketplace. Thus all commodities have economic exchange value. Commodification is the process whereby objects or activities, such as sport, become economic goods, produced not to satisfy the needs and desires of the producer, but to be bought and sold in the marketplace (**consumer culture**).

The term commodification is widely used by sociologists of sport to describe the effects of **commercialization** processes on sport in the twentieth century. This may involve changes to the rules, format or scheduling of sports events, or the increasing use of spectacle and theatricality.

The process of commodification has been evaluated in different ways. Marxists such as Bero Rigauer (**correspondence theory; Marxism**) argue that this evidence can be used to demonstrate that sport has directly grown out of capitalist social processes. Others, who might be labelled popular culturalists, argue that commodified sport is merely the desire and expression of the people – sport takes this form because that is what people demand. Those, such as Sewart, who advocate **critical theory** respond with the argument that because so few alternatives exist to modern commodified sport, popular taste is ill-informed and constrained and thus people are not free to make 'real' choices. They further argue that, whereas sport was once a partial critique of capitalism – non-utilitarian, liberating and offering scope for social resistance – sport is now determined by exchange value. Consequently, Sewart argues, sport has lost 'its intrinsic content or form ... traditional meaning and practices are ... replaced by a puerile and Barnumesque ethic of display, titillation and theatricality' (1987).

Key Reading

Guttmann, A. (1981) 'Translator's introduction', in B. Rigauer, *Sport and Work.* Columbia: Columbia University Press.
Sewart, J. (1987) 'The commodification of sport', *International Review for the Sociology of Sport*, 22 (2): 171–90.

COMPETITIVE BALANCE

Economists argue that a key feature of the appeal of, and thus demand for, sport is that in contrast to other forms of entertainment (e.g. films) the outcome of a sport tends to be relatively uncertain, something implicitly recognized by sociologists such as Stone (1955) (**play and dis-play**) and Elias and Dunning (1986) (**quest for excitement**). Economists, such as El-Hodiri and Quirk (1971), therefore argue that it is not in any team's (or competitor's) interest to become completely dominant, for this would lead to predictable results, reduced public interest in events, and thus a fall in income. A major function of a sports league, therefore, is to ensure that no team becomes excessively dominant. To this end some form of income distribution normally exists such that wealthier clubs cross-subsidize poorer clubs (**cartel**).

More recent research, by Quirk and Fort in particular, has questioned the importance of competitive balance for the economic success of a league. Quirk and Fort (1992) delineate three distinct aspects of uncertainty of outcome: (1) uncertainty over the outcome of individual matches; (2) uncertainty over a particular season; and (3) uncertainty in terms of the absence of the dominance of a single club over the long term. By testing all three of these aspects Quirk and Fort note that long-term competitive *imbalance* exists in all the major American professional team sports leagues, and that despite this, such leagues have survived and indeed flourished.

This evidence suggests therefore that competitive balance is not as important as previously assumed, and/or that the existence of practices designed to equalize wealth and playing resources has achieved sufficient competitive balance to ensure a league's success. Often overlooked in this context, however, is the fact that sport derives its appeal not solely from its uncertainty of outcome, but also from its significance as a site of identity formation (regionalism, **nationalism**, sexuality, **race**, etc.).

Key Reading

El-Hodiri, M. and Quirk, J. (1971) 'An economic model of a professional sports league', *Journal of Political Economy*, 79: 1302–19.

Elias, N. and Dunning, E. (1986) *Quest for Excitement: Sport and Leisure in the Civilizing Process*. Oxford: Blackwell.

Gratton, C. and Taylor, P. (2000) *Economics of Sport and Recreation*. London: E. & F.N. Spon.

Quirk, J. and Fort, R.D. (1992) *Pay Dirt: The Business of Professional Team Sport*. Princeton, NJ: Princeton University Press.

Stone, G. (1955) 'American sports: play and dis-play, *Chicago Review*, IX: 83–100.

COMPULSORY COMPETITIVE TENDERING (CCT)

Introduced for a range of local government services by the Conservative Thatcher government, through the Local Government Act of 1988, CCT involves the running of local authority services being put out to tender so that services are increasingly market-oriented, in line with consumer demand, and (in theory) run more economically. CCT differed from privatization, however, in that the local authority retained control over pricing, quality, programming and wider policy issues. However, the clear impetus for this policy shift was to enable the private sector to take a greater role in running public services such as sport and leisure provision. Despite resistance from such organizations as the **CCPR**, all leisure services became subject to CCT from January 1993.

Initially, CCT was deemed something of a failure as just 10 per cent of all sport/leisure contracts under the system were won by commercial organizations. The vast majority (84 per cent) were won by the existing in-house provider (the DSO (Direct Service Organization)), a great many of which were uncontested. This pattern was very similar to the introduction of CCT in many other service areas. It was speculated that commercial organizations may simply not have been ready to respond to CCT, or that many commercial organizations were put off by the size of contracts on offer (58 per cent of local authorities offered just a single contract for all their facilities with a further 29 per cent offering just two contracts), and by local authorities' retention of key powers.

However, CCT was deemed successful in that: (1) it forced local authorities to specifically identify their policy priorities; (2) it led to the rationalization of staffing and concomitant cuts in expenditure (though critics argue that this has largely been done through de-unionization of workers and lower rates of pay); and (3) it led to more flexible and creative attempts to reach policy goals. For example, providers enrolled specific user-groups, such as swimming clubs, to assume responsibility for the management and maintenance of pools, and local authorities offered cheaper hire rates in return for the provision of coaching by club members to the general public.

Despite this lack of change brought about by the introduction of CCT, the **Sports Council** expressed its concern that the greater economic emphasis of CCT had led providers to increase their charges to users of sports facilities. Other research indicated that CCT had led to reduced levels of access among disadvantaged groups (**social inclusion**). Thus CCT was thought to have hindered broader welfare goals such as increasing sports participation and **sports development**, which by their very nature were difficult to quantify in economic terms.

Because of such problems, CCT legislation was repealed in January 2000 and replaced by 'Best Value'. An aspect of the 1999 Local Government Act (brought in by Tony Blair's Labour government), this policy shift represented a move away from the primary emphasis on lowering costs, and broadened out the rationale on which local authorities could award contracts. Best Value is defined as, 'arrangements to secure continuous improvements in exercise of their functions, judged against named criteria and with regard to a combination of economy, efficiency and effectiveness'. Consequently the introduction of Best Value has been less controversial than that of CCT.

Key Reading

Nichols, G. (2000) *The Process of Best Value: Further Lessons from Leisure Pilots.* Sheffield: Institute of Sport and Recreation Management, Sheffield University.

Sports Council (1994) *Developing Sport Through CCT.* London: Sports Council.

COMPULSORY HETEROSEXUALITY

(gender; lesbians; masculinity; queer theory)

CONCENTRATION

Can be defined as the skill of focusing one's attention on a particular task and is therefore sometimes also referred to as attentional focus. Other definitions have suggested that concentration not only entails focusing one's attention on a particular task but also encompasses the skill of disregarding non-task relevant cues and thoughts. Concentration is particularly pertinent to the study of sport in that research has demonstrated a positive relationship between concentration and performance.

Nideffer's 'attentional style theory' suggests that concentration should be understood in terms of two interacting dimensions – width and directionality. More particularly, concentration may be broad or narrow (a footballer requires breadth of concentration to be aware of the position of his/her team mates; a darts player requires a more narrow focus), and may be external or internal (i.e. focus on the ball or on one's technique). Success in different sports depends upon different types of concentration. Furthermore, it is hypothesized, individuals tend to have their own preferred attentional style. Optimal performance is achieved where situational demands and the personal preference most closely match.

Weinberg and Gould (2003), however, argue that concentration in sport and exercise-settings should be conceptualized in four parts: (1) focusing on relevant environmental cues (e.g. the goal) and not attending to non-relevant cues (e.g. spectators); (2) maintaining attentional focus for the duration of an event/competition; (3) having situational awareness, e.g. of team mates, opponents, state of play, etc.; and (4) shifting attentional focus, for instance between internal and external focus, between individual skills and the broader context.

Concentration problems may stem from both internal distracters (thoughts of past or future events, narrow internal thinking about a particular skill or technique rather than the broader context, fatigue, and inadequate **motivation**) and external distracters (visual and auditory, gamesmanship by opponents, etc.). Hence concentration can be improved by focusing on the 'here and now', **goal-setting** (particularly in terms of standards of performance as opposed to outcomes such as winning), use of pre-performance routines, **self-talk** and **imagery**, breathing techniques and simulation training.

Finally, Abernethy (2001) has suggested that there are distinct attentional processing differences between experts and novices in sport. In particular, experts tend to: (1) attend more to advance information (e.g. how the ball is held rather than its movement once released); (2) attend more to the movement of opponents; (3) search more systematically for cues; (4) have a better awareness of the tactical structure of the sport; and (5) better predict the flight pattern of the particular ball (or similar equipment) used.

Key Reading

Abernethy, B. (2001) 'Attention', in R. Singer, H. Hausenblas and C. Janelle (eds), *Handbook of Sport Psychology*. New York: Wiley. pp. 53–85.

Moran, A.P. (1996) *The Psychology of Concentration in Sport Performers: A Cognitive Analysis*. Hove: Psychology Press.

Nideffer, R.M. (1976) *The Inner Athlete*. New York: Cromwell.

Weinberg, R. and Gould, D. (2003) *Foundations of Sport and Exercise Psychology*. Champaign, IL: Human Kinetics.

CONFLICT THEORY

A theory developed in opposition to **functionalism**. Conflict theorists criticized functionalists for disregarding the importance of conflict and neglecting power relations and the tendency of individuals and groups to pursue their own interests (rather than those of the social system). The core assumption of conflict theory is that social relations are characterized by coercion, exploitation and the manipulation of individuals.

Conflict theorists see sport as a corrupted form of physical exercise and contrast it to play, which is seen as spontaneous and an expression of freedom. Sport is seen as serving the needs of capitalism or other powerful (often economic) interests. Conflict theorists therefore look not only at the relationship between sport and **alienation** and sport and the perpetuation of social inequality (**class**; **gender**; **race**), but also at the effects of **commercialization**, asking who wins and loses from such processes.

Conflict theory is often seen as synonymous with **Marxism.** While it is true to say that Marxism is a form of conflict theory, some forms of conflict theory are not Marxist, drawing for instance on the work of Weber. Some forms of **feminism** could also be considered conflict theories.

The decline in the dominance of functionalism means that the identification of a theoretical perspective based on conflict has become less meaningful in sociology, and indeed such is the diversity that few criticisms can be made of conflict theory as a whole. However, it is often the case that conflict theorists underestimate the emancipatory potential of sport. If sport is so exploitative, we might ask, why is it that so many people voluntarily choose to take part in it for no obvious external reward?

Key Reading

Coakley, J.J. (2006) *Sport in Society: Issues and Controversies,* 9th edn. Boston: McGraw-Hill. esp. Ch. 2.

Gruneau, R. (1976) 'Sport as an area of sociological study: an introduction to major themes and perspectives', in R.S. Gruneau and J.G. Albinson (eds), *Canadian Sport: Sociological Perspectives.* Ontario: Addison Wesley. pp. 8–42.

CONSUMER CULTURE

Debates about consumption, consumer society and consumer culture have developed since the 1980s from a minority academic issue to a public concern. Part of the debate triggered by **postmodernism** has been the suggestion that social scientists had focused too much on the experience and effect of paid work and production and not enough on consumption. Are people increasingly addicted to spending and shopping? Does affluence create happiness? Is shopping the ultimate freedom?

One suggestion is that affluence – like poverty – is relative and hence as opportunities to spend increase so people may compare their position in society with others, e.g. with the **celebrity** lifestyles of David and Victoria **Beckham**. The fact that a professional football player (and his pop star wife) has become for some a central indicator of the 'good life' is a development that has been considered by several sociologists of sport. Aside from individual sports stars, other recent attempts to discuss aspects of sport in consumer culture have focused on fandom and fans (Crawford, 2004), advertising (Jackson and Andrews, 2005), teams (Andrews, 2004) and **megaevents** (Horne and Manzenreiter, 2006).

Reference to consumer culture, consumer society and consumption is part of the 'cultural turn' applied to the sociology of sport. The 'cultural turn' is connected to debates about **modernity**, concerning the shifting relationship between the state and the market, the transformation of the meaning of citizenship, and the implications of these developments for personal and social identities and lifestyles. The expansion of studies of consumption and consumerism since the mid-1980s is also linked to debates about **globalization**, postmodernity, and new forms of inequality mediated by taste and distinction. Two key issues are: (1) do the structures and organization of consumerism exclude, dominate and marginalize other modes of sport and leisure provision? and (2) does consumer culture heighten the manipulation of consumer agency or are consumers able to exert a degree of control (if not sovereignty)? In short, are consumers dupes, victims, rational actors or heroic communicators in consumer society?

The relationship between sport (and active bodies) and consumer culture has been noted by several social commentators. For example, John Hargreaves (1986) argued that, 'What links consumer culture with sports culture so economically ... is their common concern with, and capacity to accommodate the body meaningfully in the constitution of the normal individual.' Sport can be seen as central to the economics of late capitalist modernity. In these economies the **body** is more than an instrument for producing material goods and getting things done. The body, including the sporting and physically active body, is now portrayed as an object of contemplation and improvement in the spectacular discourses of the mass **media**, in the regulatory discourses of the state and in peoples' everyday practices. Contemporary advertisements for commercial sport and leisure clubs in the UK combine medical science and popular culture discourses evident in such phrases as 'fitness regime', 'consultation' and 'fix'. By exhorting potential consumers/members to 'Flatten your tum and perk up your bum' and reassuring us that 'Gym'll fix it', regulatory control of the body is now experienced through consumerism and the fashion industry. Sport has thus become increasingly allied to the consumption of goods and services, which is now the structural basis of the advanced capitalist countries through discourses about the model, (post)modern, consumer-citizen. This person is an enterprising, calculating and reflexive self, someone permanently ready to **discipline** her- or himself through crash diets, tanning, cosmetic ('plastic') surgery and **aerobics** and other sporting activities, in order to fit in with the demands of advanced liberalism.

There are several other developments that are conceived of as peculiar to consumer culture. These include the 'buy now pay later' belief, a concentration on form or style over function, and a growth in product disposability or planned obsolescence, all of which appear to have become embraced by consumers since the late 1950s. Is this the result of indoctrination or brainwashing, or more to do with changes in the availability of credit? Research in the USA suggests that the street life of a trendy athletic shoe has fallen in some cases to a month or even 15 days. It is suggested that one million people in the UK and five million people in the USA suffer from a shopping addiction. Reports of a riot outside a New York store selling a limited edition 'Pigeon Dunk' skateboarding trainer in February 2005 may just be one of the most visible aspects of these conditions.

There have been three main approaches to understanding consumption and consumer culture: (1) the production of consumption approach; (2) the modes of production approach; and (3) the pleasures of consumption approach. Each has been subject to criticisms: the first because it underplays human agency; and the second and third because their emphasis on the active and (apparently) powerful consumer ignores the wider structural forces of exploitation and injustice. Hence the study of sport in consumer culture focuses on familiar questions about **agency and structure**.

The three main concerns about contemporary consumer society are growing inequality, increased **commodification** and globalization. Capitalist economics and the associated ideology of consumerism became global following the collapse of the Soviet Union in the late 1980s. Commercial sports followed because: (1) driven by the profit motive the owners of sport are always looking to expand their markets and increase their profits; and (2) transnational companies, as providers of **sponsorship**, can use sport to promote their goods and services in new markets. That business strategies developed in one society may work well in other parts of the world is an argument that underpins George Ritzer's 'McDonaldization thesis'. Recently Alan Bryman has suggested that in twenty-first-century marketing and branding the 'ludic ambience' developed by the Disney Corporation increasingly acts as the ideal template for the spread of contemporary consumer cultures of advanced post-Fordist capitalism throughout the world. However, efforts to use successful sports clubs to make money may meet stiff opposition if they conflict with the social and cultural values and meanings associated with sports teams. This partly explains the protests staged by fans and the initial reticence of the board of Manchester United to embrace the offer made by American tycoon, and Tampa Bay Buccaneers owner, Malcolm Glazer.

The major issues in the study of sport in consumer culture are therefore: (1) trends in the global sports goods and services market; (2) the growth of sports coverage in the media, especially its role in the process of creating consumers out of sports audiences and fans ('consumerization'); (3) the importance of sponsorship and advertising for contemporary sport; (4) the changing role of government – concerning regulation, consumer protection and sports promotion; (5) how much, as a result of increasing consumerization, has the role of sport in the construction, maintenance and challenging of lifestyles and identities altered; and (6) how consumerization is reflected in social divisions in patterns of involvement and participation in sport (Horne, 2006).

Key Reading

Andrews, D. (ed.) (2004) *Manchester United. A Thematic Study.* London: Routledge.

Crawford, G. (2004) *Consuming Sport: Sport, Fans and Culture.* London: Routledge.

Horne, J. (2006) *Sport in Consumer Culture.* Basingstoke: Palgrave.

Horne, J. and Manzenreiter, W. (eds) (2006) *Sports Mega-Events.* Oxford: Blackwell.

Jackson, S. and Andrews, D. (eds) (2005) *Sport, Culture and Advertising.* London: Routledge.

John D. Horne

CONTENT ANALYSIS

Can be defined as the systematic study of communication. While most commonly associated with the study of the textual content of newspapers, content analysis can be performed on photographs, film/video, advertisements, speeches, music, auto/biographies, letters, diaries and public records.

In conducting content analysis, the researcher must initially decide on the sample of communication to be analysed (e.g. editions of *The Times* newspaper from the 1 to the 31 January), and then the 'unit of analysis' (a word, phrase or type of picture). Alternatively, the researcher might be interested in the prominence of particular features (e.g. the frequency of particular words in headlines) or the low prioritizing/absence of other types of data (e.g. the coverage of female sport).

Data derived from content analysis can range from qualitative to quantitative (**qualitative and quantitative research**; see also **discourse** and **semiotics**). Valgeirsson and Snyder (1986), for instance, used a cross-national quantitative analysis of newspapers to illustrate the differentiations in the structure of sport in Iceland compared to England and the US, particularly in terms of the quantification of sport (*From Ritual to Record*)

and the prominence of female and amateur sport (**amateurism**). Young (1986) undertook a qualitative or thematic content analysis of the media coverage of the **Heysel** stadium disaster to demonstrate aspects of 'deviance amplification' and **moral panic**. However, very often a combined approach is used. Clayton and Harris (2002), for instance, demonstrate that male athletes receive not only quantitatively more coverage in UK newspapers than female athletes, but also qualitatively *different* forms of coverage.

Within sports studies content analysis has largely been used in the analysis of **gender**, **race** and **nationalism**. One of the main advantages of content analysis is that research is controllable; that is to say, the communication being studied is generally fixed in space and time, not subject to the whims of humans (e.g. interviewees) who have the potential to act unpredictably. Through the **Internet** an increasing amount of media content is becoming available to researchers and electronic searches make the process quicker and more reliable (**reliability and validity**). Moreover, the availability of international media content facilitates cross-cultural studies.

One of the main potential problems with content analysis, however, lies in the **sampling**. Support for a city's bid to host an Olympic Games is likely to vary across newspapers and over time (e.g. initial support may wane as the costs to the public become more apparent). Therefore choosing the correct time frame, and the correct publication(s), is crucial to portraying this social phenomenon accurately. A second potential problem lies in validity (**reliability and validity**); i.e. does the content analysis measure what it was intended or is claimed to measure, and are the conclusions drawn correct? For instance, the communication medium may not be an accurate reflection of 'real life'. Newspapers are assembled according to tight deadlines and many factual errors are printed and not subsequently corrected. Often articles are the product of individuals' bias and subjective opinion or a deliberate attempt to be controversial and to provoke interest. Tabloid newspaper editors have at times argued that aspects of reporting are meant to be a joke, particularly with reference to nationalistic coverage of football matches (Garland and Rowe, 2001). The researcher must therefore be aware of the broader context in which the content is delivered, and its interpretation, which will be culturally specific.

Key Reading

Clayton, B. and Harris, J. (2002) 'Femininity, masculinity, physicality and the English tabloid press: the case of Anna Kournikova', *International Review for the Sociology of Sport*, 37 (3/4): 397–414.

Garland, J. and Rowe, M. (2001) *Racism and Anti-Racism in Football*. Basingstoke: Palgrave MacMillan.

Valgeirsson, I. and Snyder, E. (1986) 'A cross-cultural comparison of newspaper sports sections', *International Review for the Sociology of Sport*, 21 (2/3): 131–8.

Young, K. (1986) '"The Killing Field": themes in mass media responses to the Heysel stadium riot', *International Review for the Sociology of Sport*, 21 (2/3): 253–64.

CORRESPONDENCE THEORY

A form of **Marxism**, the application of correspondence theory to sport is epitomized in the work of German sociologist Bero Rigauer. Correspondence theorists see sport as a 'simple reflection' of the capitalist mode of production, whereby sport is seen to be completely determined by capitalism, shaped in the interests of the bourgeoisie, and an entirely alienating activity for the proletariat (Hargreaves, 1986).

Rigauer's ideas are contained in *Sport and Work* (1981), translated into English by Allen Guttmann (the preface to which provides a clear and concise critique of the Marxist approach more generally). Rigauer argues that sports under industrial capitalism, while initially pursued by elites for their own enjoyment, quickly spread down the social order and increasingly took on the characteristics of work. Most significantly, sports undergo a process of **commodification**; that is to say, they become produced to be exchanged in the marketplace, irrelevant to the needs of the producer (e.g. their personal enjoyment, fulfilment, liberation, etc.).

For Rigauer, therefore, the sportsperson is the producer, and spectators the consumers. It matters little whether the sportsperson is professional or an elite amateur for both receive rewards of some kind (and both lack control over their sporting 'careers'). The achievements of athletes are quantitatively measured – through wages or transfer fees – thus enabling exchange. Athletes must sell their product for its monetary equivalent in order to support their material needs and therefore continue to produce. Just as in conventional work forms, there are two conflicting groups: the producers of sporting achievement (athletes/proletariat) and the owners of **capital** (managers, event promoters, owners of sports teams). The latter pay the prevailing market price for the sporting achievement, sell it on to consumers and extract a profit (**commercialization**).

The sportsperson becomes known as a '4-minute miler', a 'million pound footballer', etc. Such terms dehumanize the individual, forcing his/her special (essentially human) qualities to disappear. There is little scope for individual freedom or expression in elite sports. An athlete does not work independently, but must fit in with the team, coming to perform a highly specialized role within the broader production process. Training becomes rationalized and repetitive. The worker becomes distanced from the product of his/her labours and therefore alienated (**alienation**). Commodification enables athletes to be substituted or exchanged; when they fail to meet production goals, they are replaced by another.

For Rigauer the belief that sport is a counter to work may be widely held, but this only serves to obscure sport's real function, that of reinforcing the ethic of hard work, loyalty and production necessary for the maintenance of capitalism. Thus sport corresponds almost exactly with work.

Key Reading

Hargreaves, J. (1986) *Sport, Power and Culture: A Social and Historical Analysis of Popular Sports in Britain*. Cambridge: Polity Press.

Rigauer, B. (1981) *Sport and Work*, trans. A. Guttmann. Columbia: Columbia University Press.

CRITICAL REALISM

(**realism**)

CRITICAL THEORY

In its narrowest sense, critical theory is used to describe the work of the Frankfurt School scholars, most notably, Theodor Adorno, Max Horkheimer, Herbert Marcuse and latterly Jurgen Habermas. The Frankfurt School of critical theory, a brand of neo-**Marxism**, formally existed from 1922 to 1969 but the work of its various members is diffuse and changed considerably over the authors' lifetimes. In the sociology of sport, Bero Rigauer is most closely associated with the Frankfurt School of critical theory (**correspondence theory**).

In recent years it has become normal to apply the term critical theory to any perspective which focuses primarily on power, culture and social relations. In his overview, Coakley (2006) places neo-Marxist theories, traditional critical theory, **hegemony theory**, **cultural studies**, feminist theories (**feminism**), **post-structuralism** and **queer theory** under the broad umbrella of critical theory. What groups these diverse theories together is: (1) the notion that sports are sites where society and culture are produced and reproduced; (2) the recognition that sports are socially constructed in ways that favour particular people; and (3) the desire for political action to correct inequality. Critical theorists eschew universal explanations, arguing

instead that sports and societies are constantly changing and that each context displays its own specific forms of domination and resistance. Domination may stem simply from the control of positions of political power, to the manipulation of the **media**, which effectively limits the range of voices heard, and thus the dialogue about alternatives and differences (**discourse**). Resistance may be political or institutional, or more subtle and covert.

Key Reading

Coakley, J.J. (2006) *Sport in Society: Issues and Controversies*, 9th edn. Boston: McGraw-Hill.

Inglis, D. (2004) 'Theodor Adorno on sport: the jeu d'espirit of despair', in R. Giulianotti (ed.), *Sport and Modern Social Theorists*. Basingstoke: Palgrave Macmillan. pp. 81–96.

Morgan, W. (2004) 'Habermas on sports: social theory from a moral perspective', in R. Giulianotti (ed.), *Sport and Modern Social Theorists*. Basingstoke: Palgrave Macmillan. pp. 173–86.

CULT OF ATHLETICISM

The seminal statement on the cult of athleticism can be found in J.A. Mangan's, *Athleticism in the Victorian and Edwardian Public School* (1981). Mangan's empirical study of a cross-section of public schools led him to conclude that this philosophy underpinned physical education in the English public schools from around 1860 to about 1940 (though even today it remains highly influential to many government policies promoting physical education (**national curriculum for physical education**)). The central principle of the cult of athleticism was that physical education was an effective way of 'building character' (i.e. cultivating moral values), and specifically physical and moral courage, loyalty and cooperation, the capacity to act fairly and take defeat well, and the ability to both command and obey (Mangan, 1981: 9). The cult of athleticism led to schoolboy's riotous and unruly pastimes, such as hunting and 'toozling' (the chasing and killing small birds), that had dominated in previous times being replaced by disciplined and formalized activities. While the moral worth of athleticism was a genuine and extensively held belief, the opportunity that such games provided for schoolmasters to exert control over pupils should not be overlooked.

Although Mangan focuses on athleticism in a broad sense, it should be noted that among sports, competitive team games (in particular cricket, football and rugby) were seen as primary. Physical education became compulsory and occupied a significant proportion of the school timetable. Athletic achievements outranked academic achievements and formed the basis of hierarchies of boys within the schools (**prefect-fagging system**). The leading public schools invested heavily in playing fields, as did Oxford and Cambridge universities and ambitious and aspiring grammar schools (**public school status rivalry**).

The cult of athleticism largely influenced the upper and upper-middle classes but, significantly, it was predominantly from these social groups that the personnel to organize and administer the expanding British Empire were drawn (**imperialism**). The cult of athleticism was believed to be the basis for the successful expansion of Empire, as well as the education and discipline of those colonized. The Duke of Wellington's statement that 'the battle of Waterloo was won on the playing fields of Eton' encapsulates such beliefs.

While the character built through athleticism was a distinctly English form of **masculinity**, educational institutions for females developed a parallel character-building agenda, most notably that offered by Madame **Österberg** at Dartford College at the turn of the twentieth century. Girls' colleges developed a more 'feminine' form of athleticism, based more on gymnastics than team sports, and thus remained distinctly separate from the notions of manliness developed in the boys' schools. Across the world, physical education remains more gendered than many other areas of the school curriculum (**gender**) and this is a further legacy of the cult of athleticism.

Key Reading

Hargreaves, J. (1986) *Sport, Power and Culture: A Social and Historical Analysis of Popular Sports in Britain.* Cambridge: Polity Press. esp. Ch. 3.

Holt, R. (1989) *Sport and the British: A Modern History.* Oxford: Oxford University Press. esp. Ch. 2.

Mangan, J.A. (1981) *Athleticism in the Victorian and Edwardian Public School – The Emergence and Consolidation of an Educational Ideology.* Cambridge: Cambridge University Press.

CULTURAL RELATIVISM

The belief that the practices and values of one culture *should not*, and *cannot*, be evaluated according to the standards, norms or conventions of any other culture. In part, cultural relativism can be seen to stem from the belief that all social 'realities' exist solely as a consequence of human interpretation (**objectivity and subjectivity**). Cultural relativism has the merit that it allows us to understand diverse cultural practices in their own terms, rather than dismiss and condemn them simply because they are different to our own (a practice called ethnocentricity evident, for instance, in the initial Western European perceptions of **aborigine** culture and sport). However, many see cultural relativism as a pejorative term (i.e. as a criticism) believing that the moral case against some cultural practices (such as slavery, gender inequality, etc.) is overwhelming. A key related point here is the degree to which social scientific examination should be driven by moral and political agendas, and the degree to which research should be driven by the quest for knowledge, with the researcher's values placed to one side (see also **involvement and detachment**).

CULTURAL STUDIES

A distinctive range of cross-disciplinary approaches (including sociology, history, philosophy and communication studies) which is closely associated with the Centre for Contemporary Cultural Studies (CCCS) at the University of Birmingham (UK). While the publication of the CCCS founding director Richard Hoggart's *The Uses of Literacy* (1957) and Raymond Williams's *Culture and Society* (1958) are seen as important catalysts to the cultural studies movement, many of the key concepts used in cultural studies are drawn from **Marxism** and the work of Antonio Gramsci in particular. Stuart Hall, who succeeded Hoggart in 1968, is perhaps the most well-known contemporary advocate of cultural studies.

Cultural studies is diametrically opposed to elitist conceptions of culture and much of the initial research consisted of ethnographic studies of the 'everyday world of lived reality' of the working classes (**ethnography**). Examination of these experiences, advocates of cultural studies claim, lay bare the negotiation and struggle between subordinate groups and dominant ideologies. Gramsci's influence is evident in the centrality of the concept of hegemony to cultural studies. Also, like Gramscian **hegemony theory**, cultural studies attempts to avoid the problems associated with economic determinism. Like Gramsci, cultural studies theorists have always been explicitly interventionist, seeking not only to understand oppressive relations, but to liberate the oppressed.

In relation to sport, Jarvie and Maguire (1994) identify three general aims of cultural studies research: (1) to consider the relationship between power and culture; (2) to demonstrate how sports forms consolidate, contest or reproduce broader structures of power; and (3) to highlight the role of sport as a site for popular struggle. The main proponents of the cultural studies approach in sport include Richard Gruneau, Jennifer and John Hargreaves, David Rowe and George Sage. Most of these authors have produced work which has been labelled within the **hegemony theory** tradition. Indeed, there is considerable overlap between the two theoretical approaches but hegemony theory should be considered as one variant of cultural studies; due to cultural studies' cross-disciplinary character, it should be seen as broader than hegemony theory.

Key Reading

Hargreaves, J.A. and Mcdonald, I. (2000) 'Cultural studies and the sociology of sport', in E. Dunning, and J. Coakley (eds), *Handbook of Sports Studies*. London: Sage. pp. 48–60.
Jarvie, G. and Maguire, J. (1994) *Sport and Leisure in Social Thought*. London: Routledge.

CULTURE OF RISK

(**risk**)

CYBORG SPORT

There is no one kind of cyborg; nor is there just one definition of what 'cyborg' means. As Donna Haraway, one of the most celebrated cyborg commentators puts it in *A Cyborg Manifesto* (1991), a cyborg exists when two kinds of boundaries are simultaneously problematic: (1) that between animals (or other organisms) and humans; and (2) that between self-controlled, self-governing machines (automatons) and organisms, especially humans (models of autonomy). The cyborg is the figure born of the interface of automaton and autonomy. Simply put, a cyborg is a being where the whole constitutes both machine elements and organic elements working together in a way that the machinic can affect function in the organic and vice versa, such that the (cyb)ernetic and the (org)anic working together create a new entity.

The term 'cyborg' has seen relatively narrow usage since its beginning in 1960 with reference to the kind of enhanced human who could survive in extra-terrestrial climates. This original use of the word by Manfred Clynes has led to a proliferation of science fiction generated cyborgs, ranging from the *Six-Million Dollar Man* TV series to the *Terminator* films, including 'soft' cyborgs such as Geordi LaForge from *Star Trek: the Next Generation* with his prosthetic visor, and not forgetting the proto-cyborg of Mary Shelley's *Frankenstein.*

This narrow view of the cyborg has done little to fuel purposeful debate in sports studies and has served to limit discussion to issues around performance enhancement derived from prosthetic or supplementary technologies (e.g., artificial limbs or heart valves) or, more recently, from the use of new technologies focusing on synthetic blood and genetic engineering. Even the term genetic *engineering* hints at a 'hard-metal' vision of the cyborg as a meshing of flesh and steel. The value of cyborg thinking for sports studies is greater than this.

The idea and possibility of cyborgs brings to the foreground of any discussion the nature, limits, boundaries and determinants of human being itself. At the same time, the consideration of cyborgs in sport and of cyborg-sport (whatever that means) is no less than a discussion of the meaning of sport, or, more fully, the significance to human beings of sport as a unique and identifying feature of humanity. As such, the discussion of cyborg sport can exist at several levels.

First, there is the descriptive level. There is a growing literature broadly focused around the relationship between technology and sport. At this level, the questions that predominate revolve around the definition and articulation of cyborgs in sport. To what extent, for example, is a modern pursuit cyclist like Lance Armstrong (emblematic of human and machine interdependence) a cyborg? How do we categorize athletes whose performance is enhanced (perhaps to beyond 'normal' abilities) through the use of a prosthetic limb or device that has been provided for therapeutic reasons (e.g. to replace a lost limb). Is gene therapy used for performance enhancement an 'artificial' aid and, thus, an unwanted, 'unnatural' technology? Within the discussions emanating from such questions, cyborg technologies are seen to be restorative, normalizing, reconfiguring, and enhancing. In most cases, the ensuing discussions see the notion of the cyborg stretched from its limited initial usage to a broader conceptualization allowing the interface of the cybernetic and the organic to take into account knowledge, technique, and non-game technologies. In other words, the cyborg apologist seeks to include in the discussion of cyborg sport the symbiotic relationship between humans and machines found throughout sport in the broadest application of scientific understanding to performance enhancement. The athlete undergoing remedial treatment using scanners and ultrasound, while improving their performance through complex video analysis and biomechanical modelling of technique, and controlling their emotional response to competitive stress by using biofeedback mechanisms, is every bit a cyborg.

Second, all questions at this descriptive and definitional level inevitably give rise to questions of philosophy (in its broadest sense) at the analytical level. What do we mean by human? What counts as enhancement? What is natural? At this level, many of the pseudo-ethical issues arise or are dealt with within this framework. What's wrong with enhancement (**drugs, prohibition of**)? Should genetic engineering be allowed in sport? Depending on how one tackles such questions, sports studies has neatly (if not entirely appropriately) compartmentalized these issues into the sub-disciplines of the philosophy of sport and the sociology of sport. However, the complex nature of such discussions quickly reveals that a raft of metaphysical assumptions exists within the frameworks used to analyse them. As the sociologist Raymond Williams once commented, 'nature' is the most difficult concept in the human language. To open up the discussion, one must draw equally upon the whole history of ideas: anthropology, psychology, natural science, social history, philosophy, sociology, biology and zoology, to name the most obvious. By doing so, one begins to recognize the culturally, historically and socially constructed ideas implicit in our taken-for-granted assumptions about the meaning and significance of sport in human life.

At the third and theoretical level, then, cyborg sport is an unsettling idea. It fractures and disperses meaning itself. It forces us to reconsider the plethora of dualities around which our worldview is constructed: organic–machinic; mind–body; natural–artificial; male–female; inside–outside; ego–object; us–them; self–other; primitive–developed; evolved–engineered (**binaries**). Should elite, performative sport be about discovering, uncovering, testing, realizing, achieving the fixed, pre-determined, limits of human capability bound up in the finite nature of human existence? Or is sport a measure of humankind, a barometer of our current ability to transcend our contemporary being and elevate ourselves to levels of performance in keeping with an ideal of what we want to be, not subscribed by ideas of what we are? Of course, such issues beg further questions of 'whose ideal' and is there a 'we' that can be meaningfully articulated without

reducing again to the (mere) biological ('we' as 'us human beings', however defined)? Will we finally recognize that **modern sport** is just a temporary phenomenon reflective of our temporal condition? What will then become of sporting activities, such as javelin throwing, sprinting, weightlifting and boxing, that have served to fix a particular male-centric image of the athlete as the predominant image of the embodied human being (**gender**)? As Donna Haraway (1991) says, 'whatever else it is, the cyborg point of view is always about communication, infection, gender, genre, species, intercourse, information, and semiology'.

Key Reading

Butryn, T.M. and Masucci, M.A. (2003) 'It's not about the book: a cyborg counternarrative of Lance Armstrong', *Journal of Sport and Social Issues*, 27 (2): 124–44.

Cole, C. (1998) 'Addiction, exercise and cyborgs: technologies of deviant bodies', in G. Rail (ed.), *Sport and Postmodern Times*. New York: State University of New York. Press. pp. 261–76.

Haraway, D. (1991) 'A Cyborg Manifesto: Science, Technology, and socialist-feminism in the late twentieth century' in *Simians, Cyborgs and Women: The Reinvention of Nature*. New York: Routledge. pp. 149–81.

Ryan, S. (2002) 'Cyborgs in the woods', *Leisure Studies*, 21 (3/4): 284–95.

Simon Eassom

D

DARWIN'S ATHLETES

Subtitled *How Sport has Damaged Black America and Preserved the Myth of Race*, *Darwin's Athletes* (1997) is perhaps the most controversial sports studies book to have been published in recent years. Prior to its publication its author, John Hoberman, had written relatively little on the subject of **race** relations in sport, gaining notoriety instead through his work on **drugs** and **sports medicine**, Olympism, and sport and political ideology. However, *Darwin's Athletes* launched a nationwide public debate in the United States media, prompted a walkout demonstration by black sociologists of sport at the 1997 annual conference of the North American Society for the Sociology of Sport held in Toronto, where Hoberman had been invited to give a keynote speech, and led to fierce debate in the academic community.

Darwin's Athletes is a 'racial history of modern sport'. The book starts by noting the prevalence of black athletes in the most popular American sports (and basketball and American football in particular) and argues that the **media**-generated images of sport 'probably do more than anything else in public life to encourage the idea that blacks and whites are biologically different in a meaningful way'. Hoberman starts by showing how the cult of black athleticism continues the tradition of emphasizing the physical superiority of blacks and discusses how African-Americans have bought into this collective fantasy, basking in the symbolism of black athletes' victories over whites. Hoberman then charts how the current position represents

a complete reversal from the ideologies of the European empire builders who saw their defeat and enslavement of Africans as a natural extension of their own biological superiority (**environmental determinism**; **imperialism**). The decline of such empires has been matched by the decline of white athletes. As blacks started to defeat whites in sport, the ideology adapted; though blacks possess physical superiority, whites remained dominant because of their mental superiority relative to blacks. Considerable scientific effort was devoted to 'proving' this idea in the nineteenth century (note the book's titular link to Charles Darwin, author of the seminal evolutionary theory, *The Origin of the Species*).

Hoberman noted that while whites may retreat from sport, perceiving their disadvantage to be innate, those who remain are compensated with roles of responsibility and the greater likelihood of going on to coaching or administrative power. The impact of athletic success on black communities, however, leads to peer group pressures that ridicule academic achievement and to a culture of anti-intellectualism. Moreover, the media's conflation of 'the athlete, gangster rapper and the criminal into a single black male persona', and the prominence of such images, has led to the invisibility of the African-American middle class and professionals. The black middle classes and black intelligentsia remain 'infatuated with sports' and thus 'cannot campaign effectively against racial stereotyping that preserves the black man's physicality as a sign of his inherent limitations'.

Critics of *Darwin's Athletes* argued that Hoberman was out of touch with the lived reality of African-American youths, and that his portrayal of black anti-intellectualism in particular was a crude over-generalization that would lead to the perpetuation of racist stereotypes of black mental inferiority. But Hoberman feels that at the heart of these debates is the question of whether a white middle class male could accurately analyse (and legitimately speak about) the experience of black working-class youth. Hoberman's response is that, to a degree, he clearly is at a distance from his research subject, but that this distance, this detachment, can confer unique advantages (**involvement and detachment**; **objectivity and subjectivity**). The proof, he says, is provided in the production of the book, and the fact that nothing remotely similar has been produced by those more deeply immersed in the culture.

Key Reading

Hoberman, J. (1997) *Darwin's Athletes: How Sport has Damaged Black America and Preserved the Myth of Race*. New York: Houghton Mifflin. The Mariner edition has a particularly useful preface which discusses some of the debates that surrounded the initial publication of the book.

Sandiford, K.A.P. (1999) 'Shooting hoops against Darwin's Athletes: a Barbadian response to John Hoberman', *The Sports Historian*, 19 (2): 84–111.

See also *International Review for the Sociology of Sport*, 33 (1): 83–99, for a Review Symposium on *Darwin's Athletes*.

DE-CENTRED

(**signifier and signified**)

DEEP PLAY

Anthropologist Clifford Geertz borrowed the concept of 'deep play' from Jeremy Bentham's *The Theory of Legislation* and applied it in his analysis of Balinese cock-fighting. For Bentham, deep play was a social situation/contest in which the stakes were so high that it was irrational for people to engage in it (i.e. the potential losses logically outweighed the potential benefits). The cock-fights that Geertz witnessed took place every two or three days and not infrequently involved 'centre bets' of between 100 and 250 ringgits, at a time when the average daily wage of a labourer was 3 ringgits. This centre bet between the two owners (or due to the size of the bet, more commonly coalitions), was accompanied by many more smaller side bets made between spectators (**gambling**).

The continuing cultural centrality of cock-fighting in Bali, Geertz concluded, owed much to the fact that it fundamentally involved 'a dramatization of status concerns'. Money, of course, was important, but the more of it that was **risk**ed, the more other things, such as pride, prestige, social status and **masculinity**, were at stake.

Not all cock-fights, Geertz realized, were deep play. His distinction can be summarized as follows. The more a match involved near status equals and/or personal enemies, and the more it involved individuals of high social status, the 'deeper' was the match. The deeper the match, the closer the identification of the cock and the man (the man would choose his best cock and one that people most closely associated with him). The more finely the cocks were matched, the greater **emotion** and air of tension there would be, the higher the bets would be, and the less an economic and more a status view of gaming would be involved.

A variety of unwritten, but no less pervasive, rules applied. Cock-fighting was for those involved in the everyday politics of prestige, and not for children, women or subordinates (**gender**). The centre bet coalition was always made up of the leading members of a kin group who were allies in more general terms; no outsiders were allowed in. A man would rarely bet against a cock owned by a member of his kin group and would have to bet with the kin group to show his allegiance. If his kin group was not involved, he would side with an allied kin group (**Bedouin syndrome**). The same principle was extended to inter-village matches. One would thus rarely have two cocks from the same kin group fighting each other and men rarely talked about *how much* money they had won, focusing rather on *who* was beaten. Those who had a well-known and institutionalized antipathy towards each other, would bet heavily against one another, 'in what is a frank and direct attack on the very masculinity, the ultimate ground of status, of the opponent'. Such institutionalized antipathy is normally formally initiated by betting 'against the grain'; i.e. against a previously allied kin group. If a man found that his loyalties were divided, he would wander off to avoid having to bet either way through fear of causing offence.

Consequently, cock-fighting was a way of activating rivalries. Participants came close to open and direct inter-group **aggression**, but not quite to **violence** because after all, it was 'only a cock-fight'.

Key Reading

Geertz, C. (1975) 'Deep play: notes on the Balinese cockfight', in *The Interpretation of Cultures*. London: Hutchinson. pp. 412–42.

DERRIDA

(binaries)

DEVIANCE

Most sociologists agree that deviance involves behaviour that violates social norms or rules. They are much less clear, however, about how rules/social norms are defined and when they are violated (hence deviance may sometimes be placed in quotation marks).

Conventional considerations of the relationships between sport and deviance emerged from the tradition of **functionalism**, which had a tendecy to focus on sport's potential role as a deterrent to delinquency (**functions of sport; social inclusion**). While there remains little definitive evidence of a direct causal relationship, this perspective has retained its rhetorical authority on many social policy agendas. These agendas tend to relate to perspectives which see sports, in Parsonian terms, as social systems with important socializing influences (**socialization**), or in Merton's terms, as offering alternative sources of reward that militate against the strain towards **anomie** and 'deviant' behaviour.

Early neo-Marxist interpretations of sport retained elements of this perspective, although in more critical fashion (**Marxism**). Sport was seen to reproduce social behaviour that was functionally and normatively consistent with the needs of capitalism while maintaining the illusion of sport as an autonomous liberatory domain. Ultimately, Jean-Marie Brohm's book, *Sport – A Prison of Measured Time* (1978), in adopting the terminology of 'deviance' and its control, reveals how social autonomy is actually undermined through the production of disciplined behaviour which leads to individual **alienation**.

Avoiding a focus on the capitalist 'super structure', researchers in the tradition of **symbolic interactionism** have been more concerned with the interactions that go on *within* the social worlds of 'deviant' **subcultures** and have searched for the meanings that those involved give to their actions. Within this perspective there is an understanding that meanings are established subject to constraints, such as the names and symbols associated with social groups upon which definitions are built. As such, this school has been motivated by a desire to observe people in action, revealing the complex processes through which 'deviant' practices emerge and the apparent contradictions of participants' actual behaviours that are seen to both challenge and reproduce dominant ideologies. Nevertheless, for those who have considered subcultures from within a **cultural studies** perspective, the concern has been to 'speak up' for the marginalized with the emphasis placed on counter-hegemonic resistance to wider structural changes (**hegemony theory**).

A broader conceptualization of 'deviancy' and notions of difference through a focus on gendered and racialized issues of power, domination and resistance have been offered by **feminism** (**gender**; **race**). However, feminist cultural studies of sport have themselves been blighted by a rather narrow theoretical focus documenting resistance to the dominant heterosexual masculine hegemony within sports practices. While this has produced some productive descriptions of 'deviant' behaviour among women in sport, through considerations of female subcultures and the subversion and occupation of 'male' sporting rituals and spaces, such studies continue to be hampered by a preoccupation with binary understandings of gender difference (**binaries**).

Jay Coakley has emerged as the leading exponent of attempts to synthesize these approaches. He suggests that there are two main ways in which 'deviance' in sport has been theorized: the absolutist – 'its either right or wrong' – and the relativist – 'it all depends on who makes the rules' (Coakley, 2006). The absolutist approach is represented as functionalist, laying emphasis on the deviation of behaviour from a predetermined social norm. By contrast the relativist position is represented as emanating from advocates of **conflict theory**, who present 'deviance' as a 'label' relating to certain behaviours or people identified as 'bad' on the basis of rules made by people in positions of 'power'.

For Coakley the main problem with these conceptualizations is that they ignore 'deviance' which involves an overcomformity to rules and norms, what he refers to as **positive deviance**. As such, he draws on what he calls a 'critical normal distribution approach' to distinguish between 'positive deviance' involving overconformity or unquestioned acceptance of norms, and 'negative deviance' involving underconformity or

a rejection of norms. However, this position does not seem to fully acknowledge that whether or not behaviour is considered 'deviant' – 'positive' or 'negative' – will always be contingent on the context in which the 'act' takes place and the interpretations of it which follow.

One field where a significant degree of attention has been placed on context is that of **football hooliganism**, which has seen the application of the full range of these competing theoretical perspectives. Peter Marsh's social psychological ethogenic approach concluded that much violent 'disorder' is, in fact, highly ritualized orderly behaviour constrained by tacit social rules. By contrast the 'Leicester School', grounded in **figurational sociology**, focused attention on the social characteristics of those involved in the practice of football-related violence. Mobilizing Norbert Elias's concept of the **civilizing process** and Gerald Suttles's concept of 'ordered segmentation' in slum neighbourhoods, the 'Leicester School' explored the ways in which the 'rough' working class have been the victims of a 'decivilizing spurt' that produced wider social inequalities and an upsurge in violent behaviour in Britain from the 1960s. However, while Elias's underlying metaphysics implies that football hooligans will be drawn from specific elements of the social hierarchy, more grounded interpretative ethnographies have suggested that such violence is very much contingent upon time and context, rather than being a universal attribute of particular sections of working-class men (see also **violence**).

Cultural studies theorists have been concerned with how the prominence of categories such as the 'football hooligan' is related to the organization of sport in the **media**. They have shown how viewpoints are 'mediated' through the process of news production, selection and presentation that has helped to establish the vocabulary of football hooliganism. It is in this context that the 'football hooligan' was seen to emerge as a new 'folk devil' leading to the development of a **moral panic** with future incidents appearing within this populist framework.

More recently this **commodification** has been described as a form of 'consumptive deviance'. Consumptive deviance, argue Blackshaw and Crabbe (2004), is the 'deviance' that consumers decide to buy on the back of public denunciations by establishment forces. As such, what we perceive to be 'deviant' today is often nothing more than a sophisticated and mediated commodity form, apparently performed with all the unpredictability and dangerousness we would expect, but in reality scripted and ready-made for consumption through its provocation of media attention. It is at once entertaining while 'feeling' like the real thing – the big race smashes and on-field bust-ups repeated over and again, or the titillating revelations of a sporting **celebrity**'s sexual exploits spread over the front pages. This is 'deviance' that we can 'buy' into in order to witness or feel subversive, dirty, sexy. Its distance leaves us unable to question its authenticity while leaving us safe from its consequences and responsibility for those who are caught up in the media whirlwind that surrounds it.

Key Reading

Blackshaw, T. and Crabbe, T. (2004) *New Perspectives on Sport and 'Deviance': Consumption, Performativity and Social Control*. London: Routledge.

Brohm, J.-M. (1978) *Sport – A Prison of Measured Time* trans. Ian Fraser. London: Ink Links.

Coakley, J. (2006) *Sport in Society: Issues and Controversies*, 9th edn. Boston: McGraw-Hill.

Tim Crabbe

DISABILITY

There is no universally agreed definition or understanding of disability. However, the historical development of the concept of disability provides a worthwhile contribution to our understanding of this phenomenon and the relatively recent emergence of disability sport. In ancient Judaism, for example, disabled individuals were seen to be unclean, ungodly; a punishment for the sins of the family and evidence of Satan's power over mortals. It was not until the sixteenth and seventeenth centuries – a period of significant advances in medical science – that medical practitioners challenged the explanation for impairment as a religious or spiritual phenomenon and argued that impairment was the consequence of a biological condition. Medical professionals, who were perceived to be the definers of, and providers of solutions to, disability, decided who could and could not work. This promoted the legitimacy of the medical profession in their identification and therapeutic treatment of disabled people, polarizing concepts of normal and abnormal, sane and insane, healthy and sick.

This medical model (or personal tragedy theory) of disability, embraces those definitions or perceptions which suggest that disability is an impairment owned by an individual, which results in a loss or limitation of function. Arguably, the most important post-Second World War definition of disability was introduced in 1980 by the World Health Organization (WHO). The WHO defined disability as any restriction or lack of ability (resulting from impairment) to perform an activity in the manner or within the range considered normal for a human being.

The problem with this definition (see Oliver, 1990) is that the focus on 'having something wrong' implies the need for professionals to impose their own priorities on the lifestyles of disabled people, which often relegates other personal or social needs to second place. As Oliver contends, this view does not recognize the impact that the environment and, in particular, significant others can play in the lives of those deemed to be impaired.

Such discontent led disabled people to form organizations that challenged what many perceived to be oppressive policies and the negative definitions on which they were based. The American pressure group, the Union of the Physically Impaired Against Segregation (UPIAS) suggested that to be impaired is to lack part or all of a limb, or to have a defective limb, organ or mechanism of the body. Disability is the disadvantage or restriction of activity caused by contemporary social organization which takes little or no account of people who have physical impairments and excludes them from participation in mainstream activities. This social definition is based on the notion that society *disables* people by limiting their social worth, placing additional burdens – such as negative attitudes – on impairment, which unnecessarily isolate the impaired from the rest of society.

However, while applauding the shift from medical and individual theory to social and environmental explanations of disability, critics suggest that both the medical and the social models consider bodily impairment in similar ways. If disabled people are effectively to challenge and deconstruct the political and economic structures that oppress and exclude them, they need to embrace **body** politics and accept the significance of the individual within the wider socio-political environment.

The WHO's International Classification of Impairment, Disability and Handicap (ICIDH) – developed in 2000 – took account of the criticisms of earlier definitions, and attempted to incorporate both the individual and the social models of disability. It recognized Bickenbach et al's claim that each aspect of disablement is an 'interaction between intrinsic features of the individual and that person's social and physical environment' (1999: 1183). This model allows a disability to be determined under the classifications of the body, the person in context, and the person's social and physical environment. It disabuses people of the notion that impairment is necessarily the prime disabler.

A subsequent version – the ICIDH-2 – was itself later amended and the International Classification of Functioning, Disability and Health (ICF) was launched (WHO, 2001). The overall purpose of the ICF was to 'provide a unified and standard language and framework for the description of health and health related states' (WHO, 2001: 3). However, the main criticism of the ICIDH-2 and the ICF which followed is that they continue to label those considered different to the social norm, and perpetuate the concept of disability as a natural consequence of impairment. These different perspectives on disability and the varying treatment of those with impairment help to explain the emergence and development of 'disability sport'.

Traditionally, disabled people have been marginalized from the mainstream of society and denied the attendant benefits that such a position holds. This marginalization is evident in sport and is demonstrated by the emergence and development of the Paralympics, and disability sport more generally. The Paralympics has its substantive origins in the immediate post-Second World War period when those injured in war were treated and rehabilitated in hospitals in order that they could return to the predominantly non-disabled society. While it was already well known that physical activity could play a positive role in the physiological and psychological rehabilitation of impaired individuals, it was Ludwig Guttmann, a neurosurgeon at Stoke Mandeville Hospital in England, who established international sporting competitions for disabled people using a medically based classification system. The first formally recognized national disability sport event was held at Stoke Mandeville Hospital in 1948 and provided the foundation for the Paralympic movement. While the Paralympics was originally restricted to those with spinal cord injury, it now represents the pinnacle of disability sport for a wide range of disabled people. However, despite the significant improvement in individual performances, public profile and relationships with the Olympic Games, it does not enjoy the status of the Olympics, nor do its competitors have access to the same level of support.

This structural inequality is also evident at a recreational level, as disabled people typically have far fewer opportunities than non-disabled people to participate in organized sport. Moreover, competitive sporting opportunities have traditionally been provided by disability sport organizations, and not mainstream providers of sport. Following his establishment of the Paralympic movement, and in recognition of the need for better local and regional sporting opportunities, Guttmann established the British Sports Association for the Disabled in 1961 as the coordinating body for disability sport in the UK, but since then a diverse range of disability sport organizations has emerged. Government reviews of disability sport in the UK in 1989 and 1998 criticized the lack of coordination between this growing number of disability sport organizations and, reflecting the move toward a social explanation for the causes of disability, called for the responsibility for disability sport to be shifted away from the disability sport organizations and on to the mainstream sports providers. In its 1993 policy statement, the **Sports Council** recognized that the inequalities faced by people with impairments are caused, at least in part, by a predominantly mainstream non-disabled society and that disabled people should be afforded similar opportunities to those enjoyed by their non-disabled peers. This is an indication that responsibility for fulfilling this objective lies with the mainstream sporting organizations that hitherto have typically catered only for non-disabled people (Sports Council, 1993). Concomitantly, mainstream sports organizations have begun to offer opportunities to disabled people that were hitherto only available to non-disabled people. However, while the term 'mainstreaming' has been central to the policy rhetoric espoused by both mainstream and disability sport organizations, there are different perspectives on its meaning and variable commitment to its implementation.

Key Reading

Bickenbach, J.E., Chatterji, S., Badley, E.M. and Ustun, T.B. (1999) 'Models of disablement, universalism and international classification of impairments, disabilities and handicaps', *Social Science and Medicine*, 48: 1173–87.

Oliver, M. (1990) *The Politics of Disablement*. Basingstoke: McMillan.

Sports Council (1993) *People with Disabilities and Sport: Policy and Current/Planned Action*. London: Sports Council.

Thomas, N. (2003) 'Sport and disability', in B. Houlihan (ed.), *Sport and Society: A Student Introduction*. London: Sage.

WHO (2001) *The International Classification of Human Functioning and Disability*. Geneva: World Health Organization.

Nigel Thomas

DISCIPLINE

Prior to the sixteenth century, the state operated in a largely repressive mode. Public spectacles of torture, for example, ensured the continuity of rule and social order. By the eighteenth century, larger populations and more complex divisions of labour meant that the state's primary concern was ensuring economic productivity – not through the threat of public execution, but through processes of normalization, strategies of punishment, and the use of a vast police apparatus for the management of the population. In *Discipline and Punish: The Birth of the Prison* (1977), these historical changes serve as the backdrop for Foucault's examination of the emergence of discipline, a mode of power that is exercised not via violent repression but through complex webs of relations, practices and techniques.

The emergence of discipline as a generalized mode of power was accompanied by a new view of the **body** as something that could be trained and shaped. Late eighteenth-century military manuals, for example, outlined how to convert recruits into soldiers; a soldier was not something ready-made, but was constructed through deliberate, rational and repeated exercises designed to instil appropriate bodily habits and abilities. The body and its habits, abilities, capacities and obedience are at the heart of disciplinary power.

Discipline is exercised *over* bodies; for instance, when institutions such as schools, factories, armies and prisons use scheduling, regimented exercises, functionally specific sites and **surveillance** to control and train particular bodily capacities. By organizing time (e.g., through schedules and timetables) and space (by enclosing and dividing specific zones), and by breaking down activities into function components, disciplines make it possible to observe, compare and rank bodies, and then to intervene in order to make those bodies approximate a norm. Discipline is also, crucially, exercised *through* bodies; for instance, when individuals internalize rules and habituate behaviour through the repeated pattern of exercises, schedules and routines. Thus discipline results in both productive, useful bodies and obedient, docile subjects endowed with self-restraint and self-discipline.

As with Foucault's example of military manuals, athletic training can be examined as a means for producing useful, docile individuals. Diaries, records, and programmes of graduated exercises allow coaches and athletes to assess, rank and optimize the body's competitiveness (Heikkala, 1993). School physical education employs disciplinary techniques for producing individuals who conform to sporting norms (such as the ethos of competitiveness). More importantly, however, physical education operates according to the norms of the political and economic order. Students are disciplined in order to hone those capacities (such as cooperation, respect for rules, competence in personal hygiene) deemed necessary for productive, normal citizens (Hargreaves, 1986).

Key Reading

Foucault, M. (1977) *Discipline and Punish: The Birth of the Prison*. New York: Vintage Books.
Hargeaves, J. (1986) *Sport, Power and Culture: A Social and Historical Analysis of Popular Sports in Britain*. Cambridge: Polity Press.
Heikkala, J. (1993) 'Discipline and excel: techniques of the self and body and the logic of competing', *Sociology of Sport Journal*, 10 (4): 397–412.

Jennifer Smith Maguire

DISCOURSE

While in common usage, discourse can be taken to mean a simple conversation, discussion or communication; sociologically, discourse can be seen as the way in which power relations influence that which is present (or absent) in forms of communication. Discourse can thus be applied to small-scale social interaction or to debates and public discussions about social issues. Regardless of the scale of the discourse, powerful individuals and groups seek to promote their views, possibly at the expense of others. Thus, through the analysis of a given 'text' or debate (**content analysis**), we can see which interests are being served and which are being marginalized. Moreover, discourse comes to construct and define social reality, for our understanding of a social phenomenon is shaped, limited even, by our exposure to discourse. Indeed, Foucault goes as far as to argue that, in part at least, social phenomena are only present through discourse and that there are no social phenomena outside discourse.

Discourse has been used in the study of sport in a number of ways. Particularly prominent has been the focus on the construction of **gender** and **race** relations through sports narratives, and discussion of an **obesity discourse**. Equally, John Evans has been central in examining the discourse of physical education policy (**physical education, policy in**), such as the introduction of the **National Curriculum for Physical Education** in the UK, while others have looked at the health discourse in the physical education (PE) context (**health-related physical education**). In spite of the fact that some may be critical of the tendency towards **reification** evident in discourse analysis, at the very least the notion of discourse alerts us to the fact that what we read and hear should not simply be taken for granted, but is the product of a broader conflict, and the balance of power, between interested groups.

Key Reading

Andrews, D. (1996) 'Deconstructing Michael Jordan: reconstructing postindustrial America', *Sociology of Sport Journal*, 15 (Special Issue).

Birrell, S. and Cole, C. (1990) 'Double fault: Renee Richards and the construction and naturalization of difference', *Sociology of Sport Journal*, 7 (1): 1–21.

Evans, J., Davies, B. and Wright, J. (eds) (2004) *Body Knowledge and Control. Studies in the Sociology of Physical Education and Health*. London: Routledge.

Penney, D. and Evans, J. (1999) *Politics, Policy and Practice in Physical Education*. London: Routledge.

DIURETICS

(**drugs, classes of**)

DOUBLEDAY MYTH

In December 1907 Abraham Mills, president of professional baseball's National League, issued the final report of a commission set up to establish definitively the game's origins. Prior to the publication of the commission's findings it had been widely believed that baseball developed out of the old English children's game of rounders, though curiously baseball's debt to cricket was not fully recognized (Malcolm, 2006). Mills, however, accepted the testimony of octogenarian Abner Graves who argued that Abner Doubleday, a major general in the US Army, had invented baseball at Cooperstown, New York in 1839. To commemorate the centenary of this event, the National Baseball Hall of Fame was opened in Cooperstown in 1939.

It is now widely accepted that the Abner Doubleday story is entirely mythical. Many baseball historians argue that Alexander Cartwright, founder of baseball's first team, the Knickerbocker Club of New York, is the true 'inventor' of baseball. Sociologically, however, it is more adequate to consider that baseball, like other **modern sports**, developed out of a range of antecedents which we might describe as **folk games** (see the **Webb Ellis myth** for a parallel analysis of the development of rugby football).

Once established as a myth, historians and sociologists have sought to explain the motivations behind the fabrication of this story. Many highlight the role of Albert Spalding, a former player and owner of the world's biggest manufacturer of sports goods at the time, who established the commission and publicized its findings in his 1908 *Official Baseball Guide*. Spalding was overtly patriotic, eager to establish American origins for what had become America's national game, but he also had a commercial interest in the game, and his 'American theory' was a useful marketing tool. Bloyce (2004), however, has argued that in addition to this, the Doubleday myth should be seen in the context of America's increasing world power (especially relative to Britain), and thus as an attempt by some to reject lingering feelings of inferiority relative to their former mother country (see also **imperialism** and **invented traditions**).

Key Reading

Bloyce, D. (2004) 'Baseball: myths and modernization', in E. Dunning, D. Malcolm and I. Waddington (eds), *Sport Histories: Figurational Studies of the Development of Modern Sports*. London: Routledge. pp. 88–103.

Kirsch, G.B. (1989) *The Creation of American Team Sports: Baseball and Cricket,*

1838–72. Chicago: University of Illinois Press.

Malcolm, D. (2006) 'The diffusion of cricket to America: a figurational sociological examination', *Journal of Historical Sociology*, 19 (2): 151–73.

DRAFT SYSTEM

(player reservation systems)

DRUGS

The use by athletes of substances believed to have performance-enhancing qualities can be traced back at least to the athletes of ancient Greece and Rome. In the late nineteenth century cyclists were thought to have used **alcohol** and amphetimines during endurance events; however, it is generally agreed that the widespread use of drugs in sport dates from the 1960s, a trend linked with: (1) improvements in chemical technology; (2) the increased emphasis which has come to be placed on winning; and (3) the growing involvement of physicians in the medical management of athletes.

In recent decades, increased emphasis has been placed on the importance of winning and athletes have come under mounting pressure to produce medal-winning performances. These changes have been related to a number of social developments. Of particular importance have been the politicization of sport (**boycotts; propaganda**), and the huge increases in the rewards associated with sporting success (**commercialization**).

Sport has become increasingly politicized in the period since 1945. The development of communist regimes in many parts of Eastern Europe and the emergence of superpower rivalry meant that international sporting competition took on extra significance, for sport – at least within the context of East–West relations – became an extension of the political, military and economic competition that characterized relationships between the superpowers and their associated blocs. Comparisons of the number of Olympic medals won by the United States and the Soviet Union came to be seen as a symbol of the superiority of one political system over another.

The increased emphasis placed on the importance of winning has also been associated with the growing commercialization of sport, particularly in the West. In recent years, the financial rewards associated with Olympic success have increased markedly. In many countries, Olympic gold medal winners can earn huge incomes from **sponsorship**, television commercials and product endorsement.

The growing competitiveness of modern sport and the increased rewards associated with winning have led athletes increasingly to turn for help to anyone who can hold out the promise of improving their level of sporting performance. This is an important part of the context for understanding the increasing cooperation in recent years between athletes and sports physicians; it is also an important part of the context for understanding the increasing use of drugs within sport.

The expanding involvement of physicians in the medical management of athletes has been described as the medicalization of sport. Central to this process has been the development of **sports medicine**, which is premised on the idea that highly trained athletes have special medical needs and therefore require special medical supervision.

The development of sports medicine has been associated with the development of a culture that encourages the treatment not just of injured athletes, but also of healthy athletes, with drugs. Even if the 'drugs' are simply those that are legally available, such as vitamins and food supplements, modern athletes have come to rely increasingly on medical help, drugs and supplements. This point was nicely illustrated by Robert Voy (1991), former chief medical officer for the US Olympic Committee, who recorded that a national track star was taking no fewer than 22 *legal* drugs and food supplements on a daily basis!

It is important to emphasize that the relationship between athletes and sports medicine practitioners goes beyond the treatment of sports injuries, for sports medicine is concerned not just with the prevention, diagnosis and treatment of exercise-related injuries but also with the maximization of performance. As the rewards associated with winning have increased, so the role of sports physicians in maximizing performance has become more important. One consequence of this growing concern of sports physicians with the maximization of performance has been to make top-class athletes more and more dependent on increasingly sophisticated systems of medical support. At the highest levels, the quality of medical support may make the difference between success and failure. As increased importance has been placed on winning, so athletes have increasingly turned to mechanical aids (such as exercise and massage), nutritional aids (vitamins and minerals), psychological support (discipline and transcendental meditation) and pharmacology (medicines and drugs) to increase their advantage over opponents in competition (see also **cyborg sport**). As part of this attempt to boost sporting performance, a growing emphasis has been placed on the non-medical use of banned drugs, particularly anabolic steroids, central nervous system stimulants, and analgesics (**drugs, classes of**).

Although sports medicine is a legitimate specialist area of practice, there is a substantial and well-documented history of the involvement of many sports physicians in the development and use of performance-enhancing drugs. Prominent examples of medical involvement include: (1) the central role of Dr John Ziegler, the US team doctor at the 1956 World Games in Moscow, in the development and dissemination among the weightlifting community of the first widely used anabolic steroids; (2) the systematic involvement of doctors in doping in the former East Germany; and (3) the involvement of sports medicine specialists in the development of **blood-doping**.

In 1990, the Dubin Commission of Inquiry in Canada documented the involvement of many sports physicians in providing performance-enhancing drugs to athletes in many sports and in several countries. The Commission found that, in Canada, the names of physicians willing to prescribe anabolic steroids and other performance-enhancing drugs were circulated widely in gyms, and that there were physicians in most major centres across the country who were involved in prescribing anabolic steroids and other performance-enhancing drugs to athletes. Dubin noted that the situation in the United States was similar to that in Canada, and that in Australia drugs were also readily available from physicians.

In the 1990s, *The Sunday Times* revealed that a doctor to the British Olympic men's team between 1979 and 1987 had provided steroids to British athletes and provided advice about how to avoid testing positive. Following the doping scandal in the 1998 Tour de France (which led to the establishment of the World Anti-Doping Agency, (WADA)), a great deal of information became available not just about the systematic and organized use of performance-enhancing drugs in professional cycling, but also about the pivotal role of team doctors in doping. Data from these major doping scandals point to the central role often played by sports physicians and indicate that if we wish to understand the use of performance-enhancing drugs in sport, then it is crucial that we understand the centrality of the relationship between elite level athletes and sports physicians.

Key Reading

Dubin, The Hon. C.L. (1990) *Commission of Inquiry into the Use of Drugs and Banned Practices Intended to Increase Athletic Performance.* Ottawa: Canadian Government Publishing Centre.

Houlihan, B. (2002) *Dying to Win: Doping in Sport and the Development of Anti-Doping*

Policy, 2nd edn. Strasburg: Council of Europe.

Voy, R. (1991) *Drugs, Sport and Politics*. Champaign: IL: Leisure Press.

Waddington, I. (2000) *Sport, Health and Drugs: A Critical Sociological Perspective*. London. E. & F.N. Spon.

Ivan Waddington

DRUGS, CLASSES OF

There are several classes of drugs the use of which is generally banned within sport. These include: stimulants; narcotic analgesics; anabolic steroids; diuretics; and peptide and glycoprotein hormones and analogues. *Stimulants* act on the brain to stimulate the body both mentally and physically (**arousal**). They may increase a competitor's ability to exercise at maximum levels and may reduce fatigue. *Narcotic analgesics* are the strongest form of painkillers. They may be used to reduce the pain from injury or to increase the pain threshold so that athletes can continue to compete, perhaps when to do so would **risk** more serious injury (**pain and injury**). There are also international restrictions on the supply and use of narcotics. *Anabolic steroids* are natural or synthetic compounds that act in a similar way to the hormone testosterone. They may be used by athletes to increase muscle mass, to enable longer and more intensive training, or to increase **aggression** and competitiveness. *Diuretics* help to eliminate fluid from the body. They are used in sport to lose weight quickly or to increase the rate at which urine is produced, making it more difficult to detect the use of prohibited substances. For this reason they are sometimes referred to as 'masking drugs'. *Peptide and glycoprotein hormones* (and *analogues*) are substances produced by glands in the body to control specific bodily functions. For instance, they may be used to increase growth, control pain or stimulate red blood

cell production, which increases the amount of oxygen supplied to the muscles. These drugs are particularly used by endurance athletes. Among the substances of this kind used in sport are human growth hormone and erythropoietin (EPO).

In addition to these classes of banned substances there is also a range of *prohibited methods*. These include **blood-doping**, and pharmacological, chemical and physical manipulation. Blood-doping involves the removal of blood from an athlete and the re-infusion of that blood back into the athlete before competition. This increases the number of red blood cells and therefore the amount of oxygen available to the muscles. Pharmacological, chemical and physical manipulation involves the use of substances and/or methods which may alter the integrity of a urine sample. Such methods may include catheterization, urine substitution and/or tampering, or the use of epitestosterone to mask the use of testosterone.

Key Reading

Houlihan, B. (2002) *Dying to Win: Doping in Sport and the Development of Anti-Doping Policy*, 2nd edn. Strasburg: Council of Europe.

Waddington, I. (2000) *Sport, Health and Drugs: A Critical Sociological Perspective*. London: E. & F.N. Spon.

DRUGS, PROHIBITION OF

The use of certain pharmaceutical substances (**drugs, classes of**) by participants in elite sports has been banned since the 1960s. Tests to detect those athletes using **drugs** were first introduced for the 1966 Football World Cup, held in England, and by the **IOC** at the 1968 Winter Olympic Games in Grenoble. The World Anti-Doping Agency (**WADA**) now oversees the administration of approximately 25,000 tests per year, about 1.5 per cent of which detect the presence of illegal substances. Though a relatively rare occurrence, positive tests by athletes tend to evoke high degrees of condemnation and, in the case of Ben Johnson, considerable national shame. Initially there were two main rationales for the prohibition of drugs: drugs damaged the health of athletes and their use was a form of cheating. However, many analysts have detected flaws and inconsistencies in these and subsequent arguments for the prohibition of drugs in sport.

The notion that sport, and elite sport in particular, promotes **health** (what Waddington (2000) calls the sport-health ideology) has increasingly been questioned. First, sports governing bodies are happy to accept **sponsorship** money from **alcohol** and tobacco companies, and latterly 'junk food' suppliers such as McDonalds and Coca-Cola. Second, elite sports participation entails a high **risk** of **pain and injury** (see also **risk-pain-injury-paradox**), and **violence** is also an inherent characteristic of many sports (e.g. boxing). Careers tend to be short. Post-career ailments, such as arthritis, are common among former competitors. Third, many substances that might be harmful to health are legal in sport. Most commonly cited in this regard are painkillers and anti-inflammatory drugs which enable athletes to play on with injuries, but at the risk of further and potentially more severe injury. Fourth, some banned substances (e.g. caffeine) are in wide public usage and some have therapeutic qualities (e.g. ephedrine, as found in many cold remedies). The notion that drugs should be banned because otherwise athletes will harm their health is a highly paternalistic argument which would only be convincing if athletes were incapable of making their own informed decisions.

The argument that using drugs is unfair holds more water, but remains flawed. The notion of **fair play** is integral to **modern sport**, the rules of which effectively create a 'level playing field' for participants. However, this is a very limited notion of fairness. Athletes who were born or who train at altitude may have an 'unfair' advantage. In this respect it might be argued that **blood-doping**, which provides a similar effect, should be legalized in the interests of promoting equality. Second, athletes from Western nations are likely to be supported by wealthier sports systems, and have greater access to training aids, medical facilities, etc. than their counterparts in, say, Africa. In team sports, despite the belief in the importance of **competitive balance**, measures to equalize playing resources are often limited. Is a contest between teams with radically different financial resources, such as West Ham United and Manchester United, fair? (See also **cyborg sport**.)

In more recent years, a third rationale has been introduced, which perhaps provides greater explanatory purchase. Since 1998 the **Sports Council** in the UK has noted that drug use is banned because it is harmful to the image of sport. This would explain why, increasingly, sports governing bodies have punished those using recreational drugs, and further helps us to understand why the use of drugs is seen as the very worst form of cheating (compared, say, to foul play, such as tripping or blocking opponents). There is, Waddington (2000) argues, something approaching a **moral panic** about the use of drugs in contemporary society. Drug use in sport is in many ways 'contaminated' by these fears and sports administrators are increasingly forced to respond to these broader issues. However, Cashmore (1996), argues that the rationale that drugs should be banned because athletes are role models for the young (and hence their use damages the image of sport) is also problematic because: (1) rock stars are also role models, but escape such regulation; and (2) the competitive nature of modern sport means that athletes cannot be expected to be so virtuous.

If none of these rationales are convincing, why was the use of drugs in sport prohibited and why does it remain so? The answer lies in the broader political context at the time the ban was imposed and changes in sport since. The prohibition on the use of drugs in sport began at the height of the Cold War between the Soviet bloc and the US (**propaganda**). It is notable that the IOC led the way among sporting bodies in campaigning against drug use, and that the main pressure to introduce a ban came from the US and other Western states. Increasingly being beaten by their Eastern European counterparts, their argument was that the means used were unfair. Now that such international rivalry has reduced, monetary issues stemming from **commercialization** processes have come to the fore. Sports administrators are increasingly concerned that the use of drugs will lead to negative publicity for their sports and the withdrawal of sponsors. Seen in this light, the shift from a rationale that drug use is cheating to the rationale that it is bad for the image of sport can be more readily understood.

Key Reading

Cashmore, E. (1996) *Making Sense of Sport*, 2nd edn. London, Routledge. esp. Ch. 8.

Houlihan, B. (2003) 'Doping and sport: more problems than solutions?', in B. Houlihan (ed.), *Sport and Society: A Student Introduction*. London: Sage. pp. 218–35.

Waddington, I. (2000) *Sport, Health and Drugs: A Critical Sociological Perspective*. London: E. & F.N. Spon. esp. Ch. 6.

E

EATING DISORDERS

These are extremely complex conditions variously understood and much debated across the disciplines of psychiatry, medicine, psychology, biology, sociology and epidemiology. The eating disorders anorexia nervosa and bulimia nervosa are clinically defined by diagnostic criteria, most commonly those established by the American Psychiatric Association Diagnostic and Statistical Manual (DSM-IV). Anorexia nervosa involves: (1) the refusal to maintain body weight over a minimum normal weight for age and height; (2) intense fear of gaining weight or becoming fat even though underweight; (3) disturbance in the way in which one's body weight, size or shape is experienced; and (4) may involve the restriction of food intake and the presence of amenorrhea. Bulimia nervosa involves recurrent episodes of binge eating or recurrent, inappropriate compensatory behaviour to prevent weight gain such as: (1) self-induced vomiting; (2) misuse of laxatives, diuretics or other medications; (3) fasting; or (4) excessive exercise. A large volume of literature suggests that both these conditions involve the associations of negative body image, fear of fat, and feelings of powerlessness and insecurity. For both conditions the strongest risk periods are during adolescence. These clinically defined eating disorders are therefore categorized as serious psychiatric illnesses. They are conditions which are seen to include psychological problems as well as concerns around dieting, weight and **body** image.

A number of studies indicate that eating disorders of this kind are on the increase among athletes. Sociocultural factors within sports environments are considered to play a significant role in the development of problems associated with body image, weight concerns and disordered eating attitudes. Sports emphasizing a lean physique, and those with an emphasis on aesthetics, are seen to have a higher prevalence of participants exhibiting eating disorder symptoms. Sports such as gymnastics, figure skating, dancing and synchronized swimming are reported to have a higher percentage of athletes with eating disorders for a number of reasons. First, the pressure on athletes to maintain a thin physique for these activities is reinforced by wider sociocultural demands that celebrate slenderness. Athletes in these cultures may exhibit high levels of body-dissatisfaction whereby they experience increasing levels of negative thoughts and feelings towards body image, and an excessive drive towards thinness. Second, a number of studies have highlighted that within these sports environments assumptions are often made around the performance benefits associated with particular body types; for example, that the slimmer a competitor is, the better they will perform. Research has reported athletes' use of pathogenic weight control techniques as a way to improve their performance, including self-induced vomiting, use of laxatives, smoking, starvation and over-exercising.

More recent research has highlighted the emergence of excessive weight control techniques in sports where a weigh-in is required for weight-graded competitions (such as boxing, wrestling, rowing and horse riding). These may result in cycles of weight gain followed by rapid weight loss. There is, for example, a growing literature highlighting the weight control practices of school-aged wrestlers.

There has also been a significant rise in the number of athletes possessing partial or subclinical eating disorders. A significant proportion of those participating in sport and/or physical activity are seen to exhibit disordered forms of eating or weight loss, but do not necessarily meet all of the strict diagnostic criteria as defined by DSM-IV. These behaviours are now being recognized as new conditions of disordered eating, rather than clinically defined eating disorders. These include *orthorexia*, an obsession with eating healthy foods, and *anorexia athletica*, which involves compulsive over-exercising, often alongside restrictions on food intake. While athletes experiencing these conditions may not experience the severe **health** threats associated with anorexia or bulimia, they may nonetheless experience psychological distress, body dissatisfaction, and problematic relationships with embodied identities, and thus may also be exposed to health **risks** (see Beals, 2000). The recognition of these subclinical conditions has enabled those working within sports environments to identify athletes who have disordered and potentially harmful eating patterns, even if they do not meet strict clinical criteria.

More recent research has begun to explore the ways in which new health imperatives associated with claims that there is an 'obesity epidemic' in Western culture impact upon young people's relationships with food and physical activity (**obesity discourse**). These concerns have been a major force driving changes to health education policy and practices, with schools now targeted by governments for the implementation of a range of initiatives to get young people thinner, fit and change their eating habits. Research with young women with eating disorders has highlighted how many of these policies and practices in schools may be creating cultures that may influence disordered relationships with the body, food and physical activity (Rich and Evans, 2005; Rich et al., 2004).

Key Reading

Beals, K.A. (2000) 'Sublinical eating disorders in female athletes', *Journal of Physical Education, Recreation and Dance*, 71: 23–9.

Rich, E. and Evans, J. (2005) 'Making sense of eating disorders in schools', *Discourse: Studies in the Cultural Politics of Education*, 26 (2): 247–62.

Rich, E., Holroyd, R. and Evans, J. (2004) 'Hungry to be noticed: young women, anorexia and schooling', in J. Evans (ed.), *Body Knowledge and Control: Studies in the Sociology of Education and Physical Culture*. London: Routledge. pp. 173–90.

Ryan, J. (1995) *Little Girls in Pretty Boxes: The Making and Breaking of Elite Gymnasts and Figure Skaters*. New York: Doubleday.

Smolak, L., Murnen, S.K. and Ruble, A.E. (2000) 'Female athletes and eating problems: a meta analysis', *International Journal of Eating Disorders*, 27: 371–80.

Emma Rich

ECONOMIC CHARACTERISTICS OF SPORT

For economists, sport should be analysed as a product, a commodity or a good. On this basis it is possible to view sport in three different ways: (1) as a non-durable consumption good; (2) as a durable consumption good; and (3) as a capital good. A non-durable consumption good is one that provides benefits to the consumer at the time of consumption. Examples of this include the excitement of watching a sports event or the enjoyment derived from playing a game of football. A durable good provides the consumer with benefits over time. In the case of sport, this might include **health** or feelings of well-being. A capital good is one that yields a return as part of a production process. Thus sport may improve our health and thus *enable* us to work better, which in turn may *lead* to a higher income. Taking part in sport may also lead us into a career in which we become paid directly for our sporting ability. However, the consequences of taking part in, or watching, sport may be even wider than this for they may lead us to new forms of sociability, wider networks of friends, and this, economists perceive, is a further potential yield from the production process.

Key Reading

Gratton, C. and Taylor, P. (2000) *Economics of Sport and Recreation*. London: Routledge.

ELIAS

(civilizing process; figurational sociology; involvement and detachment)

EMBOURGEOISEMENT

Refers to the process of becoming bourgeois or, more generally, middle class. Embourgeoisement is often used to refer to the way in which the British working classes became increasingly affluent and adopted the lifestyle and political attitudes of the middle classes from the 1950s onwards. The embourgeoisement thesis posited that the increased affluence of the working class and the alleviation of extremes of suffering through the welfare state would cause old class antagonisms to wither away.

However, embourgeoisement is used in a variety of senses in sports studies. Some have argued that embourgeoisement has meant the existence of a classless society, or at least a society in which **class** is not a significant marker or predictor of action. John

Hargreaves (1986), however, argues that the empirical evidence suggests that sports have not contributed to this process, that they do not embourgeoisify the working class, for sports also reproduce divisions between the social classes.

Others have argued that English football crowds have become increasingly middle class in recent years, though this is seen more as the consequence of the displacement and exclusion of traditional working-class supporters rather than the conversion of the working classes themselves. Initially this hypothesis was put forward by Ian Taylor (1971) to explain the rise of **football hooliganism** in England in terms of class conflict. Later, contrary to survey data reviewed by Malcolm et al. (2000), many academics argued that the commercialization of English football in the 1990s led to the increasing exclusion of traditional working-class supporters.

Finally, it is important to recognize the specificity of Dunning and Sheard's use of the term embourgeoisement in *Barbarians, Gentlemen and Players* (2005) to refer to the gradual emergence of the bourgeoisie as a ruling class during the nineteenth century. Based on the accumulation of wealth and on their significance for the running of the state more broadly, the industrial middle classes of this period increasingly came to challenge the aristocracy as the ruling class. The bourgeoisie started to take control of major institutions (e.g. public schools), and bourgeois values (such as **Muscular Christianity**) became increasingly dominant in their running of these institutions, and in society more broadly. This process of embourgeoisement, therefore, led to the equalization of power between the (bourgeois) masters and (often aristocratic) schoolboys in English public schools and the reform of the **prefect-fagging** system. Embourgeoisement also led to the acute levels of **public school status rivalry** between the traditionally aristocratic (e.g. Eton), and the emerging and largely bourgeois schools (e.g. Rugby). This, Dunning and Sheard argue, was central to the development of association and rugby football into their modern forms.

Key Reading

Dunning, E. and Sheard, K. (2005) *Barbarians, Gentlemen and Players: A Sociological Study of the Development of Rugby Football*, 2nd edn. London: Routledge.

Hargreaves, J. (1986) *Sport, Power and Culture: A Social and Historical Analysis of Popular Sports in Britain*. Oxford: Polity Press.

Malcolm, D., Jones, I. and Waddington, I. (2000) 'The people's game? Football spectatorship and demographic change', in J. Garland, D. Malcolm and M. Rowe (eds), *The Future of Football: Challenges for the Twenty-First Century*. London: Frank Cass. pp. 129–43.

Taylor, I. (1971) 'Football mad: a speculative sociology of football hooliganism', in E. Dunning (ed.), *The Sociology of Sport: A Selection of Readings*. London: Frank Cass.

EMOTION (PSYCHOLOGY)

Emotion is both a cornerstone of psychology (in the 'ABC of psychology', emotion is the A or affect component, B is behaviour and C is cognition) but conversely also a very general and poorly understood concept. Consequently a number of competing definitions exist, though emotion is generally thought to encompass physiological and psychological processes of fixed or limited duration. Emotion should be distinguished from mood (which is a more general feeling state, not directed at a particular thing or person), effect (which may have a longer duration and usually does not embrace physiological arousal and bodily expression) and temperament (which is viewed as a more stable attribute, like a trait or disposition).

The key conceptual differences within the psychology of emotion focus on the degrees of influence exerted by physiological and social–cognitive processes in the production of emotion (**psychology, approaches to**). Early psychological theories of emotions attributed their source to physiological disturbance (**arousal**), and suggested that emotions were an evolutionary product which served particular functions (e.g. fear and anger as self-preservation mechanisms). These theories suggested that emotions were universal, but this has not been borne out by empirical research comparing emotions in different cultural settings. Subsequently it was suggested that it was important to recognize the interaction of physiological and cognitive factors and the role of situational cues in the individual process of labelling emotions. Increasingly, emotions have been understood as complex and multidimensional processes, with more recent work placing greater emphasis on the social and cultural dimensions of emotions (see also **emotion (sociology)**).

Pychologists of sport have increasingly been influenced by Richard Lazarus's 'cognitive-motivational-relational theory'. Lazarus (1991) argues that emotions are the product of the interactional relationship between personality and environment (each may affect the other, neither variable is independent). Emotion is therefore a process in which individuals appraise situations (according to their own motives and beliefs), and make decisions about whether encounters will harm, maintain or enhance their well-being. Cognitive assessments may involve the consideration of self or ego-involvement (i.e. the significance of the event for one's identity), the effect on personal goals, appraisal of the causes of the event (e.g. whether one lost because of bad luck or the superiority of the opposition). Individuals may also have 'action tendencies' (i.e. usual responses) and, particularly relevant to sports performance, individuals may then seek to 'cope' (i.e. use deliberate and/or planned strategies) with the stressful demands. Consequently, not all stressful encounters have the same significance for mental and physical health.

In the psychology of sport the majority of emotion-related research has focused on negative emotions such as **anxiety** and its relationship to performance and **burnout**. Increasingly, however, research is investigating the relationship between emotion, physical activity and **health**. While the early indications are that physical activity may relieve **stress** and anxiety, and have a positive effect on feelings of well-being and self-perception, there is little unanimity over the mechanisms of, and the explanations for, these processes.

Key Reading

Hanin, Y.L. (ed.) (2000) *Emotions in Sport*. Champaign, IL: Human Kinetics.

Lavallee, D., Thatcher, J. and Jones, M. (eds) (2004) *Coping and Emotion in Sport*. New York: Nova Science.

Lazarus, R.S. (1991) *Emotion and Adaptation*. Oxford: Oxford University Press.

EMOTION (SOCIOLOGY)

The sociological study of emotion in sport parallels the study of the **body** in that: (1) interest in both these areas has only relatively recently emerged; and (2) both the body and the emotions are omnipresent and therefore influence all forms of human action. These two areas are further interrelated because, while emotion may be thought of as something that exists 'inside' us, it takes on sociological relevance largely due to the way it is shared with others, i.e. when it is displayed via the body.

Work on the emotions, however, is rather more clearly defined for, to date, it has centrally been concerned with the way emotions and their expression influence identity formation. Thus research has shown that, within sports **subcultures** (for instance, Donnelly's study of rock climbing and Gallmeier's study of ice hockey players), displaying the appropriate emotions is a central factor in being accepted within/rejected from those subcultures. Emotion management is also vital for female gymnasts who, while using great speed and power, are required to appear graceful and 'feminine' to the judges and audience. The study of emotion also

features in much of the work on **pain and injury** in sport, where suppression and tolerance of pain, and the display of indifference to injury, are key features of conforming to the **sport ethic**. Others have argued that alternative, extreme, or **lifestyle sports** have developed as a consequence of people's search for emotional experiences different from those that tend to characterize modern sports.

Given the close link between emotion and identity formation, research has looked at the emotional **socialization** into sport and the emotional consequences of retiring from, or leaving, sport (**retirement**). For women, sport may represent either an emotional constraint (e.g. through an obsession with body shape which leads to anxiety, self-loathing and even **eating disorders**) or emotional emancipation through empowerment achieved by bonding with other females and challenging traditional notions of femininity (**gender**). Men's identities are similarly constructed through sport and this may have emotional benefits (belonging, a heightened sense of 'manliness') or emotional costs (having to conform to an aggressive, homophobic and/or misogynist subculture). Gays and **lesbians** in sport may have to hide their sexuality (often at an emotional cost) or may participate 'openly' and enjoy emotional and/or erotic benefits.

While not entirely separate from these areas of emotion and identity formation, other scholars have looked at emotion among sport spectators, describing the motives of sports **fans**, and the emotional pleasures derived from spectating. The emotional highs of spectatorship have been discussed with reference to the release of everyday tensions (**catharsis**), the generation of feelings of community, and parallels have been drawn between the emotional significance of sport and the emotional experience of **religion** (**sport, social significance of**). Nostalgia (that is to say, positive, often romanticized, feelings of past events) and **topophilia** have been identified as key emotions for sports spectators. More critically, analysis of the sports media has been depicted as providing fetishistic, voyeuristic and narcissistic emotional pleasures.

As the above indicates, studies of emotion have the potential to embrace nearly every area of study within the sociology of sport. However, no overview of this research area would be complete without reference to Elias and Dunning who recognized the fundamental role of emotion in sport as early as the 1960s. They were the first sociologists of sport to provide a thorough analysis of emotions, notably in their work on the **quest for excitement**, and sport and leisure in the 'spare-time spectrum'. Indeed, their analysis of the emergence and development of **modern sport** forms is linked to the theory of the **civilizing process**, in which the analysis of emotional control and freedom is an inherent feature.

Key Reading

Donnelly, P. and Young, K. (1988) 'The construction and confirmation of identity in sport subcultures', *Sociology of Sport Journal*, 5 (3): 223–40.

Duquin, M. (2000) 'Sport and emotions', in J. Coakley and E. Dunning (eds), *Handbook of Sports Studies*. London: Sage. pp. 477–89.

Elias, N. and Dunning, E. (1986) *Quest for Excitement: Sport and Leisure in the Civilizing Process*. Oxford: Basil Blackwell.

Gallmeier, C. (1987) 'Putting on the game face: the staging of emotions in professional hockey', *Sociology of Sport Journal*, 4 (4): 347–62.

EMPIRE

(imperialism)

EMPIRICISM

(positivism)

ENVIRONMENTAL DETERMINISM

Dominated geographical thought from the late nineteenth to the mid-twentieth century, and can be understood as the geographical version of social Darwinism (***Darwin's Athletes***). Environmental determinism suggests that certain environmental conditions create certain habits and that these habits are then 'naturally' transmitted to successive generations (**habitus**). The theory, therefore, can be used to explain characteristics considered both 'positive' as well as 'negative'. For instance, it was believed that living in mountainous regions developed strong muscles, while people living in coastal areas became flabby. Temperature was similarly thought to be crucial – heat made people lazy and lethargic, cold climates led to vigour and strength. These environmental factors, therefore, were thought to be able to explain why Finland produced excellent long-distance runners, such as Paavo Nurmi; they were, in essence, natural products of their environment. More contemporaneously we might point to ideas about Kenyan running and altitude. Western explanations commonly attribute Kenyan success in terms of these environmental factors, ignoring counter-evidence, for example, that Kenyan runners are disproportionately drawn from certain provinces (e.g. Nandi) but not others which are geographically similarly, and that countries, like Peru, where the population tends to live at high altitudes have not produced prolific runners (**race science**).

Environmental determinism was initially used to explain the success of European, and in particular British, **imperialism**. The vigour, intelligence, courage and determination of the colonials were seen as products of their upbringing in a particular environment. However, it then became feared that British colonials going out into the hot climes of the Empire were in danger of physical degeneration. In fact, this was a key source of motivation for such colonists to play sports, such as cricket, against teams from the mother country, to demonstrate that they hadn't degenerated. Ironically, because they kept losing, this led to the integration of black players into the West Indian team, and the eventual decline of white West Indian cricketers.

Key Reading

Bale, J. (2002) 'Lassitude and latitude: observations on sport and environmental determinism', *International Review for the Sociology of Sport*, 37 (2): 147–58.

Bale, J. and Sang, J. (1996) *Kenyan Running: Movement Culture, Geography and Global Change*. London: Frank Cass.

Malcolm, D. (2001) '"It's not cricket": colonial legacies and contemporary inequalities', *Journal of Historical Sociology*, 14 (3): 253–75.

EPISTEMOLOGY AND ONTOLOGY

Epistemology is the philosophical study of what constitutes knowledge (and hence how it is acquired through research), seeking to inform us how we can know the world, or most simply asking 'what is knowledge'? Ontology is the philosophy of the nature of existence, the fundamental things that exist in the world, or most simply asking 'what is reality?' To what degree is the social world an objective, fixed reality (e.g. like a football that can be measured and weighed), or is it a social construction which therefore only exists in the perceptions and actions of people (e.g. the notion of **class**)?

On the one hand, knowledge and reality appear to be self-evident concepts but, when probed, epistemological and ontological questions become rather more complex. For instance, three key epistemological questions relate to **positivism** and interpretivism (**idealism**): (1) what is the relationship between the researcher and the subjects? Can the researcher be separated or detached from the research subjects or are the two inherently interconnected? Does each influence the other and if so, how?; (2) what can be said to be the truth/reality? Is there only one reality, or are there many different realities based on human perceptions? If there are multiple realities, are they all equally valid?; and (3) what is the most appropriate way to measure the social world? Should social scientists use the techniques of the natural sciences, or is knowledge only derived through human interpretation of what events *mean*?

The main ontological positions are divided between objectivism and constructionism (**objectivity and subjectivity**). Is it possible for researchers to provide objective representations of the social world that are not coloured by their individual perceptions, prejudices and interpretations, or do we have to accept that all portrayals of the social world are essentially personal, stemming from the *meanings* which individuals place on social phenomena?

A sporting example of these issues might be to ask whether we can understand **race** relations through statistical analysis of black athletes' participation in sport and their occupational positioning (**stacking**), or whether it is more valid to look at the messages and meanings behind the **media** presentation of, for instance, **Michael Jordan (signifier and signified**)? Ontologically, we might ask whether there is an 'objective' social reality to be observed (e.g. through personally witnessing a sports event) or whether it is more accurate to consider that individuals construct their own sets of meanings/reality (e.g. through identification with a particular team and the mediating effect this has on their understanding of that sports event). Thus, taken to its extreme, this latter position suggests that there are as many realities as there are individuals (**modernity; post-modernism; post-structuralism**).

While epistemological and ontological questions may seem unnecessarily complicated to students of sports studies, ultimately they underpin all theoretical positions and thus the validity (**reliability and validity**) of all research (**qualitative and quantitative research**) and writings.

ERYTHROPOIETIN (EPO)

(drugs, classes of)

ESSENTIALISM

The philosophical belief that it is possible to identify in objects or activities, such as sport, 'necessary properties', or an 'eternal essence' that exists separately from people and social contexts. Essentialism is generally used as a pejorative term, as most historians and sociologists argue that the socially constructed character of sports logically denies the existence of an eternal essence.

Essentialism is a widespread 'problem' in sports studies and the works of historian Dennis Brailsford and sociologist John Hargreaves are used here as illustrative examples only. Brailsford (1991) talks of 'sport's simple and eternal essence' based on a 'central psycho-social urge' of the pursuit of achievement. Similarly, Hargreaves (1986) refers to the 'nature of sport' and the existence of a 'ludic element' that cannot be altered by capitalist processes. Dunning (1999) is critical of both these authors, Brailsford for arguing at such a high level of generality that it misleadingly underplays the significant changes which **modern sport** forms represent (in contrast to traditional or **folk games**), and Hargreaves for presenting a reified notion of sport (**reification**), which suggests that sport is autonomous, rather than a social construct shaped by the relative power balances of particular social groups. Students of sports studies should be very wary of statements about the 'nature' or 'essence' of sport, for such phrases tend to ignore/obscure the fact that sports change over time and vary according to social context. Moreover, beliefs about the essence or nature of sport are most commonly ideological or value-laden statements, based on the way the author would like sport to be, rather than from the way that empirical evidence shows

sport to be structured (**involvement and detachment; objectivity and subjectivity**).

Key Reading

Brailsford, D. (1991) *Sport, Time and Society: The British at Play*. London: Routledge.
Dunning, E. (1999) *Sport Matters: Sociological Studies of Sport, Violence and Civilization*. London: Routledge. esp. Ch. 5.
Hargreaves, J. (1986) *Sport, Power and Culture: A Social and Historical Analysis of Popular Sports in Britain*. Cambridge: Polity.

ETHICS, RESEARCH METHODS

Ethics is the branch of philosophy concerned with the attempt to establish principles and codes of moral behaviour. For social scientists conducting research, ethical questions are vitally important because the knowledge that may be uncovered in the research process has the potential to alter people's lives significantly.

Many occupational umbrella groups (such as the British Sociological Association) have ethics committees and/or publish their own ethical codes which can be accessed via websites. The challenge is to draw up codes which ensure ethical behaviour, but which are not so prescriptive as to unreasonably limit the scope of social research. Though differences may exist in the specific wording that various codes use, a number of key areas are consistently discussed. First is the notion that, where possible, research subjects should give *informed consent*, i.e. that they should understand the nature and purpose of the research, and agree to be part of it. However, there are clearly cases when this is impractical, e.g. when the subjects of the research act in illegal or illegitimate ways such that they would be suspicious of being observed (users of performance-enhancing **drugs**), or where informing all subjects that they are being observed (e.g. a sports crowd) would be impractical. Researchers must also take all reasonable steps to ensure that the research data are only used for the purposes they were originally collected (albeit that no researcher is fully in control of his/her research data).

These 'exceptions' can be justified via a second ethical issue, *confidentiality and anonymity*. If it can be guaranteed that subjects will remain anonymous, and that personal information remains confidential (i.e. opinions and actions cannot be attributed to an individual and their privacy is maintained), then it is unlikely that the research subjects will come to any personal harm or experience offence as a consequence of the publication of research data (much of the research on **pain and injury** in sport has been conducted on this basis). The overriding ethical consideration here is that researchers have a duty towards respecting the interests of their research respondents. However, some would argue that it is also the duty of social researchers to subject those in positions of considerable power to relatively high levels of scrutiny (e.g. the presidents of **FIFA** and the **IOC**). Thus it might be argued that different ethical considerations should apply to research involving different subjects.

Finally, researchers should ensure that their work does not simply become a legitimating tool for powerful vested interests such as corporations and governments. Researchers should be aware of, and resist, the attempts of others to manipulate results and conclusions even if they personally stand to gain a great deal, e.g. in terms of research grants, publications, career progression, etc.

In sum, researchers should consider the effects that their research will have on others and attempt to minimize negative impacts, particularly on the less powerful/already disadvantaged social groups. Under these broad ethical considerations, it should be noted, research focusing on particular social groups, such as children, evokes different duties of care and considerations of potential harm.

Key Reading

Brackenridge, C. (1999) 'Managing myself: investigator survival in sensitive research', *International Review for the Sociology of Sport*, 34 (4): 399–410.

Sugden, J. and Tomlinson, A. (1999) 'Digging the dirt and staying clean: retrieving the investigative tradition for a critical sociology of sport', *International Review for the Sociology of Sport*, 34 (4): 385–98.

The British Sociological Association's guide to ethical research is published on their website. See www.britsoc.co.uk/equality/

ETHNOCENTRISM

(cultural relativism)

ETHNOGRAPHY

In recent years ethnography has become a popular approach to the social investigation of sporting cultures (**subcultures**). There is, however, some confusion as to what constitutes the use of ethnographic methods within the multidisciplinary field of sports studies.

The term ethnography is used within social research in two distinct ways: (1) as a verb to describe the process of doing ethnographic research; and (2) as a noun to describe an ethnographic monograph. Ethnography should not be taken to simply mean qualitative research (**qualitative and quantitative research**). As a noun, it means either a description or an aspect of a culture. As a verb (doing ethnography), it means the collection of data that may later be used to describe a culture. In this respect ethnography is simply a method of social scientific research.

Ethnography is characterized by the first-hand study of a small community or ethnic group. This form of study combines varying degrees of descriptive and analytical elements. Of key importance is that conventional ethnographies focus on one specific culture or society and consider theoretical or comparative generalizations from the standpoint of the ethnographic case study.

The origin of the modern ethnographic research tradition is generally traced to Bronislaw Malinowski (1884–1942) in the field of anthropology or the rise of the Chicago School of Sociology, where the primacy of field research and participant observation was stressed. Participant **observation** – the act of living within and being involved with a community – is at the heart of traditional ethnographic practice, but it is only one of a number of tools employed by the ethnographer. A researcher using the ethnographic 'tool kit' will, in addition to participating in and observing the community in question, conduct library-based research, and develop and employ survey techniques (**questionnaires**) and (structured and semi-structured) **interviews**. The broader aim of ethnography is the illumination of a cultural environment.

Ethnography, from the post-war period until recently, acquired a generally ahistorical perspective, concentrating on the reconstruction of a specific cultural or social system without regard to its historical development. Historical considerations were often relegated to a separate area labelled the study of social cultural change, as if this were at odds with the normal features of a cultural system. A related feature of this type of ethnography was the tendency to isolate artificially the unit of study (the tribe, the peasant community, etc.), considering it as a self-contained culture or society and failing to consider regional, national and international politico-economic and social structures with which the local community interacts. These tendencies in conventional ethnography have been criticized from many quarters. Consequently, a new type of ethnography has emerged that is conscious of both historical processes and the multilayered power structures that impinge upon the community under investigation. In sports studies, Armstrong (1998) and Klein (1993) have used this type of ethnographic tool kit to great effect in their research.

Ethnographers often refer to participant observation as fieldwork and this can lead to confusion. Fieldwork, in this sense, is synonymous with the collection of data using observational methods. However, it is the making, reporting and evaluation of observations that is the key role of the ethnographer. In order to be successful, the ethnographer must relate observations through an interpretative framework from a **sociocultural imagination**. Good ethnography attempts to avoid overt ethnocentrism (**cultural relativism**), that is the habit or tendency to judge other cultures (or communities under investigation) according to the criteria of the ethnographers' own culture.

As 'participant observation', fieldwork is an *experience* as well as a method. However, such fieldwork should never be conceived of as just an experience. The main instrument of this method is the fieldworker. The researcher must struggle to harness his/her subjectivity towards the purpose of the research; that purpose being an understanding of human experience that is somewhat systematic and objective, or more so at least than a casual impression or common sense. Nothing is less useful than an incident without meaning, an encounter without notes, and much of the data of fieldwork come through rather tedious observations and recording. The deepest insights, however, may derive from a flash of understanding that comes from engagement and encounter. As the term 'participant observation' suggests, fieldwork combines **objectivity and subjectivity**, routine and adventure, system and openness.

Though based on fieldwork, ethnography is also a way of generalizing about humanity. Like the novel, poem and parable, but also like the scientific experiment, ethnography must say more than it tells; it must imply and teach general significances through presentation of particular experiences and patterns. Among the 'truths' communicated are the ethnographer's as well as the 'native's', yet few care to read the confessional memoirs of an ethnographer (**epistemology and ontology**). A great ethnographic work is both scientific and literary, attaining a marked degree of objective precision, yet translating patterns discerned in the alien group into a form comprehensible to the reader at home (Armstrong, 1998; Klein, 1993).

In recent years there has been a trend toward what has been called auto-ethnography (Sparkes, 2002). Auto-ethnography is distinct because the self is the central vehicle for understanding the social world; the world of the ethnographer is what is being explored. Where traditionally the 'truths' of the interpretation, filtered through the experience and world view of the interpreter, but focused sharply and precisely on the world of the 'other', are the focus of ethnography, auto-ethnography is concerned largely with the position of the researcher in the world. The danger of this phenomenological position is that the truths discerned by self-examination may be too closely bound to the experience of the individual researcher and the categories of their culture, and therefore lack broader reliability (**reliability and validity**).

Obviously, it is difficult to make global generalizations based on ethnographies. It is wrong to synthesize merely substantive or 'factual' findings of ethnographic investigations, for each ethnography is more than a report, or a mere shortcut for being there. Each is an interpretation, a synthesis of questions, theories and attitudes that guide the interpreter as well as the facts reported. At the same time, the empirical or inductive approach characteristic of social scientific generalization is a necessary antidote to purely deductive or introspective efforts at reflecting on human nature (**positivism**)

Key Reading

Amit, V. (2000) *Constructing the Field: Ethnographic Fieldwork in the Contemporary World*. London: Routledge.
Armstrong, G. (1998) *Football Hooligans: Knowing the Score*. Oxford: Berg.

Hammersley, M. and Atkinson, P. (1995) *Ethnography: Principles and Practice*, 2nd edn. London: Routledge.
Klein, A. (1993) *Little Big Men: Bodybuilding Subculture and Gender Construction*. Albany, NY: State University of New York Press.
Sparkes, A.C. (2002) *Telling Tales in Sport and Physical Activity: A Qualitative Journey*. Leeds: Human Kinetics.

P. David Howe

EXAMINATIONS IN PHYSICAL EDUCATION

Arguably the most dramatic development in secondary school physical education (PE) in the UK since the mid-1970s has been the growth of General Certificate of Secondary Education (GCSE) and Advanced (A) level examinations. Unsurprisingly, given its long-standing associations with games 'playing' and physical exercise, PE has been a relatively late arrival on the examination scene. Examinations in PE have developed from a period of innovation in the early 1970s, via successive phases of consolidation in the mid- to late 1970s and rapid and sustained growth in the 1980s, to a widespread expansion and acceptance of GCSE PE and A level PE and sports studies during the 1990s. More latterly, since 2000, GCSE and A level courses have been broken down into two parts: short (Advanced Subsidiary or AS) and full (AS + A2) courses. A more recent development has been the introduction to GCSE PE of a syllabus made up of over 80 per cent 'practical'.

Since the early 1990s there has been substantial growth in examinable PE in terms of both pupil examinees and exam centres. GCSE PE more than doubled in the five-year period up to 1997. By 2005, the total number of entries for GCSE PE stood at approximately 145,000, up by over a third from two years previously. A level PE experienced equally swift expansion: from 35 candidates at its inception in 1985 to over 11,000 by 1998, and then virtually doubling to over 20,000 in the seven years to 2005.

Some issues related to examinable PE – such as a lack of appropriate resources for theory work (for example, in the form of suitable textbooks) – appear to have dissipated if not quite disappeared. Others persist, and this is particularly true for issues to do with: (1) the heavily male-dominated nature of examinable PE (at a ratio approaching 2:1); (2) the relatively low standards of attainment; (3) the tendency for GCSE PE to become separated from, rather than integral to, curricular PE; and (4) the implications for conventional PE of the ostensible academicization of the subject. Indeed, some would argue that the academicization of PE (an increasing emphasis upon the theoretical study of physical activity and sport at the expense of practical activities) reflects a 'new orthodoxy' regarding the nature, purposes and future direction of the subject. PE is said to have joined other school subjects on the academic 'treadmill'.

The case for examinable PE is typically presented as: (1) an academic opportunity for 'practically minded' pupils; (2) a motivational tool for PE teachers; (3) a marketing vehicle for schools to attract students; and (4) an opportunity for physical educationalists to improve the academic and professional status of PE. In sociological terms, the growth of examinations in PE is probably best explained as resulting from a configuration of circumstances, prominent among them being PE teachers' desires for increased professional status, the marketization of education generally, and the practical day-to-day benefits that examinable PE is perceived to have for PE teachers themselves.

Key Reading

Carroll, B. (1998) 'The emergence and growth of examinations in physical education', in K. Green and K. Hardman (eds), *Physical Education: A Reader*. Aachen: Meyer & Meyer Verlag. pp. 314–32.

Dore, R.P. (1997) *The Diploma Disease. Education, Qualification and Development*, 2nd edn. London: Allen & Unwin.

Eggleston, J. (1990) 'School examinations – some sociological issues', in T. Horton (ed.), *Assessment Debates*. Buckingham: Open University Press. pp. 57–67.

Green, K. (2001) 'Examinations in physical education: a sociological perspective on a "new orthodoxy"', *British Journal of Sociology of Education*, 22 (1): 51–73.

Ken Green

EXERCISE BEHAVIOUR

While there is considerable empirical data on the positive effects of exercising, relatively few people regularly do sufficient quantities or intensities of exercise for it to be beneficial for their **health** (see also **obesity discourse**). The main reasons why people start to exercise include the following: to control their weight (**eating disorders**); to reduce the risk of cardiovascular disease; to reduce stress and alleviate depression; for fun and sociability; and to build self-esteem. Common reasons given for not exercising include a perceived lack of time, a lack of energy, and lack of **motivation**. One of the key issues for those sport and exercise professionals concerned to increase participation rates is the problem of exercise adherence; quite simply many start to exercise but quickly (within six months) drop out.

A number of psychological models/theories of exercise behaviour have been proposed. The *Health Belief Model* suggests that a person's likelihood of exercising depends upon their evaluation of the health costs and benefits of participation/non-participation. The *Theory of Planned Behaviour* states that actual behaviour can be predicted by assessing subjective norms (beliefs about others' opinions and individual motivations), people's subsequent intentions, and also people's perceptions of behavioural control (i.e. the belief that one won't be able to devote sufficient time to exercise is likely to have a negative effect on intention). *Social Cognitive*

Theory is based on the belief that personal, behavioural and environmental factors are interacting determinants of behaviour, but that most crucially self-efficacy (that is to say, an individual's belief in their likelihood of success, in terms, for example, of exercise adherence, weight loss, etc.) is crucial to predicting behaviour.

Perhaps most influential has been the *Transtheoretical Model.* This model proposes that, in contrast to the above linear approaches, a five-stage cycle more accurately depicts the process of intention, establishment and maintenance of lifestyle changes (and thus that different interventions are appropriate at different stages). These stages are: (1) the precontemplation stage, where the person is not active and has no intention of starting to exercise; (2) the contemplation stage, where serious intention begins; (3) the preparation stage, where people begin to exercise but not regularly (defined as less than three times a week); (4) the action stage, where people exercise at least three times a week, but have done so for less than six months; and (5) where individuals exercise regularly for over six months.

The processes of change that may lead people to move from the different stages of the transtheoretical model can be divided into cognitive and behavioural processes. Cognitive processes include consciousness raising, dramatic relief (e.g. concern over health warnings), environmental and self re-evaluation (wanting to be healthier or to set an example to others), and social liberation (barriers to exercise are perceived to diminish). Behavioural processes include counter conditioning (start to exercise), helping relationships (the encouragement and enabling behaviour of others), reinforcement management (rewards for exercising), self-liberation (enabling oneself to exercise) and stimulus control (greater number of reminders to exercise).

Finally, a great deal of research has examined the specific determinants of exercising. These have been categorized as: demographic determinants (well-educated, affluent males being the most likely group to exercise); **personality** variables (self-efficacy and self-motivation, through goal-setting and monitoring of progress, being thought the most significant); behavioural variables (specifically previous exercise participation); and environmental factors such as social support, convenience of location of exercise facilities, and characteristics of the specific activity (i.e. duration, intensity, group or individual).

Key Reading

Weinberg, R. and Gould, D. (2003) *Foundations of Sport and Exercise Psychology.* Champaign, IL: Human Kinetics. esp. Ch. 18.

EXPLANATORY STYLE

Can be defined as the tendency and propensity of a person to explain and make sense of good and bad events in particular ways. Explanatory style grew out of learned helplessness research. Learned helplessness occurs when an individual comes to perceive that there is little relationship between his/her actions and subsequent outcomes. Typically, an athlete with learned helplessness will suggest that regardless of the performance they produce, they are unlikely to win (due to bad luck, fate, the actions of referees and umpires, etc.). The perception of outcome as out of one's control is a form of decreased **self-confidence.**

The theory of learned helplessness became problematic when research found that, when confronted with uncontrollable events, people behaved in a variety of ways (i.e. some did not come to perceive themselves as helpless, some did so for just a short time, some perceived helplessness only in relation to specific contexts, and others generalized helplessness from a single to a number of contexts). Explanatory style suggests that people attribute causes to uncontrollable events and that these are central to the impact such events have on **motivation** and behaviour. Specifically three dimensions of explanatory style have been suggested: internal vs. external (is the uncontrollability due to oneself or other factors?); stable vs. unstable (how long uncontrollability will last?); and global vs. specific (does the uncontrollability apply to a single event or to all phenomena?). A person with an optimistic explanatory style is likely to view events as external, unstable and specific (i.e. the opposition played well, it was a difficult shot to execute), thus leading to the view that future performances are unlikely to be influenced by these particular events.

Key Reading

Buchanan, R.M. and Seligman, M.E.P. (eds) (1995) *Explanatory Style*. Hillside, NJ: Erlbaum.

F

FAIR PLAY

The notion of fair play is one of the philosophical ideas underpinning **modern sport**. Fair play, according to Simon (1991), entails 'adherence to the letter and spirit of equality before the rules'. Since an athletic contest is designed to determine which competitor or team is best able to meet the challenge set by the sport, fair play requires that competitors do not 'intentionally disregard or circumvent the rules'. For Simon, fair play can be distinguished from 'sportsmanship' in that the latter can only be expected in pleasurable, non-serious or less competitive activities. Sportsmanship, in contrast to fair play, requires participants to conduct themselves such that the pleasure of one's opponent, and oneself, is enhanced. Thus the practice of returning a football to the opposition after a break for an injured player to receive treatment is sportsmanship rather than fair play, while the actions of a cricketer who 'walks' before being given caught out by an umpire, might more properly be defined as fair play (though this too is a 'sporting' act). For philosophers fair play (though not necessarily sportsmanship) is vital because it forms part of the implicit 'contract' entered into by all sports participants. If participants come to regard adherence to this contract as voluntary, e.g. by taking drugs (**drugs, prohibition of**), then the activity could not continue in the longer term.

Historians and sociologists take a rather different approach to fair play. Cross-cultural analyses indicate that the notion of fair play within sport is highly specific to time and place; that is to say, it seems to have developed in eighteenth- and nineteenth-century Britain. Elias, for example, notes that the sports-like activities of the **ancient Olympic Games** were governed by a warrior ethos that stressed honour and glory. Fair play, rather, is a specifically modern concept, linked to notions of democracy. This point further supports Elias's contention that **parliamentarization and sportization** should be seen as concomitant social processes. The notion of fair play was introduced as much with regard to participants, as it was to spectators and those with **gambling** interests.

For Holt (1989) the emphasis on fair play in modern sport enabled defeat to be 'useful'. If boys could be taught how to lose with dignity, the more general principle of competition – both in sport and in society more generally – was strengthened. The principle of character building through competition was fundamental to both the development of capitalism and British expansion into the Empire (**imperialism**). It is telling that CLR James in *Beyond a Boundary* rejected the political domination of Caribbean islands by the colonial power, but generally accepted the British ethos of fair play. Fair play, therefore, can be seen as a key tool in generating consent through the use of ideas, a process which enables the continued domination of subordinate groups (**hegemony theory**).

Fair play should not be seen as some kind of essential aspect of sport (**essentialism**), but as a social construct that has been formed as a consequence of broader power struggles between different people and groups. The notion of fair play often provides a legitimating ideology for the powerful. Tellingly, the use of drugs in sport is argued to be unfair, while the huge financial inequalities between Western and emerging nations are seen as an unavoidable fact of life.

Key Reading

Holt, R. (1989) *Sport and the British: A Modern History*. Oxford: Oxford University Press.

Simon, R.L. (1991) *Fair Play: Sports, Values and Society*. Boulder, CO: Westview Press.

Waddington, I. (2000) *Sport, Health and Drugs: A Critical Sociological Perspective*. London: E. & F.N. Spon. esp. Ch. 6.

FANS

According to the *Oxford English Dictionary* the word 'fan' was first used to refer to sport fans and, more specifically, to denote a follower of baseball in the US (Sandvoss, 2003). However, followers of sport have frequently been overlooked or ignored in studies of fan cultures; for instance Hills's book *Fan Cultures* (2002), though claiming to offer 'the first comprehensive overview of fans and fan theory', does not consider sports fans at all. Furthermore, the majority of academic studies and considerations of sports fans have focused largely upon supporter **violence**, or more specifically, **football hooliganism**. For instance, though Wann et al. (2001) suggest that 'fan violence' is 'relatively infrequent', and that numerous studies have shown that spectator **aggression** is actually quite unusual, they dedicate around a third of their book *Sport Fans* to this issue. Though some considerations of supporter violence have significantly contributed to our understanding of fan culture (or 'fandom' as it is sometimes known) and advanced the study of sports fans, this focus on more 'exceptional' forms of sport support has left more common and everyday forms of sport support greatly under-researched.

Beyond simplistic dictionary definitions, defining more precisely what is meant by the term 'fan' in a way that clearly establishes the subject area for study has proven to be problematic. As Hills (2002) suggests, 'fandom is not simply a "thing" that can be picked over analytically'. Being a fan is not just a label or category, it is also tied into individual and group identities and social performances, which are rarely fixed or coherent. As Crawford (2004) writes, 'much of what makes someone a *fan* is what is located within her or his personal identity, memories, thoughts and social interactions'. Hence, authors often avoid providing clear or prescriptive definitions of what or who constitutes a fan (e.g. Crawford, 2004; Hills, 2002). Instead, one way in which fans are often defined is in terms of their relationship as consumers and/or audiences.

There has been a tendency in much of the wider literature on fans to identify these individuals and groups as distinct and different from wider audiences and consumers, and to suggest that fans are different to 'ordinary' 'readers' in that fans 'actively' engage with the 'texts' they consume. A similar attitude is evident in many studies of sports fan culture, and in particular in considerations of football (soccer) fans in the UK. Numerous authors (e.g. Crawford, 2004) draw clear distinctions or dichotomies between what they define as 'traditional' fans (often white male working class) and 'new' (middle-class, often 'family'-based) consumers. However, these categories are often based upon subjective and romanticized ideas of 'authenticity', which see the celebration of one form of sport support and the rejection of all that is seen as 'new'. They are therefore problematic.

Sandvoss (2003) suggests that what identifies (though crucially does not separate out) a fan from other readers of a text is their regularity of reading. Though numerous others use levels of 'activity' as the mark of distinction between fans and non-fans (such as those who attend live sports events as opposed to so-called passive 'armchair' supporters), Sandvoss suggests that even the most active of fans will spend a great deal of time not actively engaging with the object of their fan interest. What defines a fan, for Sandvoss, is the *regularity* of engagement; that is to say, how regularly one attends games, or watches the sport/team on television.

Consequently, authors such as Crawford and Sandvoss suggest that a more profitable way forward is to locate discussions of sports fan culture within a wider consideration of contemporary patterns of consumption; recognizing that sports fans are (and always have been) primarily consumers (**consumer culture**). This approach allows links, both theoretical and empirical, to be formed with wider debates on audiences and consumption, which can inform our understanding and theorization of sports fan culture. For instance, Crawford (2003) makes no clear distinction between fans and consumers, but rather seeks to locate sports 'supporters' (a term he adopts in preference to that of 'fan') along a career path, on the basis of their degree of interest in, and involvement with, a supporter community. This approach offers a much more fluid understanding of sports fan/supporter cultures and allows consideration of how an individual's position within a particular community can change over time, along with the nature and dynamics of that community. As Crawford (2003) writes, 'as with studies of ecology, as an individual develops over time (an ontogenetical development) there will also be in process a general development of the species to which that individual belongs (a phylogenetical development)'.

An interesting and particularly useful theorization of sports fan cultures is offered by Sandvoss (2003). Sandvoss suggests that what constitutes the idea and image of a sports club is made up of numerous (often diverse) 'texts' (such as the **stadium**, its various players and staff, and its history, as well as various media texts and reading of these), making the club (to a degree) polysemic (that is to say, having several meanings). Within certain boundaries, fans can read into the object of their support (the club) a wide variety of different meanings and interpretations. This (largely) blank canvas, Sandvoss suggests, allows fans to see in the club what they value

in themselves. The club therefore becomes, like Narcissus' pool, both a self-reflection and the object of their affection. However, Sandvoss suggests that the polysemic qualities of the sports club reduce the closer the individual gets to the club, in that the more knowledge of the club a fan amasses, the more rigid the image and idea of the club becomes.

This theorization provides a useful understanding of the nature of fan affiliations and also the diversity of meanings attached to popular cultural texts (such as sports clubs) by individuals. Sandvoss (2003) also provides what numerous other authors have avoided, a definition of 'fandom': 'the regular, emotionally involved consumption of a given popular narrative or text'.

Key Reading

Crawford, G. (2003) 'The career of the sport supporter: the case of the Manchester Storm', *Sociology*, 37 (2): 219–37.

Crawford, G. (2004) *Consuming Sport: Sport, Fans and Culture*. London: Routledge.

Hills, M. (2002) *Fan Cultures*. London: Routledge.

Sandvoss, C. (2003) *A Game of Two Halves: Football, Television and Globalization*. London: Routledge.

Wann, D.L., Melnick, M.J., Russell, G.W. and Pease, D.G. (2001) *Sport Fans: The Psychology and Social Impact of Spectators*. New York: Routledge.

Garry Crawford

FEMINISM

Refers to a collection of social theories which developed in the 1960s out of concerns that 'malestream' sociology failed to seriously embrace the experiences of, and sufficiently address the issues affecting, women. Feminist ideas had a slightly later impact on sports studies, with Ann Hall (1978), Nancy

Theberge and Jennifer Hargreaves (1994) early pioneers.

The fractured character of feminism means that it is more accurate to speak of *feminisms*. Feminist theories are, however, united by three core beliefs. First, all feminists share the assumption that **gender** is one of the key determinants of life experience. Though most early feminists were women who examined women's experiences and issues, an increasing number of male sociologists of sport have adopted a feminist (sometimes called a pro-feminist) perspective to research issues related to men and masculinity. Second, though feminists disagree over the causes, methods and extent of women's oppression, all believe that women are fundamentally disadvantaged and that society is structured in such ways as to give men greater power and privilege. Third, all feminists share a political commitment to change the social condition of females (**critical theory**).

Within this consensus, there are five main schools of feminist thought relevant to sports studies: liberal feminism; radical feminism; Marxist feminism; socialist feminism/feminist **cultural studies**; and postmodern feminism.

Liberal feminism is premised on the assumption that men and women are more alike than they are different and thus both should benefit from the inalienable human rights of equality, fairness, etc. that underpin Western democracies. Liberal feminists seek to publicize inequalities and campaign for their correction but do not challenge the broader social structures (e.g. the current organization of sport) within which the sexes operate. Critics of liberal feminism argue that the concept of equality is too vague. (Equality according to what criteria: opportunity or outcome; quantitative or qualitative? Equality between whom? Which particular females should be equal with which particular males?) The reluctance to pose a more fundamental challenge to gender relations, critics argue, will result in superficial changes only.

Radical feminism is based on the premise that men and women are essentially (and markedly) different from each other and that from these inherent physical and psychological differences a system of relations – patriarchy – has developed by which men dominate women. Existing social structures, therefore, need to be replaced or overhauled from the viewpoint of women. Radical feminists thus seek the creation of distinct and separate female cultures (e.g. sports based on sharing and cooperation, rather than patriarchal characteristics such as competition and **aggression**) that have the potential to provide more liberating and humane sporting experiences. Radical feminism is not just a pro-woman stance, but asserts that women and feminine qualities are inherently superior to men and masculinity. Critics of radical feminism: (1) dispute the importance of biological relative to socially constructed differences between the sexes; (2) question whether *all* men are equally resistant to *all* women (as the notion of patriarchy implies is the case); and (3) note that the policy successes of radical feminism have been limited (where moves towards equality have been gained, they have often relied upon cooperation, rather than conflict, with men). Despites such weaknesses, a central contribution of radical feminism has been to highlight how the social world, including sport, is designed by men, for men, and celebrates and rewards typically masculine characteristics.

Subsequent schools of feminist thought moved away from the focus on gender as the *sole* category of inequality, seeking to produce a synthesis that embraces other factors – e.g. **class**, **race**, sexuality, etc. – as part of a 'matrix of relations of power'. Marxist feminism, for instance, views gender inequality as the product of economic forces of production (**Marxism**). Women are primarily oppressed through their relationship to economic production. Kept outside the labour system, women perform unpaid reproductive labour (i.e. producing the next generation of workers) and domestic labour (the function of which is to prepare male workers for more work). Women's sport and leisure opportunities are relatively limited because capitalism has no 'need' to refresh women for more work. Moreover, female sporting experiences are characterized by class oppression, i.e.

middle-class women effectively exclude their working-class counterparts in sports contexts. Gender inequality exists because of the stabilizing function it performs for capitalism and only the overthrow of capitalism can liberate women from both their class-based and gendered oppression. Critics of Marxist feminism argue that it privileges class over gender (i.e. it retains the economic determinism of Marxism), that it contains elements of biological reductionism (are males the primary workers under capitalism due to biological factors?), that it provides a static model of gender relations (how can we account for changes in gender relations during the past 200 years of capitalism?), and portrays men and women as passive recipients of sexist ideologies (**agency and structure**).

Socialist feminism (similar to feminist cultural studies) does not assume the primacy of capitalist relations over gender relations, but in relying rather more on Gramsci's **hegemony theory**, seeks to understand gender and class as mutually supporting systems (and thus refers to capitalist patriarchy). For socialist feminists, gender inequality is not caused solely by economic factors, but also by patriarchal ideologies which suggest that it is inappropriate for women to take part in certain activities (e.g. sport). By invoking hegemony, socialist feminists identify the continual negotiation and accommodation of ideas as a key social process. Critics of socialist feminism suggest that while this perspective may avoid the accusation of economic reductionism, the relationship between capitalism and patriarchy remains unclear. (Has one caused the other? Could they exist independently of each other?) Other critics, such as black feminists, suggest that the focus on class and gender is still too limited. Should, for instance, race and ethnicity be embraced as additional factors in the matrix of power relations?

Finally, the synthesis of **postmodernism** and feminism has led to the questioning of the relevance of traditional conceptions of gender and sex as categories of analysis, suggesting that the male–female, feminine– masculine, heterosexual–homosexual binaries which pervade Western thought are problematic (**post-structuralism; queer theory**). These binaries, postmodern feminists argue, are not mutually exclusive (as seen by the existence of transsexuals in sport such as Renee Richards and **David Beckham's** complex embrace of different masculine and feminine styles), and are neither causally related, nor fixed (as seen, for instance, by female adoption of masculine styles and people's changing sexual orientation over time).

Thus, while the concern with gender is a defining principle of feminism, a key tension between schools of feminist thought is the centrality of gender as a unit of analysis (the *sole*, *main*, or simply the most important factor 'in the last instance'). A critique of postmodernist feminism is that by deconstructing the categories of analysis upon which feminism is based, we may lose the *raison d'être* of feminism and thus feminism ceases to exist. How far can one move away from a focus on gender and remain a feminist?

Others have criticized the inherently subjective and value-laden basis of feminisms (**objectivity and subjectivity**). Feminism blurs conventional distinctions between politics and sociology, but the feminist retort to such accusations is that their analysis is no more or less biased or inaccurate than those of 'malestream' sociologists in opposition to whom the theoretical approach initially developed, simply that their value position is more explicit.

Key Reading

Birrell, S. (2000) 'Feminist theories for sport', in J. Coakley and E. Dunning (eds), *Handbook of Sport Studies*. London: Sage. pp. 61–76.

Cole, C. (1993) 'Resisting the feminist canon: feminist cultural studies, sport, and technologies of the body', *Journal of Sport and Social Issues*, 17 (2): 77–97.

Hall, M.A. (1978) *Sport and Gender: A Feminist Perspective on the Sociology of Sport*, CAPHER Sociology of Sport Monograph Series. Ottawa: Canadian Association for Health, Physical Education, and Recreation.

Hargreaves, J.A. (1994) *Sporting Females: Critical Issues in the History and Sociology of Women's Sports*. London: Routledge.

FIELD

The field constitutes one of three central concepts in the sociology of Pierre Bourdieu (see also **capital and habitus**), and can most simply be defined as the particular set of relations between agents operating in the same activity. The field refers to the production, distribution and consumption of goods, services and knowledge, the socially prescribed status of that activity, and the network of historical relations of power held by individuals, groups or institutions. Bourdieu points us towards three main properties of any particular field: (1) its structure; (2) its internal dynamic, characterized by competition between interested parties; and (3) its relative autonomy (its own history and specific culture).

One field identified by Bourdieu is the 'sport field' (1978). His analysis focuses on the incorporation of traditional pastimes into the English public school system by the aristocracy and bourgeoisie, which led to a more automized and rationalized set of activities, the underlying philosophies of which were masculine virtues (**masculinity**) and **fair play**. However, the entry of new agents into the field (e.g. entrepreneurs, manufacturers of sports-related products, a wider range of social classes, the sports **media**, etc.) alters the balance of power within the field. Through the concept of the field, Bourdieu encourages us to examine the sites of conflict and struggle in any given activity (e.g. **amateurism** and professionalism in sport), to locate the aspects of conflict and cooperation between respective parties, and thus to gain a clearer understanding of change within the field.

More recent applications of Bourdieu's concept of the field to sport include Defrance and Pociello's analysis of sport in France (1993), and Jennifer Smith Maguire's work on the American fitness field (2002). While in part the concept of the field is an attempt to address the traditional sociological dilemma of **agency and structure** (see also **figurational sociology**), it is not clear that the terminology which Bourdieu uses enables him to do this successfully.

Key Reading

Bourdieu, P. (1978) 'Sport and social class', *Social Science Information*, 17 (6): 819–40.

Defrance, J. and Pociello, C. (1993) 'Structure and evolution of the field of sports in France (1960–1990)', *International Review for the Sociology of Sport*, 28 (1): 1–23.

Laberge, S. and Kay, J. (2002) 'Pierre Bourdieu's sociocultural theory and sport practice', in J. Maguire and K. Young (eds), *Theory, Sport & Society*. Oxford: Jai. pp. 239–66.

Smith Maguire, J. (2002) 'Body lessons: fitness publishing and the cultural production of the fitness consumer', *International Review for the Sociology of Sport*, 37 (3–4): 449–64.

FIFA (FÉDÉRATION INTERNATIONALE DE FOOTBALL ASSOCIATION)

The governing body of world football, FIFA was founded in Paris on 21 May 1904 by seven European football associations (France, Belgium, Denmark, Netherlands, Spain, Sweden and Switzerland). Two individuals were central to the inception of FIFA, the Dutch banker Carl Hirschman and the Frenchman Robert Guérin who became the organization's first president (1904–6). In FIFA's early years both men viewed England as the *natural* leader of the fledgling federation given England's status as the 'birthplace' (or cradle) of the modern game. Thus, the English Football Association (FA) was approached on a number of occasions during the 1890s and the early years of the twentieth century with a view to taking up a leadership role in the international governance of the game. However, the FA believed that while *it* existed there was no need for another governing body. Consequently, the FA adopted an insular and somewhat arrogant attitude towards FIFA and opted to remain outside the world body.

Although the FA eventually joined FIFA in 1905, assuming a leadership role with the Englishman Daniel Woolfall holding the presidency between 1906 and 1918, Britain's early relationship with FIFA continued to be acrimonious. In the wake of the First World War, the British associations (Scotland and Wales joined FIFA as separate entities in 1910), supported by Belgium, Luxembourg and France, called for the exclusion of the former 'enemy' nations of Germany, Austria and Hungary from the FIFA fold. When FIFA's neutral associations refused to countenance these demands, the British federations withdrew. Despite being persuaded to rejoin in 1924, the British associations remained at odds with FIFA, particularly over the issue of **amateurism**. In a dispute over the IOC's decision to formally ratify **broken-time payments** for participants in the Olympic football tournament, the FA decided in 1928 to resign from the world body and, although the British still participated in international competition, it was not until 1946 that its football associations rejoined FIFA.

Despite Britain's abstentionism, FIFA's list of constituents took on an increasingly diverse character as the twentieth century progressed. During the presidency of the Frenchman Jules Rimet, the development of world soccer was particularly pronounced, with FIFA membership increasing from 20 countries in 1921 to 85 by 1954. As a consequence of this expansion, key figures in FIFA decided that it was necessary to decentralize its administrative functions and responsibilities and this led to the eventual formation of six continental confederations which took over the governance of football in their regions. Jules Rimet's other significant achievement was the creation of the World Cup, first played for in Uruguay in 1930. Since then the competition has developed into a multi-million dollar global media and marketing spectacle involving 32 teams.

The driving force behind the dramatically expanded and commercialized World Cup (**commercialization**) was the Brazilian businessman João Havelange, who in 1974 ousted the conservative Englishman Sir Stanley Rous to become the first non-European FIFA president. Until the emergence of Havelange, FIFA's leading administrative figures were all northern European (FIFA's list of presidents reads as follows: Robert Guérin, France, 1904–6; Daniel Woolfall, England, 1906–18; Jules Rimet, France, 1921–54; Rudolfe Seeldrayers, Belgium, 1954–5; Arthur Drewry, England, 1956–61; Stanley Rous, England, 1961–74). Although the numbers of affiliated members hailing from the developing world had expanded dramatically during the 1950s and 1960s following the collapse of colonialism (**imperialism**), FIFA displayed a European bias and as a result the world body's newer members from Africa and Asia found their aspirations within world football routinely frustrated. Recognizing the possibilities that FIFA's one-nation one-vote franchise provision offered, Havelange shrewdly manipulated these tensions and, in the run up to the 1974 FIFA Congress, began making a series of election promises to the game's developing constituencies. Once elected, Havelange set out to fulfil his mandate and, having secured **sponsorship** support from adidas and Coca-Cola, was able to implement his ambitious development plans and expansion programmes aimed at satisfying the Third World's calls for equity within the context of world football. Thus the World Cup Finals tournament was enlarged to 24 teams for the 1982 World Cup in Spain, and then to 32 for the 1998 competition in France. Development initiatives were set up throughout Asia and Africa and new international age group competitions were established to encourage FIFA's less-developed members to play a fuller part in international football. These developments were reflected in the game's corridors of power, with membership of FIFA's committees becoming much more globally representative.

By the mid-1990s the dissatisfaction felt by the Union of European Football Associations (UEFA) at the direction and autocratic nature of Havelange's stewardship of FIFA reached a crescendo, culminating in a bitterly fought struggle for the FIFA presidency. Havelange's decision not to stand as a candidate for the presidential vote at FIFA's 1998 Congress appeared to have left the way clear for UEFA President Lennart Johansson. However, three months prior to the election, Sepp Blatter, then FIFA's general secretary, announced that he would be standing against Johansson. With Havelange's support Blatter was duly elected, but the beginning of his reign was shrouded in controversy. In the immediate aftermath of the vote, leading figures within the world game claimed that a number of African delegates had been bribed to vote for Blatter. Although he was subsequently cleared of any wrongdoing, controversy continued to plague Blatter's first term in office. Following the collapse of FIFA's marketing partner ISL in early 2002, Blatter and his predecessor faced accusations of cronyism, corruption and financial mismanagement. UEFA sensed an opportunity to go on the offensive and they orchestrated a bid for the FIFA presidency from the head of the Confédération Africaine de Football, Issa Hayatou. Blatter proved his resilience and political nous with a resounding victory in the presidential vote at the 2002 Congress in Seoul. Since then, Blatter has been able to build on the impressive football development work associated with his predecessor and has put in place a number of programmes that should lead to an improvement in coaching and playing standards as well as boosting the grassroots of football in the game's underdeveloped regions. At present, FIFA's membership stands in excess of that of the United Nations, and FIFA has an annual turnover to match leading multinational corporations.

Key Reading

Darby, P. (2002) *Africa, Football and FIFA: Politics, Colonialism and Resistance.* London: Frank Cass.

Darby, P. (2003) 'Africa, the FIFA presidency, and the governance of world football: 1974, 1998, and 2002', *Africa Today,* 50 (1): 2–24.

FIFA (1984) *FIFA 1904–1984: Historical Publication of the Fédération Internationale de Football Association.* Zurich: FIFA.

Sugden, J. and Tomlinson, A. (1998) *FIFA and the Contest for World Football: Who Rules the Peoples' Game?* Cambridge: Polity Press.

Sugden, J., Tomlinson, A. and Darby, P. (1998) 'FIFA Versus UEFA in the struggle for the control of world football', in A. Brown (ed.), *Fanatics! Power, Identity and Fandom in Football.* London and New York: Routledge. pp. 11–31.

Paul Darby

FIGG, JAMES (1695–1734)

Accredited by a number of historians as the individual responsible for 'inventing' boxing (pugilism and prizefighting are often used as synonyms). With the backing of a patron (believed to be the Earl of Peterborough), Figg opened his 'School of Arms', or Boxing Emporium, in Tottenham Court Road, London in 1719. Figg was a fighter himself, but gained notoriety through his provision of tuition in a range of attack and self-defence arts (in addition to boxing, Figg taught the use of the broadsword and single-stick). Sociologists such as Sheard (1997, 2004) and Sugden (1996), however, reject such reductionist explanations of the genesis of boxing (see also **Doubleday myth** and **Webb Ellis myth**) arguing, for instance, that fist-fighting had long been part of folk tradition in England (**folk games**).

Figg, however, can be singled out as the man to first commercialize boxing and develop it as a business, catering largely for a rich and powerful clientele drawn from younger members of the gentry and aristocracy (**commercialization**). Sheard argues that this development indicates a movement away from duelling and sword-fighting as a way of settling disputes within these social classes, which in turn provides supporting evidence for Elias's thesis about the interlinked nature of **sportization and parliamentarization**, and the **civilizing process** more generally.

Key Reading

Sheard, K. (1997) 'Aspects of boxing in the western "civilizing process"', *International Review for the Sociology of Sport*, 32 (1): 31–57.

Sheard, K. (2004) 'Boxing in the western civilizing process', in E. Dunning, D. Malcolm and I. Waddington (eds), *Sport Histories: Figurational Studies of the Development of Modern Sports*. London: Routledge. pp. 15–30.

Sugden, J. (1996) *Boxing and Society: An International Analysis*. Manchester: Manchester University Press.

FIGURATIONAL SOCIOLOGY

Sometimes referred to as process sociology, figurational sociology developed out of the work of Norbert Elias (1897–1990). Elias is unusual among leading sociological theorists in arguing that sport and leisure are significant social phenomena in their own right, and consequently gives these practices an important role in his broader research programme.

A central Eliasian concept is the figuration. The concept of figuration simultaneously refers to living individuals and their bonds, or relationships, with others; in other words, networks of interdependency. The key to understanding society, Elias argued, is an examination of the 'networks of interdependency' in which we are all enmeshed. We are, all of us, both enabled and constrained by the networks of interdependency that include us/that we constitute.

Elias developed the concept of figuration as part of a broader critique of the prevalence of 'false dichotomies' in sociology (e.g. nature vs. nurture (see also **binaries**)), and to ameliorate problems related to the sociological use of the terms 'the individual' and 'society' (**agency and structure; macro- and micro-sociology**). Humans, Elias argued, are not closed and individualistic, but open, social, and necessarily interdependent. The concept of the figuration allows sociologists to avoid the reifying tendency in macro-sociological theories to portray 'social structures' as though they can think and act for themselves (e.g. 'the needs of capitalism', 'the functional needs of the social system' (**reification**), whilst not over-compensating by reducing social phenomena to the actions of individuals.

Certain key strands of figurational sociology flow from this. Because all humans are necessarily interdependent, power should always be conceived of as a question of relative balance. No person or group is ever all-powerful, or completely powerless. Figurations, moreover, are complex and dynamic: complex because they consist of the interweaving of the actions of (large numbers of) people; dynamic because, in the absence of a monopoly of power, power balances are always contested and therefore in flux. The complexity of networks of interdependency leads to the generation of 'blind' or unplanned social processes. Analysis of these plays a prominent role in figurational sociological research, and the dynamic nature of power leads Eliasians to stress the importance of studying social relations as processes (i.e. towards historical sociology and hence the parallel term, 'process sociology').

To illustrate these ideas, one of the first papers Elias wrote on sport was 'The Dynamics of Sports Groups with Special Reference to Football'. Here, Elias (with Eric Dunning) used the analogy of a football match to demonstrate how players' behaviour is contoured by the actions of others (encompassing both the cooperation of team mates and conflictual relations with opponents). Players adjust their actions according to the movements of team mates, and those of the opposition. In the same way, in social life, we have to consider the actions of those around us and respond accordingly. In the game, as in life, we are bound by historically and context-specific 'rules' (we might say social norms). The football analogy, Elias and Dunning (1986) note, 'shows that figurations of individuals are neither more nor less real than the individuals who form them ... Individuals always come in figurations and figurations are always formed by individuals.'

These theoretical concepts emerge out of (but could stand separately from) Elias's most influential work, *The Civilizing Process*. In volume one Elias empirically traces such things as the refinement of manners and the reduction in the use of **violence** in Western Europe from the sixteenth century onwards. Crucially, however, in volume two, Elias linked these developments to processes of state formation and the twin monopolies of violence and taxation in particular. Elias saw this work as developing a 'central theory' within the broader theoretical perspective; that is to say, as a theory towards which sociological research could, and should, be oriented. Figurational sociologists of sport have followed Elias's advice and example in this regard.

From the outset Elias (again in conjunction with Dunning) sought to explain the relationship between the relatively pacified nature of modern societies and the historically specific characteristics of sports within these societies (**quest for excitement**). Elias also looked at earlier forms of sports-like activities, such as those in ancient Greece (**ancient Olympic Games**) and the **Roman Games**, and examined the 'birth' of **modern sport** in England in the seventeenth century (**sportization and parliamentarization**). These early works are consolidated in Elias and Dunning's 1986 publication, *Quest for Excitement*. Dunning subsequently pioneered the figurational sociology of sport agenda, collaborating with Kenneth Sheard in a sociological study of the development of rugby football (*Barbarians, Gentlemen and Players*) and with Patrick Murphy and John Williams in studies of **football hooliganism**, this latter body of work leading to the formation

of the so-called 'Leicester School'. In recent years there has been a considerable increase in the number and range of figurationally informed sporting studies. Most notable in this regard has been Maguire's work on sport and **globalization** and Waddington's work on **drugs**, **health** and **pain and injury** in sport.

Critics of figurational sociology argue that Elias's work (including the concept of figuration) does not constitute a distinct approach (but is, rather, a variant of **functionalism**), and that the civilizing process is a unilinear, evolutionary theory, falsified by twentieth-century events such as the Jewish Holocaust in Nazi Germany. More specifically relating to sport, critics argue that figurational sociologists focus too centrally on issues of violence and its control, that they both ignore and are unable adequately to analyse **gender** issues, and that there is a general tendency towards a slavish and uncritical application of Elias's theory. A prominent feature of the sociology of sport in recent years has been the vigour (and at times highly personal nature) with which these criticisms have been made, and the equally robust defence that figurational sociologists have made in return.

Robert van Krieken (2001) has described *The Civilizing Process* as an 'analysis of the historical development of emotions and psychological life ... in relation to the connections ... with larger scale processes such as state formation, urbanisation and economic development'. This description highlights the importance to Elias of a developmental approach, the interconnected nature of the macro and the micro, and of the conceptualization of the 'individuals' and 'societies' as mutually constructed and mutually transformed (the rationale behind Elias's use of the term figuration). Undoubtedly there is both good and not so good sports research done by figurational sociologists (or in Elias's terms more and less adequate levels of understanding), but the best and most original work draws on these ideas to enhance our understanding of the social aspects of sport.

Key Reading

Dunning, E. (1999) *Sport Matters: Sociological Studies of Sport, Violence and Civilization*. London: Routledge.

Dunning, E., Malcolm, D. and Waddington I. (eds) (2004) *Sport Histories: Figurational Studies of the Development of Modern Sports*. London: Routledge.

Elias, N. and Dunning, E. (1986) *Quest for Excitement: Sport and Leisure in the Civilizing Process*. Oxford: Basil Blackwell.

Malcolm, D. and Waddington, I. (2007) *Matters of Sport: Essays in Honour of Eric Dunning*. London: Routledge.

Murphy, P., Sheard, K. and Waddington, I. (2000) 'Figurational sociology and its application to sport', in J. Coakley and E. Dunning (eds), *Handbook of Sports Studies*. London: Sage. pp. 92–105.

van Kreiken, R. (2001) 'Elias and Process Sociology', in G. Ritzer and B. Smart (eds), *Handbook of Social Theory*. London: Sage.

FOCUS GROUPS

A similar research method tool to **interviews**, but involve the interviewer talking to a small group (6–12) rather than to individuals. The central advantage of a focus group is that it empowers the respondents because they can swap experiences and thus gain confidence in the validity of their views (**reliability and validity**). Focus groups facilitate the emergence of issues and areas that the researcher could not/had not anticipated. Hence focus groups provide very rich, in-depth data that may not be obtainable by other means. They are particularly useful when investigating the experiences of relatively powerless or previously under-researched social groups, such as children or some minority groups.

Consequently focus groups should be loosely structured, with the researcher acting as facilitator rather than interrogator, merely guiding the discussion towards certain key areas. Researchers should ensure that all participants have the chance to contribute, and that the discussion isn't dominated by one or two people. The proceedings of a focus group are particularly complex so must be recorded, using either audiotape or, preferably, video, enabling the researcher to identify the source of a specific opinion. The key disadvantages of using focus groups are that: (1) they are difficult to arrange; (2) they are difficult to conduct effectively; and (3) they may be liable to be dominated by one or two individuals, in which case the views expressed might not be reflective of the group members experiences more broadly.

Focus groups have only relatively recently come into fashion as a research technique and thus their use in sport research has so far been limited. However, Jones and Cheetham (2001) and Fitzgerald et al. (2003) have used focus groups to examine children's views on the nature and purposes of PE and disabled young people's experiences of PE respectively.

Key Reading

Fitzgerald, N., Jobling, A. and Kirk, D. (2003) 'Valuing the voices of young disabled people: exploring experiences of physical education in sport', *European Journal of Physical Education*, 8: 175–201.

Jones, R. and Cheetham, R. (2001) 'Physical education in the National Curriculum: its purpose and meaning for final year secondary students', *European Journal of Physical Education*, 6 (2): 81–100.

FOLK DEVILS

(**moral panic**)

FOLK GAMES

Sports-like activities in which the masses partook during the European Middle Ages. Brookes (1978) argues that it is possible to outline three general types of these **medieval sports**: (1) team games in which moving players (on foot or on horseback) attempted to propel a 'ball' (or similar object) towards a 'goal' or fixed point (e.g. a church) in order to score 'points' (the antecedents of football, hockey, polo, etc.); (2) essentially individual games in which a stationary player strikes a ball into a hole, through hoops etc. (the antecedents of golf, croquet, etc.); and (3) team games in which a stationary person propelled a ball away from his/her person and scored by running between two or more fixed points (the antecedents of cricket, rounders, baseball, etc.). Such was the structure of medieval societies that identical games could have a variety of different, locally specific names, or such that an identical name could be given to a number of games played under a variety of locally specific rules.

Dunning and Sheard (2005) provide a table of 15 'structural properties' of folk games, contrasting these with the characteristics of **modern sport**. The characteristics of folk games identified are: (1) diffuse, informal organization; (2) simple, unwritten rules, legitimated by tradition; (3) game rules/customs changed on an ad-hoc or informal basis; (4) regional variation of rules, ball size, etc.; (5) no fixed limits on territory, duration or participant numbers; (6) little attempt to restrict the impact of natural (terrain, weather) and social (e.g. horse ownership) differences and inequalities; (7) low role differentiation between players (e.g. between defence and offence); (8) little distinction between playing and spectating roles; (9) low structural differentiation with several game forms (e.g. handling, kicking, players on foot and on horseback) combined within single games; (10) informal social control of players, with no outside agencies/referees to enforce rule compliance; (11) relatively high levels of socially tolerated **violence**; (12) generation of high levels of spontaneous 'battle excitement'; (13) emphasis on physical force rather than skill; (14) strong communal pressure to participate and thus demonstrate group identity; and (15) contests having local meaning only.

Folk games are a subset of what Holt (1989: 12–25) calls traditional games. Holt stresses the importance of these activities alongside **animal sports** as part of a festive culture in Britain at this time. Traditional sports were organized according to seasonal changes, holy days, the patronage of the landed classes, the rites of apprenticeship and local customs. Save for a small number of surviving events (e.g. bottle-kicking in Hallaton, England on Easter Monday) most folk game forms died out during the Victorian age. Henricks argues that three main criticisms led to their demise: (1) folk games detracted from **archery** practice (and therefore military preparation); (2) they were rowdy and entailed damage to property in urban areas; and (3) such activities clashed with **Puritan** ideals.

Dunning and Sheard accept much of this argument, citing over 30 instances of attempts by the state to ban folk football between 1314 and 1667 (arguing further, that the frequency of such bans indicates the inability of the state to impose its will on the people at this time). They also agree with Malcolmson, who argues that industrialization, which instilled a new type of **discipline** among labourers, and reduced the time and space available for such games, was also significant in the decline in folk games. However, Dunning and Sheard add to this the importance of the development of the ethos of 'equality' or **fair play** in sport, the concomitant movement towards greater social exclusivity among the landed classes, and the increasing fear of revolt amongst the lower classes, which meant that the patronage which had helped such activities to survive earlier attacks was removed. It is useful, also, to see these arguments in light of Elias's work on **sportization and parliamentarization**.

Key Reading

Brookes, C. (1978) *English Cricket: The Game and its Players through the Ages*. London: Weidenfeld and Nicolson.

Dunning, E. and Sheard, K. (2005) *Barbarians, Gentlemen and Players: A*

Sociological Study of the Development of Rugby Football, 2nd edn. London: Routledge.

Henricks, T. (1991) 'Sport in the later Middle Ages', in *Disputed Pleasures: Sport and Society in Pre-Industrial England*. Westport, CT: Greenwood Press. pp. 41–68.

Holt, R. (1989) *Sport and the British: A Modern History*. Oxford: Oxford University Press.

FOOTBALL HOOLIGANISM

Not so much a sociological or social psychological concept as it is a construct of the **media** and politicians. It is, moreover, a very imprecise term, used to cover a range of actions such as fighting, vandalism, throwing missiles, etc. Football hooliganism may take place in a **stadium**, on transport networks, in town centres, etc. It may be highly organized and involve pre-arranged **violence** or it may be spontaneous. It may or may not involve racist or Far Right sentiments (**anti-racism**; **race**). Its main common feature is that it involves fights between (predominantly) males affiliated to football clubs. While football hooliganism has, in recent years, ceased to be seen as such a pressing social issue (**deviance**), it should be remembered that during the 1970s and 1980s it was perceived to be one of the largest public order crises facing Britain and other European countries (moral panic). Indeed, the prominence of football hooliganism as a social issue can be seen as a key factor in the development of the study of sport as a legitimate sociological sub-discipline (**Heysel**; **Hillsborough**).

Contrary to earlier conceptions of football hooliganism as an 'English Disease', it has now been shown to be a world phenomenon. Moreover, while a reduction in the British media's reporting of hooliganism in recent years has led to the perception of its declining frequency, Dunning et al. (2002) argue that it is still 'alive and kicking'. The global spread of football hooliganism and its apparent waxing and waning make definitive explanations of its root causes difficult to come by. However, a number of attempts have been made.

'Popular' or media-led explanations suggest that football hooliganism is caused by: (1) excessive **alcohol** intake; (2) on-pitch events; (3) unemployment; (4) affluence; and (5) permissiveness. There is, to a greater or lesser degree, evidence to support each of these theories, but none provides a rigorous and sustainable explanation. For instance, while some fans do drink and fight, many who fight don't drink and many who drink don't fight. Some on-pitch events have sparked crowd trouble, but some hooligan incidents (such as Heysel) occur before games. Similarly, the number of hooligan incidents appears to be independent of unemployment rates, as well as affluence and permissiveness (contemporary society is probably both more affluent and permissive than it was in the late 1970s when concerns over hooliganism in Britain were at their highest).

Academics have put forward a number of competing explanations of the phenomenon. The first attempt at an explanation came from Marxist sociologist Ian Taylor (**Marxism**). Taylor argued that football hooliganism stemmed from the capitalist economy and represented a working-class resistance to the **embourgeoisement** of the game. This theory, however, proved to be historically inaccurate (Dunning et al., 1988 traced football hooliganism back to the nineteenth century, thus pre-dating football's embourgeoisement) and neglected the fact that rather than constituting a kind of **class** war, hooliganism largely entailed the working classes fighting each other.

Also developed during the 1970s, Peter Marsh's 'ethogenic' approach portrayed hooliganism as the product of innate human **aggression** which is part of the human survival instinct. Hooliganism was governed by 'rules of disorder' that limited more extreme forms of violence. Exchanges were thus ritualized, largely symbolic, and provided **catharsis**. 'Real violence' was relatively rare. Marsh's work was criticized for being ahistorical and asocial: given this explanation, how can we account for changes in patterns of hooliganism over time and the fact that not all humans engage in hooliganism?

During the 1980s the so-called 'Leicester School' emerged as the dominant perspective on football hooliganism. This approach is underpinned by a commitment to **figurational sociology**. For Dunning et al. (1998, 2002) testimony from those involved in football hooliganism demonstrates that the phenomenon involves young men, for whom fighting stems from issues of **masculinity**, territory and the generation of excitement (**quest for excitement**). They argue, moreover, that the majority of English football hooligans (around 75 per cent) are working class – or more specifically 'rougher working class' – in origin and/or current social status (**social stratification**). This pattern, they note, is similarly apparent in data on hooliganism from Scotland, Belgium, The Netherlands and Italy. Dunning et al. conclude that the **socialization** experiences in working-class communities tend to generate a **habitus** that is relatively tolerant of violence and aggression. Men in these communities come to value themselves and rank each other according to their ability to fight and use violence. An aggressive habitus is often developed where communities are highly segregated according to sex and age; that is to say, where the 'softening' pressure from females and elder males is not evident (**civilizing process**). Football is chosen as a venue for fighting because it provides regular contact with ready-made and willing opponents, and relatively good prospects of escape from detection. Finally, Dunning et al. suggest that 'fault-lines' specific to particular countries (e.g. **sectarianism**, **race** or regionalism) may also contour and fuel hooliganism, thus explaining why class and masculinity cannot always be seen to be the primary causes of hooliganism.

Based on his own ethnographic research in Scotland (**ethnography**), Giulianotti (1999) has subsequently argued that it is possible to detect different epochs of football hooliganism which he characterizes as 'traditional' disorder, 'high modernity' (from the early 1980s when the soccer 'casuals' began to emerge) and 'post-modern' (**postmodernism**). Working closely with Armstrong, Giulianotti argued that postmodern hooligan groups are not formed by narrow class or community groups. Rather they tend to be more fractured, membership tends to be more temporary and more voluntary. Hooliganism is undertaken by loose networks of small groups of friends, drawn from various backgrounds (they may come from the same community, but may equally work together, meet in pubs and clubs, etc.); in short they may be what Maffesoli has termed open-ended urban neo-tribes. Moreover, the media and politicians seek to 'de-amplify' hooliganism in their desire to host major international tournaments (**mega-events, staging of**) leading us to have a **hyperreal** understanding of hooliganism.

Giulianotti's work (both alone and with Armstrong) has been characterized by regular and bitter critiques of the Leicester School (who have responded in kind). In an interesting overview of these debates, Bairner (2007) has concluded that the main findings of Dunning et al. 'are insightful and difficult to refute'. He suggests that while there are some difficulties with Dunning et al's definition of 'rough' working class and in terms of the proportion of football hooligans who exhibit this habitus, he concludes that, 'there are no grounds for denying that the phenomenon involves young working-class men who, for a variety of reasons, either are, or else seek to be, marginal to mainstream society. Nor should we ignore the Leicester School's recognition that far from being helpless victims, these young men actively seek pleasure from their hooligan activities'.

Key Reading

Armstrong, G. (1998) *Football Hooligans: Knowing the Score*. Oxford: Berg.

Bairner, A. (2007) 'The Leicester School and the study of football hooliganism', in D. Malcolm and I. Waddington (eds), *Matters of Sport: Essays in Honour of Eric Dunning*. London: Routledge. pp. 80–96.

Dunning, E., Murphy, P. and Williams, J. (1988) *The Roots of Football Hooliganism: An Historical and Sociological Study*. London: Routledge.

Dunning, E., Murphy, P. Waddington, I. and Astrinakis, A. (2002) *Fighting Fans: Football Hooliganism as a World Phenomenon*. Dublin: UCD Press.

Giulianotti, R. (1999) *Football: A Sociology of the Global Game*. Cambridge: Polity. esp. Ch. 3.

FORMAL AND INFORMAL EMPIRE

The notion of Britain having a formal and informal Empire during the nineteenth and early twentieth centuries (**imperialism**), was initially introduced by historian Harold Perkin who subsequently used the concept to help understand why particular British sports successfully diffused to, and continue to be played in, particular countries.

According to Perkin (1989), British influence in the nineteenth century extended much further than Britain's formal possessions, for beyond the crown colonies and dominions, there was an 'informal empire' consisting of territories not under the British flag but which lay within Britain's 'sphere of influence'. Moreover, this distinction between the formal and informal empires played an important part in determining the pattern of diffusion of British sports. The formal British Empire was largely governed by members of the public school elite and, as a result, the sports that were taken to and adopted in the colonies and dominions were sports such as cricket and rugby, which, by the end of the nineteenth century, had attained a high social cachet in Britain. By contrast, the principal influence in the informal empire was exercised by members of lower status groups, such as merchants, traders, engineers and sailors, whose chief attachment was to association football. This helps to explain, Perkin argues, why soccer, now the world's most popular sport, did not become as firmly rooted in colonies like Australia, New Zealand and India, as it did in so many other parts of the world (see also **sports space**).

Empirically there are some problems with Perkin's thesis. At this time football was widely played by the public school elite, and recent historical research has revealed that the dominance of cricket in India has been exaggerated and that a significant history of football in the sub-continent has not yet been properly recorded or sufficiently recognized. However, the value of Perkin's work is that it provides the beginnings of an explanation of the differential diffusion of sports which is based on the actions, interests and relative power of different social groups and not on the 'inherent' characteristics of sport.

Key Reading

Dimeo, P. and Mills, J. (2001) *Soccer in South Asia: Empire, Nation, Diaspora*. London: Frank Cass.

Perkin, H. (1989) 'Teaching the nations how to play: sport and society in the British Empire and Commonwealth', *International Journal of the History of Sport*, 6 (2): 145–55.

FOUCAULT

(**discipline; surveillance; technologies**)

FOX-HUNTING

The prominence of fox-hunting in sports studies derives largely from the highly emotive ethical argument over whether such a pursuit constitutes a suitable sporting activity in modern, 'civilized' societies, and to a lesser extent from the sociological debate about the origins of **modern sport** forms. The anti-hunting lobby object to the harm inflicted on the fox in the name of sport; that is to say, for the enjoyment of the human participants rather than for some tangible or purposeful end, such as the supply of food (though many in the anti-hunting lobby also object to harming animals per se, including the human consumption of meat). Pro-hunters argue that fox-hunting is a humane way to limit the numbers of an animal seen as a rural pest. In the form of the *Countryside Alliance*, the pro-hunting lobby successfully widened the agenda, arguing that the attack on fox-hunting was the product of an urban majority attempting to inflict their values on a rural minority (**cultural relativism**). The infringement of civil liberties which the ban on fox-hunting represented was seen as 'the thin end of the wedge' and it was argued that once fox-hunting was banned, similar pressures on other sports, such as shooting, and perhaps fishing, would soon follow. Such was the strength of feeling among, and innovation by, the pro-hunting lobby that the legal prohibition on 'hunting with hounds' which came into force in England and Wales in 2005 has had little real effect on the number of fox-hunting meets.

Sociologically, Elias (1986) has argued that the seventeenth-century reform of the previously utilitarian, food-gathering, activity of hunting into a standardized and rule-bound activity, demonstrates an important phase in the development of **modern sport** forms (see also **sportization and parliamentarization** and **civilizing process**). Under the fox-hunting 'rules' developed by Hugo Meynell in the early eighteenth century, the kill of the fox was delegated to the hounds (where previously humans had taken a central role), and various conventions were enforced – the reluctance to pursue an edible prey (e.g. a hare), to switch foxes, or to shoot the fox. These served to enhance the centrality and *pleasure of the chase relative to the kill*. For Elias, the decline in **violence** is linked to the generation and prolonging of tension excitement and this is a general principle in the development of sports rules (**quest for excitement**).

Stokvis (1992) and Franklin (1996) have questioned the empirical basis of Elias's argument. Stokvis argues that hunting in a modern form was evident in France prior to these developments in England (and hence the link to parliamentarization is at best questionable, and at worst invalid). Franklin argues that earlier forms of hunting with hounds, and therefore the 'kill by proxy' that Elias cites as particularly important, existed in England prior to the reform of fox-hunting, and that fox-hunting was reformed as much as a consequence of the changing availability of quarry as it was a reaction to broaders social processes. Evidence from other sports, notably boxing and cricket, indicates that the hypothesized link between sportization and parliamentarization is, however, valid.

Key Reading

Elias, N. (1986) 'An essay on sport and violence', in N. Elias and E. Dunning, *Quest for Excitement: Sport and Leisure in the Civilizing Process*. Oxford: Basil Blackwell. pp. 150–74.

Franklin, A. (1996) 'On foxhunting and angling: Norbert Elias and the sportisation process', *Journal of Historical Sociology*, 9 (4): 432–56.

Stokvis, R. (1992) 'Sports and civilization: is violence the central problem?', in E. Dunning, and C. Rojek (eds), *Sport and Leisure in the Civilizing Process: Critique and Counter-Critique*. Basingstoke: Macmillan. pp. 121–36.

FRANCHISES

A franchise entails a central body (e.g. a sports league) granting permission to an individual or business (e.g. a sports team) to distribute a product or service (e.g. sports events) within a specific geographical territory. The franchise arrangement underpins the American sports league system, allowing leagues to act as **cartels**.

There were few objections to the use of franchises in the early history of American major league sports, for teams initially struggled to make a profit. Franchises therefore enabled teams to search around for markets which could sustain them. Moreover, mutually agreeing not to encroach on each other's market was as commonsensical as mutually agreeing to provide each other with regular and meaningful fixtures. However, the early years of the twentieth century saw increased competition between leagues. Leagues bought up the franchises of their rivals to maintain their monopoly position, and the exemption from **anti-trust laws** granted in 1922 effectively provided leagues with unfettered control over the supply of franchises. In recent years, the restricted supply of franchises has seen their value rise dramatically. In 1999, for instance, the New York Jets National Football League (NFL) franchise was sold for $635 million, and in 2000 the New York Islanders National Hockey League (NHL) franchise was sold for $190 million (Rosentraub, 2004).

The key debate about franchises revolves around the affect that the franchise system has on the use of public money to fund professional sport (**market failure**). Because franchises are limited, communities (**city, the**) are prepared to support the cost of ever larger fees to own a franchise, and are often seemingly held to ransom by franchise owners who threaten to move away from the city unless, for example, expensive facilities are built/subsidized (**stadium**). Indeed, such is the scale of this problem that Rosentraub estimates the total state and local debt for sports facilities in the US to be in the region of $15 billion.

Those who wish to host a franchise generally argue that there are significant economic gains to be made through this public subsidy (e.g. through employment, increased **sports tourism**, higher taxes, etc. (**multipliers**)). Critics argue that the economic arguments are, at best, unproven (Whitson et al., 2004) and that opportunity costs (i.e. the other things that such income could be spent on) are rarely considered, raising issues such as 'distributive justice' and political priorities (team owners and sports spectators are, for instance, relatively wealthy members of society and perhaps not the most deserving of public subsidy). Indeed, in recent years when

proposed subsidies have been subject to a democratic vote, they have tended to be rejected by the public.

However, the one intangible factor in all this is the importance of owning a franchise to the image of the city and the well-being of its citizens. Consequently, the greatest battles over franchises have involved the movement of ice hockey teams from Canadian to more lucrative American markets. Here, in addition to economic arguments, ideas such as national identity are evoked (**nationalism**). Does the place of ice hockey in Canadian popular culture mean that the economic costs of hosting a franchise should be borne?

Key Reading

Rosentraub, M. (2004) 'Private control of a civic asset: the winners and losers from North America's experience with four major leagues for professional team sport', in T. Slack (ed.), *The Commercialisation of Sport*. London: Routledge. pp. 101–18.

Whitson, D., Harvey, J. and Lavoie, M. (2004) 'Government subsidisation of Canadian professional sport franchises: a risky business', in T. Slack (ed.), *The Commercialisation of Sport*. London: Routledge. pp. 75–100.

FROM RITUAL TO RECORD (AND THE PARADIGM OF MODERN SPORTS)

Allen Guttmann's *From Ritual to Record: The Nature of Modern Sport* (2004) was an attempt to understand the uniqueness of **modern sport** and to identify some of the salient differences between American and European sports. The book's thesis appears most succinctly in the form of a Weberian ideal-type paradigm of modern sports (see Ch. 2).

Anterior to this paradigm are three convictions: (1) the formal-structural characteristics of modern sports are strikingly different from those of pre-modern sports; (2) pre-modern sports have tended either to acquire the formal-structural characteristics of modern sports or to survive on the margins of the mainstream of what Raymond Williams called 'residual culture'; (3) the evolution from pre-modern to modern sports can be construed as an instance of a **civilizing process** in the course of which the members of a society internalize values that reduce the level of expressive (but not instrumental) interpersonal **violence**.

Modern, as opposed to pre-modern, sports (**folk games**) can be paradigmatically defined by a set of seven interrelated formal-structural characteristics:

- *Secularism*. Modern sports are not related to the transcendent realm of the sacred. Sports in pre-modern societies frequently occurred as an aspect of religious observance (**religion**). The **ancient Olympic Games**, for example, were sacred to Zeus. Japanese *shinji-zumô* was performed at temple and shrine festivals.
- *Equality*. Modern sports require, at least in theory, that everyone – including the elderly and the disabled – be admitted to the game on the basis of his or her athletic ability (**fair play**). Pre-modern sports frequently excluded people on the basis of social class, religion, race ethnicity or gender. Medieval **tournaments**, for instance, were contests among noblemen (who were disqualified if they *wed* a commoner).
- *Specialization*. Many modern team sports (such as rugby, soccer, Australian Rules football) have evolved from earlier, less-differentiated games (such as folk football or *soule*). In addition, many team sports (such as baseball, American football) have a gamut of specialized roles and playing positions. At the elite level, individual athletes rely on ancillary teams of supportive specialists. The Dutch swimmer Inge de Bruijn, for instance, arrived in Sydney for the 2000 Olympics with two coaches, two masseuses, two physiologists, a nutritionist, a sports psychologist, and a personal trainer.

- *Bureaucratization*. Local, regional, national and international bureaucracies administer every level of modern sports from Little League Baseball to the World Cup Final (**FIFA**; **IOC**). Lacking this kind of administrative structure, pre-modern sports usually took place under the aegis of local political or religious authorities.
- *Rationalization*. Modern sports are a prime example of Weberian Zweckrationalität (instrumental rationality). Sports contests take place in purpose-built facilities (**stadium**) where scientifically trained athletes compete with technologically sophisticated standardized equipment on the basis of constantly revised rules and regulations that are perceived as the means to an end. Rationalization leads also to abstraction or what Georges Vigarello calls *déréalisation*. For example, the equestrian vaulter's whinnying, restlessly moving mount becomes the gymnast's quietly immobile 'horse' and the backyard hurdler's leafy hedges are replaced by the track athlete's lightly constructed portable rectangles. In every way, pre-modern sports exhibited a much lower level of instrumental rationality.
- *Quantification*. In modern sports, as in almost every aspect of our daily lives, performance is recorded numerically. At their panhellenic athletic festivals, the ancient Greeks measured neither the times runners ran nor the distances throwers threw (and they had no standardized units for temporal or spatial measurement in the unlikely event that they were concerned about the numbers).
- *Obsession with Records*. The sports record – defined as a hitherto unsurpassed quantified achievement – is a constant challenge to all who hope to surpass it. André Obey, a French athlete and man of letters, wrote lyrically of his hope that his daughter would 'one day recite the litany, not of battles but of records, more beautiful than the labors of Hercules'. Without the prerequisite of a quantified achievement, pre-modern athletes were unable to set – and were perhaps unable even to imagine – sports records.

For each of these generalizations about the stark contrast between the present and the past, there are exceptions. For example, the achievements of ancient Roman charioteers (**chariot races**) and seventeenth-century Japanese archers *were* quantified. There were, in other words, anticipations of **modernity** in sports as in other institutions. Wolfgang Decker, David C. Young, and a number of other scholars have cited anticipations of this sort as if they invalidated the paradigm, but isolated examples do not constitute a system. The characteristics of modernity are not a random collection of arbitrary attributes. On the contrary, they fit together like the pieces of a puzzle.

Scholars such as Colin Howell have been even more critical than Decker and Young. They have dismissed the paradigm of modern sports as a sports-historical anachronism. Their dismissal is too peremptory. It must be admitted that the paradigm can be misinterpreted to imply that the observed changes in sports occurred as part of some uniform and inevitable process that transforms each and every aspect of each and every sport in precisely the same way. The paradigm can also be misused as a facile instrument for foolishly ethnocentric value judgements – as if modern sports were somehow *better* than traditional sports (**cultural relativism**). The misinterpretation or misuse of a paradigm is, however, a poor reason to dismiss it.

If the disavowal of assumptions about the alleged inevitability, ubiquity and desirability of the evolution of modern sports seems like an inadequate response to criticism of the paradigm, one may reasonably ask: Is there a better way, in the domain of sports, to understand the contrast between a medieval game of folk football and the globally televised spectacle of football's World Cup Final? In the last analysis, the *usefulness* of the modernization paradigm is the best argument for its continued use.

Key Reading

Guttmann, A. ([1978] 2004) *From Ritual to Record: The Nature of Modern Sport*, rev. edn. New York: Columbia University Press.
See also, Guttmann, A. (2001) 'From Ritual to Record: a retrospective critique', *Journal of Sport History Review* Special Issue, 32 (1).

Allen Guttmann

FUNCTIONALISM

The dominant perspective in sociology in the first half of the twentieth century. Its roots, though, lie in the nineteenth century, mainly in the work of figures such as Auguste Comte (1798–1857), Herbert Spencer (1820–1903) and Emile Durkheim (1858–1916). Functionalism is not a unified perspective but its core, generally shared feature is an analogy between biological organisms and 'social systems'. More particularly, just as an organism consists of 'parts', such as the heart, lungs and limbs, that contribute to the working of the living organism as a whole, so societies are held to be 'systems' composed of 'parts', such as the family, the polity, the economy, religion and sport. These parts are said to contribute to the working of the society or 'system' as a whole. The contribution of a part to the whole is said to be its 'function'. For example, it is widely held that one of the functions of sport is the promotion of social cohesion. While there are few sociologists of sport who are explicit and uncritical advocates of functionalism (most notably Gunter Lüschen and Chris Stevenson, though Douglas Booth and John Loy have written some recent and largely sympathetic overviews) the principles and assumptions of the perspective appear in a range of sociological analyses of sport. Moreover, criticisms of functionalism have been used as the point of departure for the establishment of a number of subsequent theoretical perspectives.

Early functionalists sought to identify *functional prerequisites*: that is to say, those functions that necessarily need to be met for a social system to survive. Different functionalist writers have identified different processes in this regard, but among those commonly identified are: (1) adaptation to the external environment (e.g. the provision of food and housing); (2) socialization of the young into acceptable social roles; (3) social control to reward and punish desirable and undesirable behaviour; (4) reproduction of the species; (5) a shared belief system; and (6) political leadership to coordinate the actions of the population. Perhaps the most well-known formulation of functional prerequisites is the AGIL system of functional problems identified by Talcott Parsons, AGIL being an acronymn for: adaptation (see (1) above); goal attainment (the problem of achieving system goals); integration (of communities, organizations, etc. into the system as a whole); and latency or pattern maintenance (the problem, met largely by families, schools, etc., of maintaining people's commitment to common values). In both Parsons's AGIL system and the broader range of functional prerequisites identified above, we can see how sport may be functional for society, e.g. through socialization and integration of communities of players and fans, acceptance of competition, and meritocracy as 'system goals' (**functions of sport**).

Many functionalists further suggest that societies, or social systems, are characterized by *self-equilibrating mechanisms,* or mechanisms which work towards the maintenance of social stability. Changes in one area of society lead to compensatory adjustments in other areas. For instance, it might be argued that being a football **fan** in modern, relatively secular, societies fulfils those functions previously performed by more formal or traditional forms of **religion**. Societies are so highly interconnected that they can be seen to have a certain kind of unity, sometimes called *functional unity*.

The aspects of functionalism so far identified are perhaps more applicable to what is typically called the normative or 'hard' form of functionalism associated with Talcott Parsons, than the **'soft' functionalism** of Robert Merton. For Parsons, an understanding

of the conditions that maintain social stability and order is not just *a* task of sociology, it is sociology's *primary* task. Moreover, the principal source of stability, Parsons argued, is the consensus over norms and values that exists among the members of society (the consensus over the importance of sportsmanship and **fair play**, and the acceptance of these ideals in society more broadly, provide a good sporting example of Parsons's point here). Values are internalized in the course of **socialization**, and are held to be the major means by which people's behaviour is regulated and through which society is integrated. The description of this approach as 'normative' functionalism reflects the central importance attributed to norms and values in the maintenance of social order.

Four major weaknesses with functionalism, and its application to sport, have been identified. First, functionalists typically focus on the 'positive' aspects of sport, leading to an analysis which, for example, suggests that the political conflict generated by sport is less significant than the political harmony, or that the existence of **class** and/or racial barriers (**race**) to social mobility is less significant than the instances where mobility is achieved. Integration and harmony are assumed to be the normal state of affairs, while conflict and tension will be corrected by the social system within a short period of time. A key problem with functionalism, therefore, is that it stresses consensus over conflict; it has a harmonistic bias (**conflict theory**). A second weakness is that functionalist work is inherently static and ahistorical. Functionalist work tends to be present-centred. The concentration on the preservation of the system leads functionalists to overlook aspects of social change. Third, functionalist theory is based on the assumption that the needs of different groups within society are the same as the needs of the society itself. Clearly this is not the case. Sports organizations continue to be segregated along sexual/**gender** lines and, while this may satisfy the socio-emotional 'needs' of men, it is a process that, many argue, operates to the disadvantage of women (**feminism**). Many golf clubs, for example, have policies that effectively exclude those people with whom the existing members do not wish to mix. Functionalists fail to recognize that sports are usually structured to promote the interests of those with power and wealth in our society (**critical theory**). Fourth, functionalist theory tends to be pitched at a very high level of generality, and provides no scope for us to understand how human beings make decisions about what is important in their lives, and how they may seek to actively create the social world around them (**agency and structure**).

Functionalism has been so extensively and so damningly critiqued that one could be mistaken for assuming that it no longer has relevance for sports studies. However, it is a theoretical model from which many other theories borrow and an understanding of the key principles of functionalism is essential for an understanding of the sociological study of sport.

Key Reading

Loy, J.W. and Booth, D. (2000) 'Functionalism, sport and society', in J. Coakley and E. Dunning (eds), *Handbook of Sports Studies*. London: Sage. pp. 8–27.

Lüschen, G. (1967) 'The interdependence of sport and culture', *International Review of Sport Sociology*. 2: 127–39.

Stevenson, C.L. and Nixon, J.E. (1972) 'A conceptual scheme of the functions of sport', *Sportwissenschaft*. 2: 119–32; repr. in E. Dunning and D. Malcolm (eds) (2003) *Sport Critical Concepts*. Vol. 1. London: Routledge. pp. 134–46.

FUNCTIONS OF SPORT

As with **functionalism** more generally, functionalist analyses of sport have identified a range of functions that sport contributes to the society as a whole. Harry Edwards (1973), in the first North American textbook on the sociology of sport, devotes a chapter to the functions of sport, but perhaps the clearest exposition is provided by Christopher Stevenson and John Nixon (1972).

Stevenson and Nixon examined the existing sociology of sport literature and concluded that the following five major social functions of sport could be identified:

- *Socio-emotional function.* Individuals within society must be socially and psychologically well balanced. Sport promotes emotional stability in the individual: by helping with the management of tension (sport is seen as a safe place to release **aggression**); by generating feelings of community and camaraderie (with team mates or supporters of the same team); and through the 'reassurance of ritual' (the use of traditional songs, sports matches played on traditional dates at traditional venues), which serves to allay feelings of insecurity and uncertainty (see also **religion**).

- *Socialization.* Sport promotes those attitudes and values that are held to be desirable in society, for instance: self-control; cooperation; respect for the rules, authority and opponents; and the desire to better oneself. Two interdependent processes contribute towards this socialization function. *Reinforcement* of values results from the reward of appropriate behaviour (e.g. through public recognition or the appointment of a captain) and the punishment of offenders (problematic players may be transferred/sold by the club or shunned by team mates). *Modelling* provides individuals with concrete examples of desired behaviour. The functionally ideal situation (in terms of the maintenance of social stability) is for the most successful athletes to epitomize the core sporting values.

- *Integration.* Sport enables and encourages individuals to harmoniously integrate into a collectivity or group. The group may consist of the players within a team, or it may be more extensive and include spectators and supporter groups. Integration aids both the **socialization** and socio-emotional functions of sport. By developing an 'in-group consciousness' (e.g. 'I am a Manchester United supporter') integration of potentially disparate individuals within a society becomes less problematic (e.g. at times of rapid social change such as urbanization (**city, the**)).

- *Political function*. In many respects this is simply an extension of the integrative function when applied to the nation state as a collectivity. Three facets of this function are identified: the use of sport as a political means of sanctioning other nations (e.g. **boycotts** of Olympic Games); the use of sport to extend in-group friendship to other societies (e.g. the staging of the Commonwealth, or 'Friendly, Games); and the dysfunctional consequence of **nationalism** and ethnocentrism where sporting defeats take on greater political significance (for instance, the defeat of Honduras by El Salvador in a football match in 1969 is often argued to have enflamed existing tensions and led to the declaration of war).

- *Social mobility function*. Sport provides an opportunity for those with special sporting abilities to move up the social scale by acquiring wealth or prestige (**social stratification**). Social mobility provides socially disadvantaged groups (e.g. the lower **class**es, ethnic minorities) with the potential for all, and the opportunity for some, of 'improving' their life experiences. Social status in contemporary Western European societies is thought to be based largely upon an individual's achievements, and these societies are seen to be fairer than those based on ascribed status (i.e. status derived from birth or as an outcome of family relations). Sport, where the measurement of achievement is relatively objective and transparent, is thought to be a particularly 'open' route for social mobility.

There are many overlaps between the functions of sport as categorized by Stevenson and Nixon, and the functional prerequisites identified by writers within the functionalist perspective more generally. For the most part, functionalists typically focus on the contribution that sport makes to the wider society, particularly in terms of social stability. Not surprisingly, therefore, criticisms similar to those levelled at the functionalist approach more broadly have been made in relation to the literature specifically dealing with the functions of sport. Drawing on Merton's work (**'soft' functionalism**) we can see that functionalists often assume the existence of functional unity. However, sport, given its inherently conflictual character, may create as much disunity as unity. For example, is the unity among Rangers football fans more significant than their conflict with Celtic fans? Are there elements of this relationship that are dysfunctional, serving to divide rather than integrate the community? And can we really believe that the crowd and player **violence** seen in different sports across the world is always a 'harmless' release of tension and thus performs a socio-emotional function (**catharsis**)?

Key Reading

Edwards, H. (1973) *The Sociology of Sport*. Homewood, IL: Dorsey Press.

Stevenson, C.L. and Nixon, J.E. (1972) '*A conceptual scheme of the functions of sport*', Sportwissenschaft. 2, 119–32; repr. in E. Dunning and D. Malcolm (eds) (2003) *Sport Critical Concepts. Vol. 1*. London: Routledge. pp. 134–46.

G

GAELIC ATHLETIC ASSOCIATION (GAA)

Founded in 1884, the GAA is seen as one of the prime examples of sporting resistance to British colonialism (**imperialism**). The Association was the brain child of a teacher, Michael Cusack, ably assisted by the foremost Irish athlete of the period, Maurice Davin. Cusack was specifically concerned with what he viewed as the preservation of traditional Irish sporting and athletic pursuits at a time when the fashion for and popularity of the British sports of cricket, rugby and soccer threatened to destroy native sports. Cusack's call for an athletic and sporting revival of traditional Irish practices was supported by the three most important bodies in Ireland at the time: the Catholic Church, the Parliamentary Home Rule party and the Land League. They were enthusiastic supporters of the GAA as they well understood the threat that British culture posed to Ireland. If the popularity of British sports went unchecked, then indigenous culture would cease to exist. If that happened, argued the GAA's supporters, any moves towards some form of political independence for Ireland would effectively be an empty gesture because Ireland would have ceased to be, culturally at least, distinct from Britain.

After the initial meeting that founded the Association in 1884, the rules and regulations for its major team sports – hurling and Gaelic football – were published only four months later. The GAA grew to become the single biggest sporting movement in Ireland by the beginning of the twentieth century. That position has never been challenged, and despite the success of the Republic of Ireland's international soccer team in the 1990s and the popularity of provincial rugby in the professional age, the GAA has continued to flourish.

Most scholarship in recent years has sought to understand the success, or at least the appeal of, the GAA in terms of its politics. The need for such work was apparent in the 1980s and 1990s, given the political conflict in the north of Ireland. Research into the links between the GAA, **nationalism** and identity produced three major works by Mandle (1987), Sugden and Bairner (1995), and Cronin (1999). It is interesting to note that none of these four scholars were Irish. Indeed, the slow development of sports studies in Ireland, combined with the domination of political history, meant that the study of sport found no advocates within the Irish university system. With the change of the political system in the north of Ireland, and the slow transition to peace, coupled with a move away from strictly political studies of Ireland's past and contemporary situation, the focus for works on the GAA has shifted.

Becoming more numerous in recent years have been studies that have explored the workings of the GAA. As an organization the GAA has been singularly successful in marketing and selling its games for over a century, despite intense competition from other sports, the amateur status of GAA players in a world of professionalism (**amateurism**), and the potential problematic that Gaelic games are an indigenous and not a global sport. Scholars such as Bradley (1999), Darby

(2003) and others have been instrumental in pushing the study of the GAA away from the overemphasis on nationalist studies, and into areas such as the GAA and the diaspora, its links with community and the reasons for the successful spread of the games.

The Association is, to many observers, the biggest and most important mass movement in Ireland. While traditional political parties such as *Fianna Fáil* have been beset by scandal, and the Church has been reeling from the process of secularization and investigations into **child sexual abuse**, the GAA is the one truly national organization that has continued to flourish. The GAA retains amateur status for its players yet has, since the birth of the 'Celtic Tiger' (the rapid economic growth of the Republic of Ireland during the 1990s), embraced a professional attitude with respect to television **broadcasting rights** and corporate **sponsorship**. The combining of the Association with traditional Irish products and companies, namely Guinness and the Bank of Ireland, has assured the GAA a steady flow of income as well as high-profile advertising campaigns. It is the ability to combine an adherence to its traditional values, with an embrace of sporting **modernity** that has allowed the Asociation to retain its pre-eminent place in Irish society.

At the heart of the GAA, however, is the parish club: the very foundation stone that was used in the 1880s to ensure that the Association spread across the country. The parish club ensures that the games remain truly national, enabling the GAA to work on both sides of the border since partition in 1922. Another founding commitment of the Association was to support the Irish language. The GAA continues to do this, and through Irish language broadcasting of games on television (TG4) and radio (*Raidió na Gaeltachta*), the games have achieved a new synergy between sporting popularity and native tongue. Traditional culture, such as music and dance, is also supported by the Association, through its annual *Scór* competition. And in an age of increasing opportunities for women in sport, the GAA can boast

the recent centenary of camogie (women's hurling) and the steady growth of Ladies Gaelic Football since 1984 (**gender**).

As the GAA continues to change and succeed at the local level in a global sporting market, it provides plenty of scope for future researchers and commentators. Recent decisions taken by the GAA to change its rule book and end the traditional ban on members of the security forces from taking part in the life of the Association, and to open Croke Park to 'foreign' games such as soccer and rugby, are key moments in the cultural, social and political life of Ireland. The Association has succeeded as it is a community-based organization that promotes two highly engaging sports. It also reflects the debates that exist in Irish life, and mirrors the changes within the wider society.

Key Reading

Bradley, J. (1999) 'British and Irish sport: the garrison game and the GAA in Scotland', *The Sports Historian*, 19 (1): 81–96.

Cronin, M. (1999) *Sport and Nationalism in Ireland: Gaelic Games and Soccer Since 1884*. Dublin: Four Courts Press.

Darby, P. (2003) 'The next parish over from Galway Bay: Gaelic sport and the Irish diaspora in Boston – 1879–1890', *Irish Historical Studies*, 33 (132): 19–35.

Mandle, W.F. (1987) *The Gaelic Athletic Association and Irish Nationalist Politics, 1884–1924*. London: Christopher Helm.

Sugden, J. and Bairner, A. (1995) *Sport, Sectarianism and Society in a Divided Ireland*. Leicester: Leicester University Press.

Mike Cronin

GAMBLING

The average British adult spends almost £60 per year on gambling. Gambling is the single biggest item of sports-related consumer expenditure constituting 30 per cent of this market segment, and it has grown rapidly in recent years (betting on horse racing rose by 22 per cent, while expenditure on the football pools rose by 13 per cent between 1985 and 1995). Such is the economic significance of gambling that the post-**Hillsborough** reconstruction of English football grounds was partly financed by it, and a reduction in the tax levied on the football pools in particular. In some countries (e.g. the Netherlands), gambling is a relatively minor phenomenon while in others it is perhaps even more central to people's way of life than it is in Britain (e.g., Bali (**deep play**)).

Gambling is predominantly though not exclusively a sport-related activity. The first piece of legislation to address it was the 1665 Gaming Act. Often gambling among the masses occurred in relation to **animal sports**, but its influence can be seen in the first wave of 'sportization' (**sportization and parliamentarization**) in which boxing, cricket and horse racing began to take on the characteristics of **modern sport** forms. For instance, the oldest surviving set of rules for cricket dates back to 1727 and was a set of 'Articles of Agreement' between two noblemen that essentially outlined how the game, and thus the bet, could be won. At this time, gambling was central to the way in which the aristocracy expressed their identity as the social elite; gambling showed wealth which showed social status. To reduce corruption and match/race fixing, aristocrats employed boxers, cricketers and jockeys as retainers, thus ensuring their loyalty.

During the nineteenth century gamblers faced greater social censure. This was a time when the middle classes grew in power both in sport and in society more generally. Less secure of their status than the aristocrats had been, the middle class rejected gambling, partly because they were less wealthy than many aristocrats and thus could not so easily afford to lose money, partly because of scandals over match fixing, and partly on moral and religious grounds (**Puritans**).

The long and rich history of gambling in sport has made it the subject of much historical research (e.g. Vamplew, 1976). Sociologically, gambling has been researched as part of the tradition in **symbolic interactionism** of investigating sports **subcultures**, and horse racing and pool hustling in particular (Polsky, 1969). But gambling continues to be an issue in sport – from match-fixing scandals in baseball, English and Italian football and perhaps most recently international cricket – and the growth of **internet** gambling will do little to abate this trend. The prominence of gambling lies in the peculiar tension between the social significance of sport (**sport, social significance of**) and the economic gains to be made (**commercialization**), and the importance of **risk**, the uncertainty of outcome (**competitive balance**) and the **quest for excitement**. In short, those who seek to control the rewards of gambling ultimately undermine the very features of sport that make it attractive to gamblers and the public more broadly.

Key Reading

Gratton, C. and Taylor, P. (2000) *Economics of Sport and Recreation*. London: Routledge.

Holt, R. (1989) *Sport and the British: A Modern History*. Oxford: Oxford University Press. esp. pp. 179–94.

Polsky, N. (1969) *Hustlers, Beats and Others*. New York: Anchor.

Vamplew, W. (1976) *The Turf: A Social and Economic History of Horse Racing*. London: Allen Lane.

GAY GAMES

(**gender**)

GAZE

(**surveillance**)

GENDER

Refers to the socially constructed differences between women and men, while 'sex' refers to the biological and physical differences between males and females. Gender draws attention to the socially unequal distinction between femininity (characteristic behaviours and **emotions** of females) and **masculinity** (characteristic behaviours and emotions of males). Studies of sports highlight the importance of distinguishing between gender and sex even though the two concepts are used synonymously in everyday language and thought. Not all the differences between females and males are biological but, historically, beliefs about biological differences have served to justify the exclusion or limited **social inclusion** of women (e.g. in sport). Such views reflect an ideology of biological determinism where it is claimed that men are better suited to sports because men alone are inherently strong, aggressive and competitive.

Since the 1970s, research has demonstrated that sports are gendered social contexts in which, compared to girls and women, boys and men are more actively and enthusiastically encouraged to participate. Furthermore, it is demonstrated that more males than females participate in organized competitive sport and that male dominance characterizes the administration and coaching of sport. Sport, it is theorized, operates as a site for the inculcation, perpetuation and celebration of a type of masculine identity based on physical dominance, **aggression** and competitiveness. Associated with such masculine imagery, sport serves to legitimize a perceived natural superiority of men and reinforce the inferiority of females who are defined with reference to relative weakness, passivity and grace – the characteristics of femininity. Therefore, sport has often been described as a 'male preserve'.

Social changes reflecting the condition of women in society influence the status of knowledge about the relationships between and within groups of women and men in sport. Since the 1970s, one consequence of the feminist movement has been increased public awareness about the need for more opportunities for girls and women in sport (**feminism**). Subsequently, participation rates among some females increased. These developments have resulted in ongoing challenges to gender stereotyping, resistance and negotiation of established gender ideology, and the initiation of important legal and political change regarding sex discrimination in sport and society. For example, **Title IX** of the Education Amendments of the Civil Rights Act (1972) in the USA, and the Sex Discrimination Act (1975) in Great Britain were intended to counter state discrimination against women. Such legislation has been used to prevent and remove many barriers to female participation in sport.

Feminist scholars have provided the most sustained attempts at conceptualizing and understanding gender in the sociology of sport. Despite the theoretical and methodological differences between different feminisms, three key themes have driven debates about gender and sport since the 1970s. First, scholars have highlighted that the marginalization of women in sport is a legacy of (British) Victorian images of female frailty, and the dominance of white middle- and upper-class male values of physical skill and strength, mental acumen, gentlemanly conduct and **fair play**.

Second, many scholars stress the significance of the connections between physicality, power and the production of gender. Much has been written about the ways that contemporary sport reinforces a 'culturally idealized' male model of physical superiority and, at the same time, operates to oppress women through the trivialization and objectification of their physicality and sexuality (**body**; **sexualization**). The sexual harassment and vilification of women by male athletes illustrates that the use of **violence**, aggression and force is a defining feature of masculine identity, constructed and legitimated in sporting contexts. Some argue that sport maintains a culture of homophobia in which homosexuality is feared and treated with threatening behaviour (**lesbians**). Furthermore, the image of masculinity, most often represented in sport, is one that can be limiting and restrictive for some men as well as some women. There are fewer opportunities for boys and men to participate, without prejudice, in sports that are not based on strength, power and domination. Researchers have shown that boys and men who perform badly, or who do not participate in sports, experience negative feelings and disappointment.

The third key theme to emerge highlights that both women and men reinforce and challenge the dominant gender ideology in various ways. Eschewing ideas about women and men as homogeneous categories, scholars now recognize and examine difference and diversity in gendered sporting experiences both at the level of the subject, and in terms of institutional politics and practice. Such work is concerned with the relational character of gender and the idea that sport is a 'contested terrain'. This means that at any moment in history and in specific sporting contexts there are competing masculinities and femininities. There are events such as the Gay Games that allow athletes to compete in a relatively unprejudiced environment where they have less fear of derogatory and violent responses to their publicized sexual orientation. Researchers also show that sport is a context in which women can experience independence, feelings of confidence and increased self-esteem from their involvement. Participation in sport can contribute to broadening and alternative definitions of physicality that are not simply based on traditional ideals about femininity and masculinity.

The extent to which sport is oppressive and liberating for women and men is culturally specific and related to the political and economic conditions in which they live their lives. Recent research reflects increasing interest in the relationships between sport, gender, **race** and ethnicity. Such work emphasizes that questions of femininity and masculinity are inseparable from questions of race and ethnicity. Critical examinations of the historical development of sport emphasize that sport was constructed in the image of particular ideals about white masculinity. Analyses of the racial significance of sport illustrate that sporting practices can provide black males with (symbolic) opportunities for resistance to racism through the assertion of manly qualities such as athleticism, aggression and toughness. These writings also illustrate that sport reflects the historically constructed (subordinate) place of black males in (Western) societies. Dominant images of black male athleticism tend to reinforce stereotypes of black men as powerful, aggressive and hypersexual (*Darwin's Athletes*).

Scholars concerned with the relationship between sport, race and femininity increasingly challenge dominant universalistic conceptions of women in sport that, in the past, served to portray white, Western, middle-class, able-bodied, heterosexual women's experiences as representative of all sportswomen. This dominant assumption marginalized or even silenced the sporting triumphs and struggles of minority groups of females, such as those who live outside the West. A central feature of scholarship in this area is the recognition of difference between and within groups of women in relation to ethnicity, religious affiliation (**religion**), social class, sexuality, age and physical (dis)ability (**disability**). Difference is characterized by power relations operating simultaneously at the personal and institutional level. In many ways, sport can be empowering for diverse groups of females including black women, Muslim women, **aborigine** women, lesbians, disabled women and older women. At the same time, these women are incorporated into the wider social networks of power in which they may experience inequality.

Key Reading

Birrell, S. (1988) 'Discourses on the gender/sport relationship: from women in sport to gender relations', *Exercise and Sport Sciences Review*, 16: 459–502.

Connell, R. (1995) *Masculinities*. Berkeley and Los Angeles: University of California Press.

Hargreaves, J.A. (1994) *Sporting Females: Critical Issues in the History and Sociology of Women's Sports*. London: Routledge.

Scraton, S. and Flintoff, A. (2002) 'Sport feminism: the contribution of feminist thought to our understandings of gender and sport', in S. Scraton and A. Flintoff (eds), *Gender and Sport: A Reader*. London: Routledge. pp. 30–46.

Theberge, N. (2002) 'Gender and sport', in J. Coakley and E. Dunning (eds), *Handbook of Sport Studies*. London: Sage. pp. 322–33.

Louise Mansfield

GERONTOLOGY

(**retirement**)

GLADIATORS

Though initially all gladiators were slaves, their participation in the **Roman Games** led them to have an ambiguous status in Roman society. Essentially they were afforded the status of chattel or animals and deprived of any personal dignity. They were beyond the pale of respectable society and regularly compared to male prostitutes. Most died at a young age. However, following the revolt led by the gladiator Spartacus, gladiators were thought to be a security risk, a threat to social stability and therefore a group over which the emperor needed to have influence and control. Some emperors, such as Caligula, employed gladiators as bodyguards, though experiments of using gladiators in real warfare had only limited success. Some gladiators won their freedom through participating in gladiatorial fights and experienced considerable upward social mobility. Many became the subject of female infatuation and

were celebrated for their sexual promiscuity. This led some citizens to seek this 'reduced' social status and become gladiators. Roman spectators preferred 'free fighters' to slaves, presumably because they showed greater enthusiasm; indeed, Caligula himself participated as a gladiator, albeit on a part-time basis. Such was the Emporer Commodos's obvious enjoyment in participating that he was rumoured to be the offspring of his mother's affair with the gladiator Martianus, and not the son of the former emperor, Marcus Aurelius. Subsequently, a complex hierarchy developed within the gladiatorial classes and a guild was formed for the elite. Gladiators were at once the lowest of the low, and key members of Roman society.

Key Reading

Auguet, R. (1994) *Cruelty and Civilization: The Roman Games*. London: Routledge.

Grant, M. (1971) *Gladiators*. Harmondsworth: Penguin.

GLENEAGLES AGREEMENT

The 1977 Commonwealth Statement on Apartheid in Sport (otherwise known as the Gleneagles Agreement, after the place in Scotland where it was signed) stemmed from the African nations' **boycott** of the 1976 Montreal Olympic Games. The Agreement stemmed from the increasing isolation of the New Zealand government for supporting its national rugby union team's continued links with South Africa. Proposed by UK Minister of Sport Dennis Howell, the Gleneagles Agreement was an attempt to broker a more moderate, less critical position than that favoured by the heads of many African nations.

The Agreement stated that Commonwealth nations would, 'vigorously … combat the evil of apartheid by withholding any form of support for, and by taking every practical step to discourage contact or competition by their nationals with sporting organizations, teams or sportsmen from South Africa or from any other country where sports are organized on the basis of race, colour and ethnic origin'. This formal decalaration enabled the 1978 Edmonton Commonwealth Games to proceed without incident. Following New Zealand rugby union's invitation to tour South Africa in 1981, however, a code of conduct was drawn up to strengthen the Gleneagles Agreement. That a series of cricket and rugby union 'rebel tours' took place during the 1980s indicates that the Agreement was only partly successful in isolating South African sport and thus opposing **apartheid**. John Hargreaves (1986), however, is more sceptical, arguing that the Agreement enabled countries like Britain to formally appear to oppose South Africa, and thus cultivate good relations with other African nations, while informally allowing sporting links to continue and thus not alienate the South African authorities.

Key Reading

Archer, R. and Bouillon, A. (1982) *The South Africa Game*. London: Zed Press.
Hargreaves, J. (1986) *Sport, Power and Culture: A Social and Historical Analysis of Popular Sports in Britain*. Oxford: Polity Press.
Jarvie, G. (1985) *Class, Race and Sport in South Africa's Political Economy*. London: Routledge.

GLOBALIZATION

Refers to the process whereby national boundaries become less significant as the interconnectedness between people across the planet intensifies and grows stronger. Increasingly, therefore, our lives are influenced by events that occur many thousands of miles away, involving people whom we may never know or meet. While some have argued that globalization leads time and space to become compressed as technology allows us to travel or experience events many thousands of miles away, in actual fact such technologies merely speed up the movement and communication of humans, leaving time and space untouched. Globalization entails a growth in the sharing of ideas and cultures, an increasing awareness of our common identity as a species inhabiting a single planet, and a resurgence of localism and a strengthening of local identity (hence Roland Robertson's term 'glocalization'). These processes are not new (for instance, the **tournaments** of medieval Europe with international affairs), but they gained increasing momentum during the twentieth century. Neither are the effects of these processes even, in that they currently affect Western nations rather more than they do most parts of Asia and Africa.

Three key features of the globalization process are the emergence of a global economy and a global culture and the establishment of international organizations and movements. In terms of sport these aspects are manifest in the following ways: (1) the development of a global economy of sports performance (e.g. our consumption of events such as the football World Cup) and sports goods (e.g. American firm **Nike** which produces trainers in the Far East, to sell in Europe); (2) a global culture, with the acceptance of certain norms and conventions (e.g. rules and tactical innovations) and the style in which sports are staged and presented (e.g. the spectacularization of events, sometimes referred to as Americanization); and (3) the establishment of international governing bodies of sport (e.g. **FIFA**), global/multinational sports events (e.g. the Olympics, Pan-African games), and itinerant competitions such as Formula 1 Grand Prix and the ATP (Association of Tennis Professionals) tennis tour.

Following Appadurai it has become common to talk of global flows (or 'scapes'), and in particular the movement of people (athletes); technology (sports facilities, golf courses etc.); finance (prize money, endorsements, tournament **sponsorship**); images

119

(the (re-)presentation of sports events via the **media**); and ideologies (particularly nationalist ideologies, (**nationalism; propaganda**)). Following this lead, in one of the key texts on globalization, Maguire (1999) provides case studies of **sport labour migration**, the global sports industry, the media–sport production complex, and the role of sport in (national) identity formation.

Two key debates stem from these empirically observable developments: (1) how can we explain why particular sports become popular in particular social contexts (and why other sports fail to diffuse); and (2) how can we most adequately understand these global processes on a conceptual level?

Implicit in many attempts to explain the global spread of particular sports is the highly problematic concept of **sports space**. Simply stated, this notion suggests that any given society can only 'host' a limited number of sports or leisure activities. In attempts to explain which particular sports fill this space, many have cited the importance of a sport's structural properties (e.g. football is relatively simple and cheap to play, and is fluid, providing high levels of action and excitement). This argument, however, falters when exceptions exist (e.g. why is football not particularly popular in America?). Consequently, others argue that certain sports suit certain 'national characteristics' (e.g. the **violence** of rugby suits the rugged, rural or frontier character of New Zealanders and South Africans; the relative speed of baseball made it more suitable than cricket to the American temperament). However, both these arguments can be criticized for having elements of **essentialism**, and for being supported by evidence that is highly selective.

Houlihan (1994) progresses these arguments by noting that it is important to differentiate between different types of sport diffusion. While the rules and structure of a sport, he notes, may be adopted in a country, the ethos by which the game is played may be changed (e.g. the creolization of cricket in the Caribbean). In other social contexts, the sports themselves may be rejected or modified (as in Ireland with hurling or the US with baseball and American football) but the underlying ethos of how games 'should' be played may be accepted (e.g. the staunch amateur stance of the GAA). Ultimately, however, it is most adequate to consider the diffusion and globalization of sports as a mixture of the intended and unintended outcomes of purposeful action, of those who sought (or didn't seek) to introduce their sports to new people and groups, and those who attempted to resist or accept new sport forms as they were introduced to them. Centrally, the outcome is determined by the balance of power between the respective parties.

In attempting to understand global processes on a conceptual level, a number of competing theories have emerged, most notably modernization theory, imperialism, cultural imperialism and dependency theories (including **world systems theory**) and the figurational sociological approach. Modernization theories are closely linked to **functionalism** (and thus have been criticized for ignoring conflict and exploitation). They stress the homogenizing effects of globalization, with people picking and choosing from global sports culture, and societies coming to adopt the dominant Western model of sports. Theories of cultural imperialism again stress homogenization, but identify the (sometimes forceful) domination or invasion of one culture by another. Here, for instance, Olympism is seen as the product of the colonial dominance of the West and indigenous sports and cultures are marginalized or swept aside (**aborigines**). With America being the world's most powerful nation, Americanization is a term often used to portray a particular variety of cultural imperialism, one which is linked to a highly commercialized brand of sport (**commercialization**). Others, however, deny the pervasiveness of Americanization processes, arguing instead that the globalization of sport reflects the actions and interests of large multinational companies and the dynamics and logic of capitalism (e.g. breaking down nationalism, exploiting the cheaper production opportunities of less-developed economies (**world systems theory**)). These theories do not necessarily stress homogenization, but they have been criticized for their tendency towards economic determinism (**Marxism**).

Finally, there is the theory of 'diminishing contrasts and increasing varieties' forwarded by Maguire (1999) and derived from the **figurational sociology** of Norbert Elias. Maguire claims that this notion enables him to steer a path between fallaciously stressing homogenization, and overemphasizing individual choice and the production of heterogeneity. The notion of 'diminishing contrasts and increasing varieties' is meant to portray the 'double-bind' character of relationships in a global society, where each party (though not necessarily equally) can exert an influence over others. Consequently there is a commingling or interpenetration of cultures, but this two-way interplay is bounded by broader structures of power as the more powerful groups (and power is not seen as derived solely from economic factors) seek to integrate (albeit on their own terms) outsider or less powerful groups.

Two notes of caution need to be raised by way of conclusion. First, much of the work on globalization and sports globalization in particular marginalizes the experiences of women (**gender**). Second, as noted earlier, globalization affects different parts of the globe to different degrees. It is very easy for people in the West, living at the 'sharp end' of globalization processes, to form an exaggerated view of how globalization processes affect the world, and ignore the peripheral influence of these processes for much of the world's population.

Key Reading

Donnelly, P. (1996) 'The local and the global: globalization in the sociology of sport', *Journal of Sport and Social Issues*, 20 (4): 239–57.

Houlihan, B. (1994) 'Homogenization, Americanization, and creolization of sport: varieties of globalization', *Sociology of Sport Journal*, 11 (4): 356–75.

Maguire, J. (1999) *Global Sport: Identities, Societies, Civilizations*. Cambridge: Polity.

GOAL-SETTING

A goal is that which an individual is trying to accomplish, and thus goal-setting is the process of identifying and establishing what an individual is trying to achieve. Goals are common in both sport and life more generally. They are often multiple and, whilst they have the potential to contribute towards being task-focused and to provide a gauge by which progress can be measured, they may also be counterproductive leading to frustration (e.g. if their attainment comes to be seen as impossible). Ironically, while it has been suggested that goal-setting in sport is likely to be particularly productive (because by the nature of sport, goals are likely to be relatively objectively measured), research findings have been contradictory.

Two main theoretical bases have been proposed for how goal-setting can enhance performance. Locke and Latham (1990) argue that goal-setting enhances performance by: (1) directing attention; (2) mobilizing/increasing effort; (3) enhancing persistence; and (4) enabling the development of new learning strategies. Alongside these main attributes of goal-setting, Locke and Latham suggest four 'moderator variables' that impact on goal effectiveness: ability (the difficulty of goals needs to be matched to the ability of the individual); commitment (the level of commitment should match the difficulty of the goals); feedback (which may enhance perceptions of ability and progress and lead to revised goals); and task complexity (strategies need to match the complexity of the task).

Others propose cognitive explanations of goal-setting, suggesting that its effectiveness is related to the effect goals have on psychological states. A distinction is made between outcome (e.g. winning a race) and performance goals (running a specific time) and it is suggested that a greater focus on the more controllable aspects of sport (i.e. one's own performance) is likely to lower **anxiety** and increase **self-confidence**.

In drawing these strands together in the development of goal-setting interventions, Weinberg (1996) proposed 10 characteristics of a well-designed goal-setting programme. Goals should (1) be specific; (2) be challenging but realistic; (3) be both long and short term; (4) embrace both competition and practice; (5) be written down and periodically reviewed; (6) be accompanied by strategies for achieving the goal(s); (7) be related to performance not outcome; (8) relate to both the individual and the team; (9) be supported by coaches, etc.; and (10) be (re-)evaluated from time to time. Goal-setting problems commonly occur when goals are not monitored or readjusted, are not tailored to individuals, are not specific and measurable, and/or are too varied and diffuse.

Key Reading

Burton, D. (1992) 'Winning isn't everything: examining the impact of performance goals on collegiate swimmers' cognitions and performance', *The Sports Psychologist*, 3: 105–32.

Locke, E.A. and Latham, G.P. (1990) *A Theory of Goal Setting and Task Performance*. Englewood Cliffs, NJ: Prentice Hall.

Weinberg, R. (1996) 'Goal setting in sport and exercise', in R.L. Van Raalte and B.W. Brewer (eds), *Exploring Sport and Exercise Psychology*. Washington, DC: American Psychological Association. pp. 3–24.

GROUP DEVELOPMENT

Because of the complexity of the make up of groups (**group dynamics**) they are best understood as evolutionary, constantly in process, and responding to internal and external factors.

Group development is normally understood in one of three ways: as a linear process, as cyclical, or as pendular. The linear perspective suggests that each group passes through a series of stages, only advancing when the issues arising in a particular stage are resolved. The cyclical perspective suggests that groups, like living organisms, undergo birth, growth and then death but that, during the growth stage, the group prepares psychologically for its own death. The pendular perspective suggests that groups do not move in such a progressive manner, but that issues such as differentiation and conflict arise, only to be resolved, and then arise again.

Perhaps the most influential model of group development, however, has been proposed by Tuckman and Jensen. They propose an essentially linear perspective of group development, consisting of five phases:

- *Forming*. The initial phase, in which group members meet, familiarize and compare themselves with each other (e.g. in terms of fitness, technical ability), and seek to determine respective roles.
- *Storming*. A phase of resistance to, and rebellion against, the leadership and control of the group. Additionally in-fighting may occur as individuals settle into particular roles.
- *Norming*. Occurring after the conflict of stage 2 is resolved, norming involves the development of a sense of unity, cooperation and stability as roles become agreed upon and viewed as legitimate in the eyes of others.
- *Performing*. The phase when well-defined roles have been established and the group members collaborate in the pursuit of common goals and problem solving. Groups undergoing this stage are focused and channel energies in ways that benefit the team.
- *Adjourning*. The final phase involves the disbanding of a team, which may occur either as a consequence of planning (e.g. the end of a season) or through unforeseen events (inner group conflict). The former is relatively less traumatic for group members while the latter is more likely to lead to **stress**, **anxiety** and problems of adjustment.

Key Reading

Carron, A.V. and Hausenblas, H.A. (1998) *Group Dynamics in Sport: Theoretical and Practical Issues*. Morgantown: Fitness Information Technology.

Tuckman, B.W. and Jensen, M.A. (1977) 'Stages of small group development revisited', *Group and Organizational Studies*, 2: 419–27.

GROUP DYNAMICS

In contrast to psychological concepts such as **personality** and **motivation**, the focus on group dynamics is predicated on the idea that people alter their behaviour as a consequence of the presence of others. In relation to sport, empirical evidence also seems to suggest that the most successful sports teams are not necessarily those that have the best component parts, but teams which interact and work together best. As these remarks imply, a group is to be distinguished from a simple collectivity of people. Rather, groups and teams commonly exhibit characteristics such as collective identity, personal and task interdependence, and structured patterns of interaction and communication. Most centrally, however, a group or team will share goals, a sense of purpose and a common fate (**goal-setting**).

Sports psychologists argue that there are three foundations to group behaviour: group composition, group environment and group structure. *Group composition* refers to members' personal attributes (though research has provided contradictory evidence for the benefits of homogeneity of socio-economic background, residence, etc. for goal attainment) and skills and abilities (where greater heterogeneity of skills may be more desirable than uniformity).

Size is deemed a particularly important factor of *group environment*. Steiner (1972) suggested that while a larger group has a greater potential productivity, increased size may also lead to a lack of coordination and functioning. Although an optimal level exists, actual productivity either will plateau or may even decline as a result of losses due to faulty group processes. Similarly the Ringelmann Effect suggests that as the number of people in a group increases, there is a proportionate decrease in productivity per person, a phenomenon also termed **social loafing**. Additional aspects of group environment include the level of social support (the exchange of resources intended to enhance the well-being of an individual, e.g. through increasing the feelings of respect or encouragement from team mates), and perceptions of fairness and even-handed treatment.

As aspects of *group structure*, psychologists pay particular attention to group roles, norms and status, as well as the process of **group development** (i.e. the process by which a collection of individuals becomes a coherent group). *Group roles* refer to the required or expected behaviour of different group members which may serve to differentiate them from each other. Roles may be formal (such as that of the coach) or informal (such as the role of 'team joker', or the role a senior player may have in mentoring or advising junior players). Each individual in a group will have a *role perception* (a view of how they think that they should behave in a variety of situations) which they will have learnt through interaction and communication with others. In this regard, the effectiveness of the team is enhanced if there is *role clarity*; that is to say, not only do individuals know what they should be doing but others share this perception and knowledge. Additionally, *role acceptance* (personal satisfaction at fulfilling a role and legitimacy to do so in the eyes of others) enhances a group's performance. Role acceptance depends upon: (1) the opportunity to use specialized skills; (2) feedback and role recognition; (3) perceived significance of the role; and (4) autonomy of practice. Finally, roles should not be so multifaceted or demanding of time, motivation or skills/ability that *role conflict*, or the occupancy of contradictory roles, occurs.

In contrast, *norms* refer to expected behaviour that unites groups. Individuals will experience pressure to conform to group norms and norms may underpin membership of the group as a whole (e.g. initiation rites). Norms may increase the predictability of members' behaviour, increase their sense of the distinctiveness of the group, minimize the potential for individual conflict, and provide prescriptive, proscriptive, permissive and preferential guidelines for the central values of the group. However, norms may underpin differences in status within the group (e.g. deferential practices to senior players and coaches). *Status* may be prescribed formally (e.g. the appointment of a captain) or informally through age, experience, etc. Higher status individuals may have a greater impact on decision making than lower status group members.

Key Reading

Carron, A.V. and Hausenblas, H.A. (1998) *Group Dynamics in Sport: Theoretical and Practical Issues*. Morgantown: Fitness Information Technology.

Klein, M. and Christiansen, G. (1969) 'Group composition, group structure and group effectiveness of basketball teams', in J. Loy and G. Kenyon (eds), *Sport, Culture and Society*. New York: Macmillan. pp. 397–408.

Steiner, I.D. (1972) *Group Processes and Productivity*. New York: Academic.

GUTSMUTHS, JOHANN CHRISTOPH (1759–1839)

Credited with establishing (or at least being the first to lay down in writing) the founding principles of the Turnen movement. Initially a geographer, in 1786 GutsMuths took responsibility for teaching gymnastics at a school in Schnepfenthal, in what is now Germany. It was here that he developed the most complete system of physical education the world had until then seen. The significance of this system can be seen through its influence on subsequent physical educators such as Jahn and Ling.

Two of the texts GutsMuths wrote outlining his educational philosophy are particularly important. The first, *Gymnastik für die Jugend* (1793), was premised on an attack on the Church for its focus on the education of the mind, and neglect of the **body**. He identified three types of physical education – *gymnastics* (further subdivided into eight sub-types), *manual work* and *games* – and further discussed bathing, swimming, reading aloud and exercises to promote presence of mind and the senses. Finally, he provided advice for organizing exercise routines. While Gutsmuths saw such exercises as primarily for boys, in the second edition of the book he added a defence of physical education for girls. It was, however, for his teaching of gymnastics that he became most well known.

In his second main work, *Spielbuch*, GutsMuths focused on games and the nature and importance of play. Play, he argued, was vital for a child's development and games he saw as a microcosm of human life (**Homo Ludens**) in which children are relatively unrestrained by adult supervision. However, GutsMuths warned that too much game playing could exhaust children, leaving them incapable of mental activity. Games, therefore, needed to be controlled and structured through a formal educational model.

Key Reading

McIntosh, P.C., Dixon, J.G., Munrow, A.D. and Willetts, R.F. (1981) *Landmarks in the History of Physical Education*, 3rd edn. London: Routledge and Kegan Paul.

H

HABITUS

The concept of habitus is most closely associated with the work of Pierre Bourdieu (and to a lesser degree with that of Norbert Elias). Habitus refers to the physical embodiment of social relations, or, simply stated, the reason why people from different social groups (classes, sexes, nationalities) perform particular physical acts in different ways, or value particular social practices according to different hierarchies.

Habitus constitutes one of the three central concepts in the work of Bourdieu (see also **capital** and **field**). It is argued that it enables him to overcome the difficulties which stem from the traditional (false) dichotomization of the individual and society (**agency and structure**) because it demonstrates the link between personal action and broader social structures like **class**.

Bourdieu talks of habitus in terms of the predisposition, tendency, propensity or inclination towards particular tastes or desires. While taste refers to a conscious decision about preferences, habitus specifically deals with our un/subconscious leanings towards particular things (e.g. football) and away from others (e.g. polo). The notion of habitus suggests that one's tastes or inclination towards a particular view or understanding of the world are not simply the product of individual choice, but a function of one's position in the social structure. Through **socialization** and learning people come to act and react in ways appropriate to their group. Because the behavioural differences underpinning

habitus are internalized at an early age, dominated classes come to view economic and status differences between groups as unproblematic; that is to say, differences appear to be 'natural', based on individual subjective choices and not the product of social inequality. Consequently, subordinate classes see little reason to challenge the social order; habitus provides a legitimating function. Habitus for Bourdieu is both structured (i.e. determined by our social circumstances) and structuring (i.e. active in reproducing differences in the social status between particular groups).

Bourdieu (1978) uses habitus to understand why different social groups prefer (are predisposed towards) different types of sport and physical activity. It enables us to understand that different social groups will have different perceptions of the costs (economic, cultural, physical) and benefits (**health**, social mobility, symbolic benefits) of participation in particular sports. Bourdieu argues that different social groups expect that sport and physical activity will provide them with different intrinsic and extrinsic outcomes for the body. According to this view, the working and professional classes have opposing relationships to the **body**, viewed as a 'means to an end' and viewed as an 'end in itself' respectively. Hence the working classes favour sports such as boxing (where the body is used as a tool), while higher ranked social groups are more likely to embrace sports such as **aerobics** (where motivation stems from the desire to alter body shape). Different social groups also expect to accrue different 'social' profits (i.e. through the status exclusivity of particular activities, and thus heightened or consolidated prestige for the individual). Thus a person's leaning towards a particular sport stems from their socialization into, and learning of, a particular position in the social order. In turn, sports are part of the lifestyles that distinguish social classes and act as class signifiers (an excellent example of the *structured* and *structuring* nature of habitus-based sports participation). Wacquant's work on boxers (1992) is perhaps the most famous and significant use of Bourdieu's concept of habitus in a sporting context.

However, habitus is also a term used by Elias and advocates of **figurational sociology**. Perhaps more simply than Bourdieu, Elias defines habitus as 'second nature' or embodied social learning. He argues that each person develops an individual habitus which is relatively unique, as well as a series of social habituses related, for instance, to **class**, **gender** or nationality (some see this as preferential to Bourdieu's formulation of habitus which, at times, appears somewhat totalizing, with little scope for human agency). Habitus for Elias is a process, likely to develop relatively rapidly in early life and more slowly later on. While not always put in such explicit terms, the kinds of personality changes identified by Elias in *The Civilizing Process* are essentially changes in human habitus (civilizing process).

Dunning and Louise Mansfield have talked about different gender habituses, and a variant of habitus – 'habitus codes' – is central to Joseph Maguire's work on **globalization** (1999). Maguire focuses on how 'habitus codes' differ between nationalities. Sport, he argues, is one of a range of symbols that reinforce 'we-group' national identities and common belief systems (e.g. about the superiority of one nation over another). These collective 'we-group' fantasies, argues Elias, and subsequently Maguire, are a highly significant layer of habitus. National 'habitus codes' therefore act counter to **globalization** processes, for people attempt to preserve these sources of identity, for example, in the face of the development of a European identity or Americanization.

Above all else, Elias provides a historical or developmental view of habitus, showing how people's bodies, movements, **emotions** and perceptions of the body have changed over time. This is perhaps preferable to Bourdieu's view of habitus, which has been criticized for being largely class-based and static, failing to provide an explanation of how habitus relates to social change. Some, however, have argued that Elias's notion of habitus is too undifferentiated (why do people selectively apply behavioural standards according to different social contexts?) and that it contains some discrepancies in terms of time periods (why, for instance, do civilizing processes take centuries to lead to internalized behavioural norms, and such short periods to breakdown, e.g. in wartime?).

Key Reading

Bourdieu, P. (1978) 'Sport and social class', *Social Science Information*, 17 (6): 819–40.

Laberge, S. and Kay, J. (2002) 'Pierre Bourdieu's sociocultural theory and sport practice', in J. Maguire and K. Young (eds), Theory, Sport & Society. Oxford: Jai. pp. 239–66.

Maguire, J. (1999) *Global Sport: Identities, Societies, Civilizations*. Cambridge: Polity Press.

Mansfield, L. (2002) 'Feminist and figurational sociology: dialogue and potential synthesis', in J. Maguire and K. Young (eds), *Theory, Sport & Society*. Oxford: Jai. pp. 317–33.

Wacquant, L. (1992) 'The social logic of boxing in black Chicago: toward a sociology of pugilism', *Sociology of Sport Journal*, 9 (3): 221–54.

HACKING

The debate over hacking, or the deliberate kicking of opponents' shins as a way of breaking up the scrummage or as a form of tackling, was central to both the bifurcation of the rugby and association forms of football, and the subsequent establishment of a national governing body for rugby, the Rugby Football Union (RFU). The centrality of hacking within rugby was such that participants usually wore iron capped boots, or navvies, specifically for the task. The oldest surviving rules, produced at Rugby School in 1845, contained a number of clauses restricting the use of hacking (e.g. below the knee, to players in the scrummage or with the ball) and the shoes or boots allowed to be worn ('no projecting nails or iron plates').

During a series of meetings in 1863 designed to establish a single definitive set of rules for football, hacking (along with 'running in') became the central sticking point between the advocates of a Rugby-style game and advocates of a game based on the Eton rules. The latter argued that the inclusion of hacking would restrict the game's development, the former that without hacking, football would be deprived of its masculine essence (**masculinity**). The advocates of hacking, headed by the Blackheath club, withdrew rather than compromise and the Football Association (FA) was established in 1864.

During the 1860s clubs such as Blackheath and Richmond curbed the use of hacking in their locally specific codes. Dunning and Sheard attribute the development of the RFU seven years later, in 1871, to three factors: (1) the growing popularity of soccer; (2) the emergence of a variety of different forms of rugby; and (3) the growing view that hacking was a barbarous practice.

Key Reading

Dunning, E. and Sheard, K. (2005) *Barbarians, Gentlemen and Players: A Sociological Study of the Development of Rugby Football, 2nd edn*. London: Routledge.

HALLMARK EVENTS

(**mega-events, staging of**)

HEALTH

The links between physical activity and good health have been endorsed in many official publications in Britain and America. Can we conclude, then, that sport is good for one's health?

Numerous studies indicate that moderate, rhythmic and regular exercise has a beneficial impact on health. A 1996 report from the US Surgeon General concluded that regular physical activity is associated with: (1) lower levels of overall mortality; (2) decreased risk of cardiovascular, and especially coronary, disease; (3) prevention of high blood pressure; (4) decreased risk of colon cancer; (5) reduced risk of certain forms of diabetes; (6) reduced risk of falling in older adults; (7) lower levels of obesity; and (8) improved mental health. The Department of Health in Britain in 2001 listed health benefits similar to those identified in the American report. In 2004, the National Center for Chronic Disease Prevention and Health Promotion in the US reiterated all the health benefits identified in these earlier reports.

At first glance, studies like these might seem to indicate that the health-based arguments in favour of sport and exercise are overwhelming. However, it is important to note that almost all the studies which are cited to support the idea that sport is good for health refer *not* to sport, but to physical activity or exercise. But physical activity and sport are *not* the same thing. Physical activity or exercise might involve walking or cycling to work, dancing, gardening, or walking upstairs instead of taking the lift. None of these are sport. There are important differences between physical activity and exercise, on the one hand, and sport, on the other. Perhaps most importantly, whereas the competitive element is not central to most forms of physical activity, sport, in contrast, is inherently competitive (**sport, definition of**) and is becoming increasingly so. The increased competitiveness of modern sport, together with the increased emphasis on winning, mean that, unlike most people who take part in non-competitive physical activities, those who play sport are, particularly at the higher levels, frequently subject to strong constraints to continue playing while injured, 'for the good of the team', with the associated health risks this behaviour entails (**risk-pain-injury paradox**).

Many sports are also mock battles in which aggression and the use of physical **violence** are central characteristics. Many sports have, in modern societies, become enclaves for the expression of physical violence in the form of violently aggressive 'body contact'; indeed, in the relatively highly pacified societies of the modern West, sport is for many people the only activity in which they are regularly involved in aggressive physical contact with others (**quest for excitement**). In particular, professional sport is a violent and hazardous workplace. One study of English soccer found that the risk of injury to professional footballers is 1000 times greater than the injury risk in other high-risk occupations such as construction and mining.

But risks are not confined to elite sport; health costs are associated with all sports participation, even at the mass level. In assessing the health 'costs' and 'benefits' of sport and exercise, one must take into account the incidence of sports injuries (**pain and injury**). European studies suggest that every sixth unintentional injury is associated with leisure-time physical activity, mainly sports, and that around 50 per cent of people participating in team sports sustain one or more injuries over a season. At one university hospital in the Netherlands, sports injuries comprised about one-fifth of all injuries treated over a seven-year period, making sport the second highest cause of accidental injuries.

Large-scale, national studies of sports injuries are relatively rare, but a team from Sheffield University Medical School estimated that in England and Wales there are 19.3 million new injuries and a further 10.4 million recurrent injuries each year. The Sheffield researchers also estimated the economic costs and benefits of sports and exercise-related injuries to the healthcare system. The health benefits of sport and exercise (e.g.

avoidance of costs associated with the management of chronic illnesses such as those cited at the beginning of this entry) were weighed against the costs of treatment of exercise-related injuries. It was found that, while there were economic benefits associated with exercise for adults aged 45 and over, for younger adults (15–44 years old), the costs avoided by the disease-prevention effects of exercise (under £5 per person per year) were more than offset by the medical costs of treating sports injuries (approximately £30 per person per year). Thus, for every 15–44 year old adult who participates in sport, there is a net cost to the British taxpayer of £25 per year. The authors concluded that there are strong economic arguments in favour of exercise in adults aged 45 and over, but not in younger adults. A Dutch study which produced similar findings noted that this result 'contrasts heavily with statements of people who use the supposed health effect of sport as an economic argument to promote sport'.

The relationship between sport and health is complex. Injury risks vary markedly from one kind of physical activity to another; the highest risks are associated with contact sports, while the activities with the lowest injury risks are non-contact, rhythmic (and largely non-competitive) activities such as 'keep fit', swimming and diving. Moderate and regular physical activity has a beneficial impact on health but as we move from non-competitive activity to competitive sport, and from non-contact to contact sports, the health costs, in the form of injuries, increase. The injury risks associated with elite sport are particularly high. The health-related arguments in favour of regular and moderate physical activity are clear, but they are considerably less persuasive in relation to competitive, and especially contact, sport.

The injury risks associated with competitive sport are increasingly being recognized by public health specialists. Significantly, almost all the examples of physical activity recommended in the US Surgeon General's report are either lifestyle activities – such as washing a car, gardening or dancing – or non-contact, rhythmic exercises – such as water aerobics or walking; all the major competitive sports in the US (baseball, basketball and American Football), with their associated injury risks, are conspicuous by their absence from this list of recommended healthy activities!

Key Reading

Hardman, A.E. and Stensel, D.J. (2003) *Physical Activity and Health*. London: Routledge.

Nichol, J.P., Coleman, P. and Williams, B.T. (1993) *Injuries in Sport and Exercise: Main Report*. London: The Sports Council.

Waddington, I. (2000) *Sport, Health and Drugs: A Critical Sociological Perspective*. London: E. & F.N. Spon.

Ivan Waddington

HEALTH-RELATED EXERCISE

(health-related physical education)

HEALTH-RELATED PHYSICAL EDUCATION (HRPE)

Has been defined as 'the teaching of knowledge, understanding, physical competence and behavioural skills, and the creation of positive attitudes and confidence associated with current and lifelong participation in physical activity' (Harris, 2000: 2). **Health** has long been associated with physical education (PE) and with sport more generally (**cult of athleticism; muscular christianity**) but health promotion, both within PE and within society more generally, has grown in prominence since the 1980s as governments found it increasingly difficult to meet the costs of medical care, e.g. within the National Health Service (**obesity discourse; youth sport participation**).

Health-related exercise (HRE) was identified as a cross–curricular theme in the initial **National Curriculum for Physical Education** and at first there were concerns that it might be marginalized relative to the core areas of activity (athletics, dance, games, gymnastics, swimming, and outdoor and adventurous activities). Subsequent revisions have strengthened the position of HRE within the curriculum, though its delivery remains varied. Three broad approaches to the delivery of HRE in PE have been identified: (1) permeation/integration, in which HRE is delivered across the activity areas; (2) focused/discrete where particular lessons, topics or units are dedicated to HRE; and (3) a multi-method approach that combines the two (Harris, 2005).

Specific strengths and weaknesses have been identified with each approach. An overarching concern, however, is that HRE is often interpreted too narrowly; it may, for instance, be seen as a particular vigorous activity such as cross-country running. Alternatively, HRE may be seen to entail a strong focus on fitness testing, or safety and hygiene issues such as stretching and warming down, and showering. Such narrow interpretations may lead to highly regimented exercise or excessive theory, neither of which is likely to encourage longer-term participation (**exercise behaviour**). For instance, pupils may lose interest if made to do 'hard' exercises, and fitness tests may humiliate and embarrass those most in need of encouragement to participate in HRE. Behind this narrow focus may be an emphasis on the physiological rather than the psychological and social benefits of exercising. Harris argues that HRPE is often more oriented towards 'fitness for sports performance' than 'fitness for healthy lifestyles'. Such an approach seems to stem from the traditional dominance of competitive team sports within PE, and fails to embrace the growing interest in **lifestyle sports**. This kind of teacher philosophy is often nurtured in the sports science courses from which many PE teachers initially graduate. Other critics have noted that HRPE programmes often reinforce gendered practices rather than promoting equity and inclusion (Harris and Penney, 2000).

Though the political emphasis on promoting health through sport has, in many ways, helped to increase the prominence of the PE profession, there appear to be two major threats to the future unison of health and PE. First, such is the centrality of health in the broader public policy agenda that other professional bodies are increasingly competing with PE professionals over ownership. Health education professionals, for instance, claim to offer a broader perspective to physical educators, who may be perceived to be more interested in performance and excellence. Second, PE has consistently failed to engage the interests of significant numbers of pupils, many of whom cite negative experiences of sport and PE in school as a reason for their non-participation in later life. If this were to continue, public policy makers may look elsewhere for the delivery of the health agenda. In response, Fox and Harris (2003) have suggested elements of good practice which may produce more successful HRPE programmes in future. These include: (1) the greater use of individual sports and fitness activities; (2) providing activities popular within adolescent **subcultures**; (3) explaining the rationale for the role and importance of physical activity; (4) encouraging independence and self-management of leisure time; and (5) developing a sense of responsibility among students.

Key Reading

Fox, K. and Harris, J. (2003) 'Promoting physical activity through schools', in J. McKenna and C. Riddoch (eds), *Perspectives on Health Exercise*. Basingstoke: Palgrave Macmillan. pp. 181–201.

Harris, J. (2000) *Health-related Exercise in the National Curriculum. Key Stages 1 to 4.* Champaign, IL: Human Kinetics.

Harris, J. (2005) 'Health-related exercise and physical education', in K. Green and K. Hardman (eds), *Physical Education: Essential Issues*. London: Sage. pp. 78–97.

Harris, J. and Penney, D. (2000) 'Gender issues in health-related exercise', *European Physical Education Review*, 6 (3): 249–73.

HEGEMONY THEORY

At its broadest, hegemony can be used to refer to one group's exercise of power, or dominance, over another (hence, for example, hegemonic masculinity). More narrowly, some neo-Marxists have drawn on the work of Antonio Gramsci and used hegemony theory to describe the cultural and ideological domination of the proletariat by the bourgeoisie through the control of the content of cultural forms in order to engineer consensus.

More particularly within sport, hegemony theorists (e.g. John Hargreaves and Richard Gruneau) argue that these theoretical ideas have enabled them to go beyond the economic determinism characteristic of other, traditional forms of **Marxism**. While continuing to focus on economic relations as the central aspect of their analysis, hegemony theorists who have looked at sport argue that social relations cannot simply be reduced to economic relations. In keeping with this approach, their focus is not exclusively on economic processes, but on structures of power, struggle, control and resistance more generally, and on sport's role in these processes. Work on cricket in the Caribbean under the British Empire is a good example of this (***Beyond a Boundary***; **imperialism**). The initial phase of military domination was subsequently replaced by more subtle forms of persuasion of the legitimacy of colonial rule. Sport, specifically cricket, inculcated ideas that facilitated British rule (being honest, playing by the rules of the game, not questioning authority, etc. (**fair play**)).

Sport, then, is seen not as neutral ground, but as a powerful tool in shaping ideas, values and practices. It is seen as a 'contested' area of social life, which is characterized by struggles between different and opposing groups for the control of sport. But for the neo-Marxist, the exercise of control is not regarded as something that the powerful simply impose upon the less powerful. Rather, control is exercised more subtly, and in such a way that it has the appearance of being based on consent. In this context, the concept of 'hegemony' is used to describe a situation in which a dominant class or group has been able successfully to disseminate its own view of the world to subordinate groups, thus legitimating its own dominant position so that its rule is accepted by those groups.

Consequently, hegemony is never absolute, for while a dominant group is by definition more powerful than a subordinate group, its dominance is never total or absolute; indeed the dominant group have to work very hard to maintain the appearance of the legitimacy of their authority. It is this which gives sport, as well as other areas of social life, the characteristics of a 'contested terrain'. Thus the non-absolute character of hegemony means that subordinate groups are able (to a greater or lesser degree) to resist the actions of the dominant group.

For hegemony theorists, sport is part of culture and culture is no less an important feature of social life than economic or political processes. Culture is made by people through their conscious choices and actions, but as it is an inherited set of traditions and norms (formed by the choices of people in the past), it also forms and shapes the choices and actions which can be made. The balance of freedom and constraint means that sports, and indeed other cultural forms, have a degree of autonomy which in turn explains why we can empirically observe sport's own contradictions, crises and 'emancipatory potentialities'. John Hargreaves (1986) provides a number of examples: the **commercialization** of sport leads to spectacularization that may alienate audiences (**play and display**); ruthless competition leads to 'win-at-all-costs' attitudes that may lead to dull sporting encounters and 'unsporting' practices (**violence**, cheating, **drug** use), and thus blur the ideological messages that sport is virtuous, making sport a less effective instrument of social control. Further, sporting

events can be sites of disorder; **football hooliganism**, for instance, is seen as a form of resistance to a process of **embourgeoisement** of the game.

The main criticism of hegemony theory is that, counter to its claims, it does not fully solve the problems of economic determinism. Hargreaves (1986), for instance, describes hegemony as, 'an attempt to give a sense of primacy of the economic relations in social being [i.e. culture in general and sport in particular], without reducing the latter to the former'. Such phrases indicate that economic factors, if only 'in the last instance', remain more significant than any others.

Key Reading

Dunning, E. (1999) *Sport Matters: Sociological Studies of Sport, Violence and Civilization*. London: Routledge. esp. Ch. 5.

Gruneau, R. (1983) *Class, Sports and Social Development*. Amherst, MA: University of Massachusetts Press.

Hargreaves, J. (1986) *Sport, Power and Culture: A Social and Historical Analysis of Popular Sports in Britain*. Oxford: Polity Press.

Stoddart, B. (1988) 'Cricket and colonialism in the English-speaking Caribbean to 1914: towards a cultural analysis', in J.A. Mangan, (ed.), *Pleasure, Profit, Proselytism: British Culture and Sport at Home and Abroad 1700–1914*. London: Frank Cass. pp. 258–72.

HETEROSEXUAL MATRIX

(queer theory)

HEYSEL

In May 1985 the Heysel Stadium in Brussels hosted football's European Cup Final between Liverpool of England and Juventus of Italy.

Opposing fans had been allocated places on an un-segregated terrace and when Liverpool fans tried to chase their Juventus counterparts off the terrace, a wall collapsed. There were 39 killed and 454 injured, partly due to the collapse of the wall, but largely due to the crush caused by fleeing fans. The disaster is thought to have been caused by a combination of processes: (1) belligerent groups of rival fans; (2) poor policing stemming from poor communication between relevant parties; (3) poor ticketing arrangements; (4) complacent money-oriented officials; and (5) the poor repair of the stadium. The effect of Heysel was to raise **football hooliganism** more firmly to the status of an international political issue. In the immediate aftermath, English clubs were banned from European club competitions until it could be demonstrated that hooliganism was under control. The ban lasted five years, with Liverpool serving an extra two.

The reaction of the **media** to Heysel was extreme, but typical of responses to hooliganism at that time (see Young, 1985). Fans were portrayed as animals and there were calls for harsh punishments to be imposed on offenders (**moral panic**). The initial governmental response to Heysel followed this lead, and increasingly punitive policing measures were introduced, including: (1) restrictions on the consumption of alcohol; (2) increased use of CCTV (closed-circuit television); (3) the introduction of 'exclusion orders' banning those convicted of hooligan-related crimes from attending football matches; (4) the use of undercover police operations to infiltrate hooligan groups; and (5) pressure on the football authorities to introduce a football supporters' membership scheme (abandoned post-**Hillsborough**). While these measures had varying degrees of success (for instance, many argue that these measures did not stop hooliganism but merely displaced violent incidents away from the stadiums onto the transport networks), Heysel nevertheless represents a watershed in the history of contemporary football hooliganism in that it became increasingly apparent that unless the football authorities took a more active role in tackling hooliganism, the continued existence of professional football in England was in doubt. To this end, clubs set about attracting a more family-oriented, wealthier, fan base (**embourgeoisement**), which became a key feature, and a central source of debate, in English football throughout the 1990s (see also **independent supporters' associations**).

Key Reading

Chisari, F. (2004) '"The cursed cup": Italian responses to the 1985 Heysel disaster', *Soccer and Society*, 5 (2): 201–18.
Dunning, E., Murphy, P. and Williams, J. (1988) *The Roots of Football Hooliganism: An Historical and Sociological Study*. London: Routledge and Kegan Paul.
Young, K. (1985) '"The killing field": themes in mass media responses to the Heysel stadium riot', *International Review for the Sociology of Sport*, 21 (2/3): 253–66.

HIGHLAND GAMES

In his pioneering research on the Highland Games, Grant Jarvie (1991) identifies four stages or phases of development, and highlights how the development of this sporting tradition parallels broader social structural transformations in Scotland. In the first phase, from around the eleventh century to 1750, many of the folk origins of the sporting practices and cultural artefacts of what we now understand to constitute the Highland Games were evident (e.g. wearing tartan, highland dancing, the playing of pipes, running races, and strength events). These, moreover, stemmed from the specific set of social relations in existence at the time, in particular the feudal/patriarchal relations that characterized the Highland clan, and the emergence of the distinction between Highlanders and Lowlanders. In the second stage, between about 1740 and 1850, the British state sought to destroy the Highland way of life, and consequently suppressed its game forms and cultural practices (which in part led to a significant level of migration from the Highlands to North America). In the third phase, from about 1840 to 1920 the Highlands became a sporting playground for the Victorian social elite and the Highland Games became 'Balmoralized' (i.e. linked with Balmoral, royalty, and loyalty to the crown) and popularized. Highland dress, made illegal under the 1747 Act of Proscription, experienced a renaissance, there was growing interest in the sports and cultural artefacts of the Highlands, and English aristocrats became increasingly interested in the purchase of Highland land. Since 1920, in the final phase of development, the Highland Games have increasingly become organized in the style of other modern sport forms: codified, regulated, bureaucratized (*From Ritual to Record*) and commercialized (commercialization). The links made to a romanticized harmonious Highland cultural identity are a significant aspect of the Games' appeal, as are the kitsch symbols of the Highlands which characterize consumer culture.

The study of the Highland Games is important for it raises interesting questions about Scotland's dependency on England, and the uneven development of the British Isles. It also casts doubts on previous claims that tartan is an **invented tradition**. Interestingly it becomes clear, and somewhat ironic, that the development of this important icon of Scottish national identity (**nationalism**) has been heavily dependent upon English elites and the English-dominated British state.

Key Reading

Jarvie, G. (1991) *Highland Games: The Making of the Myth*. Edinburgh: Edinburgh University Press.

HILLSBOROUGH

On 15 April 1989, 95 Liverpool Football Club supporters died while attending an FA Cup semi-final at Sheffield Wednesday's Hillsborough Stadium (a ninety-sixth supporter later died in hospital). Almost all the dead were crushed due to the number and the speed with which supporters were attempting to gain access to the stand. Hillsborough was and still is the largest football stadium disaster to occur in England and it led to the landmark Taylor Report. Hillsborough and the Taylor Report are of central significance to students of sports studies because of the subsequent impact that they had on perceptions of **football hooliganism**, press coverage of football (**moral panic**), **stadium** renovation and relocation, and the relationship between football clubs and supporters more generally (**independent supporters' associations**).

The Taylor Report found that South Yorkshire Constabulary, which was in charge of policing at Hillsborough, had made a number of errors of judgement largely due to the stereotyping of football fans and an exaggerated view of the danger posed by hooligans. For instance, police denied clearly distressed supporters access onto the pitch (which would have alleviated the crushing), through the fear of a pitch invasion or that rival supporters might be attacked. In the aftermath of the Taylor Report, the obligations of the police shifted further away from a crowd-control function, and moved more towards the importance of ensuring supporter safety. Following Taylor, the then Conservative government dropped its proposed football supporter membership scheme which had, until that point, been a central plank of its anti-hooligan strategy (**Heysel**).

Many were shocked by the initial press coverage of the Hillsborough disaster, which largely blamed hooligans for the deaths. Taylor demonstrated this to be erroneous but some newspapers, in particular the *Sun*, had so offended Liverpudlians that a virtual boycott of the paper took place in the city. It subsequently became clear that football supporters, if mobilized, represented a significant consumer market which businesses neglected at their peril. Football supporters were never to be portrayed as animals or sub-human again, and their financial power became increasingly recognized and influential over the running of the game (**supporters direct**).

However, the key policy change invoked by the Taylor Report was that leading English and Scottish football clubs were forced to convert their grounds such that spectators could no longer stand to watch matches. The cost of the development of all-seater stadiums was partly met by government subsidy through the Football Trust (funded by taxation of the football pools (**gambling**)), but for most clubs this formed a relatively small percentage of their total costs. Some clubs entered ground-sharing agreements and others sold their valuable inner city sites to finance the building of new stadiums, often out of town. Most, however, sought to increase revenue by raising ticket prices (though Taylor had clearly stated that this should not be done). This movement towards improved facilities and the higher costs of attendance led many to argue that football spectatorship was increasingly following an American sports spectator model, characterized by wealthier, more middle-**class** supporters, and more family groups in attendance (**embourgeoisement**). Though not caused by hooliganism, the irony is that Hillsborough led to what many fan groups perceive to be greater levels of fan regulation and a more pacified and sanitized spectatorship experience.

Key Reading

Giulianotti, R. (1999) *Football: A Sociology of the Global Game*. Cambridge: Polity.

King, A. (1998) *The End of the Terraces: The Transformation of English Football in the 1990s*. Leicester: Leicester University Press.

Scraton, P. (2004) 'Death on the terraces: the contexts and injustices of the 1989 Hillsborough disaster', *Soccer and Society*, 5 (2): 183–200.

Taylor, P. Lord Justice (1990) *Inquiry into the Hillsborough Stadium Disaster: Final Report*. London: HMSO.

HOMO LUDENS

First published in 1938, *Homo Ludens* is German historian Johan Huizinga's (1872–1945) pioneering text on play. Huizinga starts his text by arguing that social decline has led to a situation where the term *Homo Sapiens* (man of wisdom and reason) should perhaps be replaced by *Homo Faber* (man the maker) as a descriptor of the human species. Noting, however, that other animals are also makers, Huizinga argues that the term *Homo Ludens* (man the player) might be a more valid term.

Huizinga (1949) defines play as 'an activity which proceeds within certain limits of time and space ... according to rules freely accepted, and outside the sphere of necessity or material utility'. Play engenders certain **emotion**s such as enthusiasm, it may be sacred or festive, and can be completely serious (**deep play**). But pure play, Huizinga tells us, 'is one of the main bases of civilization', because through play we learn. To argue this point Huizinga has chapters on the relationship between play and law, play and war, play and philosophy, etc. Thus all culture, Huizinga argues, arises in play. Through play, 'society expresses its interpretation of life and the world'. Huizinga concludes that civilization 'does not come *from* play like a babe detaching itself from the womb: it arises *in* and *as* play and never leaves it'. Huizinga's contribution to the study of sport is to have alerted the world to the idea that play (and thus leisure, sport, etc.) is a cultural rather than biological phenomenon, to be studied historically rather than scientifically. The study of play, therefore, is just as revealing as the study of work and many early analysts of sport justified their academic interest and research in sport on the foundations that Huizinga laid.

Key Reading

Huizinga, J. (1949) *Homo Ludens: A Study of the Play Element in Culture*. London: Routledge and Kegan Paul.

HOMOPHOBIA

(lesbians)

HYPERREAL

Jean Baudrillard uses the term hyperreal to describe contemporary Western culture. Resulting from the development of modern communications technologies, television has become all-dominant in structuring people's understanding of the social world, to the extent that Baudrillard claims that what is 'real' is not that which we personally experience, but the information that we see/receive via the **media**, and television in particular. While Baudrillard is often heavily criticized (lampooned even) for arguing that the Gulf War of the early 1990s did not occur, what he really meant in this regard was that the mediated coverage of the war presented something (almost) unrecognizable from the 'real' thing. Baudrillard argues that the current extent of media manipulation means that the media do not report reality, they construct it. Moreover, we as viewers lose our ability to differentiate between what is real and what is media presentation.

Unusually for a leading social theorist, Baudrillard provides sporting examples of his broader theoretical points. He used the example of the French public's enthusiasm for a 1978 Football World Cup qualifying match and their virtual neglect of the extradition of a German lawyer on the same day, as evidence of the seduction of the masses in contemporary society. He also criticized the media for their coverage of the **Heysel** Stadium disaster which was cynical in its glorification of **violence**, thereby providing 'fodder for TV audiences'. Lastly, Baudrillard argued that in future, football matches might be played in empty **stadiums**, with artificial images of spectators and spectator noise, as people increasingly choose to experience events on television at home, with direct experience becoming an irrelevance (**post-fandom**).

David Andrews, Geneviève Rail and Steve Redhead have perhaps been the sociologists of sport who have most embraced Baudrillard's ideas about hyperreality. Reflecting on NBC's coverage of the 1996 Atlanta Olympics, Andrews (1998) argues that, in its search for audiences, NBC manufactured a simulated model of Olympic reality (e.g. through selecting particular events to cover, and constructing particular 'stories' or narratives designed to appeal to what were perceived to be feminine interests), thus producing an event that was a reformulated and bastadized version of the 'real'; that is to say, a hyperreal presentation.

Even many of Baudrillard's supporters argue that his work is often abstract, lacking in empirical support, and aimed as much to provoke as to understand. However, his concept of the hyperreal is useful in directing our attention to the dominance of the media in the modern world, including its use, and production, of sport, and prompting us to reconsider what we mean by reality (**epistemology and ontology**).

Key Reading

Andrews, D. (1998) 'Feminizing Olympic reality: preliminary dispatches from Baudrillard's Atlanta', *International Review for the Sociology of Sport*, 33 (1): 5–18.

Andrews, D. (2000) 'Posting up: French post-structuralism and the critical analysis of contemporary sporting culture', in J. Coakley and E. Dunning (eds), *Handbook of Sports Studies*. London: Sage. pp. 106–37.

Giulianotti, R. (2004) 'The fate of hyperreality: Jean Baudrillard and the sociology of sport', in R. Guilianotti (ed.), *Sport and Modern Social Theorists*. London: Palgrave Macmillan. pp. 225–29.

IDEALISM

The school of thought which emphasizes the role of ideas in the creation of the social world; that is to say, which emphasizes that social 'reality' exists mainly through people's interpretations (and hence interpretivism is sometimes used as a synonym). People are constantly engaged in a process of interpretation of the social world and idealists argue that it is this which the social researcher should seek to understand. People are deemed to have the scope to exercise a significant degree of 'free will' (**agency and structure**). Meanings are not static or universal, but are particular (to a time and place) and constantly in process. For this reason it is not possible accurately to predict people's behaviour on the basis of the external environment, and we must reject the possibility of replicating our research findings at a later date (**reliability and validity**). Rather, idealists/ interpretivists do not strive to distance themselves from their subject matter, but accept that commitment, engagement and immersion are not only inevitable, but *desirable*. For this reason, research must be qualitative (**quantitative and qualitative research**) and is most likely to draw on the methods of **ethnography** or in-depth and loosely structured **interviews**. Donnelly and Young's classic work on **socialization** into rock climbing and rugby **subcultures** (1988), and Gallmeier's work on the staging of **emotions** in ice hockey (1987), are excellent examples of this kind of idealist/ interpretivist approach.

Critics of this position argue that it leads research findings to be characterized by high levels of subjectivity (**objectivity and subjectivity**). Critics also point to evidence which suggests that people in similar social conditions have a propensity to make similar choices and act in similar ways (e.g. people in a particular social **class** tend to participate and be interested in the same sports), suggesting that this undermines the argument about the significance of free will in determining social behaviour, relative to broader social structural influences.

Key Reading

Donnelly, P. and Young, K. (1988) 'The construction and confirmation of identity in sport subcultures', *Sociology of Sport Journal*, 5 (3): 223–40.

Gallmeier, C. (1987) 'Putting on the game face: the staging of emotions in professional hockey', *Sociology of Sport Journal*, 4 (4): 347–62.

IMAGERY

The creation or recreation of an experience through the use of imagination. While sometimes referred to as visualization or mental rehearsal, imagery may involve any or all of the senses (visual; auditory; kinesthetic, or tactile sense; and olfactory, or smell) as well as evoking moods and **emotions**. Imagery has been used to improve **concentration** and **self-confidence**, for skill and strategy acquisition and practice, for the management of emotion (e.g. **anxiety**) and **pain and injury**, and for solving problems with performance. Not surprisingly, therefore, research has indicated that between 90 and 99 per cent of Olympic athletes use imagery. Moreover, such anecdotal reports have been augmented by case study and experimentation, affirming the positive relationship between imagery and performance.

Imagery might involve surroundings, positive and negative aspects of competition and practise (hitting good and bad shots), the sights, sounds, smells and sensations of competition and practice, and may be either internal or external (i.e. the athlete viewing from their own perspective or from the perspective of the viewer). Effective imagery largely stems from practice but vividness (detail, perhaps derived from using a variety of senses) and controllability (making the imagery do what you want it to do) are the characteristics of good imagery.

There are a number of competing explanations for why imagery works. *Psychoneuromuscular theory* suggests that imagery leads the brain to emit signals to the muscles which, while less intense than the signals produced in the actual activity, prepare the way or train the body for performance. While evidence suggests that muscles *are* activiated via imagery, the problem with psychoneuromuscular theory is that it is not clear how muscle activation subsequently improves performance. *Symbolic learning theory* suggests that we learn though practice and becoming familiar with an activity, and that imagery helps create a mental blueprint for skills and performance. As support for this approach, research has indicated that imagery is more effective for primarily cognitive rather than motoric tasks. A third theory, the *psychological skills hypothesis*, argues that imagery improves performance by helping to improve psychological skills, such as reducing anxiety, and enhancing concentration. In reality it is likely that imagery works in a variety of ways.

In addition to these broad approaches, two further theories should be mentioned. The *bioinformational*, or *information processing theory*, argues that it is important to recognize that an image consists of two main types of propositions (or statements): stimulus propositions, which describe the scenario (e.g. the competition); and response propositions which describe how the athlete responds to that stimulus (e.g. scoring a goal). *Triple code theory*, as the name suggests, highlights three key components of imagery: (1) the image (the internal representation of the outside world); (2) the somatic response (the psychophysiological response stemming from the image); and (3) the meaning of the image (thus suggesting that no two people have the same imagery experience).

Key Reading

Hall, C.R. (1998) 'Imagery use by athletes: development of the sport imagery questionnaire', *International Journal of Sport Psychology*, 29: 73–89.

Munroe, K., Giacobbi, P., Hall, C. and Weinberg, R. (2000) 'The 4 W's of imagery use: where, when, why and what', *Sport Psychologist*, 14: 119–37.

Murphy, S. and Jowdy, D. (1992) 'Imagery and mental practice', in T. Horn (ed.), *Advances in Sport Psychology*. Champaign, IL: Human Kinetics.

IMAGINED COMMUNITIES

The title of Benedict Anderson's book (1983) on the origins and spread of **nationalism**. The nation, according to Anderson, is an imagined political community that is perceived to be both limited and sovereign. Communities are distinguished in terms of the 'style' in which they are imagined (e.g. whether we see ourselves as Londoners, English, European, etc.). Nations are imagined, Anderson claims, because they are so vast that members will never know, meet or even hear of their fellow members, 'yet in the minds of each lives the image of their communion'. Nations are limited because no nation's boundaries are finite, and they are sovereign as a result of the particular time of their genesis and thus dominant modes of thinking (of enlightenment and revolution) that influenced their development. Nations are also communities because a 'deep feeling' of comradeship exists between members, regardless of the inequalities that may in fact exist within each nation.

Anderson's ideas are influential in the study of nationalism and sport and have been cited, for example, by both Guiliannotti (1999) and Maguire (1999). On the one hand, Anderson usefully alerts us to the historical specificity, and the social construction, of nations. This, in turn, helps us to avoid the common but problematic conceptualization of nations as permanent and/or 'natural'. On the other hand, Anderson perhaps overstates the 'imagined' status of nations, which do, also, have many real and tangible manifestations, such as armed forces, governments and taxation systems.

Key Reading

Anderson, B. (1983) *Imagined Communities: Reflections on the Origin and Spread of Nationalism*. London: Verso.
Guiliannotti, R. (1999) *Football: A Sociology of the Global Game*. Cambridge: Polity Press.
Maguire, J. (1999) *Global Sport: Identities, Societies, Civilizations*. Cambridge: Polity Press.

IMPERIALISM

Though recently scholars have started to refer to American cultural imperialism (**globalization**), sports-related discussions of imperialism usually refer to the British Empire. Indeed, many have argued that the British use of sport in the Empire not only made colonization easier, but made post-colonial relations more harmonious. This is not, however, to deny that imperialism has often entailed the violent domination of indigenous groups, and their subsequent subordination.

Sport played a major role in the British Empire from the mid-nineteenth century onwards. Many believed that British sports were central in cultivating the moral and physical strength of individuals and in generating the work ethic and sense of self-sacrifice to the greater good demanded of would-be colonizers (**muscular christianity**). Thus the personnel sent out into the Empire were civil servants, missionaries, educators and military officers recruited from the public schools. Sport further served as entertainment for the colonists living somewhat isolated lives in sometimes hostile territories and provided a vehicle for their social interaction and the generation of solidarity. While cricket was the imperial sport par excellence, snooker, polo and badminton owe their development to sporting innovations in the imperial colonies.

Subsequently, sports came to be used as a way of building cultural bridges within and between the various territories of the Empire. Sports were used to foster friendly relations with local rulers and populations, and for the transmission of ideas about 'civilization' and the British way of life. In turn, the indigenous population could use sports to demonstrate their 'loyalty' to the Crown and their 'fitness' for collaboration with their imperial masters. Through sport the colonized were given an avenue for assimilating into the British way of life. At its extreme, this led wealthy Indian princes to send their sons to finish their education at English public schools and universities. Ultimately, a number of Indian princes – the cricketer Ranjitsinhji foremost amongst them – became honorary English gentlemen, and spokesmen for the value/ legitimacy of the Empire and the role of sport within it. Back in India, the behaviour of the ruling classes in England was closely replicated, with clear status and playing distinctions drawn between amateurs and professionals (**amateurism**).

Settlers in Australasia, Canada and South Africa could also demonstrate their loyalty to the Crown through playing sport, but for these white colonial elites (and for those in the Caribbean especially) playing sport (i.e.

cricket) enabled them to demonstrate that their residence in a hot climate had not led, as many had feared, to their physical decline (**environmental determinism**). At the same time, it should be noted that during this process of imperial expansion many indigenous sports forms were suppressed, and while some survived (e.g. Kabbadi in India), the cultural heritage of many indigenous groups was effectively destroyed (**aborigines**).

The development of international sporting fixtures allowed for the expression of a peculiar mix of commitment to Empire and national independence (**nationalism**). This was seen through the British Empire Games (subsequently the Commonwealth Games) first held in 1930. The other key sporting events were team games such as cricket and rugby, described by Holt (1989: 226) as the 'real stuff of Dominion sport' (the professionalization of football made it morally suspect, less quintessentially English, which led to its decline in the public schools and throughout the formal empire more generally (**formal and informal Empire**)).

It should, however, be remembered that within something as vast as the British Empire, reaction to and the reception for British sports and culture varied enormously. For instance, while Indian princes such as Ranjitsinhji were selected to play cricket for England, black West Indian cricketers were continually subordinated under a white West Indian captain (who often could not justify his place in terms of playing ability alone). In Ireland, British sports were rejected altogether and the formation of the **Gaelic Athletic Association** was strongly influenced by anti-British sentiment. The meanings attached to particular sports also varied from place to place. Boer interest in rugby union was in part a challenge to the British stereotyping of Boers as weak. The coexistence of three football codes in Australia (Aussie Rules, rugby union and league) derives from the nationalistic and **class** identities of different groups in the country. The 1932/3 **bodyline** cricket series tested the balance of power between the two nations.

The ironic nature of sport in the Empire is most clearly demonstrated by CLR James, in **Beyond a Boundary**. This autobiographical work us underpinned by the paradox he experienced, being brought up under the economically and politically oppressive and exploitative system of colonial rule, but through schooling and cricket instilled with a strong sense of commitment to peculiarly English ethical and behavioural codes. Despite such contradictions, sport has continued to play a significant role in the deconstruction of the British Empire, with the continuation of the Commonwealth Games a sign of solidarity, and the fierce sporting rivalries in cricket and rugby in particular, an indication of the desire of the former colonies in the late twentieth century to demonstrate the altered balance of power between nation states.

Key Reading

Holt, R. (1989) *Sport and the British: A Modern History*. Oxford: Oxford University Press.

Maguire, J. (1993) 'Globalisation, sport and national identities: "the empires strike back"?', *Society and Leisure*, 16 (2): 293–322.

Malcolm, D. (2001) '"It's not cricket": colonial legacies and contemporary inequalities', *Journal of Historical Sociology*, 14 (3): 253–75.

Stoddart, B. and Sandiford, K. (eds) (1998) *The Imperial Game: Cricket, Culture and Society*. Manchester: Manchester University Press.

INDEPENDENT SUPPORTERS' ASSOCIATION (ISA)

Since 1985, football **fans** in Britain have become increasingly well organized and politically-oriented. Formed in response to the **Heysel** Stadium disaster, in which 39 Juventus (Italy) fans died during **football hooliganism**-related incidents, the Football Supporters' Association (FSA) sought to coordinate and mobilize the views and interests of 'normal', or at least non-hooligan, fans. Their explicit goal was to thwart the proposed introduction of identity cards (or compulsory membership schemes) for football supporters, though in part they also strived to present an alternative – they argued a more representative – view of football supporters.

Once the government decided not to enforce the implementation of membership schemes FSA membership dwindled, but from this movement a range of smaller, local, associations developed that are now generally referred to under the umbrella term of ISAs. ISAs focus on local agendas, and as the 1990s progressed, such groups increasingly shifted their focus to issues such as the changes to supporter cultures imposed post-**Hillsborough** (e.g. relocation of **stadiums**, the restriction of certain styles of support), ticket pricing and the **commercialization** of the game, and broader **social inclusion** policies encompassing **anti-racism** and access for supporters with disabilities (**disability**). The most notable success of ISAs is perhaps the Independent Manchester United Supporters' Association's (IMUSA) campaign against BSkyB's attempted purchase of Manchester United (**vertical integration**), though in 2005 IMUSA was unable to prevent American tycoon Malcolm Glazer from buying a controlling interest in the club. Through the formation of **supporters direct**, football fan democracy in Britain has moved to a new level.

Nash (2001) has argued that relatively few fans become involved in ISAs (meetings are attended by between 1 and 4 per cent of average home gates), and that they tend to be dominated by an 'active minority'. Both this active minority, and ISA membership at large, is predominantly male and middle class. Consequently, ISAs have been accused of being as unrepresentative of fans as the hooligan groups whose dominance within public perceptions of football they sought to replace. Despite this, King (2003) argues that ISAs tend to have charismatic leaders who have credibility with masculine fans (including hooligans) and that these new supporter cultures should not be seen in simple middle/working-class terms, but as part of the new identities and new solidarities being formed as a consequence of Europeanization, and **globalization** more generally. Significantly, the ISA movement, while most developed in England, is becoming increasingly visible on mainland Europe.

Key Reading

Brown, A. (1998) '"United we stand": some problems with fan democracy', in A. Brown (ed.), *Fanatics: Power, Identity and Fandom in Football*. London: Routledge. pp. 50–67.

King, A. (2003) *The European Ritual: Football in the New Europe*. Aldershot: Ashgate.

Nash, R. (2001) 'English football fan groups in the 1990s: class, representation and fan power', *Soccer and Society*, 2 (1): 39–58.

INITIAL TEACHER EDUCATION (ITE)

Sometimes also referred to as Initial Teacher Training, or ITT, and of particular importance because it is during this phase of a teacher's career that many of the habits and beliefs about teaching physical education are developed. Consequently, ITE has been critiqued on a range of issues and has often been highlighted as a significant area in which to initiate policy change.

Perhaps the most notable work on ITE has been conducted by Anne Flintoff (1993) who has argued that it is responsible for the highly gendered character of PE in schools (**gender**). ITE tends to reinforce rather than challenge trainee teachers' stereotypical views of gender. Many students, for instance, leave ITE having only taught same-sex groups and it is thus of little surprise that such traditions are perpetuated, and that PE thus remains the most gender-segregated subject area in the school curriculum.

Others have expanded this critique of ITE to embrace other equal opportunity issues. McDonald and Hayes (2003) argue that while the Teacher Training Agency requires that multiculturalism and racial equality issues are addressed in ITE programmes (**race**), few institutions offer more than a 'tokenistic approach'. Similar comments have been made regarding the teaching of pupils with **special educational needs**.

In recent years ITE has developed to embrace the teaching of **examinations in physical education**. Teachers are also being educated in the provision of sports leadership awards, which are increasingly being taught in schools. Despite these changes, critics of ITE are still concerned that it often perpetuates particular pedagogical styles (**pedagogy**), especially instilling (or reinforcing) a 'skills-based' approach to teaching physical education rather than a 'teaching games for understanding' approach. Trainee teachers of PE are likely to have developed an interest in sport through personal sporting success and thus in performing sporting skills. What worked for them as pupils may not, however, be the most appropriate vehicle through which to generate interest amongst the less skilled. Similarly, trainee teachers are likely to experience only limited exposure to dance during ITE.

Finally, others have suggested that too little primary school ITE is devoted to PE and that this contributes to the relatively poor provision of PE in primary schools.

Key Reading

Flintoff, A. (1993) 'Gender, physical education and initial teacher education', in J. Evans (ed.), *Equality, Education and Physical Education*. London: Falmer. pp. 184–204.

McDonald, I. and Hayes, S. (2003) '"Race", racism and education: racial stereotypes in physical education and school sport', in S. Hayes and G. Stidder (eds), *Equity and Inclusion in Physical Education and Sport: Contemporary Issues for Teachers, Trainees and Practitioners*. London: Routledge. pp. 153–68.

Stidder, G. and Hayes, S. (2002) 'A survey of physical education trainees' experiences on school placements in the south-east of England (1997–2001)', *British Journal of Teaching Physical Education*, 33 (1): 43–8.

INTERNATIONAL RELATIONS

(boycotts; nationalism; propaganda)

INTERNET, THE

Also referred to as the World Wide Web, the Internet is often argued to be a significant factor contributing to the **globalization** of the contemporary world. The Internet enables a more rapid and more widespread flow of information than ever before. While clearly 'dominated by powerful corporate interests (companies like News Corporation, which owns BSkyB, have invested heavily in Internet companies), the Internet offers a somewhat more democratic form of communication than the **media** traditionally have and, in particular, this has meant that information can be exchanged far more freely across national boundaries, thus undermining/circumventing attempts at government control.

In relation to sport the initial, and to date main, impact of the Internet has been to increase the quantity of sports-related information available to the public. Live audio and visual feeds of sporting events can be broadcast via the Internet (**broadcasting rights**). Premiership football clubs retain the rights to broadcast delayed coverage of their games on their own websites. Unlike most television providers, a broadcast over the Internet is not limited by national boundaries, and thus this medium has a potentially global impact. Centrally, therefore, the Internet provides consumers with more choice (**consumer culture**). Indeed, such is the social significance of sport (**sport, social significance of**) that it has become one of the more important commodities (**commodification**) in the commercial expansion of the Internet. In the future, the Internet rather than television may become the main platform for the delivery of sports events. The ownership of Internet rights, therefore, may become more important than the ownership of television broadcasting rights.

However, the Internet also offers the possibility of more varied and more interactive forms of sports broadcasting. Boyle and Haynes (2000), for instance, discuss the Internet broadcast of the 1997–8 'Whitbread Around The World Yacht Race' as an example of the opportunities available. A multimedia experience, involving, audio and visual material, weather reports, email contact with crew members, etc., allowed the 'viewer' to become more immersed in the race, 'provided a more enriched narrative of events', and therefore allowed for a greater level of emotional attachment on the part of the 'viewer'. In a similar vein, the Internet seems to have increased the opportunities for sports-related **gambling**. Internet coverage of sport, therefore, may lead to a sporting experience that is more tailored to individual desires, and to a more intimate experience for viewers.

Key Reading

Boyle, R. and Haynes, R. (2000) *Power Play: Sport, the Media and Popular Culture.* Harlow: Longman.

INTERPRETIVISM

(**idealism**)

INTERVIEWS

Perhaps the most widely used research method in sports studies, interviews are particularly useful where: (1) the population being researched is relatively small (and therefore a large-scale survey isn't warranted); (2) the subject of the research is complex, focusing more on subjective issues (such as why people did things or how they felt about doing them) than objective data (questions about 'how many', 'how much' or 'when' (**objectivity and subjectivity**)); or (3) where researchers feel that they cannot

accurately predict responses, or do not fully comprehend the social phenomenon being investigated (e.g. Smith and Sparkes's research on rugby players who suffer severe spinal cord injuries (2002)).

Interviews vary according to the extent to which they are structured. Highly structured interviews may effectively be personally administered **questionnaires**. At the other extreme are so-called 'unstructured' interviews (though no interview can be entirely unstructured) in which researchers have only very general ideas about the information they wish to examine. Most commonly, researchers describe their interviews as semi-structured to indicate the existence of a standard set of questions/areas of investigation (those things that the interviewer decides are important), allied to a flexible approach and a willingness to explore those areas that the respondent sees as important. In addition to this there are group interviews, often termed **focus groups**. All interviewers must decide whether to tape-record interviews (very accurate but requires time-consuming transcription, and may be affected by technical problems) or take written notes during the interview (ensures a record is kept, but is more intrusive and thus may distract the interviewee and/or break the 'flow' of interviewer–interviewee interaction).

Good interviewers establish a rapport and trust between themselves and the interviewee and project an aura of being knowledgeable about, and empathetic to, the interviewee's world or experiences. To this end, the interviewer should ensure that the time and location of the interview are convenient for the interviewee and that his/her dress is suitable (e.g. children may find an interviewer wearing a suit and tie overly formal and representative of authority and will therefore be less forthcoming with information. Alternatively, the Chief Executive of Manchester United may consider a researcher in jeans and trainers 'unbusinesslike' and lacking seriousness). Jargon, complicated wording and leading questions (e.g. 'I suppose you were very unhappy when you were dropped from the team?') should be avoided. Good interviewers pay attention to both the flow of the interview, and the pauses required for interviewee reflection and thought. Interviewers must avoid being judgemental and imposing their own views on the interviewee, and should avoid questions that require simple 'yes–no' answers. They should use probing questions for clarification ('so are you saying that ...?') and elaboration ('can you give me an example?', 'how did you feel?'). The interviewee should find the experience of being interviewed satisfying and should see the research as worthwhile.

Advantages of interviewing include the opportunity to obtain more detailed, in-depth information, to probe more sensitive areas (e.g. about emotions experienced during instances of **pain and injury**), and to use body language etc. to sense what the respondent really means/feels. Interviews may allow for the respondent as much as the researcher to establish the research agenda. The time and cost of administering interviews, and the greater complexity required in data analysis, are sometimes viewed as weaknesses of the interview method. In addition, there is the possibility that the rapport and trust between the interviewer and interviewee are poor – leading to no useful data being obtained – that interviewers bias the interviewees into providing certain answers (interviewees give the answers they *think* the interviewer wants to hear), or that interviewees become too dominant and lead the interview into unfruitful areas. It should be remembered that interviews, like all social interaction, essentially involve a balance of power between the parties involved and getting this balance 'right' is important for both gaining useful data, and not exploiting the respondent (**ethics**; **research methods**)

Key Reading

Gratton, C. and Jones, I. (2004) *Research Methods for Sports Studies*. London: Routledge. esp. Ch. 9.

Smith, B. and Sparkes, A. (2002) 'Men, sport, spinal cord injury and the construction of coherence: narrative practice and action', *Qualitative Research*, 2 (2): 143–71.

INVENTED TRADITIONS

The notion of invented traditions is most closely associated with the Marxist historian Eric Hobsbawm (**Marxism**). Hobsbawm argues that many of today's traditions are, paradoxically, of relatively recent origin, sometimes deliberately constructed (e.g. the **Webb Ellis myth** of the creation of rugby), sometimes emerging in a less directly traceable way (e.g. the ritual of singing 'Abide with me' at the English FA Cup Final). Invented traditions, Hobsbawm argues, can be state-led or popular movements, but all are essentially processes of formalization and ritualization, characterized by reference to the past. They may inculcate certain values and norms, but their sense of permanency, and the continuity with the past that they (appear to) provide, are seen in contrast to **modernity** where change and innovation are more regular. Hence invented traditions enable social cohesion and identity at times of considerable social change. Their believed longevity provides much of the basis for their legitimacy.

Importantly for Hobsbawm (1983), 'the last three decades of the nineteenth century mark a decisive transformation in the spread of old, the invention of new, and the institutionalization of most sports on a national or even international scale'. Football in England, rugby in Wales and Gaelic football in Ireland 'provided new expressions of **nationalism** through the choice or invention of nationally specific sports' (**Gaelic Athletic Association; Doubleday myth** in relation to baseball.). International contests underlined the unity of nations and empires (**imperialism**); **amateurism** cemented **class** identities.

For students of sport, Hobsbawm's ideas are largely of interest to those researching national identity and the **globalization** of sport. Maguire (1994), in particular, has drawn links between invented traditions, English sport, and Roland Robertson's notion of 'wilful nostalgia', which appeared very prominently in media discourse in the early 1990s. In addition to this, Jarvie (1991) has shown, in his study of the **Highland Games**, that not all traditions developed in the late nineteenth century can be described as 'invented', for at times the traditions may have grown out of, or were a rebirth of, existing cultural forms.

Key Reading

Hobsbawm, E. and Ranger, T. (eds) (1983) *The Invention of Tradition*. Cambridge: Cambridge University Press.

Jarvie, G. (1991) *Highland Games: The Making of the Myth*. Edinburgh: Edinburgh University Press.

Maguire, J. (1994) 'Sport, identity politics and globalization: diminishing contrasts and increasing varieties', *Sociology of Sport Journal*, 11 (4): 398–427.

INVERTED-U HYPOTHESIS

(anxiety)

INVOLVEMENT AND DETACHMENT

Characteristic of his attempt to overcome the dichotomies that have traditionally been problematic in sociology, Elias's concept of involvement and detachment was an attempt to draw together the strengths of approaches that emphasized the conflicting concepts of **objectivity and subjectivity**.

Elias argued that one can historically trace the movement from more involved (or subjective) forms of understanding (e.g. worship of the sun) towards more detached (or objective) forms of understanding (e.g. the sun as a burning ball of gases). He therefore conceptualized the problem as *relational* – a matter of degrees of involvement and detachment – and *processual* – developing over time.

Consequently, Elias urged researchers not to seek absolute truths, merely 'more adequate' levels of understanding. Moreover, as humans can never be wholly 'detached' from their object of study (i.e. the social world), total objectivity was an unrealistic aim. On the other hand, he noted that higher levels of involvement have, historically, restricted advances in human understanding. Thus he recommended that researchers embark on a 'detour via detachment' in their research. What the metaphor of a 'detour' means is that sociologists start, like others, with specific interests to defend and an emotionally involved position, but that the sociologist should seek to control these values. Undertaking a detour *via* detachment entails – assuming one does not get lost along the way – *returning* to a more involved position. Elias spoke about the importance of a phase of 'secondary re-involvement' when, after the research process has been completed, researchers return to a politically informed position in the hope that, armed with new and more adequate knowledge, they can more successfully evoke the desired social change.

Hargreaves (1994) and Horne and Jary (1987) have been critical of Elias's notion of involvement and detachment, arguing that it essentially constitutes an 'objective' or value-neutral stance (which is thought to be unobtainable). This, however, has been vigorously rejected as a misrepresentation of Elias. Dunning has also sought to provide practical guidance for achieving such a detour (1992).

Key Reading

Colwell, S. (1999) 'Feminisms and figurational sociology; contributions to understandings of sports, physical education and sex/gender', *European Journal of Physical Education*, 5 (3): 219–40.

Dunning, E. (1992) 'Figurational sociology and the sociology of sport: some concluding remarks', in E. Dunning and C. Rojek (eds), *Sport and Leisure in the Civilizing Process*. London: Macmillan. pp. 221–84.

Hargreaves, J.A. (1992) 'Sex, gender and the body in sport and leisure: has there been a civilising process?', in E. Dunning and C. Rojek (eds), *Sport and Leisure in the Civilizing Process*. London: Macmillan. pp. 161–82.

Horne, J. and Jary, D. (1987) 'The figurational sociology of sport and leisure of Elias and Dunning: an exposition and critique', in J. Horne, D. Jary and A. Tomlinson (eds), *Sport, Leisure and Social Relations*. London: Routledge and Kegan Paul. pp. 86–112.

IOC (INTERNATIONAL OLYMPIC COMMITTEE)

Arose out of the efforts of Baron Pierre de Coubertin, a French aristocrat, who initially raised the idea of re-establishing the Olympic tradition in a speech at the Sorbonne in 1892. De Coubertin's explicit vision was the reinvention of the **Ancient Olympic Games;** however, in reality the model of the Olympics that he had a considerable role in developing was more closely based on the sporting ethos of **muscular christianity** and the **cult of athleticism** which pervaded English public schools in the late nineteenth century. Moreover, the IOC is marked by the specific context in which it was established; that is, at the height of **nationalism**, at a time when aristocratic male dominance was the norm (**class**; **gender**), and at a time when European elite classes saw themselves as having a distinct role in proselytizing and educating the people of a rapidly expanding world. Unsurprisingly, the IOC was a staunch defender of **amateurism** and was a key institution in the international diffusion of this essentially English ideology.

The IOC remains the leading body within the broader Olympic movement. It is a body of approximately 90 members, invited from the near 200 national Olympic committees (NOCs). The IOC remains predominantly male and heavily Eurocentric, with some European nations having two IOC members, and many Third World nations having none. The IOC is distinct from other international governing bodies (IGBs) of sport in that through the Olympic Charter a clear and explicit ideology is expressed, e.g. of contributing to world peace. Unlike other IGBs (**FIFA**) the IOC is therefore interested in more than just organizing sports events. The IOC has sought to spread its ideological message through the establishment of Olympic academies that organize conferences and workshops providing 'Olympic-led' education, and through sport-related aid under the Olympic solidarity programme (e.g. building facilities, scholarships for athlete coaching and administrator training). Consequently, opinion is highly divided between those who staunchly defend the movement's contribution to international affairs (Lucas, 1992), and those who cite the hypocrisy, self-perpetuating and self-aggrandizing interests of IOC members, and the undemocratic structure of the IOC (Simson and Jennings, 1992). Similarly, while some recognize the IOC's leading role in challenging the use of **drugs** in sport, others have argued that the IOC has been complicit in covering up potential drugs scandals at Olympic Games.

One of the central problems for the IOC is that political groups find the Olympic Games a particularly attractive site for conducting international relations, with **boycotts** and **propaganda** being the two most common forms of action. The modern Olympics are global in scope and, despite original intentions, essentially organized according to a nationalistic ethos. Consequently, many debates have arisen over the recognition of NOCs and hence who represents particular nation-states (e.g. when Germany was split into East and West following the Second World War, and when the communist revolution in China led the former rulers to set up government in Taiwan). High levels of **media** exposure (see also **globalization**) make it a relatively cheap and easy way to spread propaganda to a potentially huge audience (e.g. the killing of Israeli hostages at the 1972 Munich Olympics). Finally, the Olympics are ambiguous in that the ideology expressed in the Olympic Charter gives nations a rationale for nationalistic intervention (e.g. the American-led boycott of the Moscow Games) while the IOC's sporting mission can at other times enable it to claim to be above politics (and hence reluctant to support, say, the boycott of South Africa due to its **apartheid** policies).

The IOC is vulnerable to such interests for a number of reasons. First, NOCs are increasingly reliant on governments (e.g. for financial aid) and have largely followed their government's lead (e.g. over boycotts). Second, the IOC's commitment to Olympic universalism has forced it to compromise its stance of NOC independence from states. Stemming from the Cold War policies of Eastern bloc countries, increasingly, NOC members are state nominees rather than being selected by, and representative of, the IOC. Third, again stemming from its ethos of global inclusion within the movement, the IOC has increasingly become unrepresentative of its broader constituency, leading to pressures (e.g. from Africa nations) for it to become less Eurocentric. Fourth, the IOC is dependent on cities (and to some extent governments) to stage the Summer and Winter Games (**city, the**). As Olympic Games have grown ever larger, so the pool of cities capable of hosting the games has shrunk. However, such are the benefits of hosting such **mega-events** that bidding competitions have been tarnished by claims of bribery and corruption. Finally, in an attempt to free itself from an over-reliance on cities and governments, the IOC has embraced **commercialization** processes, forcing it to increasingly recognize the requests of sponsors (**TOP**) and the media.

In contrast to the polar opposite positions cited earlier (a force for good or hypocritical and corrupt), commentators such as Houlihan (1994) have argued that the IOC has taken a pragmatic approach, adapting to function as part of the international political system, continuing to stage the most significant world sporting event, and at the same time expanding its reach to be 'the global reference point for sporting organisations'.

Key Reading

Bale, J. (ed.) (2004) *Post-Olympism?: Questioning Sport in the Twenty-First Century*. Oxford: Berg.

Houlihan, B. (1994) *Sport and International Politics*. London: Harvester Wheatsheaf. esp. Ch. 5.

Lucas, J. (1992) *The Future of the Olympic Games*. Champaign, IL: Human Kinetics.

Simson, V. and Jennings, A. (1992) *The Lords of the Rings*. London: Simon and Schuster.

Young, D.C. (2004) *A Brief History of the Olympics Games*. Oxford: Blackwell.

J

JAHN, JOHANN FRIEDRICH LUDWIG CRISTOPH (1779–1852)

Built on the existing principles of gymnastics and physical education formulated by **GutsMuths**, allied them to a strong doctrine of German **nationalism**, and is credited with creating and popularizing the **Turnen** movement. Jahn was not a very successful scholar, and consequently entered the Prussian Army to fight against Napoleon at the beginning of the nineteenth century. Following defeat, Jahn resented the subsequent French occupation of Prussia and in 1810 he published *Deutsches Volkstum* ('The German Way of Life'), which was a rigorous defence of all things German. This brought Jahn considerable fame at a time when a divided German people (Germany unified as a state in 1870, relatively late in European terms) were beginning to shake off their sense of cultural inferiority.

In 1811 Jahn opened his first Turnplatz (open air gymnasium). His political objective was the strengthening of Germany's youth in order to develop an independent and unified nation. Unlike GutsMuths his physical education was for all – boys and girls, and without **class** distinctions. Jahn's system placed greater emphasis on games and weapon training than had GutsMuths's, though his biggest technical innovation was the introduction of parallel and horizontal bars. Physical education provided mental as well as physical benefits as demonstrated by the Turnen movement motto, 'Frisch, frei, fröhlich, fromm' (alert, free, cheerful, devout).

Crucially, however, Jahn stressed a meritocratic and democratic ethos, with distinctions based on physical skill rather than class or age. This, and his outspoken criticisms of the Prussian state, led him to create some powerful enemies. In 1819 the police forbade him to reopen the Hasenheide Turnenplatz after the usual winter interval. Turnen was banned in a number of states and Jahn was later imprisoned, accused of complicity in the murder of his child, and of heading a subversive movement. He was released only in 1840 when the King of Prussia died.

Key Reading

McIntosh, P.C., Dixon, J.G., Munrow, A.D. and Willetts, R.F. (1981) *Landmarks in the History of Physical Education*, 3rd edn. London: Routledge and Kegan Paul.

JORDAN, MICHAEL (1963–)

Having achieved national fame playing college basketball with the University of North Carolina (**athletic scholarships**), Michael Jordan's professional career coincided with three key social developments: (1) the rise of **Nike** and its decision to sign and heavily promote a small number of 'signature athletes'; (2) the appointment of David Stern as NBA commissioner and the game's transformed ('disneyfied') image; and (3) the emergence of sports broadcaster ESPN, which enabled increased exposure of the game.

Jordan signed for the failing Chicago Bulls in 1984 and in 1991 led them to the first of three consecutive NBA Championships. Once described as 'the most recognized American figure on the planet', Jordan is estimated to have had a $13 billion impact on the US economy.

Social research on Jordan has examined **media** representations of him, his **commódification**, and the significance (or otherwise) of his blackness/**race**. Many have argued that the portrayal of Jordan through the media served to promote notions of equality of opportunity in American society and demonstrate the possibilities of social mobility for those who appropriately applied themselves (i.e. worked hard). These ideas had particular resonance, for during this period the US experienced the 'Reaganite' shift towards neo-liberal economics and 'New right' conservatism, ideologies which emphasized that quality-of-life issues were the responsibility of the individual rather than the state. Nike's 'Be Like Mike' campaign encouraged America's youth to be aspirational and suggested that they, like Jordan, could reap the rewards.

Similarly, analysts have examined the importance of 'Jordan' as a commodity sign, and the rewards corporations have reaped from their association with it/him. Even Jordan's retirement from basketball in 1993 became a marketing opportunity for Nike, the company portraying it as a kind of purification rite, with the star wanting to escape from the rabid **commercialization** of the sport. This, however, didn't stop Jordan, when he later came out of retirement, swapping his traditional number 23 shirt for number 45, with all the additional merchandising revenue this inevitably entailed.

Final, though Jordan appeared to want to avoid the issue of race (his apolitical stance perhaps stemming from a reluctance to endanger his commercial earnings), allegedly stating that he wanted to be seen as 'neither black nor white', sociologist David Andrews (1996b) identified four distinct aspects of Jordan's racial signification (**signifier and signified**). These are: (1) Jordan's conformity to traditional racial stereotypes of physicality; (2) the consistent underplaying of Jordan's 'blackness' in an attempt to create an 'all-American' image and thus appeal particularly to basketball's largely white audience (and correlatively the notion that blackness was 'other' to being truly American); (3) the increasing emphasis that media commentaries placed on Jordan's blackness as his image became tarnished by allegations of **gambling** debts, and the perception of his selfishness and overly protective stance towards his commercial rights; and (4) the broader debate about the moral laxity of black America (epitomized by younger, black basketball stars), which seemed to be evoked as a consequence of Jordan's deteriorating image. This group, Andrews argues, were ultimately castigated for *not* 'Being like Mike'.

Key Reading

Andrews, D. (ed.) (1996a), 'Deconstructing Michael Jordan: reconstructing postindustrial America', *Sociology of Sport Journal* Special Issue, 13 (4).

Andrews, D. (1996b), 'The fact(s) of Michael Jordan's blackness: excavating a floating racial signifier', *Sociology of Sport Journal*, 13 (4): 125–58.

Smart, B. (2005) *The Sports Star: Modern Sport and the Cultural Economy of Sporting Celebrity*. London: Sage.

K

KOURNIKOVA, ANNA (1981–)

Rose to public prominence when, at the age of 15, she reached the fourth round of the 1996 US Open and then, a year later, played in a women's semi-final at Wimbledon. Though she rose as high as eighth in the tennis world singles rankings in 2000, her on-court career was essentially one of unfulfilled promise. Social scientists of sport, however, have noted that the experiences of Kournikova are revealing of the construction of **celebrity**, trends in the **commercialization** of sport, and **gender** relations.

Despite her unfulfilled promise as a player, Kournikova has been described as 'the world's most photographed/downloaded/internet searched woman' (**Internet, the**). Kournikova's **media** coverage has largely focused on her sexuality (**sexualization**). Kournikova has actively exploited this to obtain lucrative **sponsorship** and product endorsement deals. Indeed, it has been estimated that in 1999, while her on-court earnings amounted to £467,000, income from sponsors such as adidas, Yonex (a tennis equipment manufacturer), Berlei (an underwear manufacturer), and miscellaneous income from calendar and magazine shoots amounted to £7 million. Even though sports-related companies in particular were to quietly distance themselves from Kournikova once injury and poor form impaired her tennis performance, Smart (2005) has noted that she provides an example of attributed celebrity status, as opposed to achievement-based celebrity status.

Kournikova's celebrity status has been augmented by commercialization processes in sport. During her career the marketing of tennis (and indeed other sports) has increasingly centred on the eroticized bodies of leading celebrities. As one of the few, unambiguously 'female-appropriate' sports, sponsors have been attracted to tennis for its ability to fuse fashion, sportswear, glamour and sex. Moreover, the WTA (Women's Tennis Association) and tournament organizers financially rewarded Kournikova for her aesthetic appeal by ranking her highly on their 'commitment list' (which meant that regardless of performance, by merely turning up to a number of stipulated tournaments she was entitled to a $100,000 end-of-year bonus).

Finally, sociologists have argued that Kournikova provides a neat case study encapsulating trends in the media's presentation of female athletes. Harris and Clayton (2002) found that for a given period (June/July 2000) Kournikova featured in one-third of all English tabloid press stories related to female sport. While to some extent Kournikova is therefore an exception to the more general 'invisibility' of female athletes (approximately just 5 per cent of newspaper sports coverage features female sport), qualitative analysis reveals how coverage of her (and female athletes more generally): (1) places greater importance on physical appearance than on competitive success; (2) de-emphasizes athletic ability and trivializes the achievements of female athletes through the use of non-task relevant commentary; and (3) eroticizes the bodies of female athletes. Consequently, Kournikova's media coverage creates and recreates 'hegemonic femininity' (that is, dominant notions of female physicality/frailty and modes of behaviour such as notions of compulsory heterosexuality (**lesbians**). Via polarization and contrast, these ideological representations of femininity construct and maintain hegemonic **masculinity**, and hence Harris and Clayton conclude that Kournikova's '"visiblity" in the sports media is as damaging to women's sport as (women's) total exclusion'.

Key Reading

Harris, J. and Clayton, B. (2002) 'Femininity, masculinity, physicality and the English tabloid press: the case of Anna Kournikova', *International Review for the Sociology of Sport*, 37 (3/4): 397–413.

Smart, B. (2005) *The Sport Star: Modern Sport and the Cultural Economy of Sporting Celebrity*. London: Sage.

L

LEADERSHIP

Leadership is multidimensional. In sport, leaders make decisions, motivate, give feedback, direct the group and establish interpersonal relations. Leaders are distinct from managers in that, in addition to organizing and providing day-to-day structure, they are more concerned with achieving the goals of the organization. Leaders may be appointed or they may emerge from a group.

Early research on leadership was largely guided by *trait theories*, or the notion that leaders were born with particular **personality** profiles like intelligence, confidence, etc., which could be translated into various contexts. This approach, however, is now largely discredited, as a diverse, rather than a specific and limited, set of traits has been identified as contributing to successful leadership styles at one time or another and in various settings.

The *behavioural approach* suggests that leadership skills can be learnt and, moreover, that there are two central characteristics of leadership behaviour: consideration structures (e.g. friendship, trust, respect, etc.) and initiating structures (task-oriented behaviours like organization, establishment of procedures and rules, etc.). Studies of leadership in sport have suggested that successful leaders provide technical instruction, clear feedback, and encouragement, focusing more on the positive than the negative.

More recently, *interactional theories* of leadership have become more popular, predicated on the notions that: (1) no set of characteristics can ensure successful leadership; (2) different leadership styles are effective in different situations; and (3) leaders can change their leadership styles over time. Significant in advancing this trend has been Chelladurai's **multidimensional model of sports leadership**.

Key Reading

Chelladurai P. (1993) 'Leadership', in R.N. Singer, M. Murphey, and L.K. Tennant (eds), *Handbook of Research in Sport Psychology*. New York: Macmillan. pp. 647–71.

LEARNED HELPLESSNESS

(**explanatory style**)

LEICESTER SCHOOL

(**figurational sociology; football hooliganism**)

LESBIANS

Coach to prospective athlete and her parents: 'I don't allow lesbians on my team, so you can be reassured about the moral climate in our programme.'

Athletic Director checking the 'credentials' of a prospective woman coach: 'Can you tell me about any "lifestyle issues" I should be aware of with this candidate?'

Heterosexual athlete to lesbian team mate: 'The rest of the team wants you to keep your being gay to yourself. We don't want the team to get a bad image.'

Coach to player: 'You know it would be a good idea if you would take care to dress more femininely and let your hair grow longer.'

Parent of a high school athlete to college coach during a recruiting visit: 'Do you have lesbians on your team?'

Interactions like the ones above illustrate what happens in sport when discrimination and prejudice against lesbians or women perceived to be lesbians guide policy and practice. Unfortunately, despite the expansion of lesbian and gay civil rights in the larger culture, heterosexism and homophobia in sport continue to be huge problems.

Historically, sport has served a primary **socialization** function for boys and men where hegemonic values of heterosexual **masculinity** are taught and reinforced. This is particularly so for team sports such as American football, rugby, baseball, ice hockey, lacrosse and basketball. Boys and men who cannot 'measure up' to the heterosexual masculine standards of their more athletic peers are denigrated as 'sissies' or 'faggots'.

The participation of women in sport as serious athletes threatens the exclusivity of sport (**male preserve**) and challenges the idea that athleticism and competitiveness are essential components of male identity. As long as sport serves this socialization function for boys and men, all women and gay men will be trespassers in sport. The lesbian label is a social control mechanism that marks the boundaries of acceptable feminine behaviour for women. Young girls and women who are called 'dyke', 'lezzie' or 'gay' learn that their appearance or athleticism falls outside social norms for women and that they are challenging male privilege in sport. As long as lesbian identity is stigmatized, the lesbian label is

used to warn women and girls that their behaviour or appearance puts their acceptance as 'normal' women at risk. The assumption that women's sport is dominated by lesbians generalizes this stigma to denigrate all women's sports, particularly sports that are not perceived to be feminine. In this way homophobia (the fear of lesbians, in this case) serves to perpetuate heterosexism and sexism in sport.

Since the beginning of the 1980s women in sport have achieved greater equality of opportunity (**feminism; gender**). Legislation and changing gender norms have enabled greater opportunities and acceptance for athletic women. This acceptance, however, is contingent on the athlete's ability to project a heterosexual image. Fans, parents and athletes themselves are still most comfortable with women athletes who, and women's sports that, project a heterosexual, even heterosexy, image (**sexualization**). Lesbian athletes and coaches, in contrast, remain largely invisible. In this climate, lesbians in sport who are open about their identities are perceived as a threat, not only to other women in sport, but also to the image of women's sport itself. The stigma of lesbian identity and the threat of discrimination silence lesbians and reinforce the fears and prejudices of heterosexual coaches, athletes and parents.

In this atmosphere, lesbian-baiting, negative recruiting and blatant discrimination against lesbians or women perceived to be lesbians continue to be shameful parts of women's sport. Coaches lose their jobs, athletes are dismissed from teams, individual teams or entire sports are stigmatized and heterosexual athletes and coaches fear association with lesbians (Griffin, 1998; Krane and Barber, 2005).

Despite this hostile climate, lesbians have always been a part of women's sports. Earlier generations of lesbian athletes, coaches and sport administrators led the fight for equality for all women in sport. Current generations of lesbians in sport continue to distinguish themselves even as they hide their sexuality. That they are able to accomplish as much as they do from the constraints of the closet and under the threat of discrimination makes their achievements all the more impressive.

Between 1997 and 2007 a number of high-profile lesbian athletes publicly identified themselves. For example, Sheryl Swoopes (professional basketball), Rosie Jones and Patty Sheehan (professional golf), and Amelie Mauresmo, Martina Navratilova and Billie Jean King (professional tennis) have all publicly identified themselves as lesbians. More collegiate and high school athletes and coaches are also publicly coming out. Though there are many more lesbians in sport who remain hidden, the courage and visibility of these women help to dispel the negative myths and stereotypes associated with lesbian athletes that feed prejudice and fear.

Other signs of change include the increasing availability of educational and legal resources and organizations addressing heterosexism and homophobia in men's and women's sports. The Women's Sports Foundation in the United States initiative *It Takes A Team! Education Campaign for LGBT Issues in Sport* (www.ItTakesATeam.org) provides resources for coaches, athletic directors, athletes and parents. *The National Center for Lesbian Rights' Homophobia in Sports Project* (www.nclrights.org) provides legal assistance for athletes and coaches who experience anti-gay discrimination and also provides policy recommendations for athletic departments and organizations to address discrimination and harassment on the basis of sexual orientation or gender identity.

Another sign of progress is that more coaches' associations, schools and sport governing bodies are initiating efforts to educate their members about discrimination and harassment of LGBT (lesbian, gay, bisexual and transexual) people in sport. In addition, younger generations of lesbian and gay athletes and coaches are more likely to challenge discrimination. They have a greater sense of entitlement to respect and fair treatment and are more likely to take advantage of education and legal resources if they are targeted by anti-lesbian policies or practices. Another sign of social change is the increasing comfort of heterosexual athletes and coaches with

lesbians in sport. When heterosexual women in sport are able to challenge the stigma of lesbian stereotypes through education, interactions with out lesbians, or because of high-profile role models like Sheryl Swoopes coming out, their willingness to stand against discrimination and harassment becomes an important part of changing women's sports. They then become effective agents of change in defusing the power of the lesbian label to intimidate all women in sport.

Women's sport still has a way to go before athletes and coaches are judged on the basis of their accomplishments and character rather than their sexuality or femininity, but progress is being made. Athletics should be a safe and respectful place for all women, regardless of their sexuality, **race**, gender expression or **religion**. The movement to address anti-lesbian discrimination in sport is an important part of this journey toward social justice in sport.

Key Reading

Griffin, P. (1998) *Strong Women, Deep Closets: Lesbians and Homophobia in Sport.* Champaign, IL: Human Kinetics.
Krane, V. and Barber, H. (2005) 'Identity tensions in lesbian intercollegiate coaches', *Research Quarterly for Exercise and Sport*, 76 (1): 67–81.
www.ItTakesATeam.org
www.nclrights.org

Patricia Griffin

LIFELONG PARTICIPATION

Enjoyment is a critical dimension of participation in sport and physical activity. Self-evidently, people are more likely to continue doing an activity if they enjoy it. Most adherents to sport participate not for extrinsic reasons (such as health promotion) but for intrinsic reasons (such as the sheer pleasure of playing). Unsurprisingly, competence is intimately related to enjoyment. If people (and especially young people) feel that their skill levels and all-round competence in an activity are good enough or improving, they will be likely to enjoy the activity (see also **exercise behaviour**).

However, although they can be considered necessary conditions for participation, enjoyment and competence are by themselves insufficient for lifelong participation. A crucial dimension of becoming 'locked in' to sport and physical exercise appears to be the possession of a *wide sporting repertoire* or portfolio; in other words, active engagement during youth and early adulthood in several (usually three or more) sports or activities. Young people who possess wide sporting repertoires are, it seems, far more likely to become locked in to participation, motivated by a desire to repeat satisfying experiences. Some activities in individual's repertoires will endure while others will be replaced, supplemented or even dropped as their lives unfold. People's sporting and leisure portfolios or repertoires are developed, refined and even reconstructed, especially during periods of transition brought about by significant life events (such as forming relationships, starting a family, changing occupation, gaining promotion, acquiring chronic injuries, moving to live in a new area and **retirement**). Competitive forms of physical exercise (such as games) may give way to challenging forms of physical exercise (e.g. outdoor pursuits); game contests (e.g. soccer) may be replaced by game challenges (e.g. climbing). This is particularly important in relation to lifelong participation because there are large continuities in leisure interests and behaviour from youth until retirement.

Contrary to the commonsense views of government, media and other interested parties, Western European countries have experienced relatively high levels of adult sports participation as well as higher youth retention rates in recent decades (**youth sports participation**). Indeed, sports participation has, it seems, become part of present-day cultures in many Western European countries and, in particular, the UK. Roberts's comment on participation in the mid-1990s

applies equally a decade later; that is to say, 'The past Golden Age when the mass of young people were heavily involved in physically active recreation is pure myth ... young people in Britain are playing more sport than at any time in living memory' (1996: 52). The levels of sport participation among young people recorded in recent surveys in the UK (e.g. see Sport England, 2003) and Western Europe (e.g. see Scheerder et al., 2005; Telama et al., 2002) are substantially above the levels variously reported in the 1960s and 1970s. At that time, most girls did no out-of-school sport and most boys did no leisure time sport except football. The norm then was for most people to be lost to sport, probably forever, at the end of their school careers (Roberts, 1996).

Key Reading

Roberts, K. (1996) 'Young people, schools, sport and government policy', *Sport, Education and Society*, 1 (1): 47–57.

Scheerder, J., Vanreusel, B., Taks, M. and Renson, R. (2005) 'Social stratification patterns in adolescents' active sports participation behaviour: a time trend analysis 1969–1999', *European Physical Education Review*, 11 (1): 5–27.

Sport England (2003) *Young People and Sport in England. Trends in Participation 1994–2002*. London: Sport England.

Telama, R., Nupponen, H. and Pieron, M. (2005) 'Physical activity among young people in the context of lifestyle', *European Physical Education Review*, 11 (2): 115–37.

Ken Green

LIFESTYLE SPORTS

One characteristic of sport in the twenty-first century is an increase in the range and diversity of sports forms and cultures. A vivid example of this trend is the emergence and growth of what the academic and popular literature has variously termed extreme sports, alternative sports, lifestyle sports, whiz sports, action-sports, panic sports, post-modern sports (**postmodernism**), post-industrial sports and new sports. These labels encompass a wide range of participatory and made-for-television sporting activities, including residual cultural forms such as climbing and emergent activities such as paragliding and BMX biking. While these labels are used synonymously by some commentators, there are differences that signal distinct emphases or expressions of the activities (see Rinehart, 2000). Lifestyle sports are a specific type of alternative sport, including both established activities like surfing and skateboarding through to newly emergent sports like kitesurfing. Unlike some alternative and extreme sports, lifestyle sports are fundamentally about participation, not spectating, either in live or mediated settings. The term *lifestyle* reflects the terminology used by those who participate in these sports, and encapsulates the cultures that surround the activities. Despite differences in nomenclature, most commentators see such activities as having presented an *alternative* and *potential challenge* to traditional ways of 'seeing' 'doing' and understanding sport.

In the twenty-first century lifestyle sports are attracting an ever increasing body of participants and consumers. Beal (in Wheaton, 2004) notes that the growth of skateboarding in the US (as measured by sales figures) is outpacing the growth of more traditional sports like baseball. These participants/consumers include: (1) 'poseurs', buying into a desirable lifestyle; (2) the occasional participants who experience a range of different alternative and traditional sports; and (3) the 'hard core', committed practitioners who are fully familiar with the lifestyle, argot, fashion and technical skill of their activity. While some activities – such as surfing and snowboarding – are becoming increasingly popular with female participants, the majority of participants are young (or more aptly youthful), affluent, white males from affluent, Western, industrialized nations.

While each lifestyle sport has its own history, identity and developmental pattern, there are commonalities in their respective ideologies, and increasingly in terms of the transnational consumer industries which produce the commodities that underpin their cultures (**commodification**). For example, snowboarding, skateboarding, windsurfing and kitesurfing have roots in, and are all strongly influenced by, surfing. Many of these sports originated in North America and were then imported to Europe and beyond. With their roots in the counter-cultural social movement of the 1960s and 1970s, many have characteristics that are *different* to the rule-bound, competitive and masculine cultures of dominant sports (**masculinity**).

A number of characteristics define lifestyle sports (see Wheaton, 2004). Participants show high commitment in time and/or money and a style of life that develops in conjunction with the activity. They have a hedonistic individualistic ideology that promotes commitment, but often denounces regulation and institutionalization. They tend to be critical of, or ambivalent to, commercialism and formal 'man-on-man' style competition. They emphasize the aesthetic realm in which one blends with one's environment. Some practitioners refer to their activities as art. The **body** is used in non-aggressive ways, mostly without bodily contact, yet participants embrace and fetishize notions of **risk** and danger. The locations in which these sports are practised are often new or re-appropriated (urban and/or rural) spaces, without fixed or delineated boundaries.

Lifestyle sports are not solely counter-cultural but also part of the landscape of 'traditional' sports (witness snowboarding in the Olympic Games), the X-Games (see Rinehart, 2000) and increasingly a marketing tool for advertisers attracting youth audiences. Nevertheless, underpinning these forms are lived cultures that are fundamentally about 'doing it', about taking part. Research on different lifestyle sport cultures (see chapters in Rinehart and Sydor, 2003; Wheaton, 2004) has illustrated that membership, identity and status are influenced by factors including commitment, attitude, style, **gender**, **class**, and **race**. However, the 'real' or the 'authentic' tends to be defined around the performance of the activity, around 'doing it' (see chapters by Wheaton and Beal in Rinehart and Sydor, 2003). The *meaning* of participation is articulated around personal expression and gratification, such as the 'thrill of vertigo', and natural high of an adrenaline rush. As Rinehart (2000) suggests, the 'pretenders' in lifestyle sports are soon revealed.

The emergence of these sports and their associated lifestyles is related to wider issues around changing contemporary Western society (Wheaton, 2004). Theorists have represented the emergence of these sporting activities and subcultures as a new phase in the development of sports, characterized by some as 'postmodern' (Rinehart and Sydor, 2003; Wheaton, 2004). In these sports we can see some of the central issues and paradoxes of late-modern societies, such as the expression of self-identity becoming increasingly self-reflexive, fluid and fragmented, with sport and leisure increasingly becoming significant sites for identity construction (Wheaton, 2004; see also **performativity**). In these lifestyle sports, consumers are sold a complete style of life, one that emphasizes many of the aspirations of postmodern **consumer culture** (Wheaton, 2004).

Two themes are central to the research on lifestyle sports cultures (Wheaton, 2004). The first is the increasingly visible influence of global commercial forces in their development, sporting practices and identities (see also Wheaton, 2005). 'The expansion of consumer capitalism is particularly evident in the ever-expanding array of commodities linked to these activities, such as equipment, clothing, accessories, video games, videos and magazines (Wheaton, 2004). Lifestyle sports have been adopted to sell products (ranging from cars to soft drinks) to the sought after teenage male consumer audience. Commentators have therefore seen alternative sport, especially in media versions such as ESPN's X-Games, as a 'co-opted' sporting movement, increasingly controlled or dictated by transnational and media conglomerations (see Rinehart, 2000). Nevertheless, **commercialization** is not

solely a co-opting force; lifestyle sports cultures – like many youth cultures – also adapt and change, contesting subcultural meanings, spaces and identities (Wheaton, 2005). Another aspect of this 'selling-out' debate is found in participants' attitudes to the increasing institutionalization of lifestyle sports, especially in terms of feelings about formal competitions and other forms of regulation. In sports like surfing, skateboarding, snowboarding and windsurfing there have been (ideological and 'real') battles over their inclusion in traditional 'mainstream' forms of sporting competition such as the Olympic Games, and in media-driven competitions such as the X-Games (see Rinehart 2000, Rinehart and Sydor, 2003; Wheaton, 2005).

The second main research theme considers whether lifestyle sports challenge the **gender** roles, identities and power relationships in 'traditional' sports. Do these newer non-traditional sports 'offer *different* and potentially more *transformatory* scripts for male and female physicality, than the hegemonic masculinities and femininities characteristic of traditional sports cultures and identities?' (Wheaton, 2004). Chapters in Wheaton (2004) suggest that lifestyle sports present *opportunities* for more transgressive embodied social identities that differ from masculinities in traditional sports. In some lifestyle sports the boundaries of gender identity are expanded, but most sporting femininities continue to be 'framed by discourses and practices that perpetuate stereotypes of white heterosexual attractiveness, and masculinities based on normative heterosexuality and whiteness, skill and risk, working within, rather than subverting traditional patterns of gendered and bodily domination in sport' (Wheaton, 2004).

Key Reading

Rinehart, R. (2000) 'Emerging arriving sport: alternatives to formal sport', in J. Coakley and E. Dunning (eds), *Handbook of Sport Studies*. London: Sage. pp. 504–19.

Rinehart, R. and Sydor, S. (eds) (2003) *To the Extreme: Alternative Sports, Inside and Out*.

Albany: State University of New York Press.

Wheaton, B. (2005). 'Selling out? The globalization and commercialization of lifestyle sports', in L. Allison (ed.), *The Global Politics of Sport*. London: Routledge. pp. 140–61.

Wheaton, B. (ed.) (2004) *Understanding Lifestyle Sports: Consumption, Identity and Difference*. London: Routledge.

Belinda Wheaton

LING, PER HENRIK (1776–1839)

Founder of a physical education system that dominated Swedish gymnastics and spawned further influential physical education systems such as that developed by **Madame Bergman Österberg** in Britain at the end of the nineteenth century. While at the University of Lund (1804–12), Ling innovated with the system of apparatus gymnastics devised by **GutsMuths** and developed a series of free-standing exercises that formed the core of the Ling system. Alongside free-standing movements designed to correct or prevent bad posture, Ling introduced stretching and lunging exercises and exercises with a partner to provide support and resistance. Together, these formed original and far-reaching innovations in physical education.

At the beginning of the nineteenth century the ideas of GutsMuths were being well received in Sweden and the state was opening up physical training opportunities within educational establishments. Crucially Ling, who was also a poet, dramatist and leader of the Romantic movement, shared the growing national self-awareness of the Swedish middle **class** at this time. His desire to revive the ancient traditions of Nordic strength and vigour met with a receptive audience. Military defeat by Russia in 1809 appeared to increase the need for a strong Swedish youth and in part explains why Ling was motivated to establish a training school for gymnastics in 1814.

Ling was a respected fencer and gymnast and his good social standing helped his ideas to spread. Moreover, he was a keen horseman, having started riding as a youngster to aid his recuperation from a chest complaint. It has been suggested that it was this experience that probably led to his interest in developing medical gymnastics to cure ailments/disabilities. He sought links with the medical profession and argued that theory and practice should always be taught together. Here were the seeds of what we now know as physiotherapy, and many consider this innovation to be Ling's most significant legacy.

The simplicity of his system of movements, and the lack of expensive equipment, brought physical education within the reach of the masses. This was one of Ling's primary objectives. After Ling's death, his son, Hjalmar, systematized his father's work, which, on the one hand, enabled it to be taught more widely and more regularly, but, on the other, promoted a more restricted system of gymnastics than the one to which Ling himself subscribed. This led to Ling's system being seen as dull and rigid and ultimately it became less popular than the games and sports championed by proponents of the English **cult of athleticism**.

Key Reading

McIntosh, P.C., Dixon, J.G., Munrow, A.D. and Willetts, R.F. (1981) *Landmarks in the History of Physical Education*, 3rd edn. London: Routledge and Kegan Paul.

LISTED EVENTS

The term 'listed events' refers to a group of sports tournaments, matches, etc. which governments deem to be of such national significance that they should be made as freely available to the public as possible. The idea for the establishment of a set of listed events began in Britain in 1955 in anticipation of the establishment of the ITV television network alongside the BBC. It was thought that the beginnings of a competitive market would provoke an expensive battle for **broadcasting rights** and potentially deny a large section of the population access to major sports events. With the blessing of politicians, ITV and the BBC mutually agreed a list of 10 events (the English FA and Scottish FA Cup Finals, the Grand National and Derby in horseracing, test cricket involving England, the Oxford v. Cambridge Boat Race, the Wimbledon Tennis Championships, the Football World Cup, the Olympics, and the Commonwealth Games when staged in Britain) to which neither sought exclusive access (Barnett, 1990).

The establishment of listed events effectively guaranteed the BBC's monopoly over sport; they were the established broadcaster and simultaneous transmission of events reduced their commercial value to ITV. Partly because of this, and partly because sport's governing bodies objected to the significant loss of revenue that listed status entails (exacerbated by the advent of cable and satellite broadcasters), the range and status of listed events have been reviewed. Currently in the UK the 'A-listed' events are: the Olympic Games; the Football World Cup and European Nations Cup Finals; the English FA and Scottish FA Cup Finals; the Wimbledon Tennis Championships; the Grand National and Derby; the Rugby League Challenge Cup Final; and the Rugby Union World Cup Final. Membership of the A-list means that no broadcaster can be granted exclusive rights to live coverage.

In addition to this, the UK now has a B-list of events. The B-list regulations stipulate that if one category of broadcaster has coverage (free to air, or pay television plus Channel 5), there should be 'adequate and timely' secondary coverage by a broadcaster in the other category. The B-list currently consists of: England cricket test matches; non-final matches at Wimbledon; 'other' matches at the Rugby Union World Cup Finals tournament (i.e. those not on the A-list); Six Nations (rugby union) matches involving the home nations; the Commonwealth Games; the World Athletics Championship; the Cricket World Cup Final, semi-finals and other matches involving home nations; and golf's Ryder Cup and Open Championship (Sandy et al., 2004).

Germany, Italy and Denmark operate a similar system of listed events. These also include major football tournaments and the Olympic Games, but also nationally specific events such as the Italian Grand Prix, and Danish participation in handball tournaments.

Key Reading

Barnett, S. (1990) *Games and Sets: The Changing Face of Sport on Television.* London: British Film Institute Publishing.
Sandy, R., Sloane, P.J. and Rosentraub, M. (2004) *The Economics of Sport: An International Perspective.* Basingstoke: Palgrave Macmillan. esp. Ch. 6.

M

McDONALDIZATION

(consumer culture)

MACRO- AND MICRO-SOCIOLOGY

Similar to the way in which economists distinguish between macro- and micro-economic processes, meaningful distinctions can be made between sociologists who take either a macro- or a micro-sociological approach. Macro-sociologists attempt to explain social phenomena with reference to social structures or social systems (**functionalism**), such as the mode of economic production (**Marxism**). Micro-sociologists typically focus on relatively small-scale, face-to-face interaction between individuals (**idealism**; **symbolic interactionism**). The former approach tends to favour **quantitative research methods**, the latter **qualitative research methods**. Macro-sociologists tend to focus their analysis on the effects of impersonal social structures (such as **class**), while micro-sociologists stress the role of individuals in continually constructing and remodelling their identity and emotions (**agency and structure**). Finally, it should be noted that some sociologists (especially **Bourdieu** and **Elias**; **Structuration Theory**) have attempted to draw up theoretical models that bridge the macro-micro divide and provide a more holistic, reality congruent, approach.

MALE PRESERVE

The notion that sports **subcultures** may represent something of a 'male preserve' was first proposed by Sheard and Dunning in 1973 when they looked at the highly ritualized nature of the rugby club subculture, which at that time had a reputation for the regular violation of a number of taboos – for example, **violence**, nakedness, physical contact, obscenity, drunkenness (**alcohol**), etc. In order to explain this phenomenon, Sheard and Dunning note the co-relative development of rugby as a game for adults and the suffragette movement involving, respectively, men and women from the English middle and upper classes. Consequently Sheard and Dunning suggest that in the second half of the nineteenth century, particularly at this level of the social hierarchy, men increasingly came to view women as posing a challenge to men's traditional domination. Thus men from these social classes sought to bolster their own threatened masculinity by forming male preserves in which women (and homosexual men) were mocked, objectified and vilified through songs and rituals. On the one hand, women were excluded from these male preserves, either formally through the singing of songs such as 'Goodnight Ladies', or implicitly through the threatening and intimidating nature of these actions and the 'loss of status' suffered by any women choosing to remain. On the other hand, taking part in these activities increased the solidarity, the sense of unity among men.

By the early 1970s, however, Sheard and Dunning had noted that such male preserves could be seen to be declining due to financial pressures and the increasing awareness of women of their social power vis-à-vis men, power derived primarily from 'their desirability as mates'. The result has been a greater commingling of the sexes in social spaces such as rugby clubs. Where such subcultural practices continue, they exist in a less intense form than they have in the past.

The significance of Sheard and Dunning's work is that it sheds light on the way in which oppressive practices towards women are embedded in men's sport. The notion of sport as a male preserve, however, has been expanded in recent years as work on sport and **masculinity** has increasingly revealed how sport is a social activity in which masculine values are celebrated and in which males undergo **socialization** into appropriately masculine roles (see also **gender**).

Key Reading

Messner, M. (1992) *Power at Play: Sports and the Problem of Masculinity.* Boston, MA: Beacon Press.
Sheard, K. and Dunning, E. (1973) 'The rugby football club as a type of male preserve', *International Review of Sport Sociology*, 8 (1): 5–24.

MANCHESTER UNITED

(**Munich air disaster**)

MARKET FAILURE

Occurs when the balance of supply and demand in the private market leads to a situation where provision falls short of that which is deemed socially desirable. Gratton and Taylor (2000) identify two sources of **sports market** failure: efficiency-related and

equity-related market failure. Where governments identify cases of market failure, they may use this as the rationale for their intervention into the market.

Sport is believed to have social or collective benefits (such as **health** promotion and crime reduction) and thus high levels of participation are thought to contribute to a more efficient society, from which all members benefit. Private sports providers are unlikely to reduce participation costs in the interests of social welfare, however, and so either the government itself provides access to sports facilities and participation, or it subsidizes other suppliers in the commercial or voluntary sector of sport. If particular groups appear to be excluded from sports participation, governments may provide subsidies (e.g. to the unemployed) to ensure a more equitable provision of sporting opportunities on the grounds that such equity is desirable for the welfare of society more generally (**social inclusion**).

Key Reading

Gratton, C. and Taylor, P. (2000) *Economics of Sport and Recreation.* London: E. & F.N. Spon.

MARXISM

A sociological perspective rooted in the work of Karl Marx (1818–83), a nineteenth-century German philosopher, sociologist, economist and political revolutionary. The Marxist approach centres primarily on the analysis of how **class** conflict is the central dynamic of social change, and in this respect might be described as a variant of both **conflict theory** and **critical theory**.

For Marx, the key to understanding all aspects of social life lies in the economic structure of society. He argued that before we can compose music, engage in political debate, etc. – and, he might have added, play sport – we have to feed, clothe and provide shelter for ourselves. Thus, the 'material' needs of humans are the most basic needs, and the satisfaction of material needs takes priority over the satisfaction of other human needs. Consequently, 'the mode of production of material life', as Marx calls it, determines the general character of the social, political and ideological processes in a society. In short, Marx was suggesting that the economy of a society (what he termed the 'base') is the crucial determinant of its overall structure and culture (termed the 'superstructure'), and that, as a society's economy or 'mode of production' changes, so do its politics, its forms of thinking, etc. (and thus also its sport). The implication of this analysis is that sport, therefore, cannot be understood in its own terms, but can only be understood as a direct or indirect reflection of the economic 'base' of society.

Marx, therefore, developed a 'materialist conception of history' in which he distinguished between different ways of producing goods and services, or 'modes of production'. Modes of production differ in terms of property ownership and the patterns of relationships between those involved in the production process. While in the feudal system of the European Middle Ages, relations of production were based on the relationship between the lord and serf, in capitalist societies the relations of production are based on the relationship between the owners/controllers of the means of production (the bourgeoisie or capitalists) and the non-owners (the proletariat). In sport, the owners of teams and organizers of sports events are the bourgeoisie, and athletes are the proletariat.

Marx argued that all existing and past modes of production have been based on an exploitative relationship between an oppressing and an oppressed class. In all cases the production of goods is structured in such a way that the benefits accrue primarily to a property-owning minority (to whom the exploited and propertyless majority have to sell their labour power in order to survive). Central to this process is the **alienation** of workers. An ever-present class conflict arises out of these exploitative relations of production, and this constitutes the central source of

social change and historical development. For Marx, the 'history of all hitherto existing society is the history of class struggles'.

In the face of such obvious exploitation, dominant groups maintain their position in society through two key processes. The dominant class, by virtue of its ownership and control of economic production, also has control of the state and control over the production of ideas, enabling it to fight off resistance to the exploitative system of social relations (e.g. the use of sport to improve the living conditions and the **health** of the exploited). Furthermore, insofar as members of subordinate classes accept the ideology of the ruling class, they may develop a 'false class consciousness' that involves an acceptance of their exploited position (e.g. the legitimacy of a meritocratic hierarchy and ruthless competition exemplified in sport). However, Marx predicted that conflict would inevitably increase under capitalism, that the exploited would develop a revolutionary consciousness, and that the old ruling class would ultimately be overthrown. A communist society would follow in which there was no ownership of the means of production and thus no exploitation. Sport would be replaced by spontaneous, informal and liberating play (**Homo Ludens**).

The central criticism of the Marxist approach is that it exaggerates the explanatory power of economic forces. Within Marxism there has been much debate over this issue and, as a result, several different varieties of Marxism have emerged and been applied to sport. In setting out his own **hegemony theory** position, John Hargreaves (1986) also identifies **correspondence theory** and **reproduction theory** which take different positions with regard to economic determinism.

However, Hargreaves also identifies four main areas in which sport contributes to the needs of capitalism and over which there is a general consensus among advocates of these various Marxist positions:

1   Sport encourages the proletariat to accept the **discipline** and work ethos of modern production. Sport, like work, is standardized

and bureaucratized, and has a high degree of specialization. Performance/production is highly quantified and relies on science and technology.

2 Sport is commercialized (**commercialization**). Athletes and events become commodities to be bought or sold for mass consumption and bourgeoisie profit (**commodification**).

3 Sport expresses the ideologies of capitalism. These include aggressive individualism, ruthless competition, elitism, chauvinism, sexism and **nationalism**. Uncritically accepted in sport, these ideas reflect the broader structure of capitalist society so that sport can be regarded as providing an important source of ideological support for the maintenance of the capitalist system.

4 Sport is used by the state to serve the needs of capitalism. The increasing number of state interventions into the running of sport, such as the use of sport to promote a **social inclusion** agenda, is seen to be motivated not by concerns of the condition of the proletariat, but in terms of the desire to increase economic production.

Thus contemporary sport is regarded as dulling people's awareness of social inequalities and oppression. Marx described religion as 'the opiate of the masses' and it can be argued that sport performs a similar role and has, to some extent, taken the place of **religion** in increasingly secular contemporary societies. Perhaps not surprisingly, Marxists typically seek to promote radical change to structures which they regard as manipulative and oppressive. Their goal is to de-institutionalize sport, to render it more 'play-like' and to put power back in the hands of 'players', hence making sport (once again) a source of freedom and liberation.

Key Reading

Brohm, J.-M. (1978) *Sport – A Prison of Measured Time*. London: Ink Links.
Hargreaves, J. (1986) *Sport, Power and Culture: A Social and Historical Analysis of Popular Sports in Britain*. Oxford: Polity Press.
Rigauer, B. (1981) *Sport and Work,* trans. A. Guttmann. Columbia: Columbia University Press.

MASCULINITY

Sport has long since been viewed as a heavily gendered activity. Its relational dynamics, its working practices, its commercial ventures are replete with images of maleness. In the second half of the twentieth century **gender** relations in Western industrial societies witnessed a significant shift. Despite this, sport continues to be considered one of the last bastions of male domination; a '**male preserve**'.

Many of the masculine ideals attached to **modern sport** appear to have originated in the English public schools of the nineteenth century where traditional **folk games** were transformed into more orderly forms of play by the upper-class codes imposed upon them. These activities came to constitute a central element within the public school ethos, noted for their competitive and repressive qualities while at the same time viewed as a nurturing ground for the attitudes and values imperative for the maintenance of British **imperialism** (see also **muscular christianity**).

These male-dominated ideals gained much recognition during the latter part of the nineteenth century and eventually made the transition to the wider sporting sphere. Graduates of the public schools, for example, spread the games-playing ethos through a variety of social institutions, thereby enhancing the wider rationalization of sport. In addition, Pierre de Coubertin, the founder of the modern Olympic movement (**IOC**), adopted and reinforced the chauvinistic spirit of the English games-playing tradition and in so doing publicly promoted sport as a predominantly male concern.

From these early beginnings, dominant masculine images of sport persisted. The Victorian era witnessed the emergence of commonsense cultural assumptions equating manliness with sporting prowess. Where sport was concerned, women came to be seen as weak and frail, passive and emotional. Rendered ill-suited to vigorous exercise, women became the victims of an unfounded pseudo-scientific logic which located them as biologically inferior to men. Consequently, cultural values and attitudes came to determine the limits of female sporting activity, and male superiority in sport became the 'natural order of things'. Vestiges of these norms and beliefs are still evident in today's society. Research has shown that fewer females than males participate in sport, fewer women occupy positions of power in sports administration and female athletes command less **media** coverage than males (e.g. see **Anna Kournikova**). Moreover, that coverage which is afforded to women often carries sexual(ized) and/or heavily gendered connotations (**sexualization**).

One of the ways in which sport maintains and perpetuates notions of male superiority is through its relationship with the mass **media**. Important here are the contemporary marketing and advertising techniques of **consumer culture**. Sport, **health** and the **body** are key markers in consumer culture, which proffers influential ideals of youth, fitness and beauty. Sport connects intimately with consumer culture precisely because both employ the body as a central means of expression.

But how does this relationship directly affect popular conceptions of masculinity? It is argued that through its widespread use of body imagery, the media makes individuals more aware of their bodily state. The degree to which we measure up to 'the look' has come to represent the currency of social relations, our value within society and our social acceptability. Sport and exercise play a central role within this body/media nexus. To maintain one's body image is to express one's desire to lead a healthy lifestyle, to enjoy the 'good things in life' and to appeal to others. Physical fitness and participation in sports and leisure activities represent a sense of pride in oneself, a sense of cleanliness and

purification against the evils of **alcohol**, tobacco, recreational drugs and the bodily abuses of daily life. To be healthy and diet-conscious is to have some kind of sexual appeal over and above those who are not healthy and diet-conscious (eating disorders; obesity discourse).

The development of the sport/media relationship has had a dramatic impact on the way in which both male and female bodies have come to be presented and perceived. Men (as well as women) are expected to respond to the influential and persuasive forces of consumer culture, where masculinity (and femininity) is clearly defined. Emanating from film, television, books and magazines, notions of muscularity, strength and power emerge to produce images of the ideal man.

Sport also offers complex and contradictory portrayals of masculine construction in relation to sexuality. Physical bonding in the name of 'team spirit', homophobic taboos, blatant misogyny, and the objectification and vilification of women are all evident within popular forms of male sporting conquest or related social settings. Acceptable too are the practices of intimate celebration and pseudo-erotic ritual. Various commentators have cited the way in which attitudes throughout sport collectively contribute to the **reification** of heterosexuality within the sporting world in general (Pronger, 1990). The pervasiveness of dominant heterosexual/masculine norms often calls into question the femininity and sexuality of sports participants. Just as men are often labelled 'wimps' when they fail to measure up to popular images of strength, power and physical prowess, so women who pursue their sporting goals within competitive spheres are frequently seen as 'butch' and/or **lesbians**.

Thus, the relationship between masculinity and sport is grounded in both historical and contemporary social processes. Moreover, it is important that we consider these as part of the broader picture of gender identity formation; that is to say, masculine construction is not limited to sporting spheres, rather, it permeates and interweaves these and many other lifestyle areas (see also **new laddism**).

Key Reading

Hargreaves, J.A. (1994) *Sporting Females: Critical Issues in the History and Sociology of Women's Sports.* London: Routledge.

Messner, M.A. and Sabo, D.S. (eds) (1990) *Sport, Men and the Gender Order: Critical Feminist Perspectives.* Champaign, IL: Human Kinetics Press.

Pronger, B. (2000), 'Homosexuality and sport: who's winning?', in J. McKay, M.A. Messner and D.F. Sabo (eds), *Masculinities, Gender Relations and Sport.* London: Sage. pp. 222–43.

Shilling, C. (1993) *The Body and Social Theory.* London: Sage.

Andrew Parker

MASKING DRUGS

(**drugs, classes of**)

MATERIALISM

(**Marxism**)

MAXIMUM WAGE

Introduced at the beginning of the 1901/2 English football season, alongside the **retain and transfer system**, at the behest of smaller football league clubs such as Preston North End in order to limit wage bills and, by reducing the financial incentive for players to move clubs, to encourage equality of competition (**competitive balance; player reservation systems**). However, the maximum wage must also be understood in the context of **amateurism** and the concerns over the corrupting nature of **commercialization** and professionalism that pervaded sport, and English sport in particular, at this time. It was part of a system of employment regulations that enabled clubs to exert unusually high levels of control over the industry's workers (i.e. players) until recent times (see, in contrast, the **Bosman ruling**).

The maximum wage was initially set at £4 per week, but pressure from the Players' Union led to the introduction of reforms in 1910 and 1920. These reforms not only increased the maximum wage (it had risen to £20 by 1958), but made it more variable, such that clubs could reward players, for example for length of service. While to begin with the maximum wage had effectively been the wage of all first team players at the bigger clubs, these reforms made the maximum wage far from standard by the interwar years.

Clubs, moreover, were able to vary the amount that they paid players by using various alternative rewards, including: (1) benefit matches (staging a match with all proceeds given to a particular player); (2) bonuses for winning matches, league position, etc.; and (3) illegal payments (in 1957 directors of Sunderland Football Club were fined and banned from the game for making illegal payments). Individuals could also increase their earnings through international appearances and product endorsement (**sponsorship**). On this basis, Matt Taylor (2001) has estimated that, prior to the Second World War, most football league professionals were better rewarded than their average working-**class** counterparts, though their pay was probably only equal to that of professional cricketers, and considerably less than that of professionals in horseracing, boxing and, in the US, baseball.

The maximum wage was eventually abolished in 1961. Many top players considered it an unnecessary restraint on their right to earn a living. While in existence it 'shaped the occupational culture of English football' and dominated industrial relations, Taylor argues that, given the scope clubs had to infringe the regulations, its impact was symbolic rather than actual; that is to say, it never acted as an effective ceiling on earnings.

Key Reading

Mason, T. (1980) *Association Football and English Society, 1863–1915*. Brighton: Harvester.

Russell, D. (1997) *Football and the English: A Social History of Association Football in England, 1863–1995*. Preston: Carnegie.

Taylor, M. (2001) 'Beyond the maximum wage: the earnings of football professionals in England, 1900–39', *Soccer and Society*, 2 (3): 101–18.

MEDIA

So closely linked are the media and sport that there are very few sporting phenomena that can be explained without some reference to television, the press, etc. Media coverage contributes to the process of **globalization** by making accessible sports events on the other side of the world and so shrinking time and distance (or, more accurately, our perceptions of them). The collaboration of sport and the media has been described as 'a match made in heaven' or, more academically, as symbiotic (meaning that each depends on the other for their existence/survival). This, however, may be something of an over-generalization. (How reliant on TV is badminton? How reliant on sport is the satellite channel MTV?) To avoid such over-generalizations, it is important to differentiate between different media – that is to say, between newspapers and magazines, radio, television (terrestrial and satellite/cable), and increasingly the **Internet** – because each has a different relationship with, and exerts a different influence on, sport. Similarly we must be careful to distinguish between sports, for while some have a close relationship with the media (e.g. football) others remain untouched and largely ignored (e.g. netball). That said, work on sport and the media can be divided into three distinct research areas: (1) the production of sport and its effects; (2) the underlying ideologies disseminated through sports coverage; and (3) the relationship between sports bodies and the media.

Considerable work in this first area (e.g. Goldlust, 1987) has described the way that television companies 'package' sports events. This involves the use of particular camera angles, editing techniques, slow motion replays, evocative music, statistics, film footage of previous competitions and the verbal input of commentators, summarisers and experts to contribute to the build-up, fill time between breaks in play, and provide an overview/summary at the end. Consequently, the televised sports event can bear little relation to the 'live' experience (**hyperreality; post-fandom**). Television companies and producers, it is argued, use these techniques to increase the audience for their product and the net effect of these practices is to dramatize sport through providing spectacle and a narrative. We may, for instance, be shown particularly violent tackles, the goals or sprint finishes of past events, and come to understand the history of rivalry between the teams or people involved. This often leads us (the viewer) to a more empathetic understanding of events, and the feeling of having a closer connection with the participants. This has led many researchers in recent years to look at the issue of **celebrity** in sport, and some key celebrities in particular (e.g. **David Beckham**).

The second research area looks at the way in which media coverage of sport carries certain messages and meanings and examines the degree to which the audience comes to adopt such ideologies. In this, newspapers and magazines are just as influential as television and radio. Various ideological subtexts to sports coverage have been identified, such as pro-capitalist messages, nationalistic messages (**nationalism**), and messages that perpetuate stereotypes of **gender** and **race**. More specifically, sport coverage extols the virtues of many of the characteristics seen as beneficial to the workplace: teamwork; 'graft'; application; self-sacrifice (**Michael**

Jordan). International sporting events are often portrayed within the context of wider political 'battles' between nations and serve to foster a sense of nationalism and loyalty to the state. The British tabloid media's representation of England–Argentina or England–Germany football matches (framed within the discussion of the Falklands War and the Second World War respectively) is a good case in point (see also **propaganda**).

Quantitatively, gender bias in the coverage of sport propagates the notion that sport is largely a male or masculine activity. Qualitatively women's sport is shown to be different to men's, with female athletes trivialized and sexualized (**gender**; **Kournikova**; **masculinity**; **sexualization**). Similarly, the portrayal of athletes from different ethnic backgrounds may both create and foster stereotypical notions of difference: the perception of the natural ability and tactical naivety of black African footballers; beliefs about the innate **aggression** and uncontrolled character of African-American athletes. The key question when discussing any of these ideological subtexts, however, is the nature of the audience. Is it passive or active in consuming these messages? Ultimately this is a question of **agency and structure**.

Finally, research has examined the relationship between the media and sports bodies, with the central questions being: where does the balance of power lie? And in what direction is it shifting? Traditionally, televising sport has been relatively cheap in that it provides many hours of broadcasting and can draw higher viewing figures than most other kinds of programme. For advertisers these are also often the 'right' kind of viewers – young males with high disposable incomes (**sponsorship**). Initially, sports bodies were very reluctant to allow television companies to broadcast live coverage of their fixtures through fear that it would drive spectators away and lead to a loss of revenue. However, broadcasters have continually increased the fees that they are willing to pay to cover events (**broadcasting rights**) and sports bodies have increasingly complied with their demands over the timing and scheduling of competitions (**commercialization**). The result is a power struggle, but it is important to clearly distinguish between the power struggles between relatively strong and weak sports bodies (i.e. football clubs are more powerful than rugby league clubs have been) and between different broadcasters (satellite channels may be willing to pay higher fees, raised through subscription, but terrestrial channels, and national broadcasters such as ITV and the BBC in particular offer the potential for bigger audiences and therefore higher advertising revenues where applicable). International events such as the Olympics provide a different dimension to this power struggle, with, for instance, broadcasters from the wealthiest nations (the US in particular) exerting a greater influence over events than the broadcasters of smaller nations (and hence European nations negotiate together as the European Broadcasting Union).

Key Reading

Goldlust, J. (1987) *Playing for Keeps: Sport, the Media and Society*. Melbourne: Longman.

Wenner, L. (ed.) (1998) *Mediasport*. London: Routledge.

Whannel, G. (1992) *Fields in Vision: Television, Sport and Cultural Transformations*. London: Routledge.

MEDIEVAL SPORT

Information on sports forms in medieval times, also called the European Middle Ages (c.500–c.1500), largely relates to the activities pursued in England. This extremely long period encompasses the decline of feudalism and the emergence of the modern state. Some of the more significant economic and political changes during this period include the consolidation of the power of the major landowners relative to the king, and the increasing economic freedom of those at the lower end of the social scale. Significant social changes also occurred. Chivalry declined in significance and this military ethic was replaced with a civilian ethic. People became increasingly aware of the distinctions between different social classes and social **class** increasingly became dependent on wealth and property, and less dependent on military strength.

The sports of English people in the Middle Ages reflected these broader social changes. The sports pursued were highly class-specific, with **tournaments** the preserve of knights and squires (the social elite), **archery** contests the preserve of the middle classes and **folk games**, such as folk football and **animal sports**, the 'sport' of the masses or peasants. During the period we also see sport forms becoming increasingly less violent and less like war, and sport ceasing to be seen as a direct form of training for war.

Key Reading

Baker, W. (1982) 'Medieval people at play', in *Sport in the Western World*. Totowa, NJ: Rowan and Littlefield. pp. 42–55.

Guttmann, A. (1986) *Sports Spectators*. New York: Columbia University Press.

Henricks, T. (1991) 'Sport in the later Middle Ages', in *Disputed Pleasures: Sport and Society in Pre-Industrial England*. Westport, CT: Greenwood Press. pp. 41–68.

Mandell, R (1984) 'Europe, 500–1750', in *Sport: A Cultural History*. New York: Columbia University Press. pp. 106–31.

MEGA-EVENTS, STAGING OF

The study of hallmark events or mega-events became an important part of tourism literature in the 1980s. Since then, the economics of **sports tourism** at major sports events has become an increasing part of this event tourism literature. Many governments around the world have adopted national sports policies that specify the hosting of major sports events as a major objective. A broad range of benefits from staging major sports events has been suggested for both the country and the host city (**city, the**). These include: (1) urban regeneration legacy benefits; (2) sporting legacy benefits; (3) tourism and image benefits; (4) social and cultural benefits; and (5) economic benefits, which will be the main focus here. It is well known that cities and countries compete fiercely to host the Olympic Games or the Football World Cup. However, over recent years there has been increasing competition to host less globally recognized sports events in a wide range of other sports where spectator interest is less assured and where the economic benefits are not so clear-cut.

The literature on the economics of major sports events is relatively recent. One of the first major studies in this area was the study of the impact of the 1985 Adelaide Formula 1 Grand Prix (Burns et al., 1986). This was followed by Brent Ritchie's in-depth study of the 1988 Calgary Winter Olympics (Ritchie and Smith, 1991). In fact, immediately prior to these studies it was generally thought that hosting major sports events was a financial liability to host cities following the large debts faced by Montreal after hosting the 1976 Olympics. There was a general change in attitude following the 1984 Los Angeles Olympics which made a clear profit (**IOC**).

Mules and Faulkner (1996) point out that even with such mega-events as Formula 1 Grand Prix races and the Olympics, hosting does not always bring a city an unequivocal economic benefit. They emphasize that, in general, staging major sports events often results in the city authorities losing money, even though the city itself benefits greatly in terms of additional spending in the city. Thus the 1994 Brisbane World Masters Games cost the city A$2.8 million to organize but generated a massive A$50.6 million of additional economic activity in the state economy. Mules and Faulkner's basic point is that it normally requires the public sector to finance the staging of the event and incur these losses in order to generate the benefits to the local economy. They argue that governments host such events and lose taxpayers' money in the process in order to generate spillover effects or externalities.

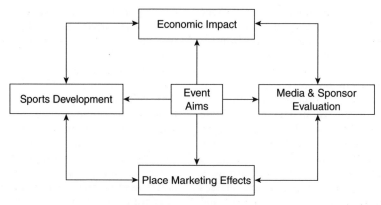

Figure 1   *The 'Balanced Scorecard' Approach to Evaluating Events*

It is not a straightforward task, however, to establish a profit and loss account for a specific event. Major sports events require investment in new sports facilities and often this is paid for in part by central government or even international sports bodies. Thus some of this investment expenditure represents a net addition to the local economy since the money comes in from outside. Also, such facilities remain after the event has finished, acting as a platform for future activities that can generate additional tourist expenditure (Mules and Faulkner, 1996).

Sports events are increasingly seen as part of a broader tourism strategy aimed at raising the profile of a city and therefore success cannot be judged on simply a profit and loss basis. Often the attraction of events is linked to a re-imaging process, and in the case of many cities is linked to strategies of urban regeneration and tourism development. Major events, if successful, have the ability to project a new image and identity for a city. The hosting of major sports events is often justified by the host city in terms of long-term economic and social consequences, directly or indirectly resulting from the staging of the event (Mules and Faulkner, 1996). These effects are primarily justified in economic terms by estimating the additional expenditure generated in the local economy as the result of the event, i.e. from the benefits injected from tourism-related activity and the subsequent re-imaging of the city following the success of the event.

Cities staging major sports events have a unique opportunity to market themselves to the world. Increasing competition between broadcasters to secure **broadcasting rights** to major sports events has led to a massive escalation in fees for such rights, which in turn means broadcasters give blanket coverage at peak times for such events, further enhancing the marketing benefits to the cities that stage them.

Although much of the literature has been concerned with the estimation of economic impacts generated through **multiplier** effects, more recent studies have emphasized additional benefits. Such benefits might include a notional value of exposure achieved from **media** coverage and the associated place, marketing effects related to hosting and broadcasting an event which might encourage visitors to return in future, or alternatively an investigation into any **sports development** impacts which may encourage young people to get more involved in sport (**youth sports participation**). Collectively these additional benefits could be monitored using a more holistic 'Balanced Scorecard' approach to event evaluation as outlined in Figure 1.

The evidence suggests that there is a wide diversity in the range of economic benefits that sports events can generate. Some events have little more than a local impact, others contribute substantially to the economic activity in the local economy as well as promoting the local area to an international

168

audience. When building a strategy for economic regeneration through sports events careful consideration should be given to which events to bid for, and the overall balance of sports events during an event year.

Local government must take a lead role not only in strategic terms but also in underwriting the operating and staging costs of sporting events because, as noted, rarely do the events themselves generate a surplus. Local government facilitates and supports such events in order to generate the real economic benefits to the local community. However, there is a distribution problem in that local taxpayers are in effect subsidizing the economic benefits that accrue to hotels, restaurants, and other leisure and tourism operators – the main beneficiaries of increased visitor spending. The rationale for this is that the local community benefits from increased employment opportunities.

Key Reading

Burns, J.P.A., Hatch, T.H. and Mules, T.J. (eds) (1986) *The Adelaide Grand Prix: The Impact of a Special Event*. Adelaide: Centre for South Australian Economic Studies.

Mules, T.J. and Faulkner, B. (1996) 'An economic perspective on major events', *Tourism Economics*, 2 (2): 107–17.

Ritchie, J.R.B. and Smith B.H. (1991) 'The impact of a mega event on host region awareness: a longitudinal study', *Journal of Travel Research*, 30 (1): 3–10.

Chris Gratton

MICRO-SOCIOLOGY

(**macro- and micro-sociology**)

MODERN OLYMPIC GAMES

(**IOC**)

MODERN SPORT

American historian Allen Guttmann (2004) and British sociologists Eric Dunning and Ken Sheard (2005) have been at the forefront of attempts to define the specific characteristics of modern sport. While different sports took their modern form at different times, the vast majority of modern sports can be seen to have derived from the period 1860 to 1900.

Guttmann, in *From Ritual to Record* (2004), identifies seven interdependent characteristics of modern sport – secularism, equality, specialization, rationalization, bureaucratization, quantification, and the quest for records – and provides contrasts between modern sports and their **medieval**, Roman (**Roman Games**), Greek (**ancient Olympic Games**), and primitive counterparts. Dunning and Sheard, in *Barbarians, Gentlemen and Players* (2005), list 15 characteristics that distinguish modern sports from **folk games**. These are: (1) specific, formal organization; (2) elaborate, written, rules legitimated by rational-bureaucratic means; (3) rules changed on a rational-bureaucratic basis; (4) national and international standardization of rules, fixed spatial boundaries, duration of play and participant numbers; (5) importance of fairness and equality (**fair play**) rather than natural or social differences; (6) high role differentiation between players (e.g. between defence and offence); (7) strict distinction between playing and spectating roles; (8) high structural differentiation of (i.e. little overlap between) game forms; (9) formal social control of players, with outside agencies to enforce rule compliancy, etc.; (10) relatively low levels of socially tolerated violence; (11) the generation of controlled, sublimated 'battle excitement'; (12) an emphasis on skill rather than physical force; (13) participation through individual choice rather than obligation to community; (14) contests which are nationally and internationally meaningful rather than just locally significant; and (15) recognized hierarchies of playing standards, often rewarded through monetization. While Dunning and Sheard provide a less abstract, more detailed set of characteristics of modern sport, the most conspicuous difference between these two competing schema is the emphasis that Dunning and Sheard place on the level of **violence** in modern sports compared to their folk antecedents.

More numerous than the descriptive typologies of modern sport, however, are the attempts to explain why and how modern sport came into being. Some historians (e.g. Vamplew, 1988) have emphasized the importance of the development of transport (and the railways in particular), reduced working hours, increased disposable income among the working classes, and the expansion of the commercial provision of leisure. These may be described as the necessary preconditions of the establishment of modern sport, but the **cult of athleticism**, and the growth of **rational recreation,** tell us rather more about why modern sports emerged in the form identified above, and why sports assumed the cultural centrality they came to hold (**sport, social significance of**). Jean-Marie Brohm and John Hargreaves, both drawing on the sociological tradition of **Marxism**, argue that these structural characteristics of modern sport developed to serve the needs of the emerging capitalist system of production in the nineteenth century. Guttmann, citing Max Weber, argues that a process of *rationalization* is the central characteristic of the development of modern societies and hence of modern sports (thus rationalization is one of Guttmann's seven key characteristics, although ultimately it underpins them all). Finally, Dunning and Sheard locate the development of modern sport within broader social changes such as industrialization and the changing **class** composition of Britain in the nineteenth century (citing the heightened **public school status rivalry** during this period) and Elias's theory of the **civilizing process**.

Key Reading

Dunning, E. and Sheard, K. (2005) *Barbarians, Gentlemen and Players: A Sociological Study of the Development of Rugby Football*, 2nd edn. London: Routledge.

Guttmann, A. ([1978] 2004) *From Ritual to Record: The Nature of Modern Sport*, rev. edn. New York: Columbia University Press.

Hargreaves, J. (1986) *Sport, Power and Culture: A Social and Historical Analysis of Popular Sports in Britain*. Oxford: Polity Press.

Mangan, J.A. (1981) *Athleticism in the Victorian and Edwardian Public School – The Emergence and Consolidation of an Educational Ideology*. Cambridge: Cambridge University Press.

Vamplew, W. (1988) *Pay Up and Play the Game*. Cambridge: Cambridge University Press.

MODERNITY

In everyday speech 'modern' is usually taken to mean 'up to date' or 'contemporary', but sociologists use the term rather differently to mean, in effect, 'not traditional'. Modernity, then, is a term that is designed to sum up the distinctiveness, complexity and dynamism of a range of social processes which developed during the eighteenth and nineteenth centuries and which, cumulatively, marked a distinct break from traditional ways of living. Although these processes were to gain worldwide influence, they initially centred on Western Europe and, although their origins may be traced back hundreds of years, it was really in the nineteenth century that recognizably modern societies and social phenomena appeared.

Some of the main features of this transformation include: (1) the development and application of more efficient forms of food production and, later, the replacement of agriculture as the dominant form of productive activity by industrial manufacture (commonly termed the Industrial Revolution); (2) the growth of the capitalist mode of production, capitalist organizations and capitalist ways of thinking; (3) population growth and movement from the countryside to the **city** (urbanization); (4) new forms of government, the growth of the state and secularization (**religion**); (5) Western colonization of the rest of the world (**imperialism**); and (6) stemming from the *Enlightenment* movement of the eighteenth century, the emergence of new, rational scientific ways of understanding the natural and social worlds which heralded an era of great medical, scientific and technological innovation and the belief in the inevitable and continual progress and advancement of humanity.

Most significantly for students of sport, **modern sport** constitutes an explicitly modern institution, developed in the same time and space as modernity more generally (nineteenth-century Western Europe), structured by many of the same ideas (progress, rationality, individualism) and undergoing many of the same processes (industrialization, urbanization, **globalization**). This is particularly well demonstrated in the work of Dunning and Sheard (2005), Hargreaves (1986) and in Allen Guttmann's *From Ritual to Record* (1978). More recently, **post-structuralism** and **postmodernism** have developed as specific critiques of the modernist construction of sport, focusing not on the economy, the state and organization of sport, but on the **body**, identity, **consumer culture**, **sexualization** and the disciplinary (**discipline**) or controlling character of sport.

Key Reading

Dunning, E. and Sheard, K. (2005) *Barbarians, Gentlemen and Players: A Sociological Study of the Development of Rugby Football*, 2nd edn. London: Routledge.

Guttmann, A. ([1978] 2004) *From Ritual to Record: The Nature of Modern Sport*, rev. edn. New York: Columbia University Press.

Hargreaves, J. (1986) *Sport, Power and Culture: A Social and Historical Analysis of Popular Sports in Britain*. Oxford: Polity Press.

MORAL PANIC

The notion of a moral panic (over groups defined as 'folk devils') expressed in Stan Cohen's classic work on mods and rockers in the 1960s (1973), was itself developed out of Howard Becker's work on **deviance**. Cohen argued that the media did not simply present the news, but that the selection of stories deemed 'newsworthy', and the 'angle' taken in news coverage, were rather more systematic, tending to reproduce the definitions and interests of the socially powerful. In particular, the exaggerated and alarmist reactions of politicians, the police, etc. towards particular social phenomena, as expressed via the **media**, serve to heighten public concern. This in turn produces a feedback loop, heightening politicians' perceptions of the need to address the phenomenon, further increasing the media coverage and thus further increasing public alarm. The dramatic and sensationalist media coverage stereotypes the groups involved and leads to the development within public perception of 'folk devils'. Consequently, the perception of the danger posed by such groups may be wholly out of proportion with its real significance.

The notion of moral panic in the context of sport was first used by Stuart Hall (1978) in his analysis of media portrayals of **football hooliganism**. Similarly, Young (1986), in his analysis of the media coverage of the **Heysel Stadium** disaster, demonstrated how the media initially sought to identify scapegoats to blame for the loss of life rather than seeking out the complex causal networks. The media further depicted the actions of football **fans** as meaningless, irrational and bestial/dehumanized, so placing them beyond the scope of understanding, and legitimating treatments that would not be suitable for 'normal' human groups (e.g. the use of electric fences to control spectators). Finally, politicians and the press called for the severe punishment of offenders and increasingly punitive law and order measures, which, in turn, heightened the public's perception that this was a social phenomenon about which 'something must be done'.

The key point of the notion of moral panic is that intended and unintended consequences of human action lead to an amplification of a social problem that far exceeds its objective status, but which results in inappropriate, and at times counterproductive, policy solutions (**Hillsborough**). More recently, Blackshaw and Crabbe (2004) have argued that the coverage of the deviant acts of professional footballers illustrates the enduring relevance of Cohen's framework.

Key Reading

Blackshaw, T. and Crabbe, T. (2004) *New Perspectives on Sport and 'Deviance': Consumption, Performativity and Social Control*. London: Routledge.

Cohen, S. (1973) *Folk Devils and Moral Panics: The Creation of the Mods and Rockers*. St Albans: Paladin.

Hall, S. (1978) 'The treatment of football hooliganism in the press', in R. Ingham (ed.), *Football Hooliganism: The Wider Context*. London: Inter-Action Imprint.

Young, K. (1986) '"The killing field": themes in mass media responses to the Heysel stadium riot', *International Review for the Sociology of Sport*, 21 (2/3): 253–64.

MOTIVATION

People use the term motivation in everyday life to refer to many things: a **personality** characteristic, an external reward or an explanation of behaviour ('we lost because we weren't motivated'). The multidimensional meaning of the term creates problems for psychologists who have sought therefore to define motivation more precisely and develop theories of motivation (**motivation, theories of**).

At its simplest, motivation can be defined as the direction and intensity of one's effort. In addition to highlighting direction (i.e. the situations, practices, etc. to which an athlete is attracted) and intensity (i.e. how *much* effort an athlete makes, how hard they try) some psychologists argue that the definition of motivation should also contain a temporal dimension (i.e. how *sustained* or lasting is that effort). While heuristically it may be useful to

separate out direction and effort, in practice they tend to be very closely related.

Psychological research on motivation tends to be guided by a number of unifying themes. Motivation: (1) is a dynamic process, changing over time and across situations; (2) is more than simply personal willpower (indeed trying harder is better conceived of as an *expression* of motivation than as a cause of it); (3) can only be fully understood through knowledge of both what an athlete enjoys and what an athlete avoids; and (4) should be viewed as an interactional process, influenced by both the self and the environment.

Within the psychology of sport and exercise there are three general perspectives on motivation. Motivation is seen as participant-centred and based on personality, needs, interests and goals. Others see motivation as situation-centred, stemming from, for example, the **group dynamics** between athletes and coaches, pleasantness of environment, etc. The most widely held theory of motivation is the interactionist view, which suggests that the best way to understand motivation is to investigate the interaction of these two sets of factors; of participant and context.

Consequently, guidelines for building motivation in sport include: (1) recognizing that both situations and personality traits explain an individual's motivation; (2) recognition that invariably people have multiple motivations, some which are commonly held, some of which are unique to the individual, but all of which may change over time; (3) that motivation can be enhanced by altering or varying the environment and that this should be sensitive to the specific individuals being motivated; (4) that the behaviour of leaders such as coaches and captains is crucial to the motivation of others; and (5) that, while it may be a more difficult task, it is possible to change the motivation of individual participants.

Key Reading

Roberts, G.C. (ed.) (2001) *Advances in Motivation in Sport and Exercise*. Champaign, IL: Human Kinetics.

MOTIVATION, THEORIES OF

Sports psychologists have produced five main theories of **motivation**. An early, but still influential, theory of motivation was the *need achievement theory*. This theory is predicated on the view that each person has two underlying achievement motivations – the desire to achieve success and the desire to avoid failure – and that behaviour is the outcome of the balance of these two **personality** characteristics (high achievers are more motivated by success than avoiding failure, while the opposite applies for low achievers). Building from this base, social (i.e. parenting and other **socialization** experiences), cognitive (ways of thinking, and perception of abilities) and developmental (i.e. how need achievement changes over time) processes have been identified as influencing the need for achievement. However, critics argue that the need achievement theory places too much emphasis on the direction as opposed to the intensity of motivation, and gives too little explanatory power to the social environment relative to intrinsic psychological drives.

Attribution theory focuses on the reasons given for success or failure. It can be argued that all attributes can essentially be categorized into four groups (ability, effort, task difficulty and luck), but Weiner's three-dimensional, locus of causality model is perhaps more influential in contemporary sports psychology. The stability, causality and controllability of attributions, Weiner argued, can be used to predict future achievement motivation. Where athletes link success to a stable factor (talent), an internal cause (personal effort, tactics) and a controllable factor (one's physical condition), they are likely to have an increased expectancy of success, increased pride in their success, and increased motivation in future. Conversely, for example, linking success to an unstable factor such as luck is likely to lead the individual to expect relatively little success in the future.

Achievement goal (orientation) theory primarily seeks to understand motivation through goals set for performance and their influence on achievement. People are thought to define success according to two types of goal: they may be oriented to the task (e.g. running a mile in four minutes) or outcome (e.g. winning a race). Also termed ego-involved goals, athletes who focus more on the outcome than the task are likely to have lower motivation orientation (particularly in practice), while those who focus on tasks are thought to work longer (especially in adverse conditions), choose more challenging tasks and work harder. Task-oriented athletes are thought to have more control over achievement.

Taking a slightly different approach, *competence motivation theory* and c*ognitive evaluation theory* share a focus on the *perception* of the individual towards tasks. Both stress the need of participants to feel competent at what they are doing allied to the need of individuals to feel that the choices (e.g. over what sport they do) are largely under their own control (the more competent and more in control an athlete feels, the more motivated they are likely to be). Importantly, these theories help to explain why the commonsense notion that increasing rewards leads to increased motivation and higher achievement is often wrong. In turn, this has led sports psychologists to look more at the way in which environment influences goal orientation and motivation.

Key Reading

Roberts, G.C. (ed.) (2001) *Advances in Motivation in Sport and Exercise.* Champaign, IL: Human Kinetics.

Weiner, B. (1986) *An Attribution Theory of Motivation and Emotion.* New York: Springer-Verlag.

MULTIDIMENSIONAL MODEL OF SPORTS LEADERSHIP (MMSL)

While Chelladurai's MMSL has been translated into a range of languages and tested via a number of empirical studies, Chelladurai himself suggests that existing research is 'piecemeal' and therefore the applicability of the model remains unproven.

The model identifies leader effectiveness as dependent on three antecedents or contingent factors: (1) environmental or situational factors; (2) leader characteristics; and (3) member characteristics (hence MMSL can be seen as part of the interactional approach to **leadership**). These factors inform three dimensions of leader behaviour: *required behaviour*, or the demands and dictates of the organizational system, norms, goals, etc.; *preferred behaviour*, that is the preferences of group members for particular types of leader behaviour, perhaps which they've experienced in other contexts, or have become used to in that context; and *actual behaviour*, or the behaviour the leader exhibits, such as initiating or consideration structures. Chelladurai hypothesizes that the closer the fit or congruence between these three types of leader behaviour, the 'better' performance and athlete satisfaction will be.

Key Reading

Chelladurai P. (1987) 'Multidimensionality and multiple perspectives of organizational effectiveness', *Journal of Sport Management*. 1: 37–47.
Chelladurai P. (1993) 'Leadership', in R.N. Singer, M. Murphey and L.K. Tennant (eds), *Handbook of Research in Sport Psychology*. New York: Macmillan. pp. 647–71.
Horn T.S. (ed.) (2002) *Advances in Sport Psychology*, 2nd edn. Champaign, IL: Human Kinetics.

MULTIPLIER

Used to assess the full economic impact derived from a specific event. Multipliers convert the initial additional expenditure stimulated, for example by the hosting of a mega-event such as the Olympics (**mega-event, staging of**), into a net expenditure figure for a fixed geographical area (e.g. the host city). The rationale behind using multipliers is the recognition that the initial financial outlay is usually just the beginning of a 'ripple effect' of expenditure.

Multipliers are particularly used in connection with **sports tourism**. There are three main types of multiplier: income multipliers; sales multipliers; and employment multipliers. Each is likely to lead to a very different assessment of economic impact (e.g. sales multipliers tend to be greater than income multipliers and thus may be used by supporters of particular events, rather than critics). However, each type of multiplier effectively seeks to measure the *direct* (i.e. the initial consumer expenditure), the *indirect* (i.e. expenditure made by local shops and restaurants etc. as a consequence of increased economic activity), and the *induced* effect (the re-spending of this stream of expenditure on locally produced goods or services). Thus, while the visitors to an Olympic Games may spend £1000 each, that economic activity will lead to an increased expenditure on goods and services by local suppliers, and an increase in the wealth of the host community, members of which will subsequently increase their own expenditure. Thus potentially the economic impact of the event can be much greater than the initial expenditure.

When calculating a multiplier one has to be very careful to consider the specific categories of expenditure and the nature of the host community. For instance, spending on petrol is likely to have a smaller overall effect on a local community than expenditure on food and drink, as the latter involves the employment of a greater number of local people in its delivery. Second, smaller communities are likely to be less self-sufficient and thus there is a greater potential for expenditure to be 'leaked'. For instance, while a large city may be able to host and service a large number of visitors, rural-based events (like golf tournaments) are likely to be too small to 'capture' all the potential economic impact, having staff, catering, etc., brought into the community for a fixed period and then leaving immediately afterwards. Because multipliers are so difficult to assess accurately, in practice most analyses simply borrow a multiplier from a similar type of event/location.

Key Reading

Gratton, C. and Taylor, P. (2000) *Economics of Sport and Recreation*. London: Routledge.

MUNICH AIR DISASTER

In February 1958, an aircraft transporting Manchester United players and officials back home from a European Cup quarter-final against Red Star Belgrade crashed during take-off after refuelling in the German city of Munich. Twenty-three people died, including eight players who were part of the talented young squad named the 'Busby Babes'.

Munich is arguably sports most remembered disaster, both publicly and within sports studies. Publicly there is much romanticizing about the players lost and the playing potential of the team. Academic analysis of the Munich air disaster, however, largely focuses on this mythologizing and on the relationship between Munich and the growth of Manchester United into one of the world's richest and most famous football teams.

Mellor has noted that Manchester United's popularity rose significantly in the period immediately following Munich. There were complaints from 'traditional' fans that the newcomers were not particularly knowledgeable, and largely came from outside Manchester. Mellor disputes the latter point, noting that concerns about the crossover of support from Manchester City to United pre-dated Munich. However, while Munich stimulated sympathy and interest in United, this was a short-lived phenomenon as United's gates dropped dramatically after 1959.

While Munich therefore had some impact on United's popularity and notoriety, Mellor

(2000) attributes the establishment of United as a 'super-club' to a number of other factors. These include: (1) United's success in European football in the mid- to late 1960s, especially their European Cup victory 10 years after Munich; (2) the decline in feelings of local identity and a strengthening national culture during the 1960s; (3) the increased ownership of cars enabling travel over greater distances; (4) the increased ownership of televisions, the televising of football, and United's prominence in this movement; and (5) the glamour and style of United's play, which made them the football club most closely connected to the burgeoning popular culture of the north of England in the 1960s, as epitomized by the fame of pop group the Beatles. This final point is underscored by the fact that United's star player, **George Best**, was sometimes referred to as the fifth Beatle.

Munich has subsequently become the subject of United folklore. United fans celebrate the efforts of manager Matt Busby in regenerating the club after Munich and cite this as the foundation of present-day success. For Mellor (2004a) Munich is 'a living cultural practice that needs to be learned and "consumed" as part of "becoming a United fan"'. It should be noted that football **fans** (mainly those of United's fiercest rivals) are critical of the mythology and romanticism that surround the Munich air disaster. Many also feel that the club has cynically exploited this incident for commercial gain – feelings exacerbated by United's financial and playing dominance (**commercialization**; **commodification**). Consequently, antipathy towards United is often expressed in relation to Munich. Thus Munich is important not only in creating the community of Manchester United fans, but also in creating the hatred which bonds together the communities of supporters of other football clubs.

Key Reading

Mellor, G. (2000) 'The genesis of Manchester United as a national and international "super-club", 1958–1968', *Soccer and Society*, 1 (2): 151–66.

Mellor, G. (2004a) '"The flowers of Manchester": the Munich Disaster and the discursive creation of Manchester United Football Club', *Soccer and Society*, 5 (2): 265–84.

Mellor, G. (2004b) '"We hate the Manchester club like poison": The Munich Disaster and the socio-historical development of Manchester United as a loathed football club', in D.L. Andrews (ed.), *Manchester United: A Thematic Study*. London: Routledge. pp. 28–42.

MUSCULAR CHRISTIANITY

Closely connected with the **cult of athleticism**, Muscular Christianity is the ideology developed by writers such as Charles Kingsley and Thomas Hughes, as exemplified in *Tom Brown's School Days* and practised in the public schools of Victorian Britain. Muscular Christianity developed in contrast to traditional, paramilitary codes of chivalry (including duelling). It extended the philosophy of the interconnected nature of a healthy body and a healthy mind, and parallel arguments that physical education necessarily entailed moral and ethical benefits, by making a more explicit link between physical activity, the **body** and Christian faith. Developing a strong body was seen as a form of bodily purification, a 'living sacrifice to God'. Physical exercise strengthened men, separated man from the animal world, produced an enlightened ruling class sensitive to modern conditions, and, in a Darwin-esque way, led to a healthier species (**health**).

Muscular Christians were similarly influential in the promotion of **rational recreation** and the diffusion of sports within the British Empire (**formal and informal Empire**; **imperialism**), believing that physical activity could combat physical and moral degeneracy among the lower social classes and the uncivilized 'races' colonized by the British (**race**). Consequently, many of the earliest sports teams founded in England were established by, or had close links with, the church, and many of the sports played within the British Empire (and especially cricket) were actively developed by church missionaries. By promoting games and physical activity Muscular Christians believed that they could increase church attendance and abate the drift towards Catholicism in the mid-nineteenth century. Dunning and Sheard (2005) argue that Muscular Christianity developed in conjunction with processes of industrialization and **embourgeoisement**.

Key Reading

Dunning, E. and Sheard, K. (2005) *Barbarians, Gentlemen and Players: A Sociological Study of the Development of Rugby Football*, 2nd edn. London: Routledge. esp. Ch. 3.

Mangan, J.A. (1981) *Athleticism in the Victorian and Edwardian Public School – The Emergence and Consolidation of an Educational Ideology*. Cambridge: Cambridge University Press.

N

NATIONAL CURRICULUM FOR PHYSICAL EDUCATION (NCPE)

Introduced in England and Wales in 1992, by John Major's Conservative government. The explicit aim was that, 'regardless of their sex, ethnic origin and geographical location', all children would share 'the same good and relevant curriculum', though part of the rationale appeared to be the government's attempt to take the control of education out of the hands of local education authorities, many of which were controlled by the opposition Labour Party.

The NCPE identified six core areas of activity – athletics, dance, games, gymnastics, outdoor and adventurous activities, and swimming – which were to be studied by all pupils, regardless of sex. Revisions to the NCPE introduced in 1995 meant that not all areas were compulsory at all age levels. In particular, post-11 years of age, some areas became voluntary while others, notably games, remained compulsory (further revisions were made in 1999).

Three main areas of research on the NCPE have emerged: (1) its influence on **gender** relations; (2) the role of **health-related physical education** (HRPE); and (3) the **discourse** of public policy and physical education (**physical education, policy in**). Many commentators were optimistic about the inclusive language of the initial policy documents, which promised to remove the traditional practice of gender segregation in PE. However, the flexibility ultimately allowed in the NCPE, the strong bias towards sports and games (which have historically been male dominated), and the marginalization of other activities (notably dance and outdoor activities) have allowed the gender differentiated curriculum to continue. The converse has happened with **health**-related activities, as initial fears that the absence of a specific activity area for HRPE would lead to the subject's marginalization have been allayed by subsequent policy statements which have encouraged it to be addressed in curriculum planning across areas of activity. Finally, Evans and Penney in particular have charted the way that contrary to the initial liberal and progressive agenda of the NCPE, government intervention in the policy process led to the promotion of the government's specific interests in and for PE, including an emphasis on team games, an agenda of restoration and keeping with tradition, and, consequently, the perpetuation of inequalities.

Key Reading

Harris, J. (2000) *Health-related Exercise in the National Curriculum. Key Stages 1 to 4.* Champaign, IL: Human Kinetics.
Penney, D. (2002) *Gender and Physical Education: Contemporary Issues and Future Directions.* London: Routledge.
Penney, D. and Evans, J. (1999) *Politics, Policy and Practice in Physical Education.* London: Routledge.

NATIONAL IDENTITY

(**nationalism**)

NATIONALISM

The existence of a close relationship between sport and nationalism is widely accepted. This relationship manifests itself in the enduring popularity of international competitions and events, in the myriad ways in which politicians and politically motivated groups have sought to harness sport to national causes and also in the very concept of national sports. Nevertheless, questions are increasingly being asked about the future of the relationship between sport and nationalism as well as about the fate of the nation itself.

Much of the literature on the relationship between sport and nationhood has been concerned with the ways in which nation states seek to promote themselves, or simply carry out their economic and diplomatic business, using sport as a useful and highly visible medium (**propaganda**). Almost since the emergence of sport in its modern form (**modern sport**), the British sought to make use of it, at least in part, in order to extend their influence in their **formal and informal Empires**. More recently, the United States has also played a significant role in the diffusion of sport, supported by the country's political and economic influence in parts of Asia and in parts of the Caribbean and Central America. In addition, during the Cold War it was apparent that the Soviet Union and most, if not all, of its East European neighbours used sport in general and especially the Olympic Games to advertise their particular brand of communism. Moreover, international rivalry was not only acted out on the athletics track or on the high beam but also impacted on the wider context of events such as the Olympics, with the United States seeking to lead a **boycott** of the Moscow Games in 1980 and the Soviet Union and its allies responding in kind when the Olympics were held in Los Angeles in 1984. Related to this is the fact that nation states also put considerable efforts into acquiring the right to host major events, which are then turned into spectacular exercises in self-promotion by the successful bidders (**mega-events, hosting of**). There can be little doubt that most national leaders in the modern world are highly conscious of the role that sport can play in boosting confidence, facilitating closer diplomatic links and securing markers of esteem.

Sport is also commonly implicated in the cultural politics of submerged nations and nationalisms. Thus within the United Kingdom, for example, sport is a hugely significant vehicle for the reproduction of distinctive national identities (Scottish, Welsh, (Northern) Irish and, increasingly, English) within the context of a multinational nation state. Similar observations can be made about Spain, Canada and other nation states where one finds varying levels of contestation between official nationalities and unofficial national identities.

In terms of both nation states and submerged nations, it is easy to see the extent to which sport, arguably more than any other form of social activity in the modern world, allows for flag waving and the playing of national anthems, both formally at moments such as medal ceremonies and informally through the activities of **fans**. The desire, particularly on the part of fans, to express their national identity in the realm of sport is clearly linked to nationalism in the broadest sense or, at the very least, to patriotism. Scottish politician Jim Sillars dismissed the attitude of his fellow Scots towards their national sporting representatives as 'ninety-minute patriotism'. Nevertheless, there is also evidence that sport can play a formidable role as an expression of cultural nationalism which either accompanies or acts as a fore-runner for fully fledged nationalist politics. The part played by the **Gaelic Athletic Association** in Ireland since its formation in 1884 is an excellent example of this.

For most sportsmen and women, even in an era when money is a major incentive for achieving sporting success, representing the nation remains important. However, it is quite conceivable that in the course of their sporting careers athletes might represent more than one nation, with neither ethnic origin nor even well-established civic connections being necessary for a move from one to another. Yet, even in an era of large-scale global migration, for the overwhelming majority of athletes engaged in international sport the matter of which country to represent remains relatively clear-cut (**sport labour migration**). For fans, things are arguably even simpler. In the modern era, following one's 'proxy warriors' into international competition is one of the easiest and most passionate ways of underlining one's sense of national identity, one's nationality or both. Needless to say, not everyone wishes to celebrate their national affiliation in this way, in most instances for the simple reason that they are not interested in sport, the nation or the relationship between the two. But just as for most active participants, for the majority of sports fans the choice is relatively straightforward. This is not to deny, of course, that in certain circumstances athletes and fans alike may well understand their nations in different ways (many England football fans exhibit little interest in/antipathy towards the national rugby union team because of its **class** connotations). Furthermore, it is not only sporting individuals who demonstrate the contested character of most, if not all, nations. Sports themselves also do so to the extent that they become 'national' in the popular imagination for a variety of reasons.

National sports take different forms and, in so doing, provide us with interesting insights into the character of particular nations. Indeed, the concept of 'national' sport not only helps us to gain a better understanding of the relationship between nations and nation states and between national identity and nationality, but also offers evidence of the ways in which some nations seek to resist **globalization**. Some 'national' sports are peculiar to specific nations. Their 'national' status is ring-fenced by their exclusivity – echoes here of ethnic nationalism. National sports and games of this type are in some sense linked to the essence of the nations in question (e.g. see **Doubleday myth**), even though their actual origins may be pre-national or at least prior to the emergence of nation states. They represent 'the nation' symbolically despite the fact that they may well have demonstrably failed to

capture the interest of most of the people who constitute the civic nation and/or the nation state. Other 'national' sports are designated as such for the simple reason that they are highly popular and, by implication, inclusive, thereby underpinning the idea of the civic nation.

There are some grounds for believing that the link between nationalism and sports is becoming weaker and that the very existence of international competition is threatened by the twin forces of globalization and consumer capitalism (**consumer culture**). For the time being, however, even though it manifests itself in a wide variety of ways, the relationship between sports and nations remains strong.

Key Reading

Allison, L. (2000) 'Sport and nationalism', in J. Coakley and E. Dunning (eds), *Handbook of Sports Studies*. London: Sage. pp. 344–55.

Bairner, A. (2001) *Sport, Nationalism, and Globalization: European and North American Perspectives*. Albany: State University of New York Press.

Cronin, M. and Mayall, D. (eds) (1998) *Sporting Nationalisms. Identity, Ethnicity, Immigration and Assimilation*. London: Frank Cass.

Miller, T. Lawrence, G., McKay, J. and Rowe, D. (2001) *Globalization and Sport*. London: Sage.

Porter, D. and Smith, A. (eds) (2004) *Sport and National Identity in the Post-War World*. London: Routledge.

Alan Bairner

NEW LADDISM

The 'New Lad' phenomenon was/is a reaction to the 1980s' 'New Man'. In contrast to 'traditional' forms of **masculinity**, 'New Man' is a more caring and compassionate partner, more actively involved in the nurturing of children and in domestic chores more generally. New Laddism also stemmed from an awareness of feminist discourse, claiming 'political correctness' through being ostensibly non-racist and respectful of femininities and **feminism**. However, the product, according to Whelehan (2000: 58) is 'almost always white; part soccer thug, part lager lout, part arrant sexist'.

New Lads were targeted, and the phenomenon promoted, by men's magazines such as *Loaded* and *FHM*. These magazines have five central characteristics: (1) they are aimed at a middle-**class** readership; (2) they are assertively heterosexual; (3) they represent an overt legitimation of consumption; (4) they promote an aspirational lifestyle; and (5) they 'implicitly depend upon a city as opposed to a rural ... milieu' (Edwards, 1997: 75–6).

Ben Carrington (1998) was the first sociologist to incorporate a discussion of New Laddism in sports-related research. He noted that David Baddiel and Frank Skinner's football programme *Fantasy Football League* exhibited many of these characteristics. In their song 'Football's Coming Home', which became the England football team's semi-official anthem during the 1996 European Football Championships, they evoked memories of England's 1966 World Cup victory. The result was an attempt to redefine the boundaries of white English masculinity, and a partial reversion to 'traditional' masculine, largely working-class, values. The concept has more recently been used by Cashmore and Parker in their discussion of **David Beckham** (2003) and by Parry and Malcolm in their work on the **Barmy Army** (2004).

Key Reading

Carrington, B. (1998) '"Football's coming home" but whose home? And do we want it?: Nation, football and the politics of exclusion', in A. Brown (ed.), *Fanatics! Power, Identity and Fandom in Football*. London: Routledge. pp. 101–23.

Cashmore, E. and Parker, A. (2003) 'One David Beckham? Celebrity, masculinity and the soccerati', *Sociology of Sport Journal*, 20 (3): 214–31.

Edwards, T. (1997) *Men in the Mirror: Men's Fashions, Masculinity and Consumer Society*. London: Cassell.

Parry, M. and Malcolm, D. (2004) 'England's Barmy Army: commercialization, masculinity and nationalism', *International Review for the Sociology of Sport*, 39 (1): 73–92.

Whelehan, I. (2000) *Overloaded: Popular Culture and the Future of Feminism*. London: Women's Press.

NIKE

Founded under the name Blue Ribbon Sports in 1964 by current CEO Philip Knight, and University of Oregon Track and Field Coach Bill Bowerman, the Nike brand emerged at the 1972 US Olympic Trials and immediately courted controversy by offering amateur athletes money to wear and promote their products (**amateurism**). Posing a challenge to the aristocratic elites and corporate bureaucracies which constitute the sporting establishment (and which were closely aligned with Nike's chief rival, adidas) has always formed the central strand of the Nike image and branding. It is now the world's largest sports shoemaker, controlling 20 per cent of the US market in 2005, with global sales of $14 billion in that year.

From the 1970s Nike sought to align itself not solely with successful athletes, but with a select few sportspeople who had personality, 'attitude' and challenged the prevailing sports system – so-called 'signature athletes' like John McEnroe and Eric Cantona. This stance is epitomized in the phrase 'Just do it', representing an absence of constraint, the promotion of individual free will and the exceptional natural talent and authenticity of Nike's sponsored celebrities. Nike are thought to have changed the rules for sports **sponsorship** by paying huge endorsements to tie athletes to using their equipment ($90 million for basketball's Lebron James, $450 million for the right to run Manchester United's merchandise and kit operation) and by 'in-your-face', aggressive advertising linking their products to the athletic success of a few high-profile individuals.

Most notably, Nike's endorsement deal with basketball superstar **Michael Jordan** led the 'Air Jordan' sports shoe to become the highest selling trainer of all time, and helped bolster the popular appeal of the NBA. Jordan became a major sports **celebrity**, and so close has this relationship been that at times the distinction between Jordan and Nike appears almost non-existent, or at least that it has become unclear who is promoting whom (see also **Tiger Woods**).

However, the Nike aura of being unconventional was dented when it subsequently moved its entire manufacturing operation out of the US in order to exploit the cheaper workforces and overheads on offer in the Far East. Initiated by workers' strike action against low pay and poor conditions, religious groups, human rights activists and corporate monitoring groups collaborated to form the Nike Transnational Social Movement (also known as the transnational advocacy network). Pressure from the Movement forced Nike to develop a 'code of conduct' for its producers, though this was subsequently dismissed as essentially a public relations move. Nike eventually announced what it called 'new labour initiatives' in May 1998, which went some way to ameliorating the Movement.

Throughout the conflict Nike complained that it was being unfairly singled out and stressed that the conditions in the factories where its products were made were little different to the production sites of many other similar companies. In part, the explanation for this heightened level of scrutiny was that Nike was both a market leader, and one of the first companies in the market sector to move production to the Far East. It was also the case that such exploitation appeared to run counter to the company's self-promotion of an anti-corporate image and this hypocrisy probably fuelled the passion with which campaigners fought against Nike. However, as the figures cited above indicate, the bad publicity stemming from these issues seems to have had little impact on sales and profits. Indeed, Nike has been described as 'a model of global postindustrial enterprise', a company that no longer produces anything itself, but merely buys up products and brands them.

Key Reading

Katz, D. (1994) *Just do it: The Nike Spirit in the Corporate World*. Holbrook, MA: Adams Publishing.

Sage, G. (1999) 'Justice do it! The Nike transnational advocacy network: organization, collective actions and outcomes', *Sociology of Sport Journal*, 16 (3): 206–35.

OBESITY DISCOURSE

The first years of the twenty-first century witnessed a notable increase in media and public concern over the issue of obesity. While on one level the definition of obesity can be seen essentially as physiological (obesity is defined as a 'score' of over 30 on the 'body-mass index' (BMI), calculated by comparing height and weight data), social scientists became particularly concerned about the social construction of obesity as an issue, and the policy and social consequences of this.

According to Gard and Wright (2004) the obesity discourse consists of the following ideas: (1) that populations are getting heavier and that average body weight is increasing rapidly; (2) that obesity is a global problem; (3) that obesity is caused by lifestyle factors (such as the excessive use of computers, watching television, etc. which lead directly to a lack of physical activity); (4) that obesity is linked to a decline in self-**discipline**, traditional family values and parenting skills; and (5) that the obesity discourse focuses particularly on children, largely on the assumption that this is a group whose behaviour can be modified and controlled. However, social scientists point out that while there is clear evidence that weight extremes (either over- or underweight) can be damaging to **health**, there is little reliable evidence regarding the health outcomes of most forms of obesity. Other evidence suggests that children are, in fact, playing more sport than ever before (**youth sport participation**), and that there is little correlation between taking part in pastimes such as watching television and playing computers, and abstaining from physical activity. There is, therefore, a considerable gap between scientific fact and public debates over the crisis of an obesity epidemic.

The rise of the obesity discourse has been attributed to a number of factors. Increasingly in contemporary societies the **body** is seen as a personal project, with individuals believing that they can actively influence their body shape and appearance (e.g. through sport, cosmetic surgery, etc.). The appearance of the body is regarded as a marker of self-worth and fat, portrayed as the very antithesis of beauty, is thus viewed as abhorrent and a signifier of moral laxity. The obesity discourse can also be seen as stemming from changes to the status of expert knowledge and the concern with **risk** in contemporary societies. In an ever changing postmodern society (**postmodernism**) there is a growing tendency for individuals to attempt to assess and manage risk, and one of the key sites over which individuals can (or believe they can) exercise control is the body. Not to be underestimated in this regard is the role of the mass **media** in creating a **moral panic**.

A central consequence of this discourse is that attention is diverted away from the social and institutional factors which contribute to poor health (e.g. poverty) while the individual is placed centre-stage in the management of what is deemed to be a 'social problem'. Anti-fatness has been described as 'the last civilized discrimination' for judgementalism, and prejudice regarding body weight far exceeds that which might normally be deemed acceptable with regard to **race** or **gender**, for example. The obesity discourse creates a climate of fear and guilt (particularly among children) and it might reasonably be concluded that this in part has led to the increase in cases of **eating disorders.**

Key Reading

Gard, M. and Wright, J. (2004) *The Obesity Epidemic. Science, Morality and Ideology.* London: Routledge.

OBJECTIVITY AND SUBJECTIVITY

Research is held to be objective if it is free of distortion from personal bias. Research which purports to be objective is based on the theoretical premise that it is possible to measure accurately all aspects of the social world, and thus to present the social world as existing independently of human perception or values. Research which is deemed to be objective is said to possess **reliability and validity**; that is to say, it gives results which are consistent and/or replicable, and it measures what it was intended/claimed to measure. The desirability of objectivity stems from the traditions of the natural sciences, in which experiments can be isolated from external events, repeated and controlled. This kind of research dominated the early social scientific study of sport, as epitomized by the work on **stacking**. Empiricism, **positivism** and **realism** are the main perspectives which promote the pursuit of objectivity.

Research is held to be subjective if it is deemed to have been influenced by the perspective of a person/the researcher. Subjectivity is often used as a term of criticism but it should be noted that some researchers insist that subjectivity is inevitable, that social reality only exists through the meanings which people attach to the world (**epistemology and ontology**). Researchers committed to a subjectivist approach focus on the *meanings* that people attach to social phenomena rather

than simply the phenomena themselves. Thus certain researchers would claim that research which focuses on the subjective understandings, e.g. of disadvantages and social exclusion faced by minority ethnic groups in sport, is more meaningful than objective measures, e.g., of the propensity of black athletes to assume certain sporting roles. However, the counter-criticism might be raised that, if social reality is essentially subjective, on what grounds can the social scientist's interpretation be deemed more valid than any other? The main perspectives that promote the pursuit of subjectivity are **idealism, interpretivism, postmodernism, post-structuralism**, and certain forms of **feminism**.

Objectivity and subjectivity is one of the dichotomies that have traditionally characterized sociology and, in truth, all social research lies somewhere on a continuum between these two poles or ideal types. A notable attempt to overcome the problems associated with making this false dichotomy is Elias's work on **involvement and detachment**.

OBSERVATION

While **interviews** and **questionnaires** are based on the assumption that researchers can elicit useful information by talking to people, observation is premised on the assumption that watching people is equally, if not more, revealing. Observation as a research method can be further categorized according to whether the researcher is overt or covert in their role as observer, and whether the researcher is a participant or non-participant in the activities being observed. Participant observation that requires a high level of immersion into the field of study is sometimes also called **ethnography**.

Observation might be used where respondents would be either unwilling or unable to relay accurately their world and experiences verbally (for instance, Charles Gallmeier (1987) used observational research methods to examine the way ice hockey players 'stage' or manufacture their **emotions** before, during and after matches). Observation is a particularly suitable method when a high level of description, rather than explanation, is required. The researcher may either record their observations on a standardized sheet (involving a very focused approach to which data are to be observed, and consequently allowing for high levels of comparability of data), or construct fieldnotes during and after observation sessions (which are descriptive and reflective).

Advantages of observational methods are that they enable the recording of human behaviour in its 'natural' environment. This solves the problem of self-reporting and inaccurate recall, which may impair data derived from other, verbal or written, research methods (e.g. interviews and questionnaires). Observation may uncover information which respondents would not be willing to discuss or behaviours about which they were not consciously aware. The disadvantages of observational methods are that: (1) they may be time consuming; (2) the presence of the observer may actually lead to the alteration of behaviour among research subjects (called the Hawthorne effect); (3) without speaking to those involved, the researcher may not fully understand the social interaction being observed; and (4) on their own, observations are unlikely to tell us *why* certain behaviour occurs, merely that it does. Especially with covert observation, taking accurate fieldnotes can be problematic in that as part of their blending into the broader environment (e.g. with football hooligan groups) researchers may be required to drink **alcohol**, take drugs, etc. Furthermore, fieldnotes may also have to be constructed some time after the observations occur, once the researcher is alone or has access to writing materials.

Key Reading

Gallmeier, C. (1987) 'Putting on the game face: the staging of emotions in professional hockey', *Sociology of Sport Journal*, 4 (4): 347–62.

Gratton, C. and Jones, I. (2004) *Research Methods for Sports Studies*. London: Routledge. esp. Ch. 10.

OLD FIRM (SECTARIANISM)

OLYMPIC MOVEMENT (IOC)

ONTOLOGY

(epistemology and ontology)

ÖSTERBERG, MADAME BERGMAN (1849–1915)

The leading nineteenth-century exponent in Britain of Swedish gymnastics, Martina Bergman, later Madame Bergman Österberg, played a pivotal role in the development of female sport/physical activities, and made a unique contribution to the feminist cause.

Österberg worked for the London School Board between 1882 and 1887, introducing her system of gymnastics to nearly 300 schools, and in 1885 founded Dartford College to provide training for physical education teachers. Her gymnastics became the official model of physical education for girls throughout English schools.

Österberg's system of gymnastics developed out of **Per Henrik Ling's** system of free-standing exercises, believed to promote **health** and provide physical therapy; a system of exercises underpinned by the concept of the 'harmonious development of the whole body'. Her gymnastics were very similar to military drill and thus required a high level of **discipline**. Cleanliness, smart dress and punctuality were seen as central. Yet, as with the **cult of athleticism**, Österberg believed that such rigorous and composed physical exercise had an impact on the individual's morality and thus she demanded from her students total commitment to the entire Österberg ethos and way of life.

Her philosophy constituted a particular version of liberal **feminism**. She was deeply commited to the social and economic freedom of women. In line with Social Darwinists, Österberg argued that the health, intellect and morality of females were vital to their ability to bear healthy children and thus the progress of the human race as a whole. A precondition of this philosophy, therefore, was that female education should be linked to a woman's role as housewife and mother; that is to say, it accepted and reinforced the existing, dominant form of **gender** relations. A further criticism that has been raised (e.g. Hargreaves, 1994) is that while middle-**class**

schoolgirls participated in Swedish gymnastics *alongside* other physical activity, for working-class girls it represented the only physical exercise available within the school curriculum. Thus, one outcome of Österberg's work was social control at the expense of freedom and expression. However, as Fletcher's work shows (1984), it is undoubtedly the case that Österberg paved the way for one of the first and most enduring professions deemed socially acceptable for women (teaching physical education) and it is perhaps in this regard that her contribution to the empowerment of women mainly lies.

Key Reading

Fletcher, S. (1984) *Women First: The Female Tradition in English Physical Education, 1880–1980*. London: Athlone Press.

Hargreaves, J.A. (1994) *Sporting Females: Critical Issues in the History and Sociology of Women's Sports*. London: Routledge.

P

PAIN AND INJURY

Various disciplines within sports science have produced research on the role of pain and injury in sport. However, it was particularly during the 1990s that the sociological study of pain and injury in sport emerged as a strong and growing research area. It has been argued that prior to this, pain and injury were often subsumed under the broader category of **violence** in sport, but this trend was probably also related to the increased incidence of injury in sport that stemmed from sport's increasing competitiveness, the social and economic costs to athletes of injuries in highly commercialized sports (**commercialization**), and the extent to which injuries were increasingly visible to sports audiences through the **media**.

Five key strands of sociological work on pain and injury have emerged. The first pointed towards the widespread acceptance of pain and injury among athletes, and argued that athletes 'normalize', rationalize and provide legitimating ideologies for their tolerance of this behaviour. The second, pioneered by Howard Nixon II, seeks to understand the structural context of pain and injury in sport. Nixon (1992) speaks of the 'culture of risk' (**risk**) in sport, and the way in which **sportsnets** serve to coerce athletes to play and train with pain and through injury. A third key strand locates playing with pain and injury within the context of **masculinity**. Authors such as Kevin Young have argued that the socialization processes which

boys and young men experience encourage them to believe that a tolerance of pain is an essential characteristic of being a 'real man' (2004). Hence, in the extremely masculine sports **subcultures**, men hide or deny their pain and injuries. In a natural extension of this work, researchers have developed a fourth strand focusing on the pain and injury of female athletes, examining whether **gender** is a significant mediating factor. This work has shown that female athletes exhibit very similar characteristics to their male counterparts, findings which rather imply that either the uncritical acceptance of the **sport ethic** is more important than masculine socialization processes, or females have become incorporated into, rather than resistant to, the dominant model of men's sport. Finally, in perhaps the most recent of the five key strands, there has been a growing focus on the providers of **sports medicine**, and their role in cooperating or conflicting with athletes who compete despite suffering pain and injury.

Key Reading

Loland, S., Skirstad, B. and Waddington, I. (2005) *Philosophical and Sociological Aspects of Sports Injury*. London: Routledge.

Malcolm, D. and Sheard, K. (2002) '"Pain in the assets": the effects of commercialization and professionalization on the management of injury in English rugby union', *Sociology of Sport Journal*, 19 (2): 149–69.

Nixon II, H.L. (1992) 'A social network analysis of influences on athletes to play with pain and injuries', *Journal of Sport and Social Issues*, 16: 127–35.

Young, K. (2004) (ed.), *Sporting Bodies, Damaged Selves: Sociological Studies of Sports-Related Injury*. Oxford: Elsevier.

PANCRATION

The most popular and most brutal event in the **ancient Olympic Games**, the Pancration was a cross between freestyle wrestling and modern day 'ultimate fighting', where participants were allowed to use any part of their body – hands, feet, elbows, knees, heads – and fight in whatever style they chose. Opponents could be tripped, strangled, choked, kicked, beaten around the head while pinned down, or have their eyes (and presumably other parts of their bodies) gouged. There was a judge, but no time limits. Rules were traditional, unwritten and, in all likelihood, enforced less strictly and less consistently than we would expect in today's sporting contests. Contests were won when an opponent conceded the bout, normally due to excessive pain. In one famous case, Arrhachion of Phigalia, who had been Olympic Pancration champion twice before, won a third crown despite being killed during a fight (strangled by his opponents legs). His last act was to break the toes of his opponent who, due to the pain, conceded the contest as Arrhachion lay dying. Arrhachion was proclaimed the winner but, apart from the loss of the crown, his opponent was neither punished for, nor stigmatized because of, his actions.

Elias (1971) (**figurational sociology**) argues that the Pancration shows us that the game contests of ancient Greece were governed by a warrior ethos (as opposed to the central ethos of **modern sport**, **fair play**), which valued bravery and valour rather than winning. Moreover, the relatively violent nature of the Pancration, and its popularity with spectators, can be explained with reference to the relatively high levels of physical **violence** experienced in everyday life (in Greek society, if murder was committed, it was the duty of the victim's kin rather than the state to punish and/or exact revenge) and the almost constant threat of war that most city states faced.

Key Reading

Baker, W.J. (1982) *Sports in the Western World*. Totowa, NJ: Rowan and Littlefield. esp. Ch. 2.

Elias, N. (1971) 'The genesis of sport as a sociological problem', in E. Dunning (ed.), *The Sociology of Sport: A Selection of Readings*. London: Frank Cass. pp. 88–115.

Finley, M. and Pleket, H. (1976) *The Olympic Games*. London: Chatto and Windus.

PANOPTICON

(**surveillance**)

PARALYMPICS

(**disability**)

PARLIAMENTARIZATION

(**sportization and parliamentarization**)

PARTICIPANT OBSERVATION

(**ethnography**)

PEDAGOGY

The term pedagogy is contested; there is no one accepted definition. Indeed, the term is often used fairly generally without being clearly defined and therefore is considered by many to be a vague concept. Even when it is defined, the definitions themselves have been described as problematic, as descriptors such as science, teaching or learning are similarly vague and unclear.

Pedagogy is variously described as an art, a craft and a science. One fairly common description is 'the science of teaching'. However, although some descriptions focus on teaching, others also take learning into account. For example, Watkins and Mortimore (in Mortimore, 1999: 17) define pedagogy as 'any conscious activity by one person designed to enhance learning in another'. For Leach and Moon (1999), the questions asked by teachers in all teaching and learning situations (i.e. 'how do I reach the children?') and those asked by pupils (i.e. 'what is the teacher trying to get at?') form the basis of pedagogy.

It is generally recognized that pedagogy is a complex activity that cannot be considered in isolation. In addition to teaching and learning, the context in which pedagogy occurs must be considered. Relevant factors include: educational goals; the aims of education and of the subject; objectives of the specific activity; the curriculum; assessment; learning activities; and the roles of teacher and learner. Pedagogy must therefore be 'fit for purpose', with teaching methods – tasks, activities and assessments – appropriate for the needs of the learner to achieve identified learning outcomes. Having high expectations of each learner, then finding the optimal level of challenge and being able to motivate each learner (**motivation**) are key pedagogical skills.

Pedagogy is 'never innocent' (Leach and Moon, 1999: 2). There are tensions between 'formal pedagogy' (multi-contextual models developed by academics) and 'vernacular pedagogy' (pedagogy developed by practitioners for a specific context). The vernacular is linked to 'folk' theories of pedagogy; those taken-for-granted beliefs that teachers and pupils bring to the teaching and learning process. Therefore, formal pedagogical theory has to compete with, modify or replace folk theories of teachers and pupils.

A teacher's folk theory and therefore choice of a specific pedagogy reflects assumptions and conceptions about the learner and the learning process, including how children learn and what is important for them to learn. Thus, for example, for teachers who view learning as the acquisition of knowledge, children's minds are receptacles to be filled. Preferred teaching styles may focus on direct teaching methods and practice to achieve competence through activities such as modelling in a relationship akin to that of master–apprentice. On the other hand, for teachers who view learning as developing conceptual understanding, a constructivist approach may be adopted, building on experiences through active learning (e.g. experiential learning, discovery learning and problem solving). Discussion and collaboration are more likely to be included.

Evidence suggests that many teachers use a limited range of teaching styles in physical education and that direct teaching methods are most frequently used. Direct teaching styles may sometimes be selected for purposes of control rather than because they are the most appropriate to achieve a specific learning outcome. Research shows that both newly qualified and student teachers rely heavily on direct teaching methods, which they perceive to be 'safer'. However, research suggests that children learn best and most in contexts where teachers are flexible, able to mix teaching methods as appropriate for the subject matter and the specific learning outcomes, and can cater for differences in ability and need.

Didactic teaching is likely to be most effective if the learning outcome to be achieved is a lower-order objective (e.g. to understand some specific information). However, overuse of direct teaching methods may restrict the attainment of higher-order objectives; for example, dealing with unpredictable situations in a game or using knowledge to form, justify and defend a position. Thus, if a higher-order objective is to be achieved, other teaching styles are more appropriate. In physical education pupils need to achieve both lower- and higher-order objectives to develop expertise and thus a range of teaching styles is needed. A range is also needed to allow for different motivations of children at different times and in different situations.

Penney and Waring (2000: 11–12) argue that the 'traditional' pedagogy of physical education in which the focus is on 'the acquisition of skills and understanding relating to performance in specific [mostly sporting] activities within the curriculum' is a barrier to learning. One result of this is that what is taught may have limited 'transfer value' from physical education to related situations outside school. Indeed, 'many young people learn to dislike participation in physical activity through participation in school physical education' (Kirk and MacDonald, 1998: 383). Thus, there are calls for alternative pedagogical models, like the situated learning model (Lave and Wenger, 1991). This is an example of a constructivist approach to learning in which the focus of attention is on the social settings that construct and constitute the individual as a learner as opposed to the learner as an isolated individual. The key to this is access by newcomers to the community of practice. Kirk and Macdonald and others identify situated learning as a possible means of improving pedagogical practice in physical education, to better equip young people for the future by reproducing in school physical education experiences of physical recreation, exercise and sport.

There is, therefore, no simple recipe for effective pedagogy. However, it is important that pedagogy is not marginalized, as Simon (in Leach and Moon, 1999) argues it is in much teaching. He argues that the focus is on classroom organization and management and on teaching skills, while ignoring the underlying pedagogy. Indeed, it has been argued that we know little about the complexity of life in physical education 'classrooms', and that more attention needs to be given to *what* physical education teachers teach than to *how* and *why*. Thus, in order to create effective pedagogies, teachers not only need to know 'how to do it' (i.e. the technical and functional skills and techniques of teaching), to enable pupils to achieve different types of learning outcome, but also need to understand the principles on which teaching is based as well as understand learners and theories of learning and their integration with specific subject matter in a specific context – with particular pupils in specific circumstances.

Key Reading

Kirk, D. and Macdonald, D. (1998) 'Situated learning in physical education', *Journal of Teaching in Physical Education*, 17: 376–87.

Lave, J. and Wenger, E. (1991) *Situated Learning: Legitimate Peripheral Participation*. New York: Cambridge University Press.

Leach, J. and Moon, B. (eds) (1999) *Learners and Pedagogy*. London: Paul Chapman Publishing in association with the Open University.

Mortimore, P. (ed.) (1999) *Understanding Pedagogy and its Impact on Learning*. London: Paul Chapman Publishing.

Penney, D. and Waring, M. (2000) 'The absent agenda: pedagogy and physical education', *Journal of Sport Pedagogy*, 6 (1): 4–37.

Susan Capel

PERFORMATIVITY

The notions of performance and performativity have their roots in **symbolic interactionism** but owe their current popularity to **post-structuralism** and the work of Judith Butler in particular. Symbolic interactionists like Goffman devoted considerable effort to analysing the ways in which people present themselves in everyday life. For Goffman, social life was like a continual drama, with social actors assuming particular roles and adjusting those roles in response to the responses of others.

Post-structuralists like Butler have extended this symbolic interactionist work. The essential difference is that these more contemporary theorists argue that the performance isn't simply the external presentation (of the self), it is the reality. Thus Butler argues that concepts like sex and gender have no meaning and no existence in abstraction from their performance, their social construction; we are not gay or straight, we are simply doing gay or straight acts at any particular time and what we come to understand by these acts is a consequence of socially constructed meanings. Performativity is said to be more prevalent in postmodern societies (see **postmodernism**), as a greater importance is attached to consumption relative to production (**consumer culture**). It is argued that identities do not exist in and of themselves (i.e we are not men and women, old and young, black and Asian, middle and working class) but that we take on these identities only when our performance is consumed (e.g. by performing the role of a young white working-class male for the consumption of our peers).

The notion of performativity has only recently been applied in sports studies. Most notable in this respect is Blackshaw and Crabbe's work (2004) which argues that performativity is a key aspect of contemporary forms of sport and **deviance**, and Giardina's work (2003) which seeks to use performativity to help understand the fluid and hybrid character of ethnic identities in a postmodern age.

Key Reading

Blackshaw, T. and Crabbe, T. (2004) *New Perspectives on Sport and 'Deviance': Consumption, Performativity and Social Control*. London: Routledge.

Giardina, M. (2003) '"Bending it like Beckham" in the Global Popular: Stylish Hybridity, Performativity and the Politics of Representation', *Journal of Sport and Social Issues*, 27 (1): 65–82.

PERSONALITY

Has been defined as consistent behaviour patterns originating within the individual. Personality therefore is relatively stable over time and is, to some extent, unique to the individual (though clearly there are commonalities, no two personalities are thought to be exactly the same). Personality is a combination of both psychological characteristics and physical manifestations (i.e. behaviour).

Typically, the personality is separated into three related levels. The *psychological core* is defined as the most basic, fundamental and deep-seated level of personality and, consequently, the most unlikely to change. *Typical responses* constitute the middle layer of personality. They are defined as the ways in which we usually respond to the external world and are thought to be highly indicative of one's psychological core. Finally, *role-related behaviour* refers to the most superficial and changeable aspects of personality, and in particular to behaviour that changes as a consequence of external factors like environmental change. Viewed in this way, personality can be seen as a continuum ranging from internally driven to externally driven behaviours.

Empirical evidence suggests that people alter their behaviour between different contexts and, consequently, theories of personality have increasingly moved from static and rigid conceptions of personality (where the psychological core is dominant) to more fluid and flexible conceptions (where the environment exerts a greater influence). Four main theoretical approaches can be detected in the literature. The *psychodynamic approach* stems from the work of the first acknowledged personality theorist, Sigmund Freud. Essentially, this approach suggests that personality is a dynamic set of conscious and unconscious processes (e.g. the id, the ego and the super ego) that constantly interact (change and come into conflict with each other) to form personality and behaviour. While usefully highlighting the role of the sub/unconscious, this approach has been criticized for underplaying the importance of the social environment, and because the theory is ultimately untestable.

The *trait approach* assumes that personality is formed by certain fundamental units – traits – which are relatively stable over time and between different social contexts, and which predispose (NB not determine) athletes to act in particular ways. Traits are distinct and independent entities (i.e. having one trait does not necessarily entail or discount having another) and their strength is indicated by the frequency, intensity and generalizability of behaviours. The trait approach led to the development of personality inventories such as Cattell's 16 PF personality test and Gill's more widely accepted 'big five' model (the five key traits being: neuroticism, extraversion, openness to experience, agreeableness and conscientiousness). Once again critics note, however, that knowledge of traits does not enable us to predict behaviour with any great degree of accuracy unless consideration of the broader environment is considered.

The third approach – the *situation approach*, or *learning theories* – is based on the assumption that individuals often exhibit behaviours shaped by environmental influences and the behaviour of other people (e.g. coaches, team mates) who they observe and with whom they interact (**social learning theory**). The obvious criticism of this approach is that it is incapable of explaining individual variance to similar environmental conditions.

This criticism has led to the development, and dominance in the field, of the *interactional approach*. This fourth theory is essentially more comprehensive, arguing that the person and the situation are co-determinants of behaviour. This leads to a focus on both 'traits' and 'states'.

Sports psychologists may measure personality (1) by listening to what an athlete says; (2) by observing an athlete in action; or (3) via tests and objective measurement instruments. In the context of sport, there may be three central rationales for the measurement and assessment of personality: (1) providing athletes with information about themselves which may relate to performance; (2) diagnosis and intervention purposes, e.g. as part of an attempt by a coach to modify the personality characteristics of an athlete and influence performance; and (3) for the purposes of predicting athletic success and selecting those most likely to succeed.

While psychologists have been unable to identify a specific personality profile which distinguishes athletes from non-athletes, evidence suggests some differences between those disposed towards team sports and those who prefer individual events. Moreover, Morgan has used a profile of mood states (POMS) to predict athletic success, arguing that an 'iceberg profile' of relatively low scores for tension, depression, anger, fatigue and confusion, and a relatively high score for vigour (thus providing the iceberg's peak in graphic form) is a good indicator of future athletic success. However, it should also be noted that the predictive powers of this model have been questioned in recent years.

Key Reading

Gill, D. (2000) *Psychological Dynamics of Sport and Exercise*. Champaign, IL: Human Kinetics.

Morgan, W.P. (1980) 'The trait psychology controversy', *Research Quarterly for Exercise and Sport*, 51: 50–76.

Schurr, K.T., Ashley, M.A. and Joy, K.L. (1977) 'A multivariate analysis of male athlete personality characteristics: sport type and success', *Multivariate Experimental Clinical Research*, 3: 53–68.

PHYSICAL EDUCATION, POLICY IN

Policy is complex. It is a term that can mean very different things to different people. Many people may still regard it as somewhat distant; something that most people involved in physical education feel the effects of, or might be required to respond to, but are not directly involved with. This reflects a commonly held view of policy as 'a thing', created by some people and implemented by others (**reification**). In recent years, research in education and in physical education has challenged simplistic portrayals of policy and has encouraged deeper thinking about *who* is involved, *how*, *when* and *where* in policy, and '*with what effects*' for curriculum, teaching and learning.

Policy in physical education needs to be understood, first and foremost, as *process*; as dynamic, and furthermore, always in a dynamic relationship with historical, social, cultural, political and economic contexts. Policy developments are simultaneously a product of those contexts *and* influential upon them. The process may be more or less *reproductive* (maintaining the status quo of curriculum and teaching in physical education and wider social structures) or *transformative* (redefining and reshaping what is taught and learnt in physical education, what and whose interests it acknowledges and addresses). Thus, policy in physical education *is never neutral*; it is always informed by, and will serve to either reaffirm or challenge particular social, cultural and political interests. Policy is inevitably and unavoidably tied to issues of equity in physical education (Penney and Evans, 1999, 2005).

To view policy '*as process*' is to acknowledge that in important respects policy is fluid and ever changing. While the publication of a policy document (such as the **National Curriculum for Physical Education** (NCPE) or revisions to it) may portray policy in physical education as fixed, the process does not end with the publication of a document. Stephen Ball's work (1990, 1993) has highlighted the need to recognize 'slippage' (in meanings, understandings and implications) as inherent and important in education policy development. In physical education, attention has been drawn to various *texts* that are produced in association with a policy such as the NCPE. Written, verbal and pedagogical texts are all *representations* of policy and can be considered 'hybrid texts' (Ball, 1990; Penney and Evans, 1999, 2005). Far from being simple or predictable, the policy process is complex, at times unpredictable and often highly political. To understand more about policy in physical education, and specifically to explore the complexities and politics of policy in physical education, the concept of **discourse** is crucial.

Discourse is a tool for analysis of policy in education, physical education and **health**. It is a concept that is fundamentally concerned with language and meanings. It serves to reveal the interests embedded in, promoted and marginalized by policy texts by virtue of what is said, how it is said, and also, by what is *not* said (Ball, 1990: Penney and Evans, 1999, 2005). What is incorporated within policy in physical education, what is excluded, and how policies are presented, all reflect the varying representation (and status) of discourses of elitism, health, **gender**, **nationalism**, and so on. There are many and varied interests in policy in physical education. The reality is that not all interests can be represented equally. Understanding that various discourses will be differentially positioned in policy is fundamental to appreciating the significance of slippage – and the ongoing dynamic of policy. Policy in physical education emerges as always subject to interpretation and *reconfigured representation*. The prominence of particular discourses will be either reaffirmed or challenged and similarly, other interests may gain a greater presence and status, as curricula are developed and lessons planned and taught.

Yet, alongside this emphasis on flexibility and ongoing change in relation to policy, there is a need to also explore notions of 'stability and control' (Penney and Evans, 1999, 2005). Some things about policy in physical education seemingly remain fixed, unable to be contested or renegotiated. As Ball (1993) has explained, policy is always and inevitably about agency *and* control, and more specifically, about the constraints to our thinking and actions that are inherent in the agency and control at any particular instance (**agency and structure**). In policy analysis we need to consider the discursive boundaries, or *frames*, within which we are acting and thinking. Frames set limits to what is thinkable (or not) as acceptable or legitimate practice in physical education (Penney and Evans, 1999, 2005).

With an appreciation of the complexities of policy it becomes evident that compromise is a further central theme of policy in physical education. What emerges as policy at any particular time or place will always be a result of compromises between competing interests in and for the subject. Again, *politics* is integral to policy: 'who can speak where, when and with what authority' (Ball, 1990: 17) is crucial in the development of policy in physical education (Penney and Evans, 1999, 2005). Not everyone is equally positioned to shape policy developments. So-called *'arrangements for policy'*, including terms of reference for policy development, selection and appointment of policy 'makers', consultation processes and timelines, will all play a part in determining what is included, excluded, privileged or marginalized in policy development (Penney and Evans, 1999, 2005). This is as true in a school or department setting as it is in government arenas.

Finally, it is worth reflecting on how policy in physical education relates to *change* in physical education. While it may be tempting to assume that policy is inherently concerned with change, it may also be concerned with reaffirming the status quo. Or, despite incorporating change agendas, policy developments may ultimately do little to challenge the status quo. 'Slippage' can take many forms and can be as much about *accommodating* new policy within long-established practices as about creative interpretations and new ways of doing things in physical education (Penney and Evans, 1999, 2005). The policy process may thus feature considerable resistance to change in physical education. Policies also actively create or constrain possibilities for change in the future. The initial development and subsequent series of revisions to the NCPE in England have illustrated the cumulative dimension to policy development. Policies set boundaries and create openings for what will be seen and thought as 'possible' as future policy in physical education. But again, there is always a need to recall that we are all active players in the physical education policy game, variously positioned to advance or suppress particular interests.

Key Reading

Ball, S.J. (1990) *Politics and Policy Making in Education. Explorations in Policy Sociology.* London: Routledge.

Ball, S.J. (1993) 'What is policy? Texts, trajectories and toolboxes', *Discourse*, 13 (2): 10–17.

Penney, D. and Evans, J. (1999) *Politics, Policy and Practice in Physical Education.* London: E. & F.N. Spon.

Penney, D. and Evans, J. (2005) 'Policy, power and politics in physical education', in K. Green and K. Hardman (eds), *Physical Education: Essential Issues.* London: Sage. pp. 21–38.

Dawn Penney

PING-PONG DIPLOMACY

(propaganda)

PLAY

(*Homo Ludens*)

'PLAY AND DIS-PLAY'

Originally published in 1955, 'American Sports: play and dis-play' is Gregory P. Stone's groundbreaking essay on post-war trends in American sport. Stone, who studied at the famous Chicago School of Sociology (**symbolic interactionism**), became the first sociologist to highlight the impact of **commercialization** on sport, though subsequently advocates of **Marxism** have been rather more active in analysing such issues.

Stone discusses the nature of the American sports industry (i.e. its growth, employment patterns, etc.) and argues that despite the prominence of the Protestant work ethic (**religion**), work and play are increasingly becoming intertwined. He notes the anomaly whereby Americans talk about sports – such as baseball, football, etc. – that are played, while the term 'sportsman' is reserved for those who take part in activities that were previously work (i.e. hunting and fishing). In his words: 'American sports that were once work are never played, but these engage the "players" – the amateurs. Sports that were never work are always played, and these engage the "workers" – the professionals' (Stone, 1955) (**amateurism**).

The sexist language of 'play and dis-play' is very much a product of its time, but Stone's citation of the 'masculine bias' of American sports, the 'taboo' on women in certain male activities (e.g. fishing trips (**male preserve**)), the importance of sport as a site for the production of **masculinity**, and the male bias in sports research and analysis are in many ways years ahead of their time. This leads Stone on to a discussion of wrestling (a sport which attracts a relatively high proportion of female spectators), which in turn leads Stone to the ideas that make this paper seminal.

It is from Stone's discussion of the spectacular elements of wrestling, but American sport more broadly, that the paper takes its title, and from which the main significance of this work stems. Stone argues that play (participating for oneself) and display (performing to onlookers), while present to varying degrees in 'sports' throughout history, are antithetical. Display, because it is spectacular, is predictable and certain, whereas the play element of games stems from their unscripted character and uncertain outcome (**competitive balance**; **quest for excitement**). Through display, play becomes dis-play. In Stone's view, therefore, the staged character of dis-play destroys the essence of sport (**essentialism**). Sport, consequently, loses its inherently 'moral' and 'ennobling' functions. This, he concludes, is 'one of the most pressing problems' facing sports studies.

Key Reading

Stone, G. (1955) 'American sports: play and dis-play', *Chicago Review*, IX: 83–100. A revised and extended version of the paper appears in E. Dunning (ed.) (1971), *The Sociology of Sport: A Selection of Readings*. London: Frank Cass.

PLAYER RESERVATION SYSTEMS

One of the two main mechanisms through which the sports labour market is restricted (the other being wage controls). Player reservation systems entail the central and administrative allocation of playing talent (as opposed to free agency, or the distribution of labour according to the demands of the market). Typically, player reservation systems mean that a player can only move to a new team if his/her existing team agrees, an arrangement which might include a transfer fee or other form of compensation (**retain and transfer system**). The first reserve systems were in baseball, and initially were secret agreements. Clubs reserved for themselves an exclusive option over a certain number of players (initially 5, subsequently 11). By 1887 the 'reserve clause' was inserted in all player contracts and remained intact until 1976.

An alternative player reservation system is the draft system widely used in North American major league sports, whereby teams take turns in selecting from the new talent graduating from college sports (**athletic scholarships**). Additionally a 'reverse order rule' operates. This provides the last placed team of the previous season with the first choice of the available players, and the first placed team with the last choice.

It is often argued that player reservation systems were introduced in an attempt to equalize access to playing talent and thus promote **competitive balance** within sports leagues. However, this perhaps overlooks the degree to which individual club owners benefit from arrangements that effectively curtail the rights of the athlete as an employee.

Indeed, Sandy et al. (2004) argue that a general pattern across sports has been: (1) the establishment of sports labour market controls; (2) the unionization of athletes and the campaign for the reform of labour market contacts; and (3) their removal/abolition and the increased rights of athletes (**Bosman ruling**). It is perhaps too early to tell whether competitive balance will be adversely affected by such changes. However, the removal of player reserve systems will undermine one of the arguments supporting the exemption of North American major league sports from US **anti-trust** laws, for these changes will mean that teams increasingly compete in an open labour market like 'normal' businesses.

Key Reading

Sandy, R., Sloane, P.J. and Rosentraub, M. (2004) *The Economics of Sport: An International Perspective*. Basingstoke: Palgrave Macmillan. esp. Ch. 4.
Staudohar, P.D. (1996) *Playing for Dollars: Labor Relations and the Sports Business*. Ithaca, NY: ILR Press.

POSITIVE DEVIANCE

Deviance always involves the violation of a norm (**deviance**). But norms do not prescribe specific actions as much as they set limits for what is defined as acceptable. Deviance, therefore, occurs when actions, traits or ideas fall outside the boundaries that mark the normal range of acceptance in a particular social world (**sport ethic, the**). Because there are normative boundaries on either side of the range of acceptance, there are two types of deviance – under-conformity, or negative deviance, and over-conformity, or positive deviance.

Negative deviance is the focus of nearly all sociological research on normative violations. It involves subnormal action that does not measure up to what is acceptable. It occurs when people ignore, reject, or fail to learn and internalize a norm. Examples of negative deviance in sports are actions such as an athlete coming late to a scheduled practice, failing to demonstrate the commitment expected by fellow athletes, or ignoring the rules of play during a contest (**fair play**). When negative deviance is chronic and pervasive to the point that violating norms becomes an end in itself among people in a social group or situation, anarchy exists.

Positive deviance has rarely been studied by sociologists. It involves supra-normal action that goes beyond what is acceptable. It occurs when people accept norms without question or qualification. An example of positive deviance in sports would be continuing to train even when it causes or intensifies **pain and injury**, disrupts family life and jeopardizes **health** and safety. When positive deviance is chronic and pervasive to the point that people uncritically follow the normative dictates of an ideology or a charismatic leader and use excessive conformity as the sole criterion for group membership, fascism exists.

The legitimacy of the concept of positive deviance has been debated among sociologists (Goode, 1991; Sagarin, 1985), although some scholars in the sociology of sport argue that the concept can be used to understand the actions of athletes who engage in supra-normal actions that cannot be explained by theories that focus only on the normal and subnormal (Coakley, 2007; Hughes and Coakley, 1991; Johns, 1998).

Excessive over-conformity may become normalized among some athletes in high-performance sport cultures. However, such action remains deviant because it falls outside the normal range of acceptance in society and among those who critically assess normative expectations in sports and acknowledge necessary limits to conformity. For example, pathogenic **eating disorders** may be common among some high-performance gymnasts, but such actions are widely defined as deviant; they represent dangerous over-conformity to **body** norms for females in sports and society at large. Similarly, performance-enhancing substances (**drugs**; **drugs, classes of**) may be used when people uncritically believe that their identity as an athlete and their membership in an elite sport culture (**subcultures**) depend on demonstrating a willingness to exceed expectations for the sake of the game, the team, and the special nature of sport. However, such over-conformity is seriously dangerous and remains deviant because it involves supra-normal action that falls outside a normal range of acceptance in society and among athletes who realize that normative boundaries are needed to curb excessive over-conformity.

Positive deviance presents challenges for social control because athletes and coaches often see it as a sign of **motivation** and commitment. When this occurs it becomes a marker of athlete identity. Collective positive deviance often creates not only strong bonds among athletes but the ideas that group membership depends on over-conformity and over-conformity is the basis for righteousness in sport culture, even though such actions are defined as deviant in society as a whole (**group dynamics**).

Key Reading

Coakley, J. (2007) *Sport in Society: Issues and Controversies*, 9th edn. Boston: McGraw-Hill.

Goode, E. (1991) 'Positive deviance: a viable concept?', *Deviant Behavior*, 12: 289–309.

Hughes, R. and Coakley, J. (1991) 'Positive deviance among athletes: the implications of overconformity to the sport ethic', *Sociology of Sport Journal*, 8 (4): 307–25.

Johns, D. (1998) 'Fasting and feasting: paradoxes in the sport ethic', *Sociology of Sport Journal*, 15 (1): 41–63.

Sagarin, E. (1985) 'Positive deviance: an oxymoron', *Deviant Behavior*, 6: 169–81.

Jay Coakley

POSITIVISM

Can be defined as any sociological approach which is premised on the assumption that the methods of the physical sciences (measurement, the search for causal factors and law-like explanations and the ability to accurately predict future events) can be applied in the social sciences. Positivists believe that as we are products of our environment, we should be able to predict human behaviour with reference to environmental factors.

The positivist approach is likely to emphasize the control of variables (e.g. income, social **class**, **gender**), replication (e.g. the ability to repeat the research under the same conditions and thus provide identical results), hypothesis testing (predicting results that are either supported or refuted by the research) and the use of statistics (e.g. chi-square tests, which assess whether a particular finding is the product of chance or is 'statistically significant'). Consequently, concepts such as feelings, **emotion**, beliefs and ideas (**idealism**) have a marginal role in positivist social research, as they are difficult to measure. Positivist research should be detached and objective and not influenced by the subjective views of the individual researcher (**involvement and detachment; objectivity and subjectivity**).

Positivism should be seen as distinct from empiricism, for while they share the belief that social reality can be measured independently of human interpretation, empiricism can be described more narrowly as the commitment to measurement. Empiricism therefore is not driven by theory, and not designed to test the accuracy of a particular hypothesis.

In an illustrative example of positivist research, Paul Pederson (2002) posited four hypotheses relating to the media's coverage of male and female athletics: (1) that more (and bigger) photographs of males were published; (2) that these were placed more prominently in papers; (3) that they were more likely to be colour photographs; and (4) that they were more likely to be 'action' shots. Pederson was able accurately to measure (quantify) his data and to isolate variables (e.g. photographs of males or females, action or posed photographs) and concluded that while the first three hypotheses could be upheld, the fourth (relating to action/posed) could not.

Beyond such **content analysis**, positivists favour research methods such as **questionnaires**, which produce **quantitative** and therefore more easily comparable data (**qualitative and quantitative research**).

Key Reading

Pederson, P.M. (2002) 'Examining equity in newspaper photographs: a content analysis of the print media photographic coverage of interscholastic athletics', *International Review for the Sociology of Sport*, 37 (3/4): 303–18.

POST-COLONIALISM

(imperialism)

POST-FANDOM

According to Steve Redhead, post-fandom developed in European football, and English football especially, following the Italia '90 Football World Cup. Post-fandom can be seen in contrast to the stereotype of the mainly male terrace culture of football supporting that dominated the game prior to the mid-1980s. For Redhead (1997: 29), post-fandom is 'fragmentary, self-conscious, reflexive, mediated, artistic (and) style-surfing'. Though aspects of this supportership style have always been present, they became more pervasive in the mid-1990s, and especially around the time of the 1994 Football World Cup in the USA.

Writing from a theoretical perspective that can broadly be described as **postmodernism**, Redhead parallels post-fandom with John Urry's work on post-tourism, in which it is argued that there is no 'real' or 'authentic' tourist experience, merely a 'multiplicity of tourist games'. Like post-tourism, post-fandom

recognizes that many football **fans** have rejected the 'authenticity' of traditional supporting styles. Rather, participatory and passive fans have increasingly become the same people, partaking in different fandom experiences at different times and in different places. The development of smaller all-seater **stadiums**, increased ticket prices, satellite broadcasters' growing interest and dominance of football (**broadcasting rights**), and the general **embourgeoisement** of the sport helped to develop the social significance of the pub football culture via which post-fandom is most clearly expressed.

Key Reading

Redhead, S. (1997) *Post-fandom and the Millennial Blues: The Transformation of Soccer Culture*. London: Routledge.

POSTMODERNISM

The central thesis of postmodernism is that beliefs and concepts, such as 'scientific rationality' and 'progress', which characterized **modernity**, have collapsed. Sport, it is argued, is a product and bears the hallmarks of **modernity** and hence, as we move to postmodernity, so we are now witnessing the emergence and development of postmodern sports forms.

Some of the key social changes that have led theorists to argue that we are entering a period of postmodernity have been identified as follows: (1) a crisis of faith in the 'big' modern ideas, such as science, progress and reason, as well as a crisis in political ideologies, such as **Marxism**, which lead postmodernists to regard all truth-claims merely as competing narratives, or rival stories; (2) changes in production and the economy with a new international division of labour, the rise of service sector employment, and post-Fordism (that is, the movement towards smaller, more flexible economic production units replacing large factories and mass production); (3) population growth and urbanization confined to the Third World, while in the First World, cities are in decline (**city, the**); (4) the growth of transnational economic (e.g. **Nike**, Coca-Cola), cultural and political activity (e.g. global anti-capitalist movements) that undermines the centrality of the nation state (see **nationalism**); (5) a growing emphasis on consumerism (**consumer culture**) and a proliferation of **media** (**hyperreal**), which lead to cultural fragmentation; and (6) the general effects of **globalization** processes, which have seen regional shifts in wealth and power from Europe to Asia and from the Atlantic to the Pacific.

In contrast to the apparent clarity of **modernity** (based on industrial manufacturing, **class** and **gender** divisions, politics linked to economic group interest, etc.), postmodernism celebrates the fragmented, the disunified and playful diversity. Contemporary societies are seen as turbulent, unstable and constantly changing, with little sense of coherence or permanence. Postmodernists argue that the distinction between 'high' and 'low' culture (and thus prestigious and popular sports) is dissolving and point towards the emergence of 'lifestyle' groupings as evidence of this. These groups and sports are not rigidly based on such categories as class, gender, etc., but on fluid identities, interpreted at a local level, and characterized by hybridity (**queer theory**; **performativity**). Indeed, postmodernists seek to break down individuals' sporting experiences such that, for example, women are not portrayed as having one unified life course. Rather, postmodernist work embraces the diversity and fractured understandings and identities that contemporary societies (and sports) foster.

Postmodernists argue that 'individualized', 'commercialized' and 'mediatized' sports forms are emerging, variously called **lifestyle sports**, extreme sports and alternative sports. They focus on the transgression of boundaries in sport, between male and female, homosexual and heterosexual, the 'natural' body and the **cyborg** (**binaries**), on the excesses of postmodern society, such as exercise

addiction, and on the decline of the 'sport for **health**' paradigm and the concomitant rise of notions of 'sport for pleasure'.

Key Reading

Andrews, D. (2000) 'Posting up: French post-structuralism and the critical analysis of contemporary sporting culture', in J. Coakley and E. Dunning (eds), *Handbook of Sports Studies*. London: Sage. pp. 106–37.

Rail, G. (1998) *Sport and Postmodern Times*. New York: State University of New York Press.

Rinehart, R. and Sydnor, S. (2003) *To the Extreme: Alternative Sports, Inside and Out*. New York: State University of New York Press.

POST-STRUCTURALISM

Refers to a group of philosophical, political and theoretical positions that emerged in France in the late 1960s and early 1970s. The leading theorists in this movement (leading at least in that their work has influenced sports studies) are Jean Baudrillard (**hyperreal**), Jacques Derrida (**binaries**) and Michel Foucault (**discipline**; **surveillance**; **technologies**).

In much the same way that **conflict theory** emerged in opposition to **functionalism**, post-structuralism emerged in what was perceived to be a crisis of **modernity**. Thus a key feature of post-structuralism is a critique of theories that searches for rationalistic, objective and scientific understandings of social life (**objectivity and subjectivity**; **positivism**). Sport in contemporary society is thought to be inextricably bound to the principles of modernity, and thus post-structuralism 'allows us to expose the *dark side* of *sporting* modernity by challenging the ethos of rational human progress embodied by – and within – modern sport culture' (Andrews, 2000: 107).

Post-structuralism is sometimes used synonymously with **postmodernism**. Andrews, however, argues that it is important to make a distinction between the two. While they share an epistemological stance which eschews the search for universal objective truths (**epistemology and ontology**), post-structuralists differ from postmodernists in that their concern is to *problematize* modernity (**queer theory**), rather than seeking to understand a new phase of social development (postmodernity) which is thought to have superseded it.

Key Reading

Andrews, D. (2000) 'Posting up: French post-structuralism and the critical analysis of contemporary sporting culture', in J. Coakley and E. Dunning (eds), *Handbook of Sports Studies*. London: Sage. pp. 106–37.

Scambler, G. (2005) *Sport and Society: History, Power and Culture*. Maidenhead: Open University Press. esp. Ch. 7.

PREFECT-FAGGING SYSTEM

Reform of the prefect-fagging system in English public schools during the nineteenth century was an important precondition to the development of football and rugby into **modern sport** forms (Dunning and Sheard, 2005). Established as charitable institutions to educate the poor, during the eighteenth and early nineteenth centuries the public schools were reformed into boarding schools for fee paying pupils from the upper and upper-middle classes. Because many of the boys were socially superior to the masters who taught at and nominally ran the schools, **discipline** and control were problems, with many rebellions and revolts (often ultimately quashed by the military) recorded.

Gradually, however, a 'dual system' of control developed through which masters were granted a degree of recognition in the classroom in return for the reciprocal recognition of the right of prefects (the older and stronger boys) to exercise control over extra-curricular activities. The result was a more stable, peaceful, school environment. The fags (described at Westminster school as, 'the small boys, the duffers and funk-sticks') provided menial and sometimes sexual services to the prefects. Fags were compelled to participate in sport, perhaps as goalkeepers or goalposts, or as markers of the boundary of the football pitch.

The prefect-fagging system at Rugby School was the first to be reformed effectively, largely because the relatively low status of the schoolboys (relative that is to, say, Eton) meant that the social distance between themselves and the masters (led by headmaster, Thomas Arnold) was relatively slight. The first written rule code for football emerged from the Rugby School Sixth Form Levee in 1845 (Levees were prefect-organized, informal assemblies/meetings). While correlation does not imply causation, the fact that Rugby was both the first school to achieve effective reform of the prefect-fagging system, and the first to commit the rules of its variant of football to writing, suggests that the two processes were closely linked.

Key Reading

Dunning, E. and Curry, G. (2004) 'Public schools, status rivalry and the development of football', in E. Dunning, D. Malcolm and I. Waddington (eds), *Sport Histories: Figurational Studies of the Development of Modern Sports*. London: Routledge. pp. 31–52.

Dunning, E. and Sheard, K. (2005) *Barbarians, Gentlemen and Players: A Sociological Study of the Development of Rugby Football*, 2nd edn. London: Routledge.

PRIMARY AND SECONDARY

RESEARCH

The term primary research refers to data originally collected by the individual, usually for a specific research project (though the individual might reuse the data in subsequent research projects). Secondary research refers to the examination of data that has been collated by other researchers and probably exists in some published form (e.g. in journal articles, government or **Sports Council** reports, etc.). The examination of newspapers (**content analysis**) or other documentary/historical sources is *not* classified as secondary research, however, for although researchers using these techniques are clearly examining data compiled by others, those data were not compiled as part of a research process.

All research should include secondary sources, if only by way of making reference to the similarity/dissimilarity between previous and current research projects and findings. Secondary research should not be seen as a priori inferior to primary research, for certain researchers may have privileged access to particular people or groups (e.g. official biographies of elite sports people), or to greater resources (e.g. government departments or the research output of commercial bodies such as Deloitte and Touche in relation to football finances or Mintel with regard to the **sports market**). Yet, when using secondary sources one must always consider the quality of the data produced and ask: Who produced it? Why was it produced? Who funded the research? Were the researchers suitably qualified to conduct such research? What **sampling** techniques were used and has this led to any bias? What assumptions and/or theoretical positions underlay the research?

Malcolm et al. (2000) provide a good example of the value of mixing primary and secondary research, combining their own primary research of surveys of, and interviews with, football fans, with a range of football fan surveys conducted by others. This combination provided a longitudinal study of football crowd composition in England between 1980 and 1995 and a rationale why, contrary to popular perceptions, the **gender** and **class** composition of football crowds did not alter very markedly during this period.

Key Reading

Malcolm, D., Jones, I. and Waddington, I. (2000) 'The people's game? Football spectatorship and demographic change', in J. Garland, D. Malcolm and M. Rowe (eds), *The Future of Football: Challenges for the Twenty First Century*. London: Frank Cass. pp. 129–43.

PRIZEFIGHTING

(Broughton, Jack; Figg, James)

PROCESS SOCIOLOGY

(figurational sociology)

PROFESSIONALISM

(amateurism; broken-time payments; commercialization)

PROPAGANDA

Can be defined as the carefully planned, systematically conducted, centrally coordinated and synchronized process of manipulating symbols, with the aim of altering human response and engendering uniform behaviour in large social groups. The intention is that this behaviour will produce immediate and effective results, compatible with the specific political interests and goals of the propaganda source.

While forms of propaganda have probably always existed, the development of the mass **media** in particular enabled propaganda to sit alongside war and diplomacy as the three central instruments of foreign policy. Consequently, it was in the lead up to, and during, the Second World War, and the subsequent 'Cold War' between the super powers of the USA and the USSR, that propaganda began to take its modern form. The use of sport for propaganda purposes has coincided with this development.

The Nazi (Berlin) Olympics of 1936 were a landmark event in this regard. Hitler attempted to use the hosting of the Games as a way of demonstrating the superiority of the Aryan race – and thus the broader philosophy of the National Socialists (Nazis) in Germany – to the people of the world. While to some extent this aim was fulfilled by cleverly manipulated events and media coverage, Jesse Owens's victory in the blue ribbon 100 metres event (plus gold medals in the 200 metres and 4 × 100 metres relay) demonstrated that the uncertainty of outcome inherent in sport made its use for propaganda purposes far from straightforward.

Post-Second World War sports propaganda was dominated by the USA and the USSR. Both sought to foster support and win allies through sporting contacts, for example through the USSR's extensive programme of sports aid to Africa and the organization of 'friendly' sporting fixtures (e.g. the 'ping-pong' diplomacy with China initiated by American President Richard Nixon). However, the superpowers also used major sporting events, most notably the Olympics, as venues through which they could demonstrate the superiority of their ideological regimes through the competitive success of their athletes (hence the extensive use of performance-enhancing **drugs** by Eastern bloc countries). Sports propaganda became most explicit, however, through the 'tit-for-tat' **boycotts** of the 1980 Moscow and 1984 Los Angeles Games by the US and the USSR respectively. However, it should be noted that almost all sports events in the late twentieth and early twenty-first centuries have been used, to some extent, for propaganda purposes including, for instance, the 2000 Sydney Olympics (**aborigine**) and the Korea-Japan Football World Cup of 2002, used as a forum to re-open debates about human rights abuses during the Japanese occupation of Korea in the Second World War.

Two key points about sport and propaganda deserve reiterating. First, sport is a useful propaganda tool because it is so prominent in the media, and because it draws such large audience interest (**sport, social significance of**). Second, sport is an unreliable propaganda tool because even the most powerful politicians cannot control sporting success and failure.

Key Reading

Hazan, B. (1987) 'Sport as an instrument of political expansion: the Soviet Union in Africa', in W.J. Baker and J.A. Mangan (eds), *Sport in Africa: Essays in Social History*. London: Africana Publishing. pp. 250–71.

Horne, J. and Manzenreiter, W. (2002) *Japan, Korea and the 2002 World Cup*. London: Routledge.

Mandell, R.D. (1987) *The Nazi Olympics*. Urbana: University of Illinois Press.

Riordan, J. (1991) *Sport, Politics and Communism*. Manchester: Manchester University Press.

PSYCHOLOGY, APPROACHES TO

There are three general approaches to the study of psychology, and therefore to sport and exercise psychology. The *psychophysiological approach* is based on the belief that physiological processes of the brain and the body provide the key to understanding performance and physical activity. Researchers within this tradition monitor physiological processes – such as heart rate, blood pressure, muscle tension, etc. – and examine how control of these factors may improve sporting performance (e.g. training pistol shooters to fire between heartbeats).

Those psychologists adopting a *social-psychological* or *behavioural approach* focus upon the interaction of the individual participant and the broader environment in which sport takes place (e.g. relations with coaches, team mates, etc.). Researchers within this perspective particularly focus on the potential to change behaviour through reinforcement (reward of desirable behaviour) and punishment (actions to decrease the likelihood of such behaviour reoccuring). Practically this might be evident in the use of team-building events and techniques (**group development**), or the highlighting of an individual who is not training well, e.g. many football clubs award a coloured bib to the player decreed to be the 'donkey of the week'.

The *cognitive-behavioural approach* emphasizes the control of the performer's thoughts and emotions as the primary means by which to alter behaviour. Researchers in this tradition seek to influence the way an athlete interprets events around him/her. Common examples of this type of work include the use of **imagery** techniques (e.g. for a goal kicker in rugby or gridiron football), or the use of **self-talk**, which convinces the individual to reinterpret a situation in a particular way (e.g. to block out the noise of the crowd or the status of the particular game).

PUBLIC SCHOOL STATUS RIVALRY

It is Dunning's contention, firstly in conjunction with Sheard ([1979] 2005) and latterly with Curry (2004), that the rivalry between Rugby and Eton Public Schools is central to the emergence and bifurcation (or the co-production) of the association and rugby forms of football. Dunning and Curry accept the evidence of Goulstone (2000) and of Harvey (1999) that football, in an incipient modern form (**modern sport**), existed outside of the public schools of nineteenth-century England, but argue that the public schools (and latterly Cambridge and Oxford universities) were the main institutional loci where these processes took place, and that status rivalry had a significant impact in determining the specifics of the game forms that continue today.

The oldest surviving set of written rules for a form of football were produced at Rugby School in 1845, a development closely linked to reforms of the **prefect-fagging** system initiated by headmaster, Thomas Arnold. Eton Public School produced a set of rules just two years later, and a number of rules (perhaps most significantly prohibition of the use of hands) were diametrically opposed to the rules produced at Rugby. The Eton rules, Dunning et al. argue, can be seen as an early prototype of association football.

It is likely, argue Dunning et al., that Eton boys produced these rules in direct response to the Rugby code. Eton saw itself as the leading public school in Britain at this time – the second oldest (after Winchester) and, being based in Windsor, closely connected to the royal court. While Rugby under Thomas Arnold was gaining notoriety as an up-and-coming institution, documentary evidence suggests that Etonians viewed it as an obscure Midlands establishment catering for parvenus (people who have recently attained their social status). The Eton rules, therefore, were designed to put the Rugby 'upstarts' in their place.

The impact of public school status rivalry can also be seen in the debates which led to the establishment of the Football Association (FA) in 1863 and the Rugby Football Union (RFU) in 1871. Students at Cambridge and Oxford universities polarized around their former public schools. Eton–Rugby rivalry remained strong and the reluctance of each side to compromise led to the establishment of the two bodies (the FA and the RFU), which ultimately standardized and codified the rules for association and rugby football, and from which the respective sports were globally diffused.

Key Reading

Dunning, E. and Curry, G. (2004) 'Public schools, status rivalry and the development of football', in E. Dunning, D. Malcolm and I. Waddington (eds), *Sport Histories: Figurational Studies of the Development* of *Modern Sports*. London: Routledge. pp. 31–52.

Dunning, E. and Sheard, K. ([1979] 2005) *Barbarians, Gentlemen and Players: A Sociological Study of the Development of Rugby Football*, 2nd edn. London: Routledge.

Goulstone, J. (2000) 'The working class origins of modern football', *International Journal of the History of Sport*, 17 (1): 135–43.

Harvey, A. (1999) 'Football's missing link: the real story of the evolution of modern football', *European Sports History Review*, 1: 92–116.

PUGILISM

(**Broughton, Jack; Figg, James**)

PURITANS

Puritanism is a religious ideology largely associated with extremist English Protestants during the late sixteenth and seventeenth centuries. While Puritans initially objected to what they saw as the excesses of the Catholic Church, the movement came to be characterized by a rejection of all luxury and sensual enjoyment, the pursuit of a spartan and simple life, and a strict adherence to moral and religious practices.

Puritans took issue with a range of leisure/sporting practices at this time. While Brailsford (1969) argues that, 'The Puritans saw their mission to erase all sport and play from men's lives', others have argued that what specifically (or particularly) offended Puritans was that these activities often occurred on a Sunday. Popular festival activities such as traversing greasy poles were thought to promote idleness. However, criticism was strongest in relation to **animal sports**, such as cock-fighting and bear baiting, which were decried as inherently cruel. Puritans further objected to the drinking of **alcohol** and the rowdiness that tended to accompany it. However, the Puritan movement in England waned after the restoration of the monarchy in 1660 (when Charles II replaced Oliver Cromwell) and many animal sports and popular pastimes continued beyond Puritanism's period of greatest influence.

Puritan hostility to sport is something of a paradox for Guttmann (2004), given his argument that the development of **modern sport**, and subsequent success in international competition, are closely linked to the influence of Protestantism (see also *From Ritual to Record*). However, Guttmann concludes that it is the scientific view of the world which developed under Protestantism that provides the greatest explanatory purchase, rather than subscription to the **religion** itself.

Key Reading

Brailsford, D. (1969) *Sport and Society*. Toronto: Toronto University Press.

Guttmann, A. ([1978] 2004) *From Ritual to Record: The Nature of Modern Sport*. New York: Columbia University Press.

Q

QUALITATIVE AND QUANTITATIVE RESEARCH

All research, and research methods, can be divided into two subsets, qualitative and quantitative. Qualitative research relies on the ability of the researcher to use words to describe and interpret the field of investigation. Quantitative research is characterized by the numerical expression of data. Debates about the relative merits of qualitative and quantitative research were initially linked to the debate over whether the social sciences could or should attempt to replicate the methods and approach of the natural sciences (**positivism; reliability and validity**). Those who said yes advocated quantitative methods. Now that the social sciences are more firmly established in their own right, these debates have become less fierce, and there is a broader acceptance that both quantitative and qualitative research methods offer the prospect of helping to advance human knowledge.

Qualitative research tends to utilize methods such as semi-structured **interviews** or **observation** and **ethnography**, while quantitative research tends to rely on surveys or **questionnaires**. By way of illustration, we can see that quantitative studies of **socialization** in sport have relied on large-scale questionnaire surveys trying to identify who or what has influenced a person to play sport and what personal characteristics stem from sports participation. Qualitative research in this area has relied on observation techniques and semi-structured interviews in seeking to provide a detailed narrative or description of how people actively make decisions about whether or not to participate in sport, how they feel about sport, and what meaning sport has in their lives.

Key Reading

Gratton, C. and Jones, I. (2004) *Research Methods for Sports Studies*. London: Routledge.

QUEER THEORY

The main epistemological (**epistemology and ontology**) standpoint of queer theory is to (a) question the 'naturalness' of common, taken-for-granted forms of identity (especially sex, **gender** and sexuality) and (b) to interrogate the boundaries between, and the production and maintenance of, hierarchical **binaries** such as heterosexual and homosexual.

Queer theory can be seen as a convergence of **post-structuralism** and **feminism**, often conspicuously influenced by Foucault (**discipline; surveillance; technologies**), Derrida and Lacan. However, the work of Judith Butler and the post-AIDS emergence of radical gay politics are perhaps more direct antecedents. Butler (1990) famously questioned the 'heterosexual matrix', arguing that while culturally we have come to think that sex/gender/sexuality is a causally related, complete package, it is not. Butler argued that we cannot assume that one category necessarily entails another (e.g. not all females are feminine), and that each of these categories is not simply a binary (e.g. people are not necessarily heterosexual or homosexual, but may choose a variety of sexualities – bisexual, transgender – through the life-course and, more controversially, that one's sex is not simply a fixed biological bipolar entity). All of these things, according to Butler, are social constructions. In addition to this, right-wing-inspired hostility to homosexuality stemming from the AIDS crisis of the 1990s was met by a gay and lesbian movement that resisted the depiction of heterosexuality as the only normal form of sexuality.

Thus queer theory can be said to *denaturalize* sexuality and gender. Queer theorists have argued that early work on **lesbians** and lesbianism in sport was ultimately premised on the notion that these women were the outsiders, and thus perpetuated the notion of heterosexuality as normal. Our understanding of heterosexuality, it is argued, is premised on the repression, exclusion and repudiation of homosexuality. To challenge this dominance politically, queer theorists argue that we need to 'queer' or interrogate heterosexuality and the practices of heterosexuals, rather than seek to conform to, and assimilate with, such practices. In this vein, Sykes (1998) has looked at how the everyday language of physical educators normalizes heterosexuality by silencing lesbian voices. Yet in some contexts heterosexuality can also be seen as 'deviant', leading the boundaries of 'normality' to be undermined. Similarly, Caudwell (2003) has looked at how football in England and Wales is both organized in such a way as to privilege what she calls 'heterofemininity', but may be used as a site to challenge the 'woman-feminine-heterosexual' order. While queer theory began as a challenge to and critique of heterosexuality, it has developed to encompass the questioning of other hierarchical forms of identity; that is to say, we also need to 'queer' the whiteness of sport.

Queer theory is a highly controversial field. Some, such as Messner (1996), argue that it denies the importance of material social relations (do the actual physical differences between the sexes not matter, and is men's

dominance of economic and political power not as significant as the dominance of ideas?). In a similar vein, others note that by undermining the coherence of categories such as sex, queer theory effectively denies the existence of sexual inequalities and thus renders feminism impotent. Most controversial perhaps is the view that the voices of minorities should be prioritized, because they have a better claim to 'truth'. Consequently, the views of others are sometimes dismissed, for instance, as 'white, male and heterosexual' as though this perspective is, in an a priori sense, fatally biased.

Sport, perhaps more than any other sphere of social life, is ordered according to sex difference. Sport, therefore, contributes significantly to our understanding of the differences between the sexes as 'natural'. Even those who recoil at the social constructionist extremes of queer theory recognize, however, that one contribution that queer theory has made to sports studies is to help us challenge sport as an institution, and develop a more critical awareness of the social sporting world.

Key Reading

Butler, J. (1990) *Gender Trouble: Feminism and the Subversion of Identity*. London: Routledge.

Caudwell, J. (2003) 'Sporting gender: Women's footballing bodies for sites/sights for the (re) articulation of sex, gender and desire', *Sociology of Sport Journal*, 20 (4): 371–86.

Caudwell, J. (ed.) (2006) *Sport, Sexualities and Queer/Theory*. London: Routledge.

Messner, M. (1996) 'Studying up on sex', *Sociology of Sport Journal*, 13 (3): 221–37.

Sykes, H. (1998) 'Turning the closets inside/out: Towards a queer-feminist theory in women's physical education', *Sociology of Sport Journal*, 15 (2): 154–73.

QUEST FOR EXCITEMENT

Elias and Dunning's original conference paper, 'The Quest for Excitement in

Unexciting Societies', developed out of Elias's earlier work, *The Civilizing Process* (**civilizing process**). One aspect of Elias's argument in *The Civilizing Process* was that people in modern societies have increasingly come to exhibit relatively high levels of individual self-restraint. In such societies, there are relatively few opportunities for people to show strong feelings or spontaneously exhibit **emotion**. People who do so inappropriately are liable to be hospitalized, criminalized or medically pacified such that they were no longer deemed to pose a 'danger' to others. Given this backdrop, how, Elias and Dunning asked, can we explain the social significance of sport and leisure in contemporary societies, and what kind of society must it be for people to be attracted to the historically specific types of physical contest of the twentieth century (**modern sport**)?

There is, it should be noted, irony in Elias and Dunning's use of the phrase 'unexciting societies'. They recognized, for instance, that in most senses modern societies were very exciting; with the range of leisure pursuits and the intellectual stimulation available to people, perhaps greater than ever before. But 'unexciting' is used in this context in a very specific sense. Modern societies are highly routinized and the opportunities for unreflective expression of excitement are limited. This leads to the possibility of 'emotional staleness'.

Consequently, there develops a socially conditioned, psychological need for pleasurable excitement; that is to say, people come to want/need situations in which tension-excitement is generated and resolved. More exactly, leisure activities in modern societies, and modern sports in particular, provide opportunities for a controlled de-controlling of emotional controls. (NB the role of leisure in *generating* tensions makes Elias and Dunning's theory quite distinctive from **catharsis** theories.)

Elias and Dunning identify two distinct types of excitement: 'real life' and mimetic excitement. Excitement may be generated in critical or dangerous situations (e.g. natural disasters, attack from animals or other humans). These situations become less common in advanced industrial societies and thus the role of mimetic excitement becomes more prominent. Mimetic excitement is the 'sibling' of the excitement generated in 'real-life' situations. While similar in kind mimetic excitement lacks the 'real', or more extreme, level of **risk** and the threat of human existence posed in 'real life'.

Thus participants in, and spectators of, invasion sports (e.g. football) experience the mimetic excitement of battle, watching the game sway to and fro on the field, safe in the knowledge that the danger of 'real' harm is minimal. Large sporting events provide some of the few opportunities for collective manifestations of strong feelings, which makes this 'controlled de-controlling' all the more enjoyable and liberating. Thus sport and leisure pursuits in modern societies take their popularity and social significance from being one of the few spheres of social life in which relatively high degrees of emotional spontaneity are afforded relatively high degrees of tolerance (**sport, social significance of**).

Key Reading

Atkinson, M. (2002) 'Fifty million viewers can't be wrong: professional wrestling, sports-entertainment and mimesis', *Sociology of Sport Journal*, 19 (1): 47–66.

Elias, N. and Dunning, E. (1986) 'Quest for excitement in leisure', in *Quest for Excitement: Sport and Leisure in the Civilizing Process*. Oxford: Blackwell. pp. 63–90.

Goodger, J.M. and Goodger, B.C. (1989) 'Excitement and representation: toward a sociological explanation of the significance of modern sport', *Quest*, 41 (4): 257–72.

QUESTIONNAIRES

A questionnaire is simply a form or list of questions administered to people to obtain specific and structured information (normally handed out, emailed, posted or delivered over the Internet for respondents to complete themselves, or delivered orally by the researcher over the telephone or in person). Questionnaires are most appropriately used where the researcher wants to ascertain relatively simple information from a large group of people, and where that information is likely to be expressed in a quantitative form (**qualitative and quantitative research**). They are therefore used more in disciplines closer to the natural sciences than to the arts (e.g. in sport psychology and sports economics rather than in sport anthropology and the sociology of sport) but have been used by social scientists to gather data, for instance, on sports spectators (**fans**).

The advantages of using a questionnaire are generally thought to be that: (1) they are a cheap and time-efficient way of contacting large numbers of people; (2) they provide standardized and structured data that can be analysed statistically and easily compared with other data-sets; (3) they involve little interpretation from the researcher, and therefore are likely to be relatively free from bias (although critics might say that the structured nature of the questions limits the range of possible responses and that this represents a form of researcher bias); (4) they provide respondents with anonymity (and hence they have been used in surveys of covert or illegal behaviour – such as drug use in sport).

The disadvantages of using a questionnaire, however, are that: (1) data tend to be simple as questionnaires do not lend themselves to the asking of complex questions (e.g. about feelings, **emotions** or motives); (2) there is little opportunity to probe why a person has answered in a particular way; (3) there may be little control over who completes the questionnaire and the sincerity of their answers; and (4) response rates tend to be low and certain groups may not be represented in the research (e.g. it has been argued that football fan surveys necessarily pass over the views of those fans excluded from attendance due to financial reasons).

Questionnaires thus should be designed and distributed to alleviate such problems. Simple, brief and concise questions, and a relevant incentive or prize for completion (plus follow-up letters), will increase response rates. Questions should not be leading, overlapping (i.e. don't ask the same thing twice and always use mutually exclusive categories) or double-barrelled (i.e. asking for two pieces of information at once). A pilot survey enables problems such as these to be eliminated before the main survey and thus will further boost the response rate. Selecting the correct **sampling** method is essential (e.g. all football fans or just season ticket holders (**reliability and validity**)). A covering letter should clearly state the purpose of the survey, the anonymity of data (**ethics**; **research methods**), who should complete the survey and how it should be completed. Closed questions (where respondents select from a limited number of choices) can be combined with open questions (requiring a brief comment from the respondent in situations where it is not possible to accurately anticipate the full range of answers) to provide both quantitative and qualitative data, thus enhancing the richness and depth of the analysis.

Key Reading

Crawford, G. (2001) 'Characteristics of a British ice hockey audience: major findings of the 1998 and 1999 Manchester Storm Ice Hockey Club supporter survey', *International Review for the Sociology of Sport*, 36 (1): 71–82.

Gratton, C. and Jones, I. (2004) *Research Methods for Sports Studies*. London: Routledge. esp. Ch. 8.

Waddington, I., Dunning, E. and Murphy, P. (1996) 'Research note: surveying the social composition of football crowds', *Leisure Studies*, 15: 209–14.

Waddington, I., Malcolm, D., and Horak, R. (1998) 'The social composition of football crowds in western Europe: a comparative study', *International Review for the Sociology of Sport*, 33 (2): 155–69.

RACE

The relationship between race and sport is complex and multifaceted. On the one hand, sport has played a central role in reproducing popular notions of absolute racial difference. Visibly identifiable variations in sports performance between different racial groups provide a commonsense rationale for the belief in race as a secure biological category that can be used to explain broader differences in human behaviour. Yet sport has at the same time been an important arena of cultural resistance for subaltern groups in resisting colonial racism. Sport has provided a modality that has enabled symbolic challenges to racial subordination. More recently, sport has become a central cultural space for wider discussions within Western societies concerning issues of multiculturalism, national belonging and identity (**anti-racism**; **nationalism**).

A critical body of sociological work on race and sport did not emerge until the late 1990s. Until then, the work within sociology, and elsewhere, was: (1) largely descriptive, examining, for example, the existence of forms of 'stacking', the placing of athletes into certain positions due to stereotypical beliefs about racial aptitude; or (2) journalistic, normally based on exposés of continuing forms of racial discrimination and overt forms of racial abuse within particular sports.

Two important exceptions to this are CLR James's *Beyond the Boundary* (1963) and Harry Edwards's *The Revolt of the Black Athlete*

(1969). For James sport, and in particular cricket, was central in mediating the anti-colonial struggles taking place in the Caribbean during the 1950s. The colonial structures of governance that were imposed throughout the British Empire, ensuring white control over black populations, were also reflected within sporting institutions (**imperialism**). This meant, for example, that up until 1960, black cricketers were barred from captaining the West Indies cricket team. The struggle to achieve racial equality within cricket and to have a black captain of the West Indies team drew upon and contributed to the wider anti-colonial independence movements of the era. Thus during the twentieth century sport became a key battlefield within the wider context of black political consciousness and social and economic emancipation.

These themes were further explored by Harry Edwards who documented the growing politicization of black athletes in the 1960s as they sought to use their public position to speak out on issues of racial discrimination within sports and also, importantly, to question the supposed racial meritocracy of American society more generally. The revolt of the black athlete was, therefore, an important part of the wider civil rights and latterly black power movements. Tommie Smith and John Carlos's famous black-gloved salute at the 1968 Mexico Olympics and the political stance of the boxer Muhammad Ali are perhaps the most well-known examples of this moment of radicalization.

Much of the work on race and sport has developed within the American context and has focused on the forms of discrimination faced by African-Americans in the slow and painful process of desegregating American sports such as baseball, basketball and track and field. More recent research has explored the Hispanic experience in sport and the use and abuse of Native American images and iconography within collegiate and professional sports (**aborigine**). This body of work has been useful as a platform for the examination of similar forms of racist practices and representations within sporting institutions and cultures in other countries. Research in Britain has shown how racist stereotypes about black physicality held by schoolteachers, coaches and sports administrators serve to push black children into certain sports and away from 'academic' pursuits because of the belief in the natural athleticism of black children. Similarly, research has suggested that those of south Asian descent have also been subject to forms of racial discrimination but conversely have been stereotyped as inherently unsuited to physical contact and competitive sports.

This widespread belief in racial stereotypes is fundamentally flawed, as it attributes to the category of 'race' an ontological validity that most biologists and geneticists argue does not exist, and further collapses the inherent heterogeneity of any racial group into an homogeneous set of crude characteristics (**race science**). In fact, modern day genetics shows clearly that there is greater genetic variation within any so-called 'race' than there is between such groups. Consequently, 'race' is viewed by sociologists as a social construct and not a biological fact. However, once these views are internalized by powerful actors within sporting institutions and by the athletes themselves, this can have a large distorting effect in producing racial variation in sports participation and performance (**self-fulfilling prophecy**). Thus that which appears, at first glance, to be biologically rooted is actually complexly related to issues of discrimination, stereotyping and identity. The end result is the widespread, if mistaken, assumptions that south Asians don't play

football, black people cannot swim or even that whites cannot jump.

Sport has also been important in signalling changes in national identity within many Western societies, as increased migration during the twentieth century has resulted in countries such as France and Britain being viewed as multicultural societies. The success of France's multiracial and multi-ethnic football team in winning the World Cup in 1998 and the European Championships in 2000 was seen as a powerful riposte to Far Right political parties which argued that only white players could truly represent France. However, the 'acceptance' of athletes of colour as representatives of 'the nation' in countries as diverse as Canada, New Zealand, Australia, Britain and France is often contingent on such athletes' continued success and is thus a precarious form of national inclusion. Some have also suggested that such success masks the continuance of racism within Western societies, giving a superficial and false image of racial meritocracy, as well as further perpetuating notions that those defined as racially other to whiteness do, after all, possess special athletic abilities. Thus contemporary scholarship on race and sport is concerned to trace this 'double bind' of how sport contributes to the continuance of dominant racial ideologies while at the same time it offers a powerful means to counter contemporary cultural racisms (see also *Darwin's Athletes*).

Key Reading

Carrington, B and McDonald, I. (eds) (2001) *'Race', Sport and British Society*. London: Routledge.

Edwards, H. (1969) *The Revolt of the Black Athlete*. New York: Free Press.

Hoberman, J. (1997) *Darwin's Athletes: How Sport has Damaged Black America and Preserved the Myth of Race*. Boston, MA: Mairner Books.

James, C.L.R. (1963) *Beyond the Boundary*. London: Serpent's Tail.

Ben Carrington

RACE SCIENCE

Refers to the set of beliefs, in part rooted in the physical sciences, which suggest that: (1) it is meaningful to talk of 'racial' groups; and (2) membership of such groups has implications for physicality and thus sports performance. Race science (**race**) forms the basis of stereotypes used to explain the prominence or absence of certain 'racial' groups in sport, and their relative success or failure in particular sports and particular playing roles (e.g. the dominance of black sprinters, and the absence of black swimmers; see also **stacking**). Moreover, these ideas are shared by physical educators and the 'gatekeepers' of sporting opportunities (e.g. coaches, scouts) and lead to a kind of **self-fulfilling prophecy**: if physical education teachers expect Asian children to be physically weak, they will therefore discourage Asian children away from sports participation, leading to them not experiencing sporting success. The lack of Asian sporting success is taken as further proof of the difference between 'racial groups'. As Hoberman has argued in *Darwin's Athletes* (1997), race science (of sport) has contributed to the continued inequalities between different 'racial' groups in America. It is fair to suggest that similar processes operate in other societies.

However, race science can be challenged in the following ways. First, *race science is conceptually weak and difficult to operationalize.* Evidence suggests that, at most, the genetic difference between 'races' is very slight, and indeed there is as much diversity within 'races' as between them. There is a lack of clarity over what 'races' actually exist and the importance of 'sub-races' (e.g. do Middle Eastern Arabs constitute a race? Are Scandinavians and Southern Europeans part of the same race?). Without clear boundaries, the assignment of individuals to particular 'racial' groups must be based on subjective judgements.

Second, *sports science research on 'race' is methodologically flawed and its objectivity is contentious.* We may accept that skin colour is linked to genes, and that sporting ability is also (partly) genetically inherited, but it does not necessarily follow that sporting ability and skin colour are themselves linked. Moreover, the sporting achievements of different groups are treated in unequal ways. Black sporting dominance (e.g. of sprinting) is often attributed to genetics, whereas white sporting dominance (e.g. yachting, skiing) rarely, if ever, is. While race science purports to be objective, it is always predicated on subjective assumptions about what the most important factors of investigation should be, and thus the commitment to a classification of races within the sports science community leads research to focus on particular areas (e.g. the search for 'fast twitch' muscle fibres) and neglect others (e.g. social factors).

Third, *race science presents as general laws, ideas that are in fact merely generalizations.* For biological notions of the difference between 'races' to hold true, there must be no exceptions, either in contemporary sport or over time. Any exceptions expose these beliefs as generalizations rather than laws and, consequently, the theoretical basis for causality between 'racial' group membership and physical ability is invalid and unreliable. For instance, while the West Indian dominance of international cricket in the 1970s and 1980s was widely attributed to the innate biological capacity that enabled black bowlers to bowl faster than anyone else, such arguments are never voiced in the 2000s now that Australia, Pakistan and England have the fastest bowlers in world cricket.

Though social scientists may have successfully de-bunked 'race science' beliefs, such ideas continue to be influential not only in sports science, but in society more generally. Consequently, they are significant in structuring the life experiences of members of minority ethnic groups.

Key Reading

Fleming, S. (2001) 'Racial science and south Asian and black physicality', in B. Carrington and I. McDonald (eds), *Race, Sport and British Society*. London: Routledge. pp. 105–20.

Hoberman, J. (1997) *Darwin's Athletes: How Sport has Damaged Black America and Preserved the Myth of Race*. New York: Houghton Mifflin.

Key Reading

Back, L., Crabbe, T. and Solomos, J. (2001) *The Changing Face of Football: Racism, Identity and Multiculture in the English Game*. Berg: Oxford.

RACIST/HOOLIGAN COUPLET

The notion of the 'racist/hooligan couplet' was introduced by Les Back, Tim Crabbe and John Solomos in their ground-breaking work on racism in English football (**race**). Back et al. (2001) note that since the 1986 Popplewell Inquiry, government inquiries and social policy have been based on the notion that racism in football is closely associated with the more general unacceptable and rowdy forms of fan behaviour, at the pinnacle of which is **football hooliganism**. They argue that, in the minds of the public and the authorities, a specific type of person – the 'racist hooligan' – emerges who is a moral pariah, against which 'acceptable' forms of behaviour can be defined (**moral panic**).

Back et al. see the consequences of the racist/hooligan couplet as twofold. On the one hand, the racist/hooligan couplet has helped galvanize otherwise disparate groups, such as the football authorities, the Commission for Racial Equality and **fan** groups, and to some extent this may account for the initial success of the Lets Kick Racism out of Football campaign (**anti-racism**). However, in the longer term, by defining racism in such a narrow way, many less extreme, everyday, practices escape being categorized as racist. For instance, those fans who racially abuse players, if they do not see themselves as fitting the racist hooligan stereotype, may not recognize the problematic status of their actions (e.g., they may argue that all opposition players are barracked and racial barracking is no different to other forms of abuse). Consequently, while many of the more overt practices have been criminalized and subsequently declined in frequency, more common, 'low-level' and institutionalized racist practices in football remain relatively untouched.

RATIONAL RECREATION

The rational recreation movement developed in the nineteenth century as a consequence of middle-**class** concerns over the way the lower classes spent their leisure time. Working-class political activism, high levels of unemployment, urban overcrowding and ethnic immigration variously made these concerns more acute between 1840 and 1890 (**city, the**). On the one hand, there was a distinct desire to wean the working classes away from drinking **alcohol**, from **gambling** and from disorderly activities perceived to be barbaric, such as **animal sports** like cockfighting. On the other hand, there was a desire to enable the working classes to enjoy some of the moral educative benefits of the **cult of athleticism** that the upper and middle classes experienced in the public schools. Consequently museums, parks and public baths were built in urban areas. Many of the early professional football clubs were also established by rational recreationists, associated either with the local church (**religion**) or with local employers/industrialists who sought to provide the physical and institutional environment through which new moral codes could be inculcated, and thus traditional working-class habits could be undermined. George Cadbury developed what was seen as a model industrial community in Bournville, England, where females were required to learn to swim, where men in 'heavy' manual jobs were required to do weightlifting, and where there was provision for a range of medical and dental care.

Of course many, and youths in particular, were resistant to the **discipline** and order that the rational recreationists demanded. Merely providing such facilities did not guarantee that the desired moral lessons were learnt and many working men would have been happy to exploit such opportunities with little concern for the motives of the providers. However, the opportunities presented proved a considerable incentive to conform to bourgeois social mores (**embourgeoisement**). There was, thus, a crucial balance between supply and demand, which led the rational recreationists to hold a significant role in diffusing **modern sport** from the social elite, across the classes. Ultimately, however, according to Holt (1989), 'the values of the marketplace undermined moral education in sport as in other forms of leisure', with the development of mass entertainment (such as professional sport) turning the working classes from participants to spectators.

Key Reading

Hargreaves, J. (1986) *Sport, Power and Culture: A Social and Historical Analysis of Popular Sports in Britain*. Cambridge: Polity Press.

Holt, R. (1989) *Sport and the British: A Modern History*. Oxford: Oxford University Press. esp. Ch. 3.

REALISM

The belief that social reality exists independently of human perceptions. Where realism departs from **positivism** is in the belief that, rather than simply collecting data about the social world, the task of the realist researcher is to expose the structure of social relations that provide the underlying explanation of the processes which inform people's actions and choices. Where realism refers to people's consciousness, it does so in so far as it advocates that consciousness is a product of the conditions under which people live. Thus people's knowledge of the social world influences their behaviour and the choices and actions they make, but in turn their knowledge is shaped by the broader environment

(there is much in realism that is reminiscent of debates about **agency and structure**). Consequently, realism borrows research strategies from both positivism and **interpretivism**. The sociological work on **pain and injury** which focuses on **sportsnets** is a good sporting example of this research tradition.

Realism differs from critical realism in that the latter is premised on the belief that some of our 'sense data' are more reliable than others (sense data are divided into primary and secondary levels). Effectively this enables critical realists to assume a position which maintains that a social reality exists beyond human perception, while also suggesting that personal interpretation and understanding play a part in structuring the social world (**epistemology and ontology**).

REIFICATION

The act of attributing human characteristics to inanimate social constructs. Common examples of reification are ideas such as 'the needs of capitalism' or 'the interests of sport'. The primary objection to such linguistic formulations is that it is misleading to speak as though, for instance, 'sport' can think or act for itself. More correctly, only people can have interests or needs, and only people can think or act in line with their interests and needs. Reification, therefore, leads to the neglect of the roles of individuals, who may ascribe various meanings or purposes to their actions. Thus reification leads one to emphasize that social structures determine social life (**agency and structure**) and to portray humans as 'cultural dupes', unable and unwilling to contest or challenge the ideas put to them.

A further problem in this regard is that reification can often also lead to the prioritizing of the actions and intentions of the most powerful groups in society, and the parallel neglect of the less powerful. When, for instance, people talk about the 'interests of sport' or the 'needs of society', they tend to be talking about the interests of those who currently run sports or those who are in relatively advantaged positions within society, for it is these voices that are heard most loudly or dominate public **discourse**. In contrast to this, the voices of the socially least powerful, and most marginalized, tend not to be heard. Thus these people's interests tend to be obscured when we reify structural concepts such as sport or society.

RELIABILITY AND VALIDITY

The two traditional measures of any scientific research are reliability and validity. Reliability refers to the extent to which results are consistent and/or replicable. For instance, a criticism often raised against **ethnography** is whether two different researchers immersed in the same social context would draw the same conclusions about the **subcultures** under investigation; that is to say, to what extent is the analysis a subjective interpretation as opposed to an objective measurement? However, quantitative methods can also be criticized on the same grounds. Would, for instance, an athlete answer the same question (e.g. about the coaching regime at a club) in the same way at two points in time, or could answers be influenced by short-lived experiences (whether or not the athlete had been selected or dropped from a team)?

Validity refers to the extent to which the research measures what it was intended or claimed to measure, and the degree to which the conclusions drawn are correct. For instance, would the medical staff of a sports club be able to provide accurate figures on the extent and frequency of injuries in the club, or would athletes conceal certain injuries? Does the media coverage of a football match against a particular nation accurately reflect what the public feels about national conflict and national stereotypes (**nationalism**)? Moreover, when assessing the conclusions of a research project, one should ask whether the claims made about generalizability are correct. For instance, are the views of members of **independent supporters' associations** generalizable to the body of football fans as a whole, or are they a somewhat unrepresentative group?

It should be noted that researchers from different theoretical positions place different degrees of emphasis on reliability and validity as criteria for evaluating research. In general, the more qualitative the approach, the less stringently such tests are applied. Some, and those influenced by **postmodernism** and **post-structuralism** in particular, argue that there simply is no objective 'truth' 'out there' to be discovered; rather there are only subjective understandings approximating to 'truth'.

RELIGION

The passion and fanaticism that many sports **fans** display towards their teams have prompted comparisons, in recent times, between sport and religion. The godlike status of athletes and the ritualized journey to the stadium each weekend have been equated to the worship of deities in holy temples. This has prompted theologian Michael Novak (1976) to argue that 'Sports is somehow a religion', while Charles Prebish (1992) definitively states that 'sport *is* a religion'. Despite such categorical statements, there are many ways in which sport and religion are dissimilar, and no matter how structurally similar the two institutions may appear, there are fundamental philosophical differences that negate such an equation. No matter how much we might love a team, we do not pray to it, nor do we expect their representatives to offer us answers to the questions of life. This really is the responsibility of one's faith.

Despite the fact that sport cannot be regarded as a religion, there is certainly clear evidence that the two institutions have engaged with one another throughout much of recorded history. Sport, at times, has been integrated into the ritualistic and religious celebrations of deities, but it has similarly been shunned by religious authorities suspicious of the way it privileges corporeal experiences over philosophical, spiritual or moral qualities. Purists might argue that 'sport' is a thoroughly modern phenomenon with its origins dating back to the mid-nineteenth century (**modern sport**), yet if the concept of sport is expanded to include ad hoc and semi-structured physical activities (**sport, definition of**), there are notable examples where these have been incorporated into religious festivals and celebrations. Many ancient societies, for example, embraced physical recreation as part of their religious celebrations. The ancient Greeks initially staged the Olympic and other games as part of larger religious festivities held to honour their gods (**ancient Olympic Games**), while half a world away, Mayan priests supervized traditional ball games on courts built next to their temples. In contemporary times, exponents of Eastern religions have used their bodies to display extreme physical feats as means of attaining religious transcendence.

While there has been a growing interest in sport and indigenous and traditional religions, particularly throughout Asia and Africa, as well as in the role of sport in both Islam and Judaism, it has been the relationship between Christianity and sport that has been scrutinized most closely. Christianity's regard for sport has fluctuated according to dominant attitudes towards the mind/body relationship. When the Church shunned the corporeal in favour of spiritual reflection, sport was relegated to the margins of human recreational activity in favour of more spiritual pursuits. When warfare and protection of the Church's material interests dominated, training the body through physical activity rose in stature. During the medieval era, the Catholic Church initially supported physical activities such as ball games in their religious festivals, yet the growing **Puritan** influence led to an uncompromising observance of the sabbath and other religious holidays. The Puritans were concerned that engaging in physical recreation would lead to the physical and moral corruption of the faithful, while the political hierarchy saw in popular amusements the roots of political unrest. Accordingly, Queen Elizabeth I mandated in 1559 and 1579 that the sabbath be set aside purely for holy contemplation, specifically banning activities including ball games, **animal sports** such as bear and bull baiting, music, drinking **alcohol**, and **gambling**. These early restrictions gradually intensified to the extent that commoners were prevented from many of the traditional activities that had characterized medieval village life (**folk games**). In the early seventeenth century, King James I responded to protests about the dearth of public gatherings and published the *Book of Sports* (1618), in which he identified activities, including dancing and **archery**, that could be lawfully pursued on Sundays. Importantly, only those who had worshipped in church were permitted to participate. The British Parliament, however, rescinded his decree, passing a bill that reaffirmed the strict observance of the sabbath, and it was not until 1633 that the book was reissued.

While the medieval church was resolute in its loathing of 'immoral' corporeal activities, by the mid-nineteenth century sport was no longer regarded as a mere physical pursuit, as educators recognized its potential to teach higher moral lessons. The English public schools, led initially by Dr Thomas Arnold at Rugby, began to implement a system of games and sports for their young charges with the expectation that the lessons learned on the playing field would transfer to other areas of life. In this philosophy, training the body was thought to be as critical as training the mind. **Muscular Christianity**, as it became known, offered sport an ethical foundation that remains current today. Concepts such as sportsmanship and **fair play** were fundamental to Muscular Christianity and were used as the basis to train future leaders for the British Empire (**imperialism**).

As Muscular Christianity spread throughout the British colonies, other organizations began to adopt its central tenet that morality could result from physical hardiness. The

Young Men's Christian Association (YMCA), founded in 1844 in England, offered the working classes a haven where they could engage in healthy, ethical, rational recreations, such as bathing, bible study and other socially beneficial pursuits. Gradually, the YMCA began offering an expanded programme of exercises and physical activities to complement their religious activities. A Jewish equivalent, the Young Men's Hebrew Association, later emerged, and for both Christian and Jewish organizations, participation in sport was an important tool for developing a worthy moral character.

Muscular Christianity slowly spread throughout the British Empire, in part because of the efforts of Christian missionaries who regarded sport as an effective means to 'civilize' the indigenous communities in which they worked. In many ways, sport remains a useful evangelizing tool, particularly in the United States where 'sports evangelism' escalated throughout the last half of the twentieth century. Here, churches commonly organize sporting competitions and leagues, using the events as opportunities to preach to the faithful or to convert new adherents. Entire organizations, such as the Fellowship of Christian Athletes founded in 1954, were established specifically to use sport as an evangelizing tool. It is now not uncommon to see devotional prayers before, during and following sporting events, though the official separation of Church and State means that in some public (state) schools, sports-related prayer has raised significant concerns.

Overall, the relationship between sport and religion is complex and not easily reduced to simplistic definitions. While structural similarities might offer a casual insight, the relationship is far more complex, hinging on changing and differing attitudes towards the **body**, secular amusements and religious authorities. Rather than simply focusing on the relationship between the two, it is useful to concentrate on how each institution has used the other to further its own interests and ends. From providing social opportunities for adherents to interact through to specific evangelizing missions, sport has offered religious communities a way of promulgating their particular doctrines. Conversely, the ethical foundations introduced into sport continue to influence contemporary sport, particularly on apparently 'moral' issues such as doping (**drugs**).

Key Reading

Higgs, R.J. (1995) *God in the Stadium. Sports and Religion in America.* Lexington: University of Kentucky Press.

Magdalinski, T. and Chandler, T.J.L. (eds) (2002) *With God on their Side. Sport in the Service of Religion.* London: Routledge.

Novak, M. (1976) *The Joy of Sports: End Zones, Bases, Baskets, Balls, and the Consecration of the American Spirit.* New York: Basic Books.

Prebish, C.S. (ed.) (1992) *Religion and Sport: The Meeting of Sacred and Profane.* Westport, CT: Greenwood Press.

Tara Magdalinski

REPRODUCTION THEORY

A form of **Marxism**, the application of reproduction theory to sport is epitomized by the work of French sociologist Jean-Marie Brohm. Reproduction theory, according to John Hargreaves, states that sport is 'related' to the capitalist mode of production and dominant social relations (as distinct from being a 'simple reflection' of them, (**correspondence theory**)). Thus within this perspective, sport can have differences to, and autonomy from, the economic base. Indeed, for reproduction theorists, it is sport's relative autonomy from the economic mode of production that enables it to contribute towards the reproduction of the dominant social relations; that is to say, sport's ideological functions rely on its popularity, which itself stems from it being different from work.

Brohm's writings are collated in his book, *Sport – A Prison of Measured Time* (1978). He states that sport emerged in England, 'the birthplace of the capitalist mode of production, at the beginning of the modern industrial epoch' (see Elias's discussion of **sportization and parliamentarization** for an alternative view). Sport means different things to different **class**es. For the bourgeoisie it is a form of distraction, whereas for the proletariat it is a means of physical recuperation. But crucially sport functions through persuasion rather than force. For the proletariat, sport has the illusion of freedom, creativity and choice but in reality, argues Brohm, sport in capitalist societies has lost all its creative, playful and spontaneous aspects. Thus, far from being an antidote to work, sport is rule-bound and structured in the interests of the dominant classes. Participants are thus 'prisoners'.

Drawing on the work of French sociologist Louis Althusser (1918–1990), Brohm sees sport as part of the 'ideological state apparatus' (as opposed to the 'repressive state apparatus'; i.e. the army, police, etc.). Sport performs certain ideological functions: (1) justifying the established social order; (2) depoliticizing the masses by holding out the illusion of positive social advancement; (3) masking international conflict by emphasizing the peaceful coexistence of nation states; (4) preparing the proletariat for industrial labour through the repression of sexuality and the domestic enslavement of women; (5) militarizing and regimenting youth; and (6) neutralizing class struggle by reducing crowds to passive 'cheering machines'.

Key Reading

Brohm, J.-M. (1978) *Sport – A Prison of Measured Time*. London: Ink Links.

RETAIN AND TRANSFER SYSTEM

The retain and transfer system, like the **maximum wage**, gave English Football League clubs tremendous power over players. Under the system, if a player wanted to change clubs his existing club initially had to agree to sell, then find a buyer and finally agree a fee. If the club *didn't* want the player to go, then the player had no option other than to stay where he was. At the end of the player's contract the club could decide whether to put the player on the retained or the transfer list. If the club wanted to keep – to retain – the player, the only stipulation was that they had to pay him the agreed minimum wages and conditions. After the Second World War football was littered with stories of wage cuts being imposed on players, refusals to accept transfer requests, and unrealistically high transfer fees being placed on players (Russell, 1997).

In 1960 the Professional Footballers Association (PFA) demanded four key changes to the employment status of footballers, including the abolition of the maximum wage and the reform of the retain and transfer system. Football club chairmen soon acceded to the players' demands to abolish the maximum wage. The PFA therefore chose to pursue the 'retain and transfer system' through the law courts, and via the George Eastham vs. Newcastle United Football Club case in particular. Eastham, a promising young player, had walked away from football when Newcastle United refused to release him. Newcastle subsequently relented and Eastham signed for Arsenal, but the PFA persuaded Eastham to allow the case to go forward as a challenge to the legitimacy of the retain and transfer system more broadly. In June 1963 Mr Justice Wilberforce declared the system 'an unjustifiable restraint to trade'. A revised contract, agreed in April 1964, enabled clubs to have first option on renewing a player's contract, but the rate of pay was to be no lower than in the previous contract. If a club did not want to keep a player, a free transfer was to be granted. Complete freedom of contract, however, was only achieved in 1978.

The players received considerable public support for their campaign and this probably reflects how antiquated employment regulations in football were, and how authoritarian football club administrators attempted to be. The ruling represents a highly significant shift in the balance of power between players and employers. The next significant advance in player power was to come with the passing of the **Bosman ruling**.

Key Reading

Russell, D. (1997) *Football and the English: A Social History of Association Football in England*, 1863–1995. Preston, UK: Carnegie Publishing.

RETIREMENT

Sociological studies of retirement from sports participation grew out of the work on sports **socialization** more generally. Just as people were assumed to need socialization *into* the norms and values of social life (e.g. of sport), so they were assumed to need socialization into the norms and values required in post-playing life.

Early gerontological work on occupational retirement (gerontology is the study of ageing and of elderly people) posed something of a contradiction. Retirement was seen as something to look forward to, a movement from the constraints of work to the freedom of leisure, yet retirement was also seen as problematic and a radical life change, requiring an adjustment of outlook and the development of coping strategies. While sociologists of sport worked from these foundations, retirement from sport differs from retirement from many other forms of social life in that, for many, it happens at a relatively young age (and thus ex-athletes generally sought secondary careers) and because most people view sport as a particularly desirable career (and hence it is likely that the changes which retirement entails would be unwelcome). Consequently, sociologists looking at retirement from sport must consider somewhat different factors to those considered by gerontologists more generally.

The study of retirement from sport, however, revealed similarly contradictory strands. Research on those leaving inter-scholastic athletics indicated that most retirees saw sport as a passing phase in their lives, and so it entailed little trauma or identity crisis. Similar patterns were found for college and university athletes. It was argued that for these people, sports were viewed as 'short-term' careers, the dynamics of which were very different to longer-term occupational careers. Early research focusing on those leaving professional sports, however, suggested a more traumatic process. Weinberg and Arond's study of retired boxers (1971) found that post-sport life was characterized by a rapid decline in prestige and income, emotional problems stemming from the fracturing of links with former friends and colleagues in the sport, and the search for new forms of employment. Subsequent studies (Swain, 1991), however, indicated that although athletes were reluctant to leave a career that had given them so much, many felt ready to move on to new things.

Two conclusions emerge. First, an individual's ability to cope with retirement is linked to their broader social structural conditions such as socioeconomic background, **gender** and **race**/ethnicity (Weinberg and Arond's sample of boxers contained a high proportion of ethnic minorities and those from economically deprived backgrounds). For instance, athletes with good educational qualifications are likely to find the transition to a post-sport career relatively straightforward compared to those with little formal education. Second, that professional athletes experience an element of relief in leaving sport seems to indicate that the desirability of sport as a career is felt more keenly by those outside than those inside sport.

Key Reading

Coakley, J. (1983) 'Leaving competitive sport? Retirement or rebirth?', *Quest*, 35 (1): 1–11.

Swain, D.A. (1991) 'Withdrawal from sport and Schlossberg's model of transitions', *Sociology of Sport Journal*. 8 (2): 152–60.

Weinberg, S.K. and Arond, H. (1971) 'The occupational culture of the boxer', in E. Dunnng (ed.), *The Sociology of Sport: A Selection of Readings*. London: Frank Cass. pp. 285–300.

RINGELMANN EFFECT

(group dynamics; social loafing)

RISK

Rose to prominence as a sociological issue with the 1992 publication of Ulrich Beck's *Risk Society*. Beck argued that as scientific knowledge expands our understanding of the world, so we also become more aware of the dangers we face. Contemporary societies are thus characterized by the prevalence of knowledge about danger and consequently all individuals, on an everyday basis, assess and attempt to manage risk. As this indicates, risk is socially and politically constructed; only certain aspects of life are defined as risky, but those that are become subject to regulation, while those not defined as such escape external intervention. Particular groups (e.g. young males) seem more tolerant of risk-taking than others. In spite of the fact that the public demands that the state works to free us from risks, people actively seek out risk within sport (and other leisure activities) and/or demand that the authorities leave them free to enjoy such risks. Risk-taking in sport is relatively protected due to the semi-autonomous nature of many sports governing bodies, the argument that risk-taking in sport is largely voluntaristic, and the active denial of risk by many sports participants.

While there may be economic risks associated with sport (e.g. **gambling**) and social risks (the risk to one's reputation and social status), of central concern has been the risk of physical injury (and death) (see also

obesity discourse). A 'culture of risk' in sport has been identified largely in the context of the widespread acceptance and normalization of playing through **pain and injury**. This culture of risk in sport will often be predicated on the notion that one must ignore the risks associated with pain and injury because they are 'part of the game' and that such self-sacrifice is for the 'good of the team'. There may be structural inducements to play when injured (such as positive feedback from coaches, team mates, the **media**, etc.) as well as structural constraints (the stigmatization and isolation of injured players, the questioning of commitment or **masculinity**). The culture of risk leads athletes to believe that the acceptance and tolerance of pain and injury is their only viable option should they wish to continue to be accepted as a sportsperson (**risk-pain-injury paradox**). Further, Frey (1991) has noted that the culture of risk effectively enables coaches and managers to transfer their own risk of failure to the athletes. The existence of the culture insulates coaches from potentially threatening questions about the legitimacy of their training routines and playing tactics, and provides management with (moral if not legal) exoneration from any responsibility for the potentially harmful effects of their working practices. The culture of risk is seen as very firmly embedded in athletic **subcultures**, and research has indicated that there are few **gender** differences in athletes' adherence to the **sport ethic**.

As central as risk is to many sporting activities (especially sports such as motor racing, mountaineering, etc; see also **lifestyle sports**), we must not forget the backdrop to Beck's concept of the risk society; that is to say, that growing concerns over risk are predicated upon advances in scientific knowledge and thus greater understanding and control over our social worlds. Indeed, recent work on pain and injury in sport has also focused on the presence of a 'culture of precaution'. Most accurately, therefore, we should seek to understand the balance between risk-taking and the existence of safety and security. Such ideas have resonance for Elias and Dunning's concept of a **quest for excitement**.

Key Reading

Donnelly, P. (2004) 'Sport and risk culture', in K. Young (ed.), *Sporting Bodies, Damaged Selves: Sociological Studies of Sports-related Injury*. Oxford: Elsevier. pp. 29–58.

Frey, J.H. (1991) 'Social risk and the meaning of sport', *Sociology of Sport Journal*, 8 (2): 136–45.

Safai, P. (2003) 'Healing the body in the "culture of risk": examining the negotiations of treatment between sport medicine clinicians and injured athletes in Canadian intercollegiate sport', *Sociology of Sport Journal*, 20 (2): 127–46.

Hughes, R. and Coakley, J. (1991) 'Positive deviance among athletes: the implications of overconformity to the sport ethic', *Sociology of Sport Journal*, 8 (4): 307–25.

Nixon II, H.L. (1993). 'Accepting the risks of pain and injury in sport: mediated cultural influences on playing hurt', *Sociology of Sport Journal*, 10 (2), 183–96.

Young, K., White, P. and McTeer, W. (1994) 'Body talk: male athletes reflect on sport, injury and pain', *Sociology of Sport Journal*, 11: 175–94.

ROMAN GAMES

Consisted of combat events between **gladiators**, mass executions of criminals, and the theatrical reconstruction of battles and historical pageants that brought the great moments of Roman history back to life. Animals such as elephants and lions were transported from around the Empire to take part in the Games. Events were staged in arenas that seated tens of thousands of spectators, the best known of which were in Rome, namely the Colosseum, and the Circus Maximus where **chariot races** were staged.

The Roman Games developed out of religious burial rites thought to satisfy the dead man's need for blood (***From Ritual to Record***; **religion**). Initially confined to the aristocratic families that dominated public life and public office, these 'sports' became democratized and spectacularized as individuals sought to strengthen their own political position. For an aspiring politician, the organization of a lavish show was an excellent way in which to ensure electoral success.

The reign of Caligula represented a watershed in the history of the Roman Games. His predecessor, Tiberius, reduced expenditure for such shows, and then turned his back on Rome to live in Capri. Caligula learnt from Tiberius' subsequent unpopularity, celebrating his accession by staging many great shows. Subsequently, he bought the people's affection with gifts of food. It is from this

RISK-PAIN-INJURY PARADOX

The notion of the risk-pain-injury paradox has developed out of various sociological works on **pain and injury** in sport, including that of Curry (1993), Hughes and Coakley (1991) and Young et al. (1994), but is most clearly expressed in the work of Howard Nixon (1993). Stemming from the notion of a 'culture of risk' (**risk**), where playing with pain and injury is normalized as a necessary 'sacrifice' if one is to seek sporting success, Nixon notes that such practices are likely, in the long run, to actually reduce one's chances of athletic achievement and thus sporting success. That is to say, desire for sporting success leads athletes to play through pain and with injury, a situation in which, paradoxically, the chances of sporting success are reduced. More broadly, such risk-taking conflicts with what Nixon perceives to be 'commonsense' assumptions about the relationship between sports participation and **health** promotion. This paradoxical situation, however, appears to be a largely accurate portrayal of the culture of elite sport.

Key Reading

Curry, T.J. (1993) 'A little pain never hurt anyone: athletic career socialization and the normalization of sports injury', *Symbolic Interaction*. 16: 273–90.

point that Juvenal's famous dictum *panem et circenses* (bread and circuses) derives.

Successive emperors sought to outbid each other in terms of the splendour and the number of events staged during their reign. Staging events demonstrated the emperor's goodwill and generosity, but it was not enough simply to arrange for the Games to be held; it was important that the emperor attended, and that he performed in front of the crowd both as a deity and as 'one of the people'. His power to decide on a participant's life or death – particularly if done in an arbitrary manner – reinforced the notion of the emperor as god. Yet, contrary to Juvenal, these events were no 'opiate of the masses', but occasions at which the people could cheer (and thus give support to) particular politicians, demand reductions in taxation, call for the liberation of a particular gladiator, or even express hostility towards the emperor himself. Emperors such as Caligula and Nero responded by humiliating political opponents and forcing them into the arena to fight. The people derived pleasure from witnessing the games, and the ritual of the event enabled the construction of the collective self-consciousness of Romans; that is to say, a mechanism by which they could come to think of themselves as a community rather than as a collection of individuals.

To modern eyes these events seem extremely barbaric, but it should be remembered that Rome at this time was a city of great inequalities of wealth, where the luxury of a few was matched by densely populated, insanitary, harsh and generally violent conditions for the many. As Auguet (1994) notes: 'To confront death was not an exceptional act of heroism; it was the normal way of proving oneself a Roman.' Inequality was central to the organization of events: animals pitted against humans, women against dwarfs, **gladiators** armed with one type of weapon against gladiators armed with another (**fair play**). It should also be remembered that, initially at least, **gladiators** were slaves or criminals and, consequently, occupied the status of chattel or animals. Indeed, the Roman Games involved a reversal of the principles of the ancient Greek Games; where slaves had previously watched freemen compete, now freemen watched the performances of slaves.

Key Reading

Auguet, R. (1994) *Cruelty and Civilization: The Roman Games*. London: Routledge.

Hardy, S. (1977) 'Politicians, promoters and the rise of sport: the case of Ancient Greece and Rome', in *Canadian Journal of History of Sport and Physical Education*, 1977, 8 (1): 1–15.

Harris, H.A. (1972) *Sport in Greece and Rome*. London: Thames and Hudson.

S

SAMPLING

It is not unusual in social research, normally due to time or cost constraints, for the population under investigation to be too large or inaccessible for researchers to investigate in its entirety. Consequently, the vast majority of sports studies research relies on investigating a subset, or a sample, of the broader population and extrapolating from the results.

Sampling techniques are normally categorized into two types, probability and non-probability. Probability sampling is an attempt to conduct research on a representative group of the broader population. There are four main types: (1) *random sampling*, in which a list of the entire population is drawn up, and then research subjects are chosen at random (using a randomizing technique, e.g. assigning each person a number and then using a random number table, or computer, to select the sample); (2) *systematic sampling*, in which cases are selected according to a pattern (e.g. every tenth spectator who passes through the turnstile at a sports event); (3) *stratified random sampling*, in which the population is divided into sub-groups (e.g. social classes) and then random sampling is used within each of the groups; and (4) *cluster sampling*, in which the population is already distributed into convenient groups (e.g. school classes or sport teams) and respondents are picked by selecting particular clusters.

Non-probability sampling does facilitate the generalization of findings to the broader population, but may more commonly be used to lend weight to or support an existing hypothesis (pending further research). Categories of non-probability sampling include: (1) *convenience sampling*, in which the nearest (or cheapest to access) respondents are used; (2) *snowball sampling*, in which the initial respondents are used to gain access to subsequent respondents; (3) *quota sampling*, in which, for instance, one wants to interview footballers from across a range of football leagues and thus selects a relatively even number from each; and (4) *purposive sampling*, in which typical, extreme or just well-suited cases are selected for the research. For instance, one might interview members of **independent supporters' associations** to try to understand how fans feel about the relocation of **stadium**s. These interviewees would not be representative of fans as a whole, but they would be likely to have the most thought-out and coherent opinions. Often, non-probability sampling techniques are used concurrently. In Malcolm and Sheard's research on injuries in elite rugby union (2002), interviewees were selected using convenience, snowball and quota sampling.

The degree to which one can extrapolate – or generalize – from a piece of research is dependent upon how representative the sample is, and this in turn relies on the accuracy with which the characteristics of the entire population are known to the researcher (e.g. while we could generate an accurate list of all professional footballers in a country, it would not be feasible to draw up a list of all athletes using performance-enhancing drugs). Where the broader population is known, probability sampling will be more appropriate, but where it is not, non-probability sampling is equally valid.

Key Reading

Gratton, C. and Jones, I. (2004) *Research Methods for Sports Studies*. London: Routledge. esp. Ch. 7.

Malcolm, D. and Sheard, K. (2002) '"Pain in the assets": the effects of commercialization and professionalization on the management of injury in English rugby union', *Sociology of Sport Journal*, 19 (2): 149–69.

Waddington, I., Malcolm, D. and Horak, R. (1998) 'The social composition of football crowds in western Europe: a comparative study', *International Review for the Sociology of Sport*, 33 (2): 155–69.

SECTARIANISM

The concept of sectarianism could in theory be applied to any relationship in which one particular group (or sect) acts or is perceived to act in a harmful way towards another group. To that extent, the word could be used to describe discriminatory practices based on **gender**, **race**/ethnicity, sexual orientation, and so on. In practice, however, both in the sociology of sport and more widely, the concept of sectarianism is associated with conflictual relationships between different religious groups. In many instances, however, what separates the rival sects has less to do with **religion** than with political differences. Nevertheless, religious labels are often used to define the warring factions. In sports studies, the concept has been applied most frequently to Northern Ireland and Scotland.

In the case of Northern Ireland, it can be demonstrated that sport is one of the most important signifiers of religious or political affiliation. Gaelic games such as hurling, Gaelic football and camogie (**Gaelic Athletic Association**), are played almost exclusively by Catholics (or Irish nationalists), whereas 'British' games such as cricket, rugby union and (men's) field hockey are played predominantly although not exclusively by Protestants (or Ulster unionists). In addition, global sports such as boxing and golf are enjoyed by members of both traditions with relatively little evidence of sectarianism. On the other hand, association football, which is also played and watched by Catholics and Protestants, has long been implicated in sectarian practices. More generally, the game also acts as a cultural signifier inasmuch as members of the two communities tend to support different teams. Most Catholic football **fans** favour the Republic of Ireland's national side, Celtic in the Scottish Premier League and, in very small numbers, Cliftonville and a couple of other clubs in the Irish League. For their part, Protestants give their support to the Northern Ireland team, to Celtic's rivals, Rangers, and to leading Irish League clubs, notably Glentoran and Linfield. The situation as regards fans becomes more confused, however, in relation to English football, with Catholics and Protestants alike supporting major clubs such as Arsenal, Everton, Liverpool and Manchester United.

Although attempts have been made to use sport as a vehicle for improving community relations in Northern Ireland, this has proved difficult, not least because sport has contributed for so long to the reproduction of cultural difference and, more prosaically, because many administrators feel, not unreasonably, that their main responsibility is to ensure the well-being of their respective sports and not to engage in social engineering.

In Scotland, the concept of sectarianism is used most frequently to describe the relationship between Celtic and Rangers football clubs – the so-called Old Firm – and their fans, although the Scottish parliament has acknowledged that sectarianism impacts on other areas of Scottish society. Celtic's support base is mainly, although not exclusively, Catholic, while Rangers are followed almost entirely by Protestants (again using these religious descriptors purely as a matter of convenience). Followers of the two clubs often highlight their differences by way of songs and symbols, most of which are linked to the historic conflict between the two political traditions in Ireland. Some commentators are inclined to attribute sectarian motives to one club more than the other. Some suggest that the existence of the Old Firm provides a useful safety valve allowing for the expression of residual sectarian attitudes that are otherwise increasingly less common in Scotland (**catharsis**; **functions of sport**). Others argue that the massive popularity of the two clubs reflects the fact that the tensions between the two traditions have not been resolved, a fact from which the Old Firm benefit financially.

It is conceivable that religious tensions within Indian cricket or between separate linguistic groups in Belgian sport could also be described as sectarian. However, this is not how social scientists of sport generally approach such issues. It is worth noting, however, that Sir Donald Bradman, a Protestant and arguably the world's greatest ever cricketer, was accused, most notably by Bill O'Reilly, of behaving in a sectarian manner towards his Catholic team mates.

Key Reading

Bairner, A. (ed.) (2005) *Sport and the Irish: Histories, Identities, Issues*. Dublin: University College Dublin Press.

Bradley, J.M. (1995) *Ethnic and Religious Identity in Modern Scotland: Culture, Politics and Football*. Aldershot: Avebury.

Cronin, M. (1999) *Sport and Nationalism in Ireland: Gaelic Games, Soccer and Irish Identity since 1884*. Dublin: Four Courts Press.

Murray, B. (2000) *The Old Firm: Sectarianism, Sport and Society in Scotland*. Edinburgh: John Donald Publishers.

Sugden, J. and Bairner, A. (1993) *Sport, Sectarianism and Society in a Divided Ireland*. Leicester: Leicester University Press.

Alan Bairner

SELF-CONFIDENCE

Psychologists define self-confidence as the belief that one can successfully perform a desired behaviour. Some have further refined this definition in suggesting that self-confidence can be viewed as both a trait (i.e. a stable part of one's make-up, a tendency or disposition to either be confident or lack confidence) and a state (i.e. something that is context-specific and thus subject to change). In addition to this, it is important to recognize that self-confidence may be influenced by organizational and sociocultural factors. As the broadening of this definition suggests, self-confidence in sport is an imprecise term incorporating everything from a gut feeling to a psychological concept.

Self-confidence is a particularly important concept for psychologists of sport because research has consistently demonstrated a positive relationship between confidence and performance. Confidence has been found to aid **concentration** and is thought to enable the arousal of more positive **emotions** (such as relaxation) and foster a more positive approach to negative emotions such as **anxiety**. The more confident a person the more challenging self-imposed goals are likely to be, the more effort is likely to be expended in the pursuit of those goals, and the more ambitious will be one's tactics and strategies within a game. However, it should be noted that while self-confidence has a largely positive effect on performance, it is possible to be overconfident; to be so optimistic about one's success that the impact is negative (e.g. fostering a lack of effort, poor preparation, etc.). Finally, the reciprocal nature of self-confidence and behaviour should be noted; that is to say, self-confidence alters behaviour (e.g. improves performance), and behaviour (e.g. exercise adherence) improves self-confidence.

Bandura, critical of the vagueness with which the term self-confidence had been used, developed *self-efficacy theory* (1997) on which much sport-related work in this area is now based. Self-efficacy theory is a situation-specific form of self-confidence that focuses not simply on the skills one has, but on *one's judgements* about what one can do with those skills. There are six key sources of self-efficacy: (1) performance accomplishments (e.g. victories in previous sporting events); (2) vicarious experiences (e.g. seeing others being successful. This is a four stage process, involving the initial attention given to observing, the retention of that information, the motor reproduction of the activity and the motivation to learn about and repeat that skill); (3) verbal persuasion (both from others and in the form of self-persuasion); (4) imaginal experiences (**imagery**); (5) physiological states (the interpretation of states of **arousal** as either enabling or constraining performance); and (6) emotional arousal (e.g. positive emotional states such as happiness have been shown to enhance efficacy judgements). However, a central tenet of self-efficacy theory is that each of these potential sources must be cognitively appraised by the individual and that this therefore accounts for differential levels of self-efficacy among people who may experience the same efficacy-building experiences (**explanatory style**).

Key Reading

Bandura, A. (1997) *Self-efficacy: The Exercise of Control*. New York: Freeman.

Feltz, D.L. (1988) 'Self-confidence and sports performance', *Exercise and Sport Sciences Reviews*, 16: 423–57.

SELF-FULFILLING PROPHECY

Robert Merton, in *Social Theory and Social Structure* (1957), described the self-fulfilling prophecy thus: 'in the beginning, a false definition of the situation evoking a new behaviour which makes the originally false conception come true'. Within the sociology of sport the self-fulfilling prophecy has been mostly used to explain the relatively high numbers of blacks and African-Americans competing at the elite level of sport. This works in two ways. First (false, or certainly as

yet unproven), beliefs about the innate biological superiority of blacks (**race science**) lead black athletes to have increased **self-confidence** about their sporting abilities and thus practise more and work harder to achieve success. Correlatively, it is believed that these beliefs, augmented by the empirical dominance of black athletes in sport, lead white youngsters to assume that they cannot compete and thus are less likely to see sport as a viable career option. Thus the false belief (innate biological difference) evokes a new behaviour (relative levels of commitment to sport) that leads to the originally false conception coming true (disproportionate numbers of successful black and African-American athletes in elite sport).

It has also been argued that tabloid press reporting of **football hooliganism** contains elements of self-fulfilling prophecy. In this instance, the **media** present football as a dangerous event that attracts others oriented towards **violence**. Moreover, responding to tabloid calls for draconian measures, politicians introduce policies that have the unintended consequence of exacerbating the problem, e.g. the segregation of crowds, leading to the creation of football 'ends', and strong feelings of territoriality (**moral panic**).

Key Reading

Loy, J.W. and Booth, D. (2004) 'Social Structure and social theory: the intellectual insights of Robert K. Merton', in R. Giulianotti (ed.), *Sport and Modern Social Theorists*. London: Palgrave Macmillan. pp. 33–42.

Merton, R. (1957) *Social Theory and Social Structure*, rev. and enl. edn. New York: Free Press of Glencoe.

SELF-TALK

A form in intrapersonal communication, but more simply it occurs whenever we think about something. Self-talk can be categorized as essentially positive ('You'll win the next point') or negative ('I'm going to lose'), as well as motivational, instructional, mood-related and self-affirming. However, in the sporting context self-talk is usually used to refer to the technique of replacing negative thoughts which lead to diminished performance with more positive thoughts. As a thought modification technique, self-talk can be used as a mediator between an event and one's response, enabling athletes to appraise situations differently. Hence, rather than chastizing oneself for missing a putt (which might lead to anger, or a sense of impending defeat), one might use instructional self-talk to guide oneself through the mechanics of putting (leading to calmness and improved preparation for the next putt). Suggested techniques for self-talk include: (1) use of cue words; (2) use of short and specific phrases; (3) use of the first person; and (4) use of the present tense. Self-talk should be positive, kind, said with meaning and attention, and repetitive. Thought stopping (focusing on the undesired thought for a period and using a cue to switch attention to something else) and changing negative self-talk to positive self-talk (recognizing and seeking to alter negative thoughts rather than attempting to remove them from one's mind) are two commonly recommended self-talk techniques. Self-talk in sport has, in particular, been identified as contributing to enhanced **concentration**, increased **self-confidence**, and as playing an important part in an athlete's rehabilitation from injury.

SEMIOTICS

(**signifier and signified**)

SEXUALITY

(**gender; lesbians; masculinity**)

SEXUALIZATION

It is mundane to observe that sexuality is an important phenomenon in all areas of human society, and, therefore, that the domain of sport will be no exception. Given the corpo-reality of sport – bodies (**body**) performing under the close **surveillance** of spectators – it is not surprising that sex and sport will have a close and, in a variety of ways, difficult relationship. If it can be safely concluded that sport is always already sexual, what does it mean to say that it is also undergoing 'sexualization'? The answer is that, rather than being a simple, necessary component and by-product of sport as a social phenomenon, sexualization is the systematic, commercially inspired intensification of the sport–sex nexus.

Sexualization involves the promotion of certain forms of sexuality, especially those of a heterosexual nature, because sport in this form is regarded as highly marketable. By contrast, some subjects and practices are repressed and so 'de-sexualized' – for example, homosexuality in mainstream sport (**lesbians**). Sexualization in sport is, therefore, both strategic and contested – a marketer's ideas about using sex to attract spectator interest, especially through the **media**, and often a source of conflict for some, especially women, who see in such an approach a subjugation of sporting excellence through sexual exploitation.

The issue of sexualization has, historically, been deeply gendered (**gender**). The masculine domination of sports culture, especially its emphasis on men's performative superiority in most of the high-profile, strength- and speed-based sports (such as the various codes of football), and male control over the institution of sport have made it difficult for women to find a secure and elevated place in the sports hierarchy (**masculinity**). The **commercialization** of the sports industry has tended to reproduce women's subordination – as sport has become industrialized and, crucially, 'mediatized', what have women been able to sell to male-dominated corporate sponsors, media organizations, sports bodies, and spectators? The answer has been a traditionally patriarchal one – their sexuality. As the relationships between sport, media, image and advertising are now routinized and sophisticated, 'playing the sex card' is a common strategy in women's sport.

The main justifications for sexualizing women in sport are that: (1) it helps provide the necessary economic resources to pursue their sport that would otherwise be unavailable in a sexually segregated sports market; (2) once spectator (especially male) attention has been gained by sexual attractiveness, exposure to the sporting skills of women will lead to a new appreciation that is not dependent on physical appearance and appeal; (3) objections to the use of sexual address by sportswomen are condemned as prudish and commercially naive – the sexualized **body** is a part of life to be celebrated, it is argued, and any attempt to prevent individual women from maximizing their competitive sexual advantage in the sports market is an unwarranted restraint of trade.

The main counter-arguments against the sexualization of women's sport are, in turn, that: (1) it merely reproduces the perceived inferiority of women's sport and their dependence on sex for status and remuneration; (2) it is naive to believe that a sexual mode of address will not ultimately dominate and obscure women's sporting excellence; and (3) the sexualized behaviour of individual sportswomen has negative consequences for all women, irrespective of their own personal attitudes and demeanour.

Sexualization of women's sport can take many forms – including artfully designed, revealing sportswear, photoshoots in men's 'soft core' and 'lad's mags' (**new laddism**), glamour photography, nude calendars, or merely through journalists' emphasis on their conventional sex appeal (or lack thereof). Perhaps the most notoriously overt sexualization of women's sport is the swimsuit issue of *Sports Illustrated* magazine, the biggest selling annual issue that seems to confirm the sexualized place of women in sport's culture. The most frequently cited symbol of sexualized women's sport in the early twenty-first century is **Anna Kournikova**, a tennis player whose prominence as an endorser of products such as underwear, and earnings from the marketing of her image, far outweigh her success as a tennis player, and the rewards given to other, better-performed but less photogenic women's tennis players like Lindsay Davenport. Such media- and advertising-inspired sexualization is often given strong support by senior (mostly male) sports administrators – such as Sepp Blatter and Lennart Johannsson, current president of **FIFA** and former president of its European counterpart UEFA respectively – who have called for women's football to adjust its mode of presentation in order to capitalize on its potential sex appeal.

Women's sport has had to deal with the issue of sexualization for many decades as both symbol and cause of gender inequity in sport. A relatively new development, however, is the sexualization of sportsmen. This process is also inspired by marketing and image, with male sport celebrities becoming increasingly conspicuous across contemporary culture, as opposed to being largely confined to sport-loving men (**celebrity**). Sexualized male sport has been increasingly 'pitched' to women, who, as a large potential media sports audience in their own right and as controllers of many key decisions on household expenditure, are vital to the development of sports and ancillary industries. In 2007, **David Beckham**, the England footballer, is not only the most prominent of sexualized sportsmen and their potentially symbolic status for 'new men' everywhere, but also the subject of substantial discussion about his innovations in the presentation of masculine style. The significance of this shift in imaging should not, then, be discounted – as sexual objectification is traditionally associated with women, it presents the possibility of both the feminization and the subordination of men. It also brings to the fore questions of the homo-erotic gaze usually suppressed in hegemonic masculine discourse (a lesbian gaze has been similarly marginalized with regard to women).

The institution of sport, which has traditionally exhibited a heterosexual masculinist dominance sustained by such strategies as the exclusion of women (gay and straight) and homosexual men (**male preserve**), and the (hetero)sexualization of women, is currently experiencing considerable challenge and change. These emanate less from sport's propensity for progress and reform from within than from the late capitalist forces that restlessly seek new ways of exploiting sport's 'sign value'. Sexualization in sport is symptomatic of an older institutional order that, when extended beyond its familiar boundaries, prompts newly emergent forms of sports power and identity.

Key Reading

Davis, L.R. (1997) *The Swimsuit Issue and Sport: Hegemonic Masculinity in Sports Illustrated*. Albany: State University of New York Press.

Guttmann, A. (1996) *The Erotic in Sports*. New York: Columbia University Press.

Miller, T. (2001) *Sportsex*. Philadelphia: Temple University Press.

David Rowe

SIGNIFICANT OTHER

(socialization; symbolic interactionism)

SIGNIFIER AND SIGNIFIED

Originating from the linguistic studies of Saussure, the signifier refers to a sign (for instance a letter, a sound or a word) and the signified refers to what people understand by that sign. Saussure's semiology (the study of systems of signs) recognized that there was no necessary or immutable connection between the sound of, for instance, the word football, and what we commonly understand by that term. Moreover, what we understand by the word football, we only understand in relation to *what it does not mean*, and therefore in opposition to, e.g. rugby, tennis, cricket, etc. (**binaries**). Thus the meaning of a sign is arbitrary, historically and culturally specific, and derived from its place in the broader signifying system (from this, it can be argued that the meaning of a subject is 'decentred', or removed from the subject itself).

Saussure's work was given broader applicability by Roland Barthes, who used Saussure's methods to understand a range of social signifying systems such as fashion, art, but most notably for students of sport, wrestling and the Tour de France. By studying the relationship between the signifier and the signified, argued Barthes, we could further our understanding of the 'mythologies' of everyday life, and expose the social interests that lay behind them (and for Barthes, capitalist interests were particularly influential (**Marxism**)). However, in Barthes's later work, he came to the conclusion that the meaning of signs could not be 'contained' (limited) and that therefore texts must be read as constant streams of signifiers, and that the conventional idea of the separation of the producer and consumer of texts must be rejected.

The use of signifiers in the sociology of sport most commonly relates to studies of sport and **race**. For instance, in David Andrews's work (1996) on **Michael Jordan** as a 'racial signifier' (which also draws on the work of French post-structuralist Jacques Derrida (**post-structuralism**)), it is suggested that the basketball star's imagined persona is 'floating' (i.e. unstable and with various manifestations), and that while he was largely distanced from the historically grounded racial stereotypes (e.g. of a threatening, potentially violent, black **masculinity**) which structure the lives of many African-Americans, the consequence of the mediated image was to reinforce such stereotypes.

Key Reading

Andrews, D. (1996) 'The fact(s) of Michael Jordan's blackness: excavating a floating racial signifier', *Sociology of Sport Journal*, 13 (2): 125-58.

Andrews, D. (2000) 'Posting up: French post-structuralism and the critical analysis of contemporary sporting culture', in J. Coakley and E. Dunning (eds), *Handbook of Sports Studies*. London: Sage. pp. 106-37.

Rojek, C. (1985) *Capitalism and Leisure Theory*. London: Tavistock.

SOCIAL EXCLUSION

(**social inclusion**)

SOCIAL INCLUSION

The political goal tackling *social exclusion*, which became widely used in British government policy following the election of the Labour government in 1997. Many Western political bodies had previously sought to eliminate poverty, but a general rise in living standards had eliminated many of the extremes of deprivation. However, significant social inequalities remained untouched. The notion of social exclusion broadens the policy focus away from simply tackling poverty and financial inequality. As a concept it is much more wide ranging and refers to a lack of access to four key social systems: democracy, welfare, the labour market, and family and community. The rise of social inclusion policies is predicated on this, and also the recognition that the (traditional) forms of social disadvantage, e.g. poverty, unemployment, poor health and family breakdown, are often linked to each other, providing a compounded or combined set of problems for the individual or community. Social inclusion thus attempts to confront this range of problems, viewing improved health, improved educational achievement, improved employment prospects, improved physical environment and reduced crime as inherently linked. Groups identified as being particularly vulnerable to social exclusion include: young people, old people, low-income families, people from minority ethnic groups (**race**), people with disabilities (**disability**), the long-term unemployed and the homeless.

As an activity that has traditionally been linked to the promotion of health and the building of moral character, sport has been identified as having the potential to make an important contribution to the social inclusion project. Groups with an interest in promoting sport have seized on this opportunity. As a consequence, significant amounts of government money have been directed into sport and social inclusion projects, perhaps most notably the Positive Futures programme. Active partners in social inclusion projects include government departments, local councils, sports governing bodies, the police, schools, professional football clubs and various charity groups.

Researchers, however, have come to be somewhat sceptical about the merits of using sport for these ends. Most agree that the value of sport in this context is simply that it is an activity which engages people's interests (and thus, for example, music could provide an equally successful vehicle). To this end, sport can provide young people in particular with a fruitful diversion from anti-social activities. However, it has been pointed out that such diversions are often temporary or short-lived, and that there is, for instance, no necessary or logical link between engaging in sport and abstaining from **drug** use, indeed quite the opposite; many sports have a strong **alcohol** culture, and increasingly the media report footballers' use of recreational drugs. Other critics argue that the link between **health** and sport is far from unproblematic. Furthermore, it has been argued by Tess Kay for instance, that sport and social inclusion policies often centrally focus on males, while policies developing women's sporting opportunities tend to disproportionately advantage wealthier females (Collins and Kay, 2003). Consequently, one key aspect of social disadvantage – **gender** – remains largely untouched. Finally, other critics argue that many groups have simply repackaged existing sports programmes to embrace the social inclusion agenda in search of finance, and this has led such things as anti-drugs education to be merely 'tagged-on' as an afterthought.

The motives for some groups to be included in social inclusion projects are not always entirely altruistic. For instance, professional football clubs have been utilized to deliver after-school education to children, but many remain suspicious that the clubs' real motives for doing this are to attract a new generation of football fans and thus make a commercial gain for the club. Consequently, a great deal of caution needs to be used when making claims about the positive effects that sport can have to alleviate broader social problems.

Key Reading

Collins, M. and Kay, T. (2003) *Sport and Social Exclusion*. London: Routledge.
Crabbe, T. (2000) 'A sporting chance? Using sport to tackle drug use and crime', *Drugs: Education, Prevention and Policy*, 7 (4): 381–91.
Houlihan, B. and White A. (2002) *The Politics of Sports Development*. London: Routledge.

SOCIAL LEARNING THEORY

While Julian Rotter is sometimes referred to as the 'father of social learning theory', the approach is more commonly associated with Albert Bandura and his classic 1960s' 'Bobo Doll study'. In this study, Bandura showed nursery school children a short film of an adult being violent towards a doll. Half the children were shown a film which ended with the violence being rewarded and praised by another adult, while half the children watched an ending in which the violent adult was reprimanded and punished. Subsequently given a Bobo Doll to play with, those children who had seen the violence rewarded were more

likely to exhibit aggressive behaviour (**aggression**) towards the doll themselves (interestingly, it is unlikely that this experiment would be permitted by modern ethical committees (**ethics; research methods**)).

The relevance of this study, and social learning theory more generally, is to highlight not only the role that significant others have in shaping an individual's behaviour, and the importance of learning vicariously from the actions of others, but also the role of reinforcement of learning through the rewards and punishment for specific behaviours.

In relation to sport, researchers have looked at the way in which athletes learn 'sportsmanship' from those around them (**fair play**), how **violence** in professional sport (perhaps observed on television) provides a model for young players and then becomes incorporated into their own behaviour (**habitus**), and at the way in which the non-punishment of (perhaps minor) aggressive and/or violent acts may encourage athletes to increasingly use aggressive strategies.

Key Reading

Bandura, A. (1965) 'Influence of models' reinforcement contingencies on the acquisition of imitative responses', *Journal of Personality and Social Psychology*, 1: 589–95.
Sheldon, J.P. and Aimar, C.M. (2001) 'The role aggression plays in successful and unsuccessful ice hockey behaviour', *Research Quarterly for Exercise and Sport*, 72: 304–9.
Shields, D.L.L. and Bredemeier, B.J.L. (2001) 'Moral development and behaviour in sport', in R. Singer, H. Hausenblas and C. Janelle (eds), *Handbook of Sport Psychology*. Champaign, IL: Human Kinetics.

SOCIAL LOAFING

In contrast to theories of **group dynamics** which suggest that groups fail to produce maximal performances due to problems of coordination, social loafing refers to individuals' reduction in effort (or **motivation**) as a consequence of working in a group. Research suggests that social loafing occurs in a wide range of different sports and/or particular tasks requiring a range of different skills (i.e. physical, cognitive, perceptual and evaluative), and in a range of different cultures.

Social loafing has been identified as most common in situations where: (1) the contribution and effort of individual group members are not identified or acknowledged; (2) the contribution of some is not deemed to be essential to the goals of the group as a whole; and (3) the contributions of some group members are seen to have disproportionate significance (e.g. where teams are divided into 'stars' and 'bit-part' players or journeymen).

Social loafing can be contagious within groups and can lead to serious dissension and conflict between team members. Consequently, to reduce social loafing in sports teams, coaches should increase the scrutiny and monitoring of individuals' performances, educate members of the value of the input of others, perhaps rotating players between positions periodically, and highlight the importance of each aspect of the team for the performance and success of the whole.

Key Reading

Everett, J.J., Smith, R.E. and Williams, K.D. (1992) 'Effects of team cohesion and identifiability on social loafing in relay swimming performance', *International Journal of Sport Psychology*, 23: 311–24.

Hardy, C.J. (1990) 'Social loafing: motivational losses in collective performance', *International Journal of Sport Psychology*, 21: 305–27.

Karau, A. and Williams, K.D. (1993) 'Social loafing: a meta-analytic review and theoretical integration', *Journal of Personality and Social Psychology*, 65: 681–706.

SOCIAL NETWORK THEORY

(**sportsnet**)

SOCIAL STRATIFICATION

Stratification refers to the different layers of hierarchically organized social groups, which make up all known societies. Social scientists study stratification to identify inequalities, examining how membership of particular strata contours people's life chances and lifestyles, and to understand how inequalities and differences between groups are generated and maintained over time. With reference to sport, social scientists examine how social stratification impacts on sports participation and involvement, as well as the ways in which different social groups use sports to establish and reinforce the social boundaries between themselves and others.

Sociologists commonly believe that there are three main forms of stratification in contemporary societies – **class**, **gender** and **race**/ethnicity (though valid claims have also been made for age and **disability**). While initially the tendency was to examine these forms of stratification in isolation, increasingly it has been recognized that it is more adequate to see these strata as intertwined. For instance, while more men take part in sport and physical activities than do women, and while those in middle-class occupations participate more than do those in working-class occupations, British research indicates that middle-class women take part in sport more regularly than do working-class men (see also **feminism**).

Different sociological perspectives understand stratification in different ways. Within **functionalism** social stratification is seen as a means of allocating rewards according to the functional needs of the social system, and thus is permanent, necessary and inevitable. In **conflict theory** (see also **Marxism**) stratification is a mechanism of exploitation, which results in the combining of political power and social status with economic power. While some forms of **feminism** suggest that gender is the single most significant form of social stratification, **postmodernism** is predicated on the assumption that the 'old' forms of stratification which characterized **modernity** are declining in significance.

Certainly, forms of social stratification vary over time and between societies. For instance, most twentieth-century sociologists have identified social class as particularly significant, but such distinctions were largely irrelevant in ancient Greek societies, which were essentially stratified into two groups, slaves and citizens. The former were excluded from sports participation, while for the latter, participation was almost obligatory. Similarly in India, caste, based on beliefs in the Hindu **religion**, has been a more significant determinant of social life than class (and thus caste has become a significant unit of analysis for historians of Indian cricket). However, while there is considerable speculation that contemporary Western democracies are becoming 'classless', the evidence from social studies of sport suggests that this is far from being the case.

Key Reading

Horne, J., Tomlinson, A. and Whannel, G. (1999) *Understanding Sport: An Introduction to the Sociological and Cultural Analysis of Sport*. London: E. & F.N. Spon. esp. Ch. 5.

SOCIALIZATION

Refers to the processes through which humans learn the norms and values of a particular social context. In short, socialization can be described as the transmission of culture. In contrast to some natural scientists and psychologists, who stress the significance of 'natural' behavioural characteristics or instincts, sociologists, to varying degrees, lay greater emphasis on learnt social characteristics and thus socialization.

Initially, sociologists viewed socialization as a process that was centrally experienced by children, but latterly a distinction has been made between primary socialization (what happens to young children) and secondary socialization (what happens when people grow older). This distinction is based on the 'significant others' (i.e. the people most influential in transmitting norms and values, e.g. parents, friends, work colleagues) at a given point in time. More accurately, however, we should conceive of socialization as a lifelong process and we should reject the narrow compartmentalization of socialization as the categories of primary and secondary suggest (**habitus**).

Reflecting this, sociologists of sport started by looking at who participated in sport, how they came to be involved in sport, why they chose to do so, and what the effects of participation were (e.g. in terms of character building). Much of this research was targeted at children. Subsequently, broader questions were asked that linked sports participation to broader social issues. How was sports participation mediated by **gender**, **class** and **race** (see also **social stratification**)? How was it tied to identity? What accounted for the choices made by people at various points in their lives? And how did broader cultural factors affect the choices that people made? Thus, it has been argued that particular class backgrounds affect one's propensity to be drawn towards particular sports, that socialization processes are responsible for instilling 'commonsense' notions about the appropriateness of particular activities for particular sexes (i.e. for boys, sport is positively associated with heterosexual **masculinity**, whereas girls risk being viewed as unfeminine and/or **lesbian** through sports participation) and that, particularly through schooling, black males may be socialized into thinking that they have a natural aptitude for sport (and correlatively are not academically talented). Key socializing agents in these processes include the family, educational establishments and the **media** (television, magazines, etc.).

These different areas of research reflect different theoretical interpretations of socialization (**agency and structure**). The early approaches, Coakley (2006) calls them 'socialization-as-internalization' approaches, can be divided into two further groups: those informed by **functionalism** and those by

Marxism. Both consider socialization processes to be highly deterministic, in which people are passive receivers of messages. A division arises, however, in that functionalists tend to view the adoption of social norms and values as 'good', or functional for society, while Marxists view the adoption of these characteristics as 'bad', or serving the needs of capitalism, and reproducing the exploitation and **alienation** of the working class. Both these approaches encountered problems when research indicated that sport did not necessarily build the character traits that were claimed for it; that is to say, sports participation did not necessarily lead to better academic achievement, reduced delinquency and **deviance**, or strong moral character.

In response to this, approaches which Coakley (2006) terms 'socialization-as-interaction' developed. These are largely based on **symbolic interactionism** and **cultural studies**, and have in common the rejection of the idea that humans, in any simple way, are simply the products of social forces and, instead, depict individuals as more active in interpreting and responding to socialization experiences. These approaches view participation in sport as just as problematic as non-participation. Thus studies have looked at the socialization processes involved in becoming an elite athlete, which tend to involve the acceptance of a 'culture of risk' (**risk**), and playing with **pain and injury**. For instance, Donnelly and Young's classic study of rock climbers and rugby players (1983) identified four stages of socialization: (1) pre-socialization; (2) selection and recruitment; (3) socialization; and (4) acceptance/ostracism. They argued that those seeking to gain membership of a **subculture** consciously adopted the mannerisms and styles of dress, behaviour, etc. of that group. However, invariably this adoption is inaccurate or imperfect, and established members test the newcomers, who in turn may or may not modify their behaviour. Thus Donnelly and Young concluded that socialization is an ongoing process, involving continued construction/reconstruction of identity and continued confirmation/reconfirmation of identity by other members of the subculture.

This latter strand of socialization research has gone some way towards correcting the mis-portrayal of socialization as an homogenizing and all-embracing process. However, there is still a tendency to use 'socialization' in an over-generalized way. While it is true that, ultimately, more or less all social behaviour can be explained by reference to socialization, this statement lacks detail and thus tells us very little. Therefore, when talking about socialization, we must always strive to identify the specific socialization processes involved, and the specific groups or factors involved in that socialization. Moreover, we need to be aware of the range of different outcomes that can stem from seemingly very similar socialization processes; that is to say, the variety of ways in which individuals can perceive and react to socialization. Despite these limitations, socialization remains a key term in the sociology of sport, for it enables us to see that behaviour is socially produced, and not simply natural or innate.

Key Reading

Coakley, J. (2006) *Sports in Society: Issues and Controversies*, 9th edn. New York: McGraw-Hill. esp. Ch. 4.

Donnelly, P. and Young, K. (1988) 'The construction and confirmation of identity in sport subcultures', *Sociology of Sport Journal*, 5 (3): 223–40.

Horne, J., Tomlinson, A. and Whannel, G. (1999) *Understanding Sport: An Introduction to the Sociological and Cultural Analysis of Sport*. London: E. & F.N. Spon. esp. Ch. 5.

SOCIOLOGICAL IMAGINATION

The Sociological Imagination is C. (Charles) Wright Mills's classic text critiquing what he saw as the 'grand theory' and 'abstract empiricism' that dominated American sociology in the 1950s, and setting out the guidelines for a radical sociological approach. Mills stressed the need to make connections between (our) personal problems and public issues, between the interconnected nature of the historical, structural and biographical. His work has been highly influential across all sociological sub-disciplines including (but largely implicitly) the sociology of sport.

Mills's sociological imagination focuses on three interrelated notions: *consciousness*, *craft* and *commitment*. He argued that the sociological imagination involved a *consciousness*, which has been said to consist of four sensibilities: historical (based on historical knowledge and comparison), cultural (based on an awareness of human diversity), structural (based on an understanding of the relationship between **agency and structure**) and critical (based on being sceptical and reflexive about social life). *Craft* refers to the tools (theoretical models, empirical inquiry and language), tactics (working from one's life experiences, using literature to locate as many viewpoints on a subject as possible) and techniques (recording ideas, being reflexive) that sociologists might employ. *Commitment*, Mills argued, stemmed from an appreciation of social injustices. The sociological imagination holds the potential to improve the quality of human life.

As noted above, Mills argued that the sociological imagination could/should enable the sociologist to understand how personal troubles are linked to broader public issues. This is especially relevant in the sociology of sport because so many of the leading writers in the area are or have been involved in sport, as spectators and as elite and not so elite performers. The influence of Mills can be seen in the work of writers such as Jennifer and John Hargreaves, Richard Gruneau, Alan Ingham and Grant Jarvie; writers who in particular have been concerned to call for changes in sports-related social policies.

Key Source

Bramham, P. (2002) 'Rojek, the *sociological imagination* and leisure', *Leisure Studies*, 21 (3/4): 221–34.

Guttmann, A (1984) 'The sociological imagination and the imaginative sociologist', in N. Theberge and P. Donnelly (eds), *Sport*
and the Sociological Imagination. Refereed Proceedings of the 3rd Annual Conference of the North American Society for the Sociology of Sport, Toronto, Canada, November 1982. Fort Worth, TX: Texas Christian University Press, pp. 4–20.

Loy, J. and Booth, D. (2004) 'Consciousness, craft, commitment: the sociological imagination of C. Wright Mills', in R. Giulianotti (ed.), *Sport and Modern Social Theorists*. Basingstoke: Palgrave Macmillan, pp. 65–80.

Gruneau, R. (1983) *Class, Sports, and Social Development*. Amherst, MA: University of Massachusetts Press.

'SOFT' FUNCTIONALISM

A term largely associated with the work of Robert Merton (1910–2003), and used in contrast to Parsonian 'hard' functionalism. Originally a student of Parsons, Merton developed a theoretical framework that, while still being recognizably functionalist, attempted to address the major weaknesses of the functionalist approach. Some consider that Merton produced the most theoretically sophisticated form of functionalism, while others argue that his work effectively provides nothing more than a very clear statement of the inherent weaknesses of the approach. Whichever position one takes, an understanding of Merton's work provides valuable insights into **functionalism** as a whole.

Merton's contribution can be seen through his identification of 'three false postulates', which he argued could be found in the work of many functionalists. They are: (1) the postulate of the functional unity of society; (2) the postulate of universal functionalism; and (3) the postulate of indispensability. More specifically, these postulates respectively hold, first, that standardized social practices (institutions) are functional for the *whole* society; second, that *all* institutions fulfil social functions; and third, that these institutions are consequently *indispensable*. Recognizing the erroneous nature of these postulates is useful to sports sociologists in that it enables a functionalist framework to embrace: (1) the fact that sports participation is highly fractured in modern societies (i.e. along the lines of **race**, **class**, **gender** and **disability**) and therefore cannot be functional for the whole of society; (2) the idea that sport or some aspects of sport fulfil no social function (e.g. **violence** and **aggression** amongst players and **fans**); and (3) that the **functions of sport** (e.g. **socialization**, social integration) could be performed by alternative social institutions (e.g. the Church (**religion**)).

Connected with these three false postulates are Merton's ideas of *dysfunctions, manifest and latent functions*, and the role of *unintended consequences*. The term dysfunction allows Merton to understand social practices that do not contribute to the social system as a whole. Consequently, **football hooliganism** does not have to be understood as a release of tension (or **catharsis**), but as something that actually poses a danger to the social system. The distinction between manifest functions (the objective consequences of human action which contribute to the maintenance of the social system, and which are both intended and recognized) and latent functions (those consequences that were neither intended nor recognized) allows Merton to highlight that conscious motivations may not be the same as objective consequences. Merton thus points out that people are rarely aware of all the consequences of their actions and that social life is so complex that almost all our actions have *unintended consequences*. For instance, an unintended consequence of the intentional act of opening up American team sports to African-American participants has been the over-representation in these sports of members of this minority ethnic group (**stacking**).

Key Reading

Loy, J.W. and Booth, D. (2004) 'Social structure and social theory: the intellectual insights of Robert K. Merton', in R. Giulianotti (ed.), *Sport and Modern Social Theorists*. London: Palgrave Macmillan. pp. 33–48.

SPECIAL EDUCATIONAL NEEDS

In many countries the inclusion of pupils with special educational needs (SEN) in mainstream education and thus physical education (PE) has become a key government policy objective since the late 1980s. However, this is a long-term and ongoing process, the roots of which can be traced back as far as the mid-nineteenth century.

In Britain, the concept of SEN was first introduced in the 1978 Warnock Report and then included in the 1981 Education Act to prevent the sharp distinction between two groups of pupils – the 'handicapped' and the 'non-handicapped'. In this regard, SEN is a legally defined term which refers to the school-based learning needs of pupils, some of whom have disabilities, that arise from a wide range of difficulties – including cognitive, physical, sensory, communicative or behavioural difficulties (**disability**) – as well as those who are perceived to be specially gifted in one way or another. In short, while there is no common definition of SEN in educational policy, students are typically considered to have a SEN 'if they have a learning difficulty which calls for special educational provision to be made for them' (DfES, 2001: 6). It is also recognized that not all students who have an SEN in subjects such as science and mathematics will necessarily have an SEN in PE, while those students who have an SEN related to some or all aspects of PE may not have an SEN in other curriculum subjects. It is often the case, of course, that some pupils will have an SEN in PE and in other subjects.

The introduction of the term SEN resulted in a move away from using those categories of handicap that had previously been the basis for the provision of special educational services for those students who needed them (such as the educationally subnormal, blind and maladjusted), while simultaneously greatly extending the range of students considered to have SEN. While the previous categories of handicap applied to approximately 2 per cent of the school population – many of whom were educated in special schools – this reclassification of pupils, which apparently focused more fully on the individual's needs, led to the identification of as many as 20 per cent of students in mainstream education considered to have SEN.

More recently, in light of the growing numbers of students with SEN who are now taught PE in mainstream schools, the revised **National Curriculum for Physical Education** (NCPE) 2000 for England (DfEE/QCA, 1999) featured for the first time a detailed statutory statement on inclusion and outlined how such pupils should be enabled to participate as fully and effectively as possible within PE lessons. Numerous studies have indicated, however, that in contrast to the supposed educational benefits that inclusion would have for all pupils, it would appear that many pupils with SEN currently experience a narrower range of sports and activities within NCPE compared to other students, and are at times engaging in different activities to, and sometimes taught separately from, those students in lessons. Among other things, this appears to be strongly associated with: (1) the alleged privileging of competitive team sports over more individualized physical activities in NCPE; (2) the diverse range of SEN presented by pupils; and (3) the ability of teachers to meet those needs. In policy terms, these findings are important for they raise serious questions about the extent to which pupils with SEN are being, and even can be, fully included within mainstream PE lessons (Smith and Green, 2004; Smith and Thomas, 2005).

Key Reading

DfEE/QCA (Department for Education and Employment/Qualifications and Curriculum Authority) (1999) *Physical Education: The National Curriculum for England*. London: HMSO.

DfES (Department for Education and Skills) (2001) *Special Educational Needs Code of Pratice*. London: DfES.

Morley, D., Bailey, R., Tan, J. and Cooke, B. (2005) 'Inclusive physical education: teachers' views of teaching children with special educational needs and disabilities in physical education', *European Physical Education Review*, 11 (1): 84–107.

Smith, A. and Green, K. (2004) 'Including pupils with special educational needs in secondary school physical education: a sociological analysis of teachers' views', *British Journal of Sociology of Education*, 25 (5): 593–608.

Smith, A. and Thomas, N. (2005) 'Inclusion, special educational needs, disability and physical education', in K. Green and K. Hardman (eds), *Physical Education: Essential Issues*. London: Sage. pp. 220–38.

Andy Smith

SPECIALIST SPORTS COLLEGES

In Britain, as in many other Western societies, there has been over the last decade or so growing concern over the supposed decline in young people's participation in sport and physical activity via school-based physical education (PE) (**youth sports participation**). Many believe there to be a relationship between sports participation rates and, among other things, a lack of international sporting success, and declining standards of **health** and educational attainment. It was within this context that a plethora of policy initiatives aimed at young people have been developed. In England, one of the more recent policy initiatives to have been introduced has been the specialist schools programme that was launched in 1994, ostensibly in order 'to help secondary schools to develop strengths and raise standards in a chosen specialism' (OFSTED, 2005: 5); in effect, to act as centres of excellence for particular subjects such as sport, technology or science. The first Specialist Sports College (SSC) was designated in 1997 and since then, largely in conjunction with the publication of a series of PE-related sport policies such as the Physical Education and School Sport Club Links (PESSCL) strategy, the total number of

SSCs has increased to 345 in June 2006, just short of the government's target of 400 to be established by the end of that year.

By seeking to establish a more efficient national infrastructure for PE and school sport, the main objectives of the SSC policy include: (1) improving participation and achievement in PE and school sport among students of all abilities; (2) raising standards of teaching in schools; (3) providing a structure through which students can progress to careers in sport and PE; and (4) promoting the development of young talented athletes through SSCs' links with other schools, sporting agencies, clubs and the regional centres of the UK Sports Institute (DfES/DCMS, 2003; OFSTED, 2005).

To what extent have these objectives been achieved? In a recent evaluation of the specialist schools programme, OFSTED (2005: 15) claim that 'the majority of sports colleges have improved the curriculum in PE and are offering a wide range of accreditation opportunities ... suited to the needs of a wide range of pupils'. They also note that since 1998, 'pupils aged 16 in specialist schools have performed significantly better in external examinations than those in other schools' (OFSTED, 2005: 6). Moreover, all SSCs were said to have 'effective links with other schools, sports clubs and national sports bodies in their communities' (OFSTED, 2005: 28), and some 'use specialist coaches to support activities, sometimes in less accessible activities, such as ice-skating, horse-riding, martial arts and golf, both in lessons and out of school' (OFSTED, 2005: 29).

Despite this generally positive evaluation of the specialist schools programme, it should be noted that while the establishment of SSCs may be 'significant in contributing to the achievement of objectives associated with the regeneration of individual schools and the wider regeneration and reinvigoration of local communities' (Houlihan, 2000: 190), evidence for the other elements of the SSC policy is more mixed. Indeed, because such a policy has, among other things, several potentially mutually exclusive and overly ambitious objectives, and is based on a rather

limited understanding of the complexities involved in the achievement of those objectives (e.g. using PE and school sport as a vehicle through which to promote young people's mass participation in sport and physical activity while, simultaneously, increasing the proportion and success of talented school-aged children at the elite level of sporting competition), it remains to be seen whether SSCs will have the desired long-term impact upon young people's participation in, and experiences of, PE and sport.

Key Reading

DfES/DCMS (Department for Education and Skills/Department for Culture Media and Sport) (2003) *Learning Through PE and Sport: A Guide to the Physical Education, School Sport and Club Links Strategy.* London: DfES/DCMS.

Houlihan, B. (2000) 'Sporting excellence, schools and sports development: the politics of crowded policy spaces', *European Physical Education Review*, 6 (2): 17–93.

Loughborough Partnership (2005) *School Sport Partnerships. Annual Monitoring and Evaluation Report.* Loughborough: Institute Youth Sport/Loughborough University.

OFSTED (2005) *Specialist Schools: A Second Evaluation.* London: HMSO.

Andy Smith

SPONSORSHIP

The payment of cash (or in kind) that a company may make to a league, team, event, individual or activity, for the right to exploit the commercial potential of being associated with that activity. The sponsorship of sports events accounts for about three-quarters of all sponsorship in the UK.

There are many problems related to attempts to estimate the market size for sports sponsorship including: (1) firms and sports bodies are reluctant to release commercially sensitive data; (2) the market is highly fragmented, ranging from Olympic Games (**TOP**) to local sports teams; and (3) expenditure on sponsorship is often consumed within firms' broader marketing and publicity budgets. However, in 1999, it was estimated that the sports sponsorship industry was worth $20 billion per year globally, with an annual rate of increase of 10 per cent. The significance of sports sponsorship is such that all major sports events are now, to some extent, reliant on sponsorship income.

Businesses may have one or a combination of the following four motives for sponsoring sports events: (1) image enhancement (for instance, Brylcream's sponsorship of **David Beckham** was designed to rid the company of its 'old-fashioned' image); (2) increased product or company awareness (public awareness of Cornhill Insurance was dramatically raised through the company's sponsorship of cricket); (3) to use the linked hospitality opportunities to entertain current and potential clients; and (4) product trial and sales opportunities (e.g. computer firms that supply scoring or timing services to events and so publicly demonstrate their technical expertise).

Sport provides companies with a number of specific benefits from sponsorship. Sports events attract huge audiences of both 'live' spectators and those who consume sport via the media. Because sports occupy many hours of broadcasting, a sponsoring company may appear on the television screen for many hours at a fraction of the equivalent cost of TV advertising. Moreover, they may then enjoy secondary exposure, as newspapers and television news programmes report on the sports events. It was for these reasons that tobacco firms in particular were attracted to sports sponsorship from the 1970s until being banned by the European Union from 2001 (fully implemented in 2006). Moreover, sport, perhaps more than any other aspect of popular culture, bears the hallmarks of **globalization**. Thus a firm like Coca-Cola with global sales will find sponsoring international sporting events such as the Olympics a particularly suitable medium for promoting itself. Sports also attract sponsors because of the widespread acceptance of the ideology that links sport with good **health**, morality and worthwhile endeavour. Sponsors hope that such positive values will rub off onto the public's perception of their goods and services (and conversely many sponsors questioned their involvement with cycling teams in the Tour de France following the **drugs** scandals which rocked the event in the late 1990s and early 2000s).

The benefits to the sport are fairly self-evident in that income is received, but sports may also benefit from increased publicity as sponsors seek to exploit the relationship to its full potential (e.g. through advertising, competitions, etc.). This can lead to greater media interest for the sport, and therefore the increased value of sponsorship (a virtuous circle). But there may also be costs for the sport, the image of which may suffer if the increased level of **commercialization** leads to a questioning of the integrity of the sport, or a compromise over rules or the timing of events. Sponsorship can also lead to onerous demands on particular participants, as companies focus their attentions on a select few athletes (**celebrity**), but it can also lead to significant financial inequalities between competitors (**Jordan**; **Kournikova**; **Nike**). There can also be problems over clashes between sponsors of individuals and sponsors of events, especially where companies are direct competitors (**ambush marketing**; **Beckham**). Finally, sponsorship income is very volatile and unreliable for the sports body, as the benefits accruing to a company may diminish over time (leading the sponsor to withdraw). Moreover, companies in financial trouble are likely to cut sponsorship budgets before making cutbacks in other areas.

Key Reading

Gratton, C. and Taylor, P. (2000) *Economics of Sport and Recreation*. London: Routledge.

Horne, J. (2006) *Sport in Consumer Culture* Basingstoke: Palgrave Macmillan.

SPORT, DEFINITION OF

In everyday speech, we tend to use words like 'sport', 'play' and 'game' rather loosely, sometimes treating them as synonyms. However, for students of sports studies, accuracy of language is very important. Linguistic precision is essential for effective communication and while it may not be problematic when talking about sport in an everyday sense, when we come, for example, to talk about the **functions of sport**, the differences between sport, play and games can be quite dramatic. For instance, while sports participation and spectatorship may generate very different types of **emotion** to those generated by non-competitive play activities, participation in physical exercise may be considerably more beneficial to **health** than sports participation (**pain and injury**).

In attempting to define and classify sports, most scholars start by distinguishing them from related activities such as play and games. In an excellent definitional statement, Allen Guttmann (2004) suggests that *play* is the most general category of action that we are concerned with in this field. Play, argues Guttmann, is any non-utilitarian physical or intellectual activity that is pursued for its own sake; that is to say, the pleasure is in the doing rather than the achievement of some objective. Play, in short, is 'autotelic', engaged in as an 'end in itself' and not as a means towards the achievement of some external end such as health, character development, money, etc. It follows from this definition that physical education in schools, and professional sport, are not 'play'.

Play, Guttmann continues, may be spontaneous or organized. If it is organized, play becomes a *game*. Games, however, may be competitive or non-competitive. Competitive games, argues Guttmann, are *contests* and contests, in turn, can be divided into intellectual contests and physical contests. While sports have an intellectual component, fundamentally they are physical contests. Moreover, unlike, say, 'real' fights and wars, they are playful. Guttmann accordingly

reaches the conclusion that sports can be defined as organized contests of a playful, non-utilitarian character in which the physical demands outweigh the intellectual components.

Barry McPherson et al. (1989) provide a similar, though slightly different definition of sport. First, sport, they say, is *structured*, meaning that even the most informal forms – e.g. children playing soccer in the street or baseball in the park – are governed by rules of some kind, while the more formal forms – e.g. the Football World Cup – are 'highly structured' in the sense of being controlled by large bureaucratic organizations. Second, they say that sports are *goal-oriented*, meaning that they are directed towards achievement and that, whatever the particular goals or standards the participants may be striving to achieve, the criteria for determining success and failure are usually clear. Third, sport is *competitive* and contest-based, whether the contest involves just individual competitors or teams. Finally, sport, they say, is 'ludic', a term derived from the Latin word, *ludus*, meaning 'play' or 'game' (**Homo Ludens**). Sports, therefore, are structured, goal-oriented, competitive forms of play.

However, as each of these definitions depends upon 'degrees' of difference (e.g. of physicality, competitiveness), it is not productive to spend too much time debating whether, for example, synchronized swimming, ice dance, or chess are sports. Moreover, while seeking analytical clarity through such definitions, it is important to avoid the charge of **essentialism** and portraying sport as some kind of unchanging, asocial, construct. A good example of this approach is provided by Elias and Dunning who, while not disagreeing with the above definitions, attempt to define sport *developmentally*. Rather than stressing notions of organization, competitiveness and/or goal orientation, Elias and Dunning (1986) note that sports as we know them today (**modern sport**) refer to a pattern of competitive physical activities which began to emerge for the first time in Britain and Ireland in the seventeenth and eighteenth centuries, particularly in England in the eighteenth century. The word 'sport' they note, is derived from the Anglo-French 'desporter', and emerged in the English language in the seventeenth and eighteenth centuries in conjunction with a quite specific change of structure, function and meaning; i.e. the greater stress on notions such as **fair play**, respecting one's opponents, abiding voluntarily by rules and not cheating (**sportization and parliamentarization**). From this definition of sport we take the adjective 'sporting'.

Key Reading

Elias, N. and Dunning, E. (1986) *Quest for Excitement: Sport and Leisure in the Civilizing Process*. Oxford: Basil Blackwell.

Guttmann, A. ([1978] 2004) *From Ritual to Record: The Nature of Modern Sport*, rev. edn. New York: Columbia University Press.

McPherson, B.D., Curtis, J.E. and Loy, J.W. (1989) 'Defining sport', in B.D. McPherson, J.E. Curtis and J.W. Loy (eds), *The Social Significance of Sport*. Champaign, IL: Human Kinetics.

SPORT ENGLAND

(**Sports Council**)

SPORT ETHIC, THE

The concept of the sport ethic was developed to represent the core norms used by athletes to assess identity and group membership in high-performance sport cultures. Initial research by Hughes and Coakley (1991) identified the following four norms as constituting the sport ethic:

1   Athletes are dedicated to 'the game' above all else and demonstrate dedication through unwavering commitment, making sacrifices to play, and meeting the expectations of fellow athletes.
2   Athletes strive for distinction in that they relentlessly seek to improve and achieve perfection; winning becomes important as a marker of achievement and one's willingness to push limits.
3   Athletes accept **risk**s and play through pain to show that they will not succumb to pressure or fear in any situation in which the game and fellow athletes depend on their continued participation.
4   Athletes accept no obstacles as they pursue possibilities in their sport, even when the odds are against them.

These norms are not unique to sport; they are taught to children by parents, incorporated into academic curricula, emphasized in motivational speeches and self-help books, and portrayed on posters hung on the office walls of business managers and executives. However, the importance of these norms is magnified in sport cultures. Locker room slogans, pep talks by coaches, and media commentary by former athletes and coaches contain many references to them. Athletes use them to assess themselves and others as they engage in processes of making identity claims and assessing the identity claims of others who seek membership in elite sport groups (**subcultures**).

The identity implications of conforming to the norms of the sport ethic are so significant in many sport cultures that there are many athletes who accept them without question or qualification as they seek to have their identity claims acknowledged, accepted, and continuously reaffirmed over time. This, in turn, serves as a foundation for pervasive patterns of dangerous normative overconformity in which athletes put the **health** and well-being of their bodies on the line. Examples include pathogenic eating and weight reduction patterns among athletes in, for example, distance running, gymnastics, wrestling and horse-racing (**eating disorders**); the use of unapproved and often dangerous performance-enhancing substances (**drugs**); and playing with injuries that could result in lifelong pain and **disability** (**pain and injury**). An abundance of similar examples illustrates that athletes take seriously the sport ethic. Even retired athletes speak in romantic and respectful terms about those players who were willing to overconform to the norms of the sport ethic and, in the process, establish their identities in sport lore (**positive deviance**)

Although winning, wealth and fame are seen by many people outside of elite sport cultures as the central **motivation**al factors in athletes' lives, those inside sport cultures realize that such factors are important to athletes primarily because they enable them to continue playing the game and remain among those few people in the world who can reaffirm the identity that is central to their self. This is true in sports where wealth and fame are rare, as well as in highly publicized media sports where external rewards are great. Therefore, an awareness of and commitment to the sport ethic may be found among athletes at certain skateboard parks as well as on the football pitch at World Cup matches.

Key Reading

Hughes, R. and Coakley, J. (1991) 'Positive deviance among athletes: the implications of overconformity to the sport ethic', *Sociology of Sport Journal*, 8 (4): 307–25.

Jay Coakley

SPORT LABOUR MIGRATION

Though initially a topic addressed by sports geographer John Bale in his book *The Brawn Drain* (1991), sport labour migration became established as a central topic of academic research through Bale and Maguire's (1994) edited collection, *The Global Sports Arena*. While historians (notably Lanfranchi and Taylor, 2001) have contributed to this area, it has largely been sociologists through the broader analysis of **globalization** processes who have been at the forefront of this research tradition. Some of the key questions examined include: (1) sport migrants' **motivation**s; (2) the methods of recruitment; (3) the experiences and problems encountered by migrants in the host country; (4) the legal status and rights of migrants; and (5) the consequences of this changed status for social identity. While the bulk of this work has focused on professional footballers, other sports studied include rugby union, cricket, ice hockey, basketball and baseball.

Two somewhat overlapping, but also competing, typologies of sports migrants have emerged. Maguire (1999: 106) identifies five overlapping, ideal type groups: settlers (typically lasting four or five years), mercenaries (driven by money with no attachment to place), nomadic cosmopolitans (seeking new and varied experiences), returnees (e.g. pro-tennis players), and pioneers (those with the missionary zeal to develop a particular sport in the host nation). Magee and Sugden (2002) also identify the mercenary, the settler, and nomadic cosmopolitans, but cite three other categories: ambitionists (who move to further their careers), exiles (who opt to leave their 'home' country, perhaps for political or personal reasons) and the expelled (those forced to leave their 'home' country).

Key Reading

Bale, J. (1991) *The Brawn Drain: Foreign Student-Athletes in American Universities*. Urbana, IL: University of Illinois Press.

Bale, J. and Maguire, J. (1994) *The Global Sports Arena: Athletic Talent Migration in an Interdependent World*. London: Frank Cass.

Lanfranchi, P. and Taylor, M. (2001) *Moving with the Ball: The Migration of Professional Footballers*. Oxford: Berg.

Magee, J. and Sugden, J. (2002) '"The world at their feet": professional football and international labour migration', *Journal of Sport and Social Issues*, 26 (4): 421–37.

Maguire, J. (1999) *Global Sport: Identities, Societies, Civilizations*. Cambridge: Polity.

SPORT, SOCIAL SIGNIFICANCE OF

Historically, sport has been viewed as a subject not worthy of serious academic study. There are a number of reasons for this: (1) the prevalent view in the West, derived from Descartian philosophy, that the mind is distinct from, and superior to, the **body** (and that sport is essentially a bodily activity); (2) the short-term view that sociology should be concerned with changing the world rather than contributing to knowledge more generally (and that sport has marginal political significance); and (3) following Marx, the prioritization of interest in production and the economy rather than leisure and 'non-productive' features of social life (such as sport). However, partly as a rethinking of some of these ideas (e.g. the declining interest in **Marxism**, the growing sociological interest in consumption as well as production, (**consumer culture**; **postmodernism**)), and partly due to radical changes in sport itself, there has in recent years been a growing acknowledgement that sport is of great social significance. For simplicity's sake it is common to argue for sport's significance on a number of separate fronts – economically, politically and culturally – though in reality the three are closely related.

In recent years, rapid **commercialization** has made sport economically more significant. Key aspects of this are the development of **sponsorship** and the growth of **media** coverage of sport. Consequently, more people are employed in sport-related industries and an even wider range of goods relies on sport for the development/continuance of their market (e.g. **Nike**, Coca-Cola). That contemporary societies have increasingly become consumption-oriented has impacted considerably on the economic growth of sport.

Similarly, during the twentieth century politicians increasingly came to recognize the political importance of sport. Sport was used to build solidarity and a coherent national identity (**nationalism**), to foster links between countries, to ostracize countries (**boycotts**) and to demonstrate the superiority of one political system over another (e.g. in the Cold War between the US and the USSR (**propaganda**)). The relatively advanced stage of the **globalization** of sport further contributes to both the political and the economic significance of sport.

In combination with these processes, sport has come to occupy a more central cultural position. Sport, it has been argued, has to some extent come to replace the role of religion in contemporary societies, serving as a site for mass gatherings and the generation of feelings of community. The far-reaching nature of the media coverage of sport has created the phenomenon of the sports **celebrity**, which extends beyond the appeal of sport itself. The achievements of women in sport have led many to rethink conceptualizations of **gender** and stereotypical beliefs about the 'innate' abilities of the sexes. Sport is seen as a tool through which the **body** can be altered, and increasingly sociologists have recognized the importance of physical appearance for the way we see ourselves and the way others judge us (**obesity discourse**).

As stated, it is most adequate to view the economic, political and cultural areas as closely interrelated. First and foremost, sport is socially significant because it engages the passions of people (**quest for excitement**) and has become a central feature of the way in which many people in contemporary Western societies construct and express their identity. It is the recognition of this fact by commercial bodies and political organizations that leads to the use of sports for economic, political and indeed religious ends (see also **religion**). In turn, these interventions heighten the cultural centrality of sport.

Key Reading

Dunning, E. (1999) *Sport Matters: Sociological Studies of Sport, Violence and Civilization*. London: Routledge. esp. Ch. 1.

SPORTIZATION AND PARLIAMENTARIZATION

Sportization is the term used by Elias to describe the process by which **folk games** became transformed into their **modern sport** forms (see also **sport, definition of**). More specifically, the sportization process involves the development of more precise and explicit rules, which are written down and enforced in a stricter and more efficient way. Because sports rules invariably restrict the means by which individuals can achieve sporting success (e.g. the prohibition on the use of hands in football, restrictions on the number of forward passes allowed in American football), the sportization process necessarily entails the development of stricter personal self-control and self-**discipline** among participants (and thus entails a civilizing 'spurt' (**civilizing process**)).

Elias (1986) notes that this process first occurred in eighteenth-century England, involving sports such as boxing, cricket, horse-racing and **fox-hunting**, and attempts to explain why this should be the case (a 'second wave' involving soccer, rugby, tennis, etc. followed in the nineteenth century (**Barbarians, Gentlemen and Players**)). His answer lies in what he calls the 'parliamentarization of political conflict'. The end of the seventeenth and beginning of the eighteenth centuries saw the development of relatively peaceful means for deciding political issues in England with, for example, the development of parliamentary rules, high levels of mutual trust, and mechanisms for the peaceful transference of power between political parties. In contrast, England's neighbours remained relatively disunited (e.g. Germany and Italy) or highly centralized and subject to a form of absolute rule (e.g. France). The dominant class of English landowners formed both political clubs and sports clubs and hence the Jockey Club and the Marylebone Cricket Club (MCC) became the national governing bodies for horse-racing and cricket respectively (note that sports associations and unions like the FA, **FIFA** and the RFU were formed 100 years later). Elias did not argue that parliamentarization *caused* sportization, or indeed that sportization *caused* parliamentarization, rather that these concomitant processes involved the *same people* and that the ideas that structured the way they organized their working lives similarly informed the way they structured their leisure time. In many respects, these processes derive from a shift in **habitus**.

Elias used fox-hunting as the main empirical case study to support these ideas. Under the fox-hunting 'rules' developed by Hugo Meynell in the early eighteenth century, argued Elias, levels of **violence** decreased and tension excitement was prolonged. This prolonging of tension excitement, he argued, is a more general characteristic of the development of sports rules (**quest for excitement**) and a key feature of modern sport forms. While Elias's empirical work on fox-hunting has been criticized for being limited and inaccurate (see Franklin, 1996; Stokvis, 1992), studies of boxing (Sheard, 1997) and cricket (Malcolm, 2005) provide confirmatory evidence of the link between sportization and parliamentarization.

Key Reading

Elias, N. (1986) 'An essay on sport and violence' in N. Elias and E. Dunning, *Quest for Excitement: Sport and Leisure in the Civilizing Process*. Oxford: Basil Blackwell. pp. 150–74.

Franklin, A. (1996) 'On fox-hunting and angling: Norbert Elias and the "sportisation" process', *Journal of Historical Sociology*, 9 (4): 432–56.

Malcolm, D. (2005) 'The emergence, codification and diffusion of sport: theoretical and conceptual issues', *International Review for the Sociology of Sport*, 40 (1): 115–18.

Sheard, K. (1997) 'Aspects of boxing in the western "civilizing process"', *International Review for the Sociology of Sport*, 32 (1): 31–57.

Stokvis, R. (1992) 'Sports and civilization: is violence the central problem?' in E. Dunning, and C. Rojek (eds), *Sport and Leisure in the Civilizing Process: Critique and Counter-Critique*. Basingstoke: Macmillan. pp. 121–36.

SPORTS COUNCIL

Established by Royal Charter in 1966, with a remit to coordinate and lead central government influence over sport in the United Kingdom. The Sports Council was initially divided into 10 regional councils, supported by the Scottish and Welsh Sports Councils. It was responsible for both elite level sport and mass participation. As quangos (quasi-autonomous non-governmental organizations), and reflecting the long-held belief that sport and politics 'should not mix', these sports councils have traditionally had considerable freedom to act, though to some extent this has declined in recent years.

In 1996, following the publication of *Sport: Raising the Game*, the Sports Council was reorganized. Most significantly, this saw the creation of a UK Sports Council (UK Sport), plus an English Sports Council (now Sport England) to work alongside its Scottish and Welsh counterparts. The respective roles have similarly been clarified, with UK Sport having responsibility for elite level sport. Its primary goal is stated as 'World Class Performance' and thus athletes who deliver international victories. It also has two supporting goals: 'Worldwide Impact', that is to say, to play a leading role in the international politics of sport and to support UK bids to host major international sporting events (such as the Olympics (**mega-events, hosting of**)); and 'World Class Standards', promoting ethically fair and **drug**-free sport (**drugs**; **fair play**).

The focus of Sport England's efforts (and those of Sport Scotland, and the Sports Councils of Northern Ireland and Wales) is mass participation in sport (though there is a recognition that this, in part, leads to international success). Sport England's objectives are threefold. They aim to get people to: '*Start* – to improve the health of the nation, particularly for disadvantaged groups, *Stay* – through a thriving network of clubs, coaches and volunteers and commitment to equity, and *Succeed in Sport* – via an infrastructure capable of delivering world class performers'. Sport England seeks to build partnerships with others involved in the delivery of sport and provide evidence that can be used to justify sport's role in broader social policies, such as promoting **social inclusion**. Both UK Sport and its national counterparts distribute funds allocated to sport that are raised by the National Lottery, but the majority of this money is distributed through Sport England.

Key Reading

www.sportengland.org/Home page of Sport England.
www.uksport.gov.uk/Home page of UK Sport.

SPORTS DEVELOPMENT

Providing a concise and generally acceptable definition of sport has always proved problematic and academics and practitioners have had to accept the inherent vagueness and contested nature of the concept (**sport, definition of**). However, the problems of definition are compounded when the concept of 'sport' is coupled with the equally vague notion of 'development'. While all public policy areas have blurred edges indicating the limits of government interest or overlap with other policy areas, most have a recognizable core of objectives that define the service in the eyes of users, the public and politicians. Core objectives are often manifest in a recognizable pattern of practices, professions and institutions which, over time, become part of the established fabric of public services. Unfortunately, the policy area of sports development is far less distinct. There are four main reasons for this:

1 In those countries that engage in sports development it is a sub-area within broader sport policy which, itself, was only acknowledged by non-communist European governments as a legitimate and regular focus for public expenditure and policy from around the late 1960s.

2 Sports development has been characterized by a high degree of instability of objectives which, given its short history, has made it difficult to establish the continuity of practice that often provides a foundation of a public profile.

3 Sports development has normally been low on the government's policy agenda. Only rarely over the last 20 years has sports development been a salient issue for governments, often prompted by crisis, such as urban disturbances, with a sports development response seen as a cheap, high-profile palliative.

4 Sports development is often located in a sector of government activity that is crowded with services that are both relatively resource rich and politically weighty such as education, children's services, **health** and urban renewal (**city, the**).

The paradox is that while sports development is an activity that is a recognized element in the spectrum of services within the public and often the voluntary sectors (**sports market**), precise definition remains elusive. A common attempt at definition, that sports development is 'getting more people to play more sport', has the virtue of brevity but begs more questions than it answers. Collins provides a definition that attempts to capture the processual character of sports development. For Collins, sports development is 'a process whereby effective opportunities, processes, systems and structures are set up to enable and encourage people in all or particular groups and areas to take part in sport and recreation or to improve their performance to whatever level they desire' (quoted in Houlihan and White, 2002: 3). A similar and frequently quoted definition was provided by the British Sports Council in 1993 which stated that, 'Sports development is about ensuring the pathways and structures are in place to enable people to learn basic movement skills, participate in sports of their choice, develop their competence and performance, and reach levels of excellence' (Sports Council, 1993).

These two definitions draw attention not only to the scope and ambition of sports development but also to the extent of ambiguity. In terms of scope, sports development refers to those not currently involved in sport as well as those already active, and also refers to the grassroots or mass participant and performance objectives focused on the aspiring international athlete. Sports development has been conceptualized as an activity preoccupied with the service inputs (facility provision) and the creation of opportunities, but it has also been conceptualized as an activity the proper focus of which is on service outcomes and the maximization of benefit. In addition, at different times the emphasis in sports development has varied between reactive and proactive strategies: on the one hand, creating opportunities to meet demand, on the other, actively intervening in a more paternalistic manner to encourage people to participate in sport in order to generate personal health benefits or community benefits, such as enhanced social **capital**. The most significant tension running through the policy and practice of contemporary sport development is therefore between *development through sport*, with the associated emphasis on social objectives for the individual and the community, and *development of sport*, where there is less deliberate emphasis on the instrumental capacity of sport and a greater willingness to value the more intrinsic outcomes of participation. In recent years the emphasis on the instrumental interpretation of sports development has been further strengthened by the increasing concern with public health and the rise in obesity levels generally (**obesity discourse**), but especially among children. As a result, there has been a further broadening of the concept of sports development to incorporate the even more loosely defined notion of physical activity. Sport England has coined the term 'Everyday Sport' to encompass its drive for higher levels of physical activity, which would include walking, jogging and keep fit activities (**Sports Council**).

The extent of variation between definitions of sports development can be frustrating but is not so different from the problems faced in defining other areas of government activity, for example the recurring debate over whether the primary purpose of education is to meet the needs of the economy or to ensure that children fulfil their potential. While most policy areas are characterized by long periods of relative stability none remain static, and a definition of sports development will reflect the past and current mix of objectives, practice, principal agents of implementation and sources of resources which in turn have been affected by the broader factors such as the political salience of sport and sports development and also by policy movement in contiguous areas.

In summary, the Sports Council definition of sports development, which emphasizes the establishment of pathways, structures and opportunities for skills acquisition and progression, is probably as concise as it is possible to achieve. However, what is most striking about the definition is its scope, for if sports development can apply to the acquisition of generic movement skills in primary school and the training of Olympic champions, it is difficult to see what form of sport-related policy intervention is excluded. In addition, the gradual incorporation of physical activity objectives and strategies within the ambit of sports development policy is testing the flexibility of current definitions, perhaps to the point of destruction.

Key Reading

Green, M. and Houlihan, B. (2005) *Elite Sport Development: Policy Learning and Political Priorities*. London: Routledge.

Houlihan, B. and White, A. (2002) *The Politics of Sport Development: Development of Sport or Development Through Sport?* London: Routledge.

Hylton, K., Bramham, P., Jackson, D. and Nesti, M. (eds) (2001) *Sports Development: Policy, Process and Practice*. London: Routledge.

Sports Council (1993) *Black and Ethnic Minorities and Sport: Policy and Objectives*. London: Sports Council.

Barrie Houlihan

SPORTS MARKET

For economists the sports market can be identified as the combined demand for and supply of sporting opportunities. On the supply side there are three main providers of sport: the public sector (local and national governments), the voluntary sector and the private or commercial sector. Governments contribute through the funding of both grassroots and elite sport as well as providing finance for both local and national sporting facilities (**market failure**), though they are also active in taking revenue from sport in the form of taxation. The voluntary sector contributes largely through the provision of unpaid labour (coaches, referees, bar staff) on which all non-professional sports clubs rely. The commercial sector supplies opportunities for spectator 'participation' via professional sports teams, many fitness and **health** facilities, and finance in the form of **sponsorship** (from companies like **Nike**, promoting sports products, and companies like Coca-Cola in the non-sports commercial sector).

The demand for sport is the aggregate of the demand for opportunities to participate and the facilities required for participation, the demand for equipment, shoes, etc., and increasingly the demand for sports-related travel (**sports tourism**). It is also important to embrace the demand for spectatorship, which itself can be broken down into 'live' and mediated forms. At the extreme, this places the demand for sport, and thus the sports market itself, on a global scale.

Key Reading

Gratton, C. and Taylor, P. (2000) *Economics of Sport and Recreation*. London: Routledge.

SPORTS MEDICINE

The sports medicine discipline can be traced to the 1928 Winter Olympic Games in

St Moritz, Switzerland, and the founding of the Association Internationale Médico-Sportive. German physicians were to the fore of this movement, with sports medicine in English-speaking nations developing somewhat more slowly. For example, the first English language book to use sports medicine in its title was published 29 years after its German counterpart and the first British professional association for sports medicine, the British Association of Sports Medicine (now British Association of Sport and Exercise Medicine – BASEM), was founded in 1953. The American College of Sports Medicine was established in 1954. Despite advances towards a coherent medical sub-discipline in recent years (e.g. the establishment of scholarly journals and accredited training programmes), there remains some ambiguity over which specific skills sports medicine should encompass (e.g. what combination of orthopaedic surgery, nutrition, epidemiology, sports safety and sports physiology are desirable).

Two excellent histories of the development of sports medicine currently exist. In *Mortal Engines*, John Hoberman argues that the early practitioners of sports medicine viewed athletes as mere curiosities, and as interesting sources of physiological data which could progress understanding of the functioning of the human body per se. As the twentieth century progressed, however, doctors and those in the sporting community came increasingly to see sports medicine as offering the potential to improve athletic performance. These developments have put 'physiology in the service of sport' (Hoberman, 1992: 78). Waddington (1996) largely concurs with this view, but focuses specifically on the role of sports medicine in relation to the use of performance-enhancing **drugs** in sport. Through an examination of the development of **blood-doping**, Waddington suggests that the common perception of sports medicine doctors being the antithesis of drug cheats and the enforcers of anti-doping policies should be refined. In his view the development of performance-enhancing drug use in sport and sports medicine are inseparable.

More recently the sociological understanding of sports medicine has been extended through research into the practices of doctors and medical staff associated with sports teams. In a seminal piece, Stephen Walk argued that there were grounds to suggest 'that medicine is practiced differently, more competently, and/or more ethically in non-sports contexts' (1997: 24). Subsequent research has indicated that sports clinicians experience extensive bargaining and negotiation with athletes over treatment (**pain and injury**), and has further exposed numerous elements of poor medical practice in sport (e.g. disregard for athletes' longer-term health, breaches in patient confidentiality). While we conventionally think of doctors as powerful and authoritative figures, it appears that within the sports context they are often rather subservient to athletes and coaches (Malcolm, 2006).

Key Reading

Hoberman, J. (1992) *Mortal Engines: The Science of Performance and the Dehumanization of Sport*. New York: Free Press.

Malcolm, D. (2006) 'Unprofessional practice? The status and power of sports clinicians', *Sociology of Sport Journal* 23 (4): 376–95.

Waddington, I. (1996) 'The development of sports medicine', *Sociology of Sport Journal*, 13 (2): 176–96.

Walk, S.R. (1997) 'Peers in pain: the experiences of student athletic trainers', *Sociology of Sport Journal*, 14 (1): 22–56.

SPORTS SPACE

The notion of sports space effectively suggests that any given society can only 'host' a limited number of sports, or that people only have the time and/or enthusiasm for a limited number of leisure activities. In discussions of the diffusion or **globalization** of sport, therefore, the claim is often made that one sport did not become popular because another one did (and thus there was not 'room' for both). On this basis, Markovits and Hellerman (2001) argue that football has not become popular in the US because the sports space has been filled by baseball, American football, and, more latterly, basketball. Mason (1986) has used similar arguments to explain why football did not become popular in Australia ('crowded out' by rugby league, rugby union and Australian Rules football), New Zealand and South Africa (cricket and rugby), and on the Indian sub-continent (cricket and field hockey). Malcolm (2006) notes that many historians suggest that cricket failed in America because baseball succeeded.

While seemingly commonsensical, arguments based on a notion of sports space are highly problematic. As the above examples indicate, when we cross-reference ideas about sports space we can see that it seems to vary between societies; in places one sport is enough to fill the sports space, in others three or four may be needed. What this shows is that researchers' assignment of sports space is either arbitrary or teleological. That is to say, we cannot measure or predict the sports space of a particular place, only make judgements in retrospect. Sports space, therefore, is determined by the number of sports that are *currently* popular. It therefore provides a very problematic concept on which to explain why particular sports did not become popular in a particular culture in the first place.

Key Reading

Malcolm, D. (2006) 'The diffusion of cricket to America: a figurational sociological examination', *Journal of Historical Sociology*, 19 (2): 151–73.

Markovits, A.S. and Hellerman, S.L. (2001) *Offside: Soccer and American Exceptionalism*. Princeton, NJ: Princeton University Press.

Mason, T. (1986) 'Some Englishmen and Scotsmen abroad: the spread of world football', in A. Tomlinson and G. Whannel (eds), *Off the Ball: The Football World Cup*. London: Pluto Press. pp. 67–82.

Waddington, I. and Roderick, M. (1996) 'American exceptionalism: soccer and American football', *The Sports Historian*, 16 (1): 28–49.

SPORTS TOURISM

Has been defined as, 'All forms of active and passive involvement in sporting activity, participated in casually or in an organized way for non-commercial or business/commercial reasons, that necessitates travel away from home and work locality' (Standeven and DeKnop, 1999). On one level this all-embracing definition enables as wide an array of activities as possible to be covered by the term. However, it involves no more than combining established definitions of tourism and sport and simply describes 'sport away from home', where 'away from home' is taken to include day-trips. Weed and Bull (2004: 37) have suggested a different approach, arguing that sports tourism is constructed as much around experiences as activities, and that people and places interact with activities to construct such experiences. Consequently, Weed and Bull (2004: 37) suggest the following *conceptualization* of sports tourism: 'a social, economic and cultural phenomenon arising from the unique interaction of activity, people and place'.

Sports tourism is a diverse and heterogeneous phenomenon that encompasses a wide range of differing activities and product niches. Five overlapping and non-mutually exclusive 'types' of sports tourism are proposed by Weed and Bull (2004):

1 *Tourism with sports content* has as its defining characteristic that sport is an 'incidental' activity and is not the prime purpose of the tourism trip. Given such a defining characteristic, this category may overlap with sports event tourism and luxury sports tourism, where it may also be possible that sport is not the prime purpose of the trip.

2   *Sports participation tourism* essentially refers to sports holidays (including sports day-trips), and is probably the 'common-sense' understanding of the term sports tourism. As with the previous category, there is some overlap with other sports tourism types, particularly luxury sports tourism.

3   *Sports training tourism* is much narrower than the previous two types, comprising, quite simply, sports tourism trips where the prime purpose is sports instruction or training. This might range from a weekend instruction course for beginners on how to sail a dingy, to an elite training camp at altitude for a national athletics squad.

4   *Sports event tourism* refers to tourism where the prime purpose of the trip is to take part in sports events, either as a participant or as a spectator. Sports events can range in size from mega-events such as the Olympics (**IOC**) and Football World Cup, to the smallest of local events, such as a five kilometre fun run. Each will attract a quantity of travelling spectators and/or participants.

5   *Luxury sports tourism*, unlike any of the previous categories, is not defined by reference to the nature of the activity involved. Rather it is the quality of the facilities and the luxurious nature of the accommodation and attendant facilities and services that define this type of sports tourism. Consequently, it overlaps with all the other categories, as it simply caters for the luxury end of the market in each case.

There is, unquestionably, a wide range of impacts resulting from sports tourism provision, of which the economic impact is perhaps the most obvious. Sports tourism is a dynamic and expanding economic sector. Sports-related facilities, activities, places and events are capable of generating visitors from outside the local area, and this generates economic benefit locally from sales of accommodation, food, beverages (**alcohol**), gifts, admission fees, other spending at facilities, hire fees, use of transport, etc. Sports, particularly sports events, may also generate

sponsorship income, inward investment, **media** exposure, ongoing tourist appeal and secondary **multiplier** effects.

In the mid-1990s, it was claimed that it was not unreasonable to estimate that 10–15 per cent of domestic holidays in northern Europe were sports-oriented. However, the need for a more specific and consistent focus on this information gap in future tourism data collection was identified. At the turn of the century, Mike Collins and Guy Jackson (cited in Standeven and DeKnop, 1999) presented a 'conservative' estimate for the value of sports tourism in the UK which suggested an overall value of over £2.5 billion annually.

It has tended to be in the area of sports events that most economic impact research has been conducted. The obvious direct benefits of major sporting events (new facilities and visitor spending) are supplemented in most cases by pre- and post-event tourism boosts. Resulting publicity and the positive influence on local tourism are clear advantages of staging such events (**mega-events, staging of**).

Sports tourism has also made a number of significant impacts in rural areas over recent years. Despite the evident sensitivity of rural environments and the fact that there will be some negative impacts of development, sports tourism has for the most part maintained a reputation as 'soft' tourism, capable of contributing to the rural economy in a range of contexts across the world. As traditional rural economic contributors such as farming are in decline in many areas, sports tourism has been seen as a way to boost rural economies. Countryside pursuits, such as hiking, climbing, orienteering, fell running and cycling, all increasingly contribute to the rural economy.

The nature of contemporary sports tourism is such that it is no longer possible to view it as a tourism market niche. It is a multifaceted phenomenon that comprises a range of heterogeneous areas. Obvious differences within sports tourism are between: (1) those who watch and those who actively take part; (2) those who travel with sport as the prime purpose and those for whom sport is an incidental tourism activity; (3) those for whom sports tourism involves competition and those for whom involvement is recreational; and (4) those for whom different aspects of the activity, people and place interaction are important. There are, of course, many other dimensions on which sports tourists differ and this serves to illustrate the multidimensional nature of the sports tourism experience, to which providers must respond. Sports tourism, as both a phenomenon and an area of academic interest, has developed considerably in recent years, and the indications are that it will continue to grow still further.

Key Reading

Standeven, J. and DeKnop, P. (1999) *Sport Tourism*. Champaign, IL: Human Kinetics.
Weed, M. and Bull, C. (2004) *Sports Tourism: Participants, Policy and Providers*. Oxford: Elsevier.

Mike Weed

SPORTSMANSHIP

(**fair play**)

SPORTSNET

The sportsnet is a term introduced to the sociology of sport by Howard L. Nixon II through his ground-breaking work on **pain and injury**. Applying a variant of social network theory, Nixon defines sportsnets as the webs of interaction that 'directly and indirectly link members of social networks in a particular sport or sports setting'. While he does not specify which groups of people might be included within a sportsnet, it appears from his published work that a sportsnet may include athletes, coaches, physicians and physiotherapists (**sports medicine**), sports administrators and, in US sport, college alumni.

Nixon conceives of the sportsnet as a 'communication network' within which, information is filtered and meanings modified. In his work on pain and injury, sportnets are biased, giving athletes the illusion of self-control while masking any sense of risk related to their training and playing practices. This leads to the 'normalization' of playing hurt or, more broadly stated, the acceptance of a 'culture of risk' (**risk**).

On the one hand, the emphasis on interaction in sportsnets leads to a number of similarities with **symbolic interactionism**. On the other, Nixon points to the 'structural properties' of sportsnets, arguing that athletes are more likely to be enmeshed in the sportsnet and receptive to the messages given within it, where they are:

> a) larger (and athletes are more easily replaced); b) denser (network members have more contacts with each other than with people outside the sportsnet); c) more centralized in their control over the flow of information and resources; d) higher in the reachability of athletes to coaches and other authorities; e) more closed for athletes (or more restricted in permissible contacts with people outside the sportsnet); f) more homogeneous in the transactional content of member relations; g) more stable in their social relational patterns. (Nixon, 1992, pp. 131–32)

Consequently, Roderick (1998) has pointed to the similarities between Nixon's use of the sportsnet and Elias's concept of the figuration (**figurational sociology**), but he is critical of Nixon on a number of points. These include the lack of clearly defined boundaries to the sportsnet, Nixon's ahistorical and non-processual chararacterization of sportsnets, and his one dimensional conception of power in the sportsnet, such that athletes are simply 'receivers rather than sources' of messages about the desirability to play with pain and through injury.

Key Reading

Nixon II, H.L. (1992) 'A social network analysis of influences on athletes to play with pain and injuries', *Journal of Sport and Social Issues*, 16 (2): 127–35.

Roderick, M. (1998) 'The sociology of risk, pain and injury: a comment on the work of Howard L. Nixon II', *Sociology of Sport Journal*, 15 (1): 64–79.

STACKING

Can be said to be a sporting manifestation of broader social patterns of racial prejudice and discrimination (**race**). The emergence of significant numbers of black athletes in elite sport in the United States in the 1960s and 1970s, led many to accept the popular ideology that, as an area of social life, sport is relatively free from 'racial' discrimination. However, sociologists of sport questioned whether it is correct to equate this representation with an absence of discrimination. Initiated by Loy and Elvogue in 1970, a series of studies have illustrated how, in a variety of team sports, there is a tendency for members of minority ethnic groups to experience 'stacking'; that is to say, sportspeople of African-Caribbean, Asian, Latin-American descent, etc. tend to be disproportionately over-represented in certain roles while remaining somewhat excluded from others. Further, the tendency is for sportspeople from minority ethnic groups to be 'stacked' into roles that can be classified as relatively peripheral (in a physical sense, for example wingers) and/or less significant to the outcome of the game. Conversely, white athletes tend to dominate those positions that are deemed to be the most 'central' or tactically significant.

The vast majority of studies of stacking have been produced with reference to the United States (see earlier editions of Coakley, e.g. 1990), but others have attempted to apply the notion of stacking to, for example, French-Canadians in ice hockey, Australian-Aborigines in rugby league, blacks and Asians in English cricket (Malcolm, 1997), and the British-black population in soccer (Maguire, 1991), rugby union, rugby league and basketball. In most cases, patterns of stacking have corresponded to popular beliefs about the physical and mental traits of different so-called 'racial' groups. Commonly, black athletes dominate positions that require speed and strength while white athletes dominate positions that require mental skills and decision-making capabilities.

Popularly, many believe stacking to be a consequence of physical differences between 'racial' groups. In a similar vein, others have argued that different 'races' are psychologically suited to different sports roles. Yet despite the extensive search for such genetic differences, and theories based on 'fast-twitch' muscle fibres, the denser bones of blacks (which reduce buoyancy and impair swimming), the genetic advantage of living and training at altitude, and the 'coolness' of blacks under pressure, there is no concrete evidence to support the idea that stacking is biologically based (**race science**). Moreover, there is much counter-evidence that casts doubts on these hypotheses. (What biological explanations can be given for Swiss and Austrian dominance of skiing? Why do Peruvian athletes, born and trained at altitude, lack international success in endurance sports?) Rather, these arguments tend to be teleological; that is to say, they derive from the racial stereotypes that they are seeking to explain, and they are not based on a reliable evidence base that demonstrates causality.

Sociological explanations have largely been based around the idea that the recruitment and selection of players by coaches, scouts, etc. are influenced, either consciously or subconsciously, by beliefs which stem from racial stereotypes. Thus, when selecting a position that is thought to require speed and agility, coaches are inclined to look more favourably upon black or African-Caribbean athletes. A related idea is that the athletes themselves also contribute to stacking in that they 'self-select' (on the basis of their own acceptance of racial stereotypes of biological difference) positions which they feel give them the best chances of sporting success. While these arguments are more intuitively sound than the biological and/or psychological explanations (and also supported by a range of cross-cultural examples), once again they have little by way of concrete supporting evidence (beyond a few anecdotal quotes from coaches and managers).

An alternative, historically based, explanation for stacking is offered by Malcolm (1997). Using the example of cricket in the Caribbean and on the Indian sub-continent, he argues that the playing roles into which the respective 'racial' groups are currently 'stacked' are the result of the broader power and **class** differences that influenced their initial entry into the game in the eighteenth century. Particular roles develop particular meaning for particular social groups, and these meanings are transmitted across generations (**habitus**).

While stacking continues to exist in some elite sports, the numerical dominance of black athletes in many of America's leading team sports, and the increased internationalization of European sports such as football, have led to this pattern becoming less distinct. In addition to this, some writers (e.g. Birrell, 1989) have noted that studies of stacking tend to be repetitive, largely descriptive, and provide little by way of theoretical advancement. Others have criticized studies of stacking for being overly empiricist (**positivism**). Some leading textbooks have subsequently ceased to discuss stacking per se, and focus more broadly on the structures of power which disadvantage minority ethnic athletes and the ways in which minority ethnic groups experience this disadvantage. Stacking, where it continues to exist, is merely one, possibly waning, manifestation of these broader power struggles.

Key Reading

Birrell, S. (1989) 'Racial relations theories and sport: suggestions for a more critical analysis', *Sociology of Sport Journal*, 6: 212–27.

Coakley, J. (1990) *Sport in Society: Issues and Controversies*, 4th edn. St Louis: Mosby.

Maguire, J. (1991) 'Sport, racism and British society: a sociological study of England's elite male Afro/Caribbean soccer and rugby union players', in G. Jarvie (ed.), *Sport, Racism and Ethnicity*. London: Falmer Press. pp. 94–123.

Malcolm, D. (1997) 'Stacking in cricket: a figurational sociological re-appraisal of centrality', *Sociology of Sport Journal*, 14 (3): 265–84.

STADIUM

Sports stadiums have antecedents in the arenas of Greece (**ancient Olympic Games**) and Rome (**Roman Games**) but in their modern guise are products of the eighteenth and nineteenth centuries. They are of considerable sociological significance, attracting as they do crowds of supporters (**fans**) who these days are far from neutral in the teams that represent them in stadium-sited sports. Indeed, it is the partisanship of sports supporters that has led to a number of 'social problems', notably (but far from exclusively) in connection with football (**football hooliganism**). The stadium is a site of power in which bodies are controlled and subject to various forms of **surveillance**. What is more, it is a secure site for the incarceration of a large number of bodies. Not without reason has the stadium been likened to a prison and it is hardly surprising that Jean-Marie Brohm (1978) has read sport per se as 'perhaps the social practice which best exemplifies the "disciplinary society", analysed by M. Foucault' (**discipline**).

The sports stadium has evolved over time. From being a relatively unconfined space on which games could be played, it became enclosed with the establishment of spatial rules that controlled where 'play' should take place. In other words, an explicit line separated players from spectators, replacing the pre-modern tradition of **folk games** with permeable boundaries. However, while rules were central to the bureaucratization of 'players', few if any rules were applied to the behaviour of spectators. As sport became commodified (**commodification**), a degree of social segregation emerged with the ability of some spectators to pay for superior accommodation, resulting in the establishment of grandstands. These were followed by basic forms of seating, though well into the 1950s most spectators stood throughout games and spectators could move from end to end and were not confined to a specific place.

The gradual decline in intra-stadium mobility resulted in large part from the desire of police and club authorities to control all spectators (and hence the move to all-seater stadiums). This individualization of spectators resulted from the spurious argument that seating was safer than standing. In Britain, this was a response to the crisis in football, the result of the Bradford fire disaster and a number of disasters resulting from uncontrolled crowding (**Hillsborough**). The all-seater stadium can also be read as a response to the 'hooligan problem' and to a more general '**civilizing process**' in urban structures generally.

The modern stadium not only is a response to changes in architecture – the old wooden grounds being replaced by concrete and glass stadiums – but also is typified by advances in horticulture (or 'turf-science') and land use. Traditionally, the stadium was a mono-cultural space given over to a single sport; it was a *football* ground or a *cricket* ground. Changes in technology and architecture have turned the 'ground' into a stadium. It is today a multi-purpose facility that can be used for many sporting and non-sporting events. Weddings, banquets, conferences, religious gatherings (**religion**), museums, the ubiquitous franchising of clothes and equipment, and hotels are part and parcel of the stadium (or 'tradium') complex. For spectators this is leisure laced with spending (**consumer culture**).

The stadium (the word 'ground' or 'park' is less commonly used in the UK these days) serves to not only segment space but also conquer nature. The domed stadium or the retractable roof, exemplified by the Sky Dome in Toronto and the Millennium Stadium in Cardiff, can eliminate the effects of rain or temperature; floodlights can change day into night and synthetic surfaces can replace the vagaries of grass (though synthetic surfaces have been rejected in many places

due to the various injuries that result from their unforgiving surfaces). The outcome of the rationalization of the stadium is that it comes closer to the sporting ideal, a normative space as adumbrated by the philosopher Paul Weiss (1969) 'Ideally a normal set of conditions for a race is one in which there are no turns, no wind, no interferences, no interval between signal and start, and no irregularities to the track – in short, no deviations from a standard situation' (*From Ritual to Record*). Here, Weiss is talking about athletics but his words could be applied to any other sport. Sports find the physical environment an intrusion that interrupts the ideal game; hence the desire to 'eliminate' nature as a form of 'noise' by the interiorization of sport and the artificiality of its stadiums.

In recent years stadium-based sports have faced increased competition from television (**media**). Paradoxically, a modern stadium is incomplete without the presence of large television screens that transmit in slow motion or as action replays repeats of the movements on the field. Such a phenomenon suggests the postmodern condition of the simulation being superior to the reality (**hyperreal**), and has led to the suggestion by some postmodern scholars such as Jean Baudrillard and Paul Virillio that fans should be removed from stadiums and that sports should become a purely televisual experience (**postmodernism**). After all, like nature, fans can be seen as extraneous 'noise' that influences the outcome of a game as well as providing the danger of crowd misbehaviour and hooliganism. Although the world of stadiums has not yet reached this stage, it is far from an implausible scenario.

The Marxist view (**Marxism**) of the stadium is that of a modern version of '**bread and circuses**'. However, resistance to change in stadium development is frequently found in the activist groups that have opposed such 'developments' as those noted above (i.e. all-seating, relocations, '**embourgeoisment**', etc.). The relocation of stadiums is often perceived by local fans as a loss of 'their' home team (**independent supporters' associations**). However, in the UK – as opposed to the USA (**franchises**) – team relocation has generally been over very short distances.

Finally, the stadium has implications for urban land use (**city, the**). Writing in 1928 the German anglophile, Rudolf Kircher contrasted the private nature of the main sports stadiums in the UK (and the US) with the municipally funded arenas in much of mainland Europe. He also recognized that in much of Western Europe the stadium was part of an urban leisure zone, whereas in Britain stadiums were often sited in residential areas. During the 1980s and 1990s a substantial change has occurred in the urban geography of sports stadiums. In the US there has been a tradition of club relocation over intra-continental distances. In the UK, club relocation has been at the intra-urban scale, either to sub-urban or to brownfield sites. Fans have sometimes tried to oppose stadium change, but such opposition has been unsuccessful and supporters have come to accept the modern, all-seater stadiums (see also **topophilia**).

Key Reading

Bale, J. (2001) *Sport, Space and the City.* Caldwell, NJ: Bradford Press.

Bale, J. and Moen, O. (eds) (1995) *The Stadium and the City.* Keele: Keele University Press.

Inglis, S. (1983) *The Football Grounds of England and Wales.* London: Willow Books.

Inglis, S. (2000) *Sightlines: A Stadium Odyssey.* London: Yellow Jersey Press.

John Bale

STRESS

Can be defined as a person's inability to respond to particular physical or psychological demands, and thus is narrower in scope than related terms such as **arousal** and **anxiety**. Stress may stem from general life events (e.g. death of a friend) or from sports-specific events such as performance and team selection. Stress is thought to be determined by situation or context. For instance, the more an athlete perceives an event to be important, and the more uncertain the

athlete feels about events, the more stressful the situation will be (e.g. the more uncertain the length of time it will take to recover from injury, and the greater the chance that injury will lead an athlete to miss a major fixture, like a cup final, the more stressful will be the experience for the athlete). However, the stress personally experienced will also depend on **personality** dispositions such as trait anxiety, levels of self-esteem and, specifically to sport, anxiety/**self-confidence** over one's physique (for sport normally involves the potential for one's physique to be evaluated by others).

McGrath's Stress Process describes the four interrelated stages that lead to stress. Stage 1 involves *environmental demand* (e.g. playing a match). Stage 2 is the *perception of demand*, a stage which recognizes that people will not perceive the same environmental demand in identical ways. In stage 3, *stress response*, we see the individual's physical and psychological stress response (e.g. worry, heightened levels of **concentration**). Stage 4, *behavioural consequences*, refers to the effect of stress on the performance (improved or deteriorated). The behavioural consequences then feedback into Stage 1.

Key Reading

Jones, J.G. and Hardy, L. (eds) (1990) *Stress and Performance in Sport.* New York: Wiley.

McGrath, J.E. (1970) *Social and Psychological Factors in Stress.* New York: Holt, Rinehart & Winston.

STRUCTURATION THEORY

Anthony Giddens's (1984) structuration theory is most notable in its attempt to 'resolve' the sociological dilemma of **agency and structure**. Through the formulation of a theoretical framework which accords primacy to neither structure nor agency, Giddens seeks to overcome the false dichotomy inherent in the use of the two terms. Rather, Giddens states that agency and structure are not independent phenomena (i.e. a dualism) but more accurately a duality (though critics have argued that to some extent this is just word play). More usefully he talks of structure as both the medium for, and the outcome of, social action. For Giddens it is important that structure is not seen as determinant, but that we are sensitive to contingencies, the 'unacknowledged time/space conditions', and the unintended consequences of individual action. Structure, Giddens says, should be conceived of as both enabling and constraining.

A number of criticisms of structuration theory have been raised, not least that Giddens's own work remains biased towards agency. Yet Giddens is arguably the most influential British sociologist of his era and it is perhaps surprising that his work has largely been neglected in the field of sports studies. There are no clear or obvious reasons for this. However, Gruneau has fruitfully used structuration theory in his work (1983), conveying the notion that sport can at the same time be both liberating (facilitating the formation of political and cultural groupings) and constraining (contributing to the perpetuation of the capitalist mode of production). John Horne and David Jary (1987, 2004) have also called for the more widespread adoption of Giddens's work in the sociology of sport, initially in preference to the Eliasian concept of **figuration** (though oddly, Horne has not subsequently used Giddens extensively in his own empirical work). Ironically, Giddens wrote his MA thesis on 'Sport and Society in Contemporary Britain' and briefly worked at the University of Leicester at the time when Elias and Dunning (also at Leicester) published their first essays on sport.

Key Reading

Dunning, E. (1992) 'Figurational sociology and the sociology of sport: some concluding remarks', in E. Dunning and C. Rojek (eds), *Sport and Leisure in the Civilizing Process: Critique and Counter-Critique*. Basingstoke: Macmillan. pp. 221–84.

Giddens, A. (1984) *The Constitution of Society*. Cambridge: Polity.

Gruneau, R. (1983) *Class, Sports and Social Development*. Amherst, MA: University of Massachusetts Press.

Horne, J. and Jary, D. (1987) 'The figurational sociology of sport and leisure of Elias and Dunning: an exposition and critique', in J. Horne, D. Jary and A. Tomlinson (eds), *Sport, Leisure and Social Relations*. London: Routledge and Kegan Paul. pp. 86–112.

Horne, J. and Jary, D. (2004) 'Anthony Giddens: structuration theory, and sport and leisure', in R. Giulianotti (ed.), *Sport and Modern Social Theorists*. London: Palgrave Macmillan. pp. 129–44.

SUBCULTURES

Because much of the early research on subcultures dealt with delinquents and 'deviants' (**deviance**) it was sometimes thought that the 'sub' in subculture referred to a cultural unit that was less than or inferior to the larger culture. It is now more generally accepted that subcultures refer to smaller units of larger cultural groupings, but even this simple confusion in meaning signals a need for caution in using the term. Just as Raymond Williams suggested that 'culture' is one of the most complex words in the English language, we should not expect the various usages of the term 'subculture' to be any less complex.

Just in the case of sport has the word been used to describe all of sport (the subculture of sport; the athletic subculture (**sport ethic**)) or the culture of a single team. Most commonly, in the case of sport and leisure, subculture refers to the culture – the meanings and ways – that develops in association with a specific activity: the subculture of aircraft modellers; the subculture of ballroom dancers; the subculture of skateboarders. Even this covers a great diversity of subcultural types, and Loy et al. (1978) attempted to classify sport and leisure subcultures into three overlapping groups: occupational subcultures, avocational subcultures, and deviant subcultures. Avocational subcultures include all of the sport and leisure subcultures, but they interface with occupational subcultures (coaches, professionals, **sports medicine** staff, etc.) at the professional and high-performance levels, and with deviant subcultures in areas such as **gambling**, hustling and **football hooliganism**.

Early research on delinquent subcultures in the United States led to the first general theory of subcultures, which argued that subcultures were formed by interacting individuals as problem-solving mechanisms (to deal with poverty, **violence**, etc). A rather more sophisticated understanding of the processes of subculture formation developed in the UK in the 1960s and 1970s. The 'new criminology' that emerged from the National Deviancy Conference, and the Centre for Contemporary Cultural Studies also studied delinquency (**cultural studies**), and extended that research to include the various youth subcultures in Britain at the time (mods, rockers, skinheads, hippies, etc.; see also **moral panics**). It became apparent that the ideas they developed about leisure and style could be transferred to the analysis of sport and leisure subcultures. In addition to research and theories grounded in studies of delinquency, the various interpretive sociologies also studied social actors and social formations such as subcultures in their concern with the way in which social actors make sense of the world. Interpretive sociologies take the actors' meanings and definition of the situation as the basis for social analysis (**idealism**; **symbolic interactionism**). Interpretive sociologies and British youth culture research came together in the 1980s to drive what has been referred to as the 'cultural shift' in the sociology of sport. Before this 'cultural shift' studies of sport subcultures tended to be descriptive analyses of various sports 'careers', including studies of professional boxers, wrestlers, ice hockey players, pool hustlers, and the various careers associated with horse-racing.

Careers analyses reached a peak in 1975 with the publication of Ball and Loy's important collection, *Sport and Social Order*, which included theoretical work on occupational subcultures in sport, a study of the career patterns and career contingencies of professional baseball players, and two innovative comparative studies: ice hockey players and

Hollywood musicians, and professional wrestlers and physicians. Although subcultural research of this type continued after 1975, there was a subtle change in the notion of 'career'. Careers in sport came to be thought of less as the work of a 'professional' career, and more as analyses of an individual's period of involvement in sport. Thus, a youth's involvement in community and/or high school soccer could be considered as a 'career', and there was a growing interest in **socialization** in the study of sport subcultures. The processes of becoming an athlete and becoming an adult person, and the way these two interact, were addressed to a certain extent in some of the 'career' subculture studies. However, the socialization process came to the fore as a result of the 'cultural shift'.

Subcultural studies during this period began to deal with the processes of becoming involved in sport, maintaining involvement in sport and **retirement** from sport. For example, Donnelly and Young (1988) examined the way in which rookie athletes constructed appropriate subcultural identities for themselves, to be confirmed (or rejected) by established athletes in the subculture. Research also began to go beyond descriptive and interpretive analyses to examine the relationship of subcultures to the larger culture. In addition to an appropriate subcultural identity, researchers also began to recognize the ways in which sport and leisure subcultures were involved in social **class**, **race**, and **gender** identities.

The 'cultural shift' was accompanied by a 'critical shift' in the sociology of sport, and subcultural studies of sports and leisure practices began to show how some activities are involved in the reproduction of social inequalities, while others represent radical and challenging attempts to transform those social inequalities. Research reflecting the influence of this change includes studies of British football hooligans, bodybuilders, baseball players in developing nations, US high school football, US university basketball players, women professional golfers, boxing, male team sport locker rooms, women's softball, women's ice hockey, skateboarding and **aerobics**. Thus subcultures in sport could be seen in three ways: (1) as carriers of residual cultural values – some progressive, such as ideas about sportspersonship and **fair play**, some more regressive in terms of stereotypical notions about race and gender; (2) as entities that maintained the status quo of dominant sports and national cultures (**nationalism**); and (3) as active sites of cultural production, developing new meanings and ways and challenging traditional and established meanings and ways. It is the latter elements of resistance and transformation that have attracted most interest from sport sociologists, as evidenced in the large number of studies dealing with new, 'alternative' and 'extreme' sports (**lifestyle sports**). The complexity of subcultures is evident in that the same subculture may be seen in more than one of the above ways.

The study of subcultures shows not only how sports and other leisure practices are socially constructed and socially defined activities, meaningful only to the extent that meaning is attached to them by the participants, but also, as Gruneau (1981) noted, how 'subcultures, with their various "establishment" and "countercultural" emphases, have been constitutively inserted into the struggles, the forms of compliance and opposition, social reproduction and transformation, associated with changing patterns of social development'. Writing in 1972, Arnold suggested that 'sport and hobby subcultures ... [may] have a sociological importance in and of themselves'. Research in the sociology of sport in the last 35 years has proven him correct.

Key Reading

Donnelly, P. (1985) 'Sport subcultures', in R.L. Terjung (ed.), *Exercise and Sport Sciences Reviews*, Vol. 13. New York: Macmillan. pp. 539–78.
Donnelly, P. (1993) 'Subcultures in sport: resilience and transformation', in A.G. Ingham and J.W. Loy (eds), *Sport in Social Development: Traditions, Transitions and Transformations*. Champaign, IL: Human Kinetics. pp. 119–45.

Donnelly, P. and Young, K. (1988) 'The construction and confirmation of identity in sport subcultures', *Sociology of Sport Journal*, 5 (3): 223–40.
Loy, J.W., McPherson, B.D. and Kenyon, E. (1978) *Sport and Social Systems: A Guide to the Analysis, Problems and Literature*. Reading, Mass: Addison-Wesleyn.
Wheaton, B. (ed.) (2004) *Understanding Lifestyle Sports*. London: Routledge.

Peter Donnelly

SUBJECTIVITY

(objectivity and subjectivity)

SUPPORTERS DIRECT

Launched at Birkbeck College, London, in September 2000 with the explicit aim of enabling the democratization of football clubs in England (and latterly Scotland). The seeds of the idea for a body of this kind were sown in an early report published by the Football Taskforce, *Investing in the Community*, but it was in the Taskforce's final report, *Football: Commercial Issues*, that the details of the proposal became more concrete. As this indicates, Supporters Direct is best seen as a response to the **commercialization** of football in England during the 1990s.

Supporters Direct builds on the (more or less) popular movements of football fans, commonly referred to as **independent supporters' associations** (ISAs), and seeks to provide legal and organizational advice, and banking assistance, to enable **fans** to establish supporters' trusts (of which well over 120 have been established) and consequently take a more influential role in the running of clubs. Through the purchase of shares by fans, and the pooling of voting rights, supporters are able to exploit the relatively new business-like structures of professional football clubs in England in opposition to which both Supporters Direct and ISAs have largely developed. The ultimate goal is full mutual ownership of football clubs through a restructuring of share ownership, but a more minor, though significant, achievement to date includes the election of supporter representatives on to the boards of various clubs. This has most commonly been the case at clubs in the lower leagues which have faced financial difficulties, and subsequently have been 'saved' largely through the actions of, and finance raised by, fan groups.

Key Reading

Hamil, S., Michie, J., Oughton, C. and Warby, S. (2000) *The Changing Face of Football Business: Supporters Direct*. London: Frank Cass.
www.supporters-direct.org/Home page of Supporters Direct.

SURVEILLANCE

In his examination of discipline, Foucault (1977) suggests that control over visibility is a key element in the exercise of power; to be made visible is to be made subject to the exercise of disciplinary power (see also **performativity**). As an illustration, Foucault discusses Bentham's design for a Panopticon, a circular prison with cells arranged around a central guard tower, the windows of which are covered with blinds that make it impossible to know where (and if) guards are looking. Because of the blinds, inmates never know if they are being observed, and because of the spatial arrangement of cells, they are always able to be observed. Thus, power in the Panopticon is both visible (in the figure of the tower) and invisible (because of the blinds). The significant result is that inmates must always act *as if* they are being observed; they become, in effect, their own guards and take up the responsibility for their own surveillance.

The Panopticon is more than a prison design; for Foucault, it captures a generalized disciplinary logic at work in everyday life (**discipline**). This logic can be found in the design of places, such as schools, hospitals, factories and gyms, in which spatial organization divides and controls the location of bodies, thereby making surveillance possible and, ideally, inescapable. Bodies are not simply observed but are subjected to a normalizing gaze; they are examined, measured and ranked (against a **body** shape subjectively defined as normal). Furthermore, the constant surveillance associated with these disciplinary spaces induces in the individual the habit of self-surveillance. By internalizing the normalizing gaze, individuals – far more effectively than any guard, teacher, doctor, manager or coach – constantly police their actions and attitudes, thereby ensuring the automatic and continuous exercise of disciplinary power.

Foucauldian analyses of sport and physical activity are thus sensitive to two interconnected aspects of surveillance. The first concerns the various techniques that facilitate the surveillance of bodies. This can include sporting spaces structured by the principle of visibility (as with the sports **stadium**s); mechanisms of observation that are part of physical culture settings or systems (for example, elevated referee platforms in sports such as tennis and volleyball, and mirrors in dance studios and **health** clubs (**aerobics**)); and techniques and tools for employing a normalizing gaze (such as the criteria and benchmarks against which bodies and their capacities are evaluated in the context of a physical exam or sporting contest).

The second and related concern is with the ways in which self-surveillance is adopted and exercised by individuals. This can be as an outcome of repeated observation – like the inmate, the sport participant may come to act *as if* the instructor is always watching. Self-surveillance can also be the outcome of virtual or implied observation. For example, beauty and fitness magazines are filled with images and articles that encourage individuals to scrutinize their bodies, assess their failings and then work towards a particular norm via prescribed exercises, diets and fashion choices (**obesity discourse**).

Key Reading

Ashton-Shaeffer, C., Gibson, H.J., Autry, C.E. and Hanson, C.S. (2001) 'Meaning of sport to adults with physical disabilities: a disability sport camp experience', *Sociology of Sport Journal*, 18 (1): 95–114.

Duncan, M.C. (1994) 'The politics of women's body images and practices: Foucault, the Panopticon, and Shape magazine', *Journal of Sport and Social Issues*, 18 (1): 48–65.

Foucault, M. (1977) *Discipline and Punish: The Birth of the Prison*. New York: Vintage Books.

Jennifer Smith Maguire

SURVEYS

(**questionnaires**)

SYMBOLIC INTERACTIONISM

There are a number of loosely associated approaches which might be described as micro-sociological, interpretative or interactionist perspectives (**idealism**; **macro- and micro-sociology**). These include ethnomethodology, which focuses on the 'everyday' methods that people use to understand and create coordinated interaction, and Goffman's dramaturgy, where social life is seen as a form of theatre. Of these micro-sociological approaches, symbolic interactionism has probably had the greatest influence in the sociology of sport.

Symbolic interactionists are concerned with the way in which an individual makes sense of, or interprets, the world in which he or she lives. The focus of symbolic interactionism is typically on the symbolic significance of signs, gestures, shared rules and written and spoken language, and the way in which the use of symbols assists us to make sense of our own and one another's behaviour. The starting point for symbolic interactionists is the fact that, because of the comparatively high level of development of the human vocal apparatus and nervous system, humans have a distinctive capacity to communicate in a symbolic manner; hence 'symbolic interaction'. This distinctiveness consists of the fact that, via the use of symbols, we are able to interpret or 'define' each other's actions, instead of merely reacting to each other in mechanistic ways.

Central to symbolic interactionism is the idea that the human being has a 'self' and that, through the use of symbols, we can be the object of our own actions. G.H. Mead (1863–1931), for example, distinguished between three aspects or functions of the self – the 'I', the 'me' and the 'generalized other'. The 'I' is the active, initiating aspect of the self, the 'me' is the self as object, and the 'generalized other' is the social part of the self that consists of learned moral rules and an awareness of how the roles one performs fit in with the roles of others. The interpersonal processes involved in developing and sustaining particular identities or self-images are the central object of investigation for symbolic interactionists.

Developing and sustaining a self-image involves an ongoing process of symbolic communication and negotiation with others (and with ourself). We attempt to convey to others particular images of how we would like them to see us, and of how we would like to see ourselves. Others, in turn, accept, reject or modify the image that we seek to convey, thus reinforcing or undermining our preferred self-image. Self-images are continually being produced and modified as part of the process of social interaction; we help to form the self-image of others, just as others contribute to our own self-image. Symbolic interactionists use the term 'significant others' to describe the most important people in determining our identity (e.g. partners, team mates, coaches, etc.).

Donnelly (2000) has argued that sociologists of sport have used symbolic interactionism (or more broadly 'interpretive' approaches) in two main, but overlapping, ways: (1) to understand sports **subcultures**; and (2) to understand **socialization** processes. In terms of subcultures, many of the early studies focused on the 'careers' of professional sportspeople such as boxers and wrestlers. Subsequently, research focused on leisure-based subcultures, such as those relating to surfing, rock climbing and playing rugby. Within subcultures, symbolic interactionists considered the possible conflict or complementarity of the identities: How do people come to construct their identities as athletes? What part do others play in this process? And what happens when self-identity is threatened? Gallmeier (1987) in his study of professional ice hockey players in the United States, examines the 'emotional performances' of players before, during and after games, focusing in particular on the social processes involved in the mental or emotional preparation the players undergo in getting 'psyched up' and in 'putting on a game face'. He shows how the 'staging' or managing of emotional performances is influenced by significant others (primarily by the coach, but also by the trainer and the **fans** and by interaction with team mates) who evoke rapidly shifting emotional expressions for each game situation.

Some symbolic interactionists focus much more centrally on the entry, or *socialization* into sports subcultures. In their classic study of rugby players and rock climbers, Donnelly and Young (1988) use a four-stage career model, describing how (potential) group members move through the following phases:

pre-socialization, selection and recruitment, socialization, and acceptance/ostracism.

The main criticisms of the symbolic interactionist approach are that it overemphasizes individual agency and that it neglects the broader impact of structural factors on social phenomena (**agency and structure**). Similarly it has been argued that, given the premise that each individual constructs his/her own understanding, results could not be generalized (e.g. Gallmeier's study concerned hockey players from just one team), and that researchers' accounts were highly subjective (**objectivity and subjectivity**). Taken to its logical conclusion, the argument that all human action is subject to individual interpretation leads to a situation in which no single interpretation could be identified as more or less adequate than any other (thus making sociology redundant). It has also been argued that some ethnographic researchers (**ethnography**) have 'gone native'; that is to say, empathized so closely with their subjects that they are unable to critically scrutinize their actions (**cultural relativism**).

Key Reading

Donnelly, P. (2000) 'Interpretative approaches', in J. Coakley and E. Dunning (eds), *Handbook of Sports Studies*. London: Sage. pp. 77–91.

Donnelly, P and Young, K (1988) 'The construction and confirmation of identity in sport subcultures', *Sociology of Sport Journal*, 5 (3): 223–40.

Gallmeier, C (1987) 'Putting on the game face: the staging of emotions in professional hockey', *Sociology of Sport Journal*, 4 (4): 347–62.

TARTAN ARMY

The name given to the football fans who travel to watch the Scottish (male) national team play international fixtures and who, despite a historical legacy of fan **violence** (**football hooliganism**), have more recently been perceived as relatively passive, inclusive and hedonistic. While Giulianotti (1991) notes that some Tartan Army members locate the group's origins to a fixture in Israel in 1981, popularly and academically the Tartan Army became visible at the Italia '90 Football World Cup, and through UEFA's presentation of the 'Fair Play Award' at Euro '92 to around 5000 Scottish fans for their exemplary behaviour and contribution to the tournament.

The contemporary behaviour of the Tartan Army is contrasted with pre-1980 stereotypes which presented Scottish football fans as macho, drunken and violent (**alcohol**; **masculinity**). Since then, Scottish football fans have developed an image as gregarious (which is part based on the continued link with alcohol consumption), self-promoting, raucously good-humoured, and friendly. Scottish football fans put aside their local club rivalries and deeper sectarian divisions in favour of a collective anti-Englishness (**Bedouin syndrome**; **sectarianism**). Persuasive or forceful self-policing methods quieten the more abusive and aggressive forms of behaviour. Through this process, the English become stigmatized as hooligans while the Scottish supporters exhibit many of the characteristics of **carnival**.

Key Reading

Guiliannotti, R. (1991) 'Scotland's tartan army in Italy: the case for the carnivalesque', *Sociological Review*, 39 (3): 503–27.

Finn, G.F. and Giulianotti, R. (1998) 'Scottish fans, not English hooligans!: Scots, Scottishness and Scottish Football', in A. Brown (ed.), *Fanatics! Power, Identity and Fandom in Football*. London: Routledge. pp. 189–202.

TAYLOR REPORT

(Hillsborough)

TEBBIT 'CRICKET TEST'

Named after Norman Tebbit, a senior Conservative politician in the Thatcher government. Speaking in Los Angeles in 1990, Tebbit argued that if a British immigrant, or one of his/her descendants, chose to support a team such as India or the West Indies when that team was playing cricket against England, this could, and indeed should, be used as a gauge of his/her patriotism and thus acceptability as a British citizen. Talking specifically about British Asians (though Tebbit viewed the 'test' as more generally applicable), Tebbit asked, 'which side do they cheer for ... were they still harking back to where they came from or where they were?' Tebbit's statement served to heighten the public debate over **race** and national identity issues (**nationalism**) and, in particular, calls for greater restrictions to be imposed on the number of immigrants accepted into the UK. While Tebbit argued that the comments were designed to promote national integration, they effectively forwarded the argument that assimilation (i.e. that immigrants should forsake their ethnic roots and be subsumed into the culture of the host nation), as opposed to multiculturalism (i.e. the celebration and promotion of ethnic diversity within a nation), should form the basis of British race relations policy (see also **anti-racism**).

Key Reading

Carrington, B. and McDonald, I. (2001) *'Race', Sport and British Society.* London: Routledge.

Malcolm, D. (1997) 'Stacking in cricket: a figurational sociological reappraisal of centrality', *Sociology of Sport Journal,* 14 (3): 265–84.

Marqusee, M. (1998) *Anyone but England: Cricket, Race and Class.* London: Two Heads Publishing.

TECHNOLOGIES (OF DOMINATION/OF THE SELF)

Over the course of his career, Foucault was concerned with two types of connection between bodies and power: (1) technologies of domination, which are largely institutional; and (2) technologies of the self, which are exercised by the subject. Foucault was interested in how these two types of technologies interact in the constitution and distribution of authority and influence, and the governance of society. The concept of 'technologies' is significant, as it foregrounds questions of *how* things are accomplished; by what means are bodies invested with power, made productive and useful, and at the same time, made governable? Foucauldian analyses of sport and physical culture thus tend to be empirically grounded and historically sensitive. They are focused upon the regular and repeated practices, procedures and rules that are developed and deployed over time to target and train bodies, endowing them with particular skills, capacities and attitudes.

Technologies of domination are means by which institutions direct the conduct and capacities of individual bodies towards certain ends. The objective of these multiple techniques, **discourses** and forms of knowledge is to train individuals to be productive in ways that, more often than not, reproduce the social order. However much they may constrain choice, such technologies are 'positive' in the sense that they affirm the **body**'s vital energies and seek to optimize its productivity.

In *The History of Sexuality: An Introduction* (1978), Foucault outlines two different, yet interlinked, technologies of domination – one individualizing (an 'anatomo-politics'), the other totalizing (a 'biopolitics') – that work through a rationality of optimization through normalization. In the individualizing mode, various disciplines separate individual beings and skills from each other in order to better train them to meet an established goal. For example, athletic training programmes use skill isolation, drill repetition and performance measurements in order to hone capacities such as speed, endurance or precision. In the totalizing mode, regulatory procedures make possible a cataloguing of different groups of bodies in order to better monitor and manage their performance relative to particular benchmarks. For example, national physical fitness tests and statistics allow specific groups to be identified as 'at **risk**' and subsequently targeted with exercise, diet and other **health** promotion campaigns (**obesity discourse**).

Technologies of domination are intertwined with technologies of the self – various means by which individuals are encouraged to focus their attention on themselves, monitor and work on their conduct, and develop particular forms of self-knowledge. For example, through disciplinary training techniques, such as skill detection and correction, an athlete may develop self-scrutiny and self-discipline that lead to a heightened conformity to a 'winning' norm. However, interactions between technologies of domination and the self are far from predictable. The body, invested with power via technologies of domination, may then employ its productive capacities and self-knowledge to abandon, disrupt or modify the norms towards which its self-**discipline** is directed. For example, Markula's examination of instructors of 'mindful' fitness (2004) highlights how technologies of the self hold open the possibility of a radical ethical practice of freedom, through which individuals may challenge or change the dominant feminine body discourse.

Key Reading

Foucault, M. (1978) *The History of Sexuality: An Introduction.* New York: Vintage Books.

Maguire, J.S. (2002) 'Michel Foucault: sport, power, technologies and governmentality', in J. Maguire and K. Young (eds), *Sport, Theory & Society.* Oxford: JAI Press. pp. 293–314.

Markula, P. (2004) '"Turning into one's self": Foucault's technologies of the self and mindful fitness', *Sociology of Sport Journal,* 21 (3): 302–21.

Jennifer Smith Maguire

THEORY OF THE LEISURE CLASS, THE

Originally published in 1899, Thorstein Veblen's *The Theory of the Leisure Class* is a commentary on the consequences of capitalism as manifest in late nineteenth-century America (**class**). Veblen noted that capitalism created a wealthy elite and, furthermore, that this class of people developed leisure forms largely modelled on how they imagined previous historical elites had used their leisure time. The non-productive use of time (i.e. a life of leisure) was deemed to be irrefutable evidence of wealth and power and thus bolstered the elite class's status. Moreover, members of this class used their conspicuous consumption of leisure time as a way of distancing themselves from work-like activities and thus other social groups (who, of course, had to work). Veblen noted that a range of leisure pursuits – travel, collection of art work, etc. – could serve the elite class's purposes in this regard. However, he regarded sport as particularly important as this form of leisure enabled the elite to demonstrate their physical superiority over other social groups, to express links with a supposedly 'chivalrous' and noble past, to socialize children and build 'character', and to provide a forum in which aspirant classes could 'prove' themselves. The close relationship between sport and war (expressed through similar terminology, organization of competing sides, displays of **emotion**, etc.) reinforced many of these ennobling and enriching characteristics of sport.

As well as bolstering social status, conspicuous leisure, and thus sports, helped to foster a common cultural identity among the wealthy elite. Moreover, such class consciousness was particularly useful at times of rapid social change and when increased social mobility threatened to undermine existing forms of **social stratification**. This, Veblen argued, was one reason why sports grew in both number and social significance during the late nineteenth century.

Key Reading

Horne, J., Tomlinson, A. and Whannel, G. (1999) *Understanding Sport: An Introduction to the Sociological and Cultural Analysis of Sport.* London: Routledge. esp. Ch. 4.

Veblen, T. (1899) *The Theory of the Leisure Class: An Economic Study of Institutions.* New York: Macmillan.

TITLE IX

Passed by the US Congress, Title IX of the 1972 Educational Amendments was a key legislative event in the attempt to improve **gender** equality. Title IX was intended to remove any bias or discrimination on the basis of sex, in any federally funded educational programme or activity (the closest UK equivalent to this legislation is the 1975 Sex Discrimination Act). This, of course, clearly encompassed and had specific ramifications for sport.

Before the passing of Title IX, huge inequalities in spending (50:1 in favour of males) and participation rates (for every girl participating in US high school sports there were 12 boys) existed in US sport. It was on this basis that liberal feminists campaigned for the introduction of Title IX or similar legislation (**feminism**). Many institutions delayed its implementation for as long as the law allowed them (five years), but Title IX was eventually effective in reducing funding inequalities and thus increasing opportunities for females to participate in sport (**athletic scholarships**) both in terms of numbers, and in terms of opening up new sports for women (the remarkable growth of women's soccer in the US is a tribute to this).

However, there have been a number of forms of resistance to these changes that have held back further strides towards equality. The central unintended consequence of the implementation of Title IX has been that as many men's and women's sports programmes have merged, men have increasingly taken the most powerful positions, something which has effectively disadvantaged women to a greater extent than was the case pre-Title IX. Related to this, there has been an actual decline in the number and proportion of female head coaches and administrators since 1972 and, it has been argued, the removal of these female role models serves to reinforce 'commonsense' notions about sport being a masculine domain, and reduce female aspirations to secure their futures within sport. Moreover, American universities with large (Gridiron) football programmes almost always fall short in tests of Title IX compliance. Because of a reluctance to cut the 'flagship' of a university's sports programme, and because of the revenue from alumni and boosterism that this attracts, other male sports have been disproportionately affected. This has led the men in these sports to feel that Title IX has directly reduced their opportunities to participate in sport, and thus has fuelled the opposition to increased gender equality. Title IX illustrates a central dilemma in sports-gender policy; namely while separation of the sexes in sport is likely to lead to the continued disadvantage of women in sports (e.g. in terms of funding), closer contact between male and female sport is likely to reduce female autonomy, and create new forms of inequality.

Key Reading

Carpenter, L.J. and Acosta, R.V. (2005) *Title IX*. Urbana, IL: Human Kinetics.

TOP (THE OLYMPIC PARTNER PROGRAMME)

The **IOC**'s vehicle for maximizing revenue from **sponsorship**. Established in 1985, and first introduced at the 1988 Calgary Winter Olympics, TOP emerged under the presidency of Juan Antonio Samaranch and with the assistance of ISL, a marketing company established by adidas owner, Horst Dassler. TOP has become so successful in recent years that it is now the Olympic movement's single biggest source of revenue. The key to this success was Dassler's ability to persuade leaders of the (at that time) 150-plus national Olympic committees (NOCs) that significant amounts of additional revenue could be generated by pooling the ownership rights to Olympic symbols (such as the rings). Previously these rights had resided with each individual NOC within the particular territories that they represented.

A maximum of 12 'partners' join TOP for each summer and winter Games. These sponsors receive exclusive marketing rights for their product category (partners are chosen such that they have discreet markets and thus can be seen to work together, rather than in opposition with one another) on a worldwide basis. They can use all the Olympic imagery (e.g. the Olympic rings), exploit hospitality opportunities at the Games, and have preferential access to all Olympic broadcast advertising. Consequently, TOP partners tend to be companies with a global market for their products, such as Coca-Cola, Kodak, Visa, McDonald's, etc. Despite the growth in **ambush marketing** in recent years, the IOC boasts that the success of TOP is indicated by the very high rates of sponsor renewal (i.e. the same companies return Games after Games). Along with the impact of the **media**, TOP has been singled out as one of the key features of the **commercialization** of the Olympic Games in recent years.

threatened closure of a ground or a team's relocation to another or a new stadium can lead these emotional ties to be converted to resistance and activism. Consequently, it was only following the widespread upheaval in the location of English football clubs stemming from the Taylor Report into the **Hillsborough** disaster of 1989 that topophilia became a concept commonly used by social scientists of sport. Significantly, topophilia represents the centrality of **emotion** in sports studies, and the impact of cultural geographers on the area.

Key Reading

Bale, J. (1994) *Landscapes of Modern Sport*. Leicester: University of Leicester Press.

Bale, J. and Moen, O. (eds) (1995) *The Stadium and the City*. Keele: Keele University Press.

Giulianotti, R. (2005) *Sport: A Critical Sociology*. Cambridge: Polity. esp. Ch. 8.

TOPOPHILIA

Literally means the love of, or affection for, a place. Less commonly used in sports studies is the opposite term, topophobia, which describes feelings of fear or **anxiety** related to a particular place.

Topophilia (and topophobia) is a term most closely associated with the work of the American geographer Yi-Fu Tuan, but in the study of sport the concept has been most regularly and thoroughly discussed by British sports geographer, John Bale. In sport, the love of place usually centres on the home **stadium** of a particular team. The supporter does not necessarily need to find the stadium aesthetically pleasing to evoke topophilia, for such emotions are likely to be triggered by memories of past events (e.g. particularly significant games). In this way, it is argued, topophilia is central to the way in which contemporary **fans** construct their identities.

While generally, sports fans are relatively passive in expressing their topophilia, the

TOURNAMENTS

The Tournament was a **medieval sport** form through which the elite knighthood class competed for economic and social status. Tournaments involved two distinct forms of combat – mêlées and jousts – with the former declining, and the latter growing in significance as the period progressed. Changes to tournaments during this period provide an excellent illustration of the broader social transformations in the European Middle Ages (c. 500–c.1500).

Initially, when mêlées dominated, the distinction between the tournament and 'real' war was very slight. Knights and their respective entourages of squires and other servants would fight each other, seeking not only immediate glory through victory, but also financial gain through the imprisonment of the loser who may have subsequently been released on payment of a ransom. Typically held in an open field, mêlées were not regulated in any way. In the early years the number of participants could reach up to 100 but, as the cost of maintaining and equipping a large entourage increased, this number reduced. In contrast to **modern sport** forms, participants could enter the combat as they pleased. For instance, Philip, Count of Flanders, was noted for his tactic of waiting until two combatants had tired each other, and then swooping down on the exhausted participants. Reports indicate that in some instances up to 50 knights could be killed at one event. Developments in war technology and tactics – most notably **archery** – meant that mêlées became increasingly removed from and thus redundant as a way of training for war.

In the course of time, more highly organized and rule-bound jousts replaced these rather spontaneous free-for-all clashes as the central events of a tournament. Tournaments also became increasingly spectacular, display-oriented, and more dominated by pageant. Grander tournaments (e.g. to celebrate a royal birth) were advertised months, possibly years, in advance and were accompanied by days of banqueting, parades through towns, stands and pavilions for spectators, and extensive tented villages. Increasingly, tournaments were staged closer to, or even in, urban areas. Smithfield in London was one such site. Females became central figures in the events, being hostesses for the dances and festivities or presenting the prizes that had replaced ransoms as the knight's form of pecuniary reward. Complex scoring systems were introduced putting greater emphasis on the display of individual skill as opposed to the physical wounding or even death of an opponent. The 'tilt' or central barrier was introduced to prevent the collision of horses but also, probably, to provide a more conspicuous show of skill. This enabled the more explicit glorification of a knight's achievements, who would then be held in higher esteem by both his peers and the female spectators.

While initially, knights had competed alongside their entourages, events became increasingly focused on, and restricted to, the knights themselves. This served to create social distance between themselves and the emerging bourgeois class. When, on occasion, bourgeois groups tried to copy their superiors, they were chastised and even beaten for so doing. Thus knights, while declining in number due to broader social and economic changes, became a group who were increasingly aware and protective of their own status position, which in turn contributed to the development of a new sense of solidarity. Tournaments aided the move towards social exclusivity and provided a forum for the display of individual honour. Military might – both personal and in terms of the size of the entourage a knight could muster – became less important. These processes reflect the growing pacification of societies during this period and the rising importance of wealth and property as opposed to physical force (**civilizing process**).

Key Reading

Baker, W. (1982) 'Medieval people at play', in *Sport in the Western World*. Totowa, NJ: Rowan and Littlefield. pp. 42–55.

Guttmann, A. (1986) *Sports Spectators*. New York: Columbia University Press.

Henricks, T. (1991) 'Sport in the later Middle Ages', in *Disputed Pleasures: Sport and Society in Pre-Industrial England*. Westport, CT: Greenwood Press. pp. 41–68.

Mandell, R. (1984) 'Europe, 500–1750', in *Sport: A Cultural History*. New York: Columbia University Press. pp. 106–31.

TRIANGULATION

The name given by Norman Denzin to the process whereby researchers use a number of complementary research methods in an attempt to produce results of greater **reliability and validity**. The theory behind triangulation is that by looking at a social phenomenon from a number of different vantage points, one can more accurately 'locate' that phenomenon. These vantage points might also include different types of data-set (e.g. **questionnaires interviews**), different theoretical perspectives, the use of different researchers to interpret the same material, or the examination of a social phenomenon on a variety of levels (**macro- and micro-sociology**). Thus, for instance, one might argue that the dynamics of social **class** and sport can best be understood by generating quantitative data from large-scale surveys of sports participation, and largely qualitative data from interviews with people about their interest/ disinterest in certain sports and/or their experiences of inclusion/exclusion. Notably the **football hooliganism** research of the 'Leicester School' relied on triangulation, namely **observation** at matches, ethnographic work in the communities from which many known hooligans came (**ethnography**) and **content analysis** of newspapers to provide the historical context of the 'hooligan problem'. Ironically, however, Denzin later changed his position as a consequence of embracing **postmodernism** and came to argue that, in fact, the local knowledge, feelings and **emotion**s of the research subject should be given priority.

TURNEN

Has its roots in the educational philosophies of **GutsMuths** and **Jahn**, but it was in the 1840s (after GutsMuths had died and when Jahn had entered old age) that the Turnen movement became popular throughout Germany. At this time, the German populace became convinced of the importance of physical **health** within education more broadly, and increasingly committed to democratic ideals such as those Jahn had made as the cornerstone of his practice. The Turnen movement at this time also became increasingly anti-clerical (there was considerable debate over the inclusion of the word 'from' – meaning devout – in the movement's motto (**religion**)) but the emphasis on democratic principles and German **nationalism** meant that Turnen appealed to a cross-section of the middle and working classes. A simple and natural way of life was stressed. Spirits, tobacco and coffee were shunned. Turnens saw themselves as a social elite, not unlike the Japanese Samurai.

In keeping with the nationalistic principles of the movement, the various regional bodies founded the *Deutscher Turnerbund* (German Gymnastic Association) in 1848. However, conflict arose, when the more radical sections of the movement wanted to make an explicit statement about the importance of the principles of liberty, equality and fraternity in the development of a united Germany. However, more conservative sections of the *Turnerbund* feared that such an overtly political stance would invoke the anger of the state and regional princes and thus limit the spread of Turnen. This split resulted in a period of stagnation and legal restriction for the movement during the 1850s.

In the 1860s the Turnen movement was reinvigorated by a renewed French threat. The Prussian military preferred the **Ling** system to Turnen, but was eventually overruled by the state authorities. A key factor in this was the increasing influence of Adolf Spiess who advocated a more systematized, regulated form of gymnastics which appealed to the authorities in a way that Jahn's voluntaristic and democratic principles did not. Though the Turnen movement was never to recover from its period of radicalism in the 1840s, it became increasingly utilized in Prussian schools at this time.

The ultimate demise of Turnen was due to the rather spontaneous uptake of sporting activities in Germany from the 1880s to the First World War. Clubs and governing bodies for a range of English sports and games (such as football, athletics, tennis and rowing) were established during this period, many by English businessmen or students (**formal and informal Empire**). Memberships grew rapidly. The *Deutsche Turnershaft* alone grew from 170,000 members in 1880, to 1.25 million in 1914. Sports were decried as un-German, overly dominated by record-keeping and measurement (*From Ritual to Record*) and morally weak (unlike Turnen, having no higher moral purpose such as German nationalism). But Turnen had become a largely indoor, formal and restrictive activity under the philosophy of Spiess, with much of Jahn's emphasis on games, rambling and outdoor activities being lost. Sports and games provided participants with greater freedom and, with the development of the Olympic movement in 1894, greater international resonance. Turnen came to be seen as a narrowly patriotic movement, subsequently split by anti-Semitic debates. In contrast, the German Athletic Sports Authority, under the leadership of Carl Diem, embraced the international sporting community and became ascendant.

Key Reading

McIntosh, P.C., Dixon, J.G., Munrow, A.D. and Willetts, R.F. (1981) *Landmarks in the History of Physical Education,* 3rd edn. London: Routledge and Kegan Paul.

U

UNCERTAINTY OF OUTCOME HYPOTHESIS

(competitive balance)

URBANIZATION

(city, the)

US COLLEGE SPORTS

(athletic scholarships)

UTILITY MAXIMIZATION

The idea of utility maximization was initially applied to English professional football by the Political and Economic Planning research group in 1966, and subsequently adopted by Peter Sloane in 1971. In sharp contrast to the explicit goal (and sometimes aggressive pursuit of) profit maximization in American team sports and capitalist corporations more generally, utility maximization was a term adopted by economists to explain the objectives of (especially) football club owners in England. Prior to the 1990s the majority of football clubs operated at a loss and only survived as economic entities due to directors' donations, supporter club activities, and transfer fee revenues. Clearly, it was argued, the objective of an English professional football club was not to maximize profit, but to achieve playing success while remaining solvent. The existence of a football club was regarded as a utility for the local community.

These economists were perhaps searching for an economically rational explanation for economically irrational behaviour. Profit, of course, is linked to playing success and it is not clear that football club directors eschewed profit maximization for utility maximization, merely that they were involved in what was, at the time, a fundamentally unprofitable activity. Directors were often (and still are) fanatical supporters who see sports patronage as a hobby, and regard the prestige, privilege, fame and reflected glory of being involved with a leading sports team as their reward. Such rewards, however, are difficult to measure in economic or quantifiable terms. While some English elite professional sports teams are now profitable (i.e. because of increased income from **sponsorship**, merchandising and **broadcasting rights**), it remains the case that often we can only explain aspects of decision making in English professional team sports with reference to personal aggrandizement and broader social benefits.

Key Reading

Gratton, C. and Taylor, P. (2000) *Economics of Sport and Recreation*. London: E. & F.N. Spon.

Sloane, P.J. (1971) 'The economics of professional football: the football club as a utility maximiser', *Scottish Journal of Political Economy*, 18: 121–46.

V

VALIDITY

(reliability and validity)

VERTICAL INTEGRATION

Entails the merger of companies acting at different stages of the production, or value, chain. Vertical integration may be desired for reasons of: (1) organizational efficiency through greater cost-effectiveness; (2) technical efficiency; and (3) to increase market power.

In sport, vertical integration is most clearly evident in the attempts of **media** companies to own or take part ownership of professional sports teams. In 2000, 29 teams in the North American major leagues were partially or wholly owned by media groups, as were 10 teams in the English FA Premiership and a number of others across Europe (Gerrard, 2004). Such vertical integration profits media companies that bid for **broadcasting rights** through the 'toehold effect', as part of any payment will ultimately be returned to the bidder. This enables a higher bid to be made (making success more likely) but also forces competitors (who will be aware of this) to increase their bid (meaning that even if the vertically integrated company loses, their net income is increased).

However, rather than these economic gains, a more important driver of vertical integration in sport seems to be the importance of increasing market power through securing access to broadcasting rights. To a company such as satellite broadcaster BSkyB, the ownership of broadcasting rights is vital to their economic survival. Ownership of teams provides security of access. Interestingly, however, perhaps the most famous case of (attempted) vertical integration – that is BSkyB's attempted takeover of Manchester United in 1999 – was not rejected by the Monopolies and Mergers Commission because of the 'toehold' effect, but because it was feared that the merger would increase United's playing dominance and thus reduce **competitive balance** within the league. In this regard, many sports governing bodies have rules that limit the extent of club ownership by individuals and companies. The English FA, for instance, forbids the ownership of more than 10 per cent of the shares in more than one football club, and though legally challenged in 1999, UEFA prohibits clubs owned (defined as the possession of 51 per cent of shares) by the same company from competing in the same competition (e.g. the Champions League).

Key Reading

Gerrard, B. (2004) 'Media ownership of teams: the latest stage in the commercialisation of team sports', in T. Slack (ed.), *The Commercialisation of Sport*. London: Routledge. pp. 247–66.

Sandy, R., Sloane, P.J. and Rosentraub, M. (2004) *The Economics of Sport: An International Perspective*. Basingstoke. Palgrave Macmillan.

VIOLENCE

Widely perceived to be a negative phenomenon, a social problem that should be addressed. Commonly, violence is defined in relatively narrow terms. Smith (1983: 7), for instance, defines violence as 'physically assaultive behaviour that is designed to, and does, injure another person or persons physically'. Sports-related violence, however, is a multifaceted phenomenon. The key distinction to be made is between *crowd violence* and *player violence*. However, we should also consider the following issues: (1) the relationship between violence perpetrated within and outside sporting arenas (e.g. male athletes' involvement in sexual violence towards women); (2) different degrees of intention (how can we tell if the tackler in rugby intends to injure an opponent or merely get the ball?); and (3) different degrees of legitimacy (punching is an inherent feature of boxing, tolerated in ice hockey, and prohibited in baseball). As such examples show, the distinctions between violence and **aggression**, and violence and **deviance**, are far from clear-cut. In order to properly understand violence and sport, therefore, we need to look at violence as a social rather than a psychological phenomenon, and as something that varies both historically and cross-culturally (Young, 2000).

Coakley (2006) argues that *crowd violence* is related to three factors: (1) the action of, and the tensions arising from, the event itself; (2) crowd dynamics such as **alcohol** consumption, crowd demographics, and the location, importance and historical background to the event; and (3) the broader social, economic and political context in which the event takes place (e.g. ethnic tensions (**race**), the assertion of community identity, the socially constructed need for **catharsis**).

However, the vast majority of research on sport and violence has focused specifically on **football hooliganism**. This research has shown that crowd violence is not a new phenomenon and that various forms exist in a number of different cultures. The dominance of this research area has, however, tended to obscure the fact that sports crowd disorder is not limited to football but evident at sports as diverse as cricket, horse-racing and American football. While various explanations have been proposed for the existence of football hooliganism, and while there is little agreement between researchers about its root causes, this body of work consistently stresses the importance of Coakley's third (and to a lesser degree second) set of factors in explaining sports crowd violence.

Classically, researchers of *player violence* cite Smith's fourfold typology (1983). Accordingly, player violence can be categorized as: (1) *brutal body contact*, including tackles and collisions inherent to many 'contact' sports; (2) *borderline violence*, including the use of bouncers in cricket, shirt pulling in football, 'raking' in rugby union, actions which lie outside the rules of the sport, but which are largely tolerated as part of the game; (3) *quasi-criminal violence*, including acts which lie outside the rules of the sport, the law of the land, and the norms of participants, for example tackles that result in serious injuries; and (4) *criminal violence*, involving either clearly premeditated and/or extreme forms of violence including post-match assaults.

While traditionally, sports organizations have sought to 'deal' with violent incidents within the game itself (e.g. through fines and suspensions), in recent years legal intervention to regulate sports violence has become more common. Young's analysis of these legal cases (1993) indicates that the most common defence against such charges tends to rely on the 'voluntary assumption of risk'; i.e. that participants effectively consent to be exposed to relatively high levels of violence simply through their participation in the sport.

Explanations for the occurrence of player violence focus on four key themes:

1 Some suggest that **commercialization** in sport, which has led to increased rewards to be associated with winning, has increased the propensity of participants to use violence. Moreover, the media promote and glamorize violence to increase spectator interest. The central problem with this

explanation, however, is that player violence is common in grassroots sports and historical evidence indicates that player violence was probably more common prior to the twentieth century and the most dramatic phase of the commercialization of sport (**ancient Olympic Games**).

2   Scholars such as Messner have pointed to the relationship between sports violence and the construction of hegemonic **masculinity**. Messner (1990) notes that the **socialization** experiences of boys involve learning that 'real' men both can personally tolerate, and are able to inflict, pain and violence.

3   Researchers point to violence as a central characteristic of sports **subcultures**. Sport is an occupation in which careers are short and often terminated by injury (**retirement**). Through his work on the **sport ethic** and **positive deviance**, Coakley (2006) argues that sports participation entails the normalization of **risk** and broad acceptance of violence and **pain and injury**. Players are told to play 'until the bone sticks through the meat', and coaches berate players who do not conform as 'sissies', i.e. as not masculine.

4   Acting either in conjunction with or separate from the above factors, researchers have pointed to the link between violence and the **media**. In much the same way that studies of football hooliganism have examined the amplification and de-amplification of the 'problem' of hooliganism in the press (**moral panics**), researchers have looked at the potential 'spill-over' effect whereby the portrayal of player violence in the media leads to higher levels of violence in grassroots sport and in society more generally (**social learning theory**). However, a cause–effect relationship has been difficult to conclusively prove, and it is probably more adequate to view the audience for violence as heterogeneous, structured by factors such as **class**, **gender** and **race**. Such a heterogeneous audience is likely to perceive and respond to violence in markedly different ways.

The most sustained focus on violence in sport has come from the perspective of **figurational sociology** (indeed, part of the critique of figurational sociology is that it over emphasizes the role of violence). Violence is inherent to Elias's study of the **civilizing process** and to his work on the **quest for excitement**. This body of work suggests that contrary to contemporary perceptions, violence has largely decreased in Western societies in the last 500 years. This is evident in the rule structures and conventions governing sports as diverse as boxing, rugby and cricket. Moreover, rather than perceiving violence as a 'negative' thing, figurational sociologists argue that the very appeal of sport in contemporary societies (**sport, social significance of**) rests on the fact that it is characterized by relatively high degrees of violence.

Key Reading

Coakley, J.J. (2006) *Sport in Society: Issues and Controversies*, 9th edn. Boston: McGraw-Hill. esp. Ch. 6.

Messner, M.A. (1990) 'When bodies are weapons. Masculinity and violence in sport', *International Review for the Sociology of Sport*, 25 (3): 203–14.

Smith, M. (1983) *Violence and Sport*. Toronto: Butterworths.

Young, K. (1993) 'Violence, risk, and liability in male sports culture', *Sociology of Sport Journal*, 10 (4): 373–96.

Young, K. (2000) 'Sport and violence', in J. Coakley and E. Dunning (eds), *Handbook of Sports Studies*. London: Sage. pp. 382–407.

VISUALIZATION

(**imagery**)

W

WADA (WORLD ANTI-DOPING AGENCY)

Formally established on 10 November 1999 with the mission 'to promote, coordinate, and monitor at the international level the fight against doping in sport in all its forms'. Initially located in Lausanne (Switzerland), though now with a permanent home in Montreal (Canada), **IOC** Vice-President Richard Pound became WADA's first president chairing an 'executive board' made up of five members of the Olympic movement and five representatives of public authorities, and a full 'board' of 30 members drawn from various sports organizations (such as the IOC, NOCs, etc.) and public bodies (such as the European Union and the Council of Europe).

The impetus for the establishment of WADA was the doping scandal that occurred during the 1998 Tour de France (see Waddington, 2000). Partly in response to the French government's intervention into issues previously considered to be the domain of sports governing bodies, the IOC convened a World Anti-Doping Conference in Lausanne in February 1999. Here, it became clear that sport's governing bodies were suspicious of governments which, they perceived, sought to exploit sport for **propaganda** purposes. Conversely, governments clearly lacked confidence in the ability or willingness of sport's governing bodies to tackle doping issues. There was, however, a consensus over the need for a body with global representation and coverage that would strengthen the fight against doping and increase public confidence

in doping control measures prior to the 2000 Sydney Olympic Games.

It was decided that, 'The Agency's principle task will be to co-ordinate a comprehensive anti-doping program at international level, develop common, effective, minimum standards for doping control ... commission unannounced out-of-competition controls ... (and) promote the harmonization of anti-doping policies and procedures.' WADA was also to be responsible for the annual publication of a list of prohibited substances, the accreditation of testing laboratories, and the development of educational material and programmes. The main area of debate focused on the independence of WADA from the IOC. Consequently, WADA's Executive Committee and Board have significant public body representation, and the funding of WADA is shared equally between governments and the IOC.

All but two International Sports Federations within the Olympic movement initially signed up to the WADA anti-doping code; cycling's Union Cycliste International (UCI) and **FIFA**. Through threat of exclusion from the Olympic Games, these bodies have now largely fallen into line (though FIFA in particular has negotiated some significant exemptions for footballers). WADA immediately increased the number of out-of-competition tests by 10 per cent, and the creation of the 'Office of Independent Observer' was deemed a success in improving the transparency and accountability of drug testing at the Sydney Olympic Games.

WADA sees the harmonization of anti-doping policies as a central priority for the future (though Waddington argues that anti-doping policies should be sensitive to the particular sporting context in which they are to be applied). Though WADA represents a significant advance in the fight against doping in sport, a number of challenges to further progress remain: (1) the mutual suspicion between the IOC, sport's governing bodies and governments; (2) the fragmentation of sports (e.g. commercial and non-commercial, Olympic and non-Olympic); (3) the establishment of criteria for the acceptable level of harmonization; and (4) the monitoring of compliance.

Key Reading

Houlihan, B. (2002) *Dying to Win: Doping in Sport and the Development of Anti-doping Policy*, 2nd edn. Strasbourg: Council of Europe Publishing.

Waddington, I. (2000) *Sport, Health and Drugs: A Critical Sociological Perspective*. London: E. & F.N. Spon. esp. Ch. 9.

http://www.wada-ama.org/ Home page of the World Anti-Doping Agency

WEBB ELLIS MYTH

In the grounds of Rugby School there is a commemorative stone in honour of William Webb Ellis who, it is alleged, 'with a fine disregard for the rules of football as played in his time, first took the ball in his arms and ran with it, thus originating the distinctive feature of the rugby game, AD 1823'. Dunning and Sheard, in **Barbarians, Gentlemen and Players** (2005) were the first to question the validity of this story, but it is now commonly accepted that this version of the creation of the game is a myth (see also baseball's **Doubleday myth**).

Dunning and Sheard note that the Webb Ellis myth was first proposed by Matthew Bloxam in the Rugby School magazine, *Meteor*, in 1880. That the report appeared 57 years after the event was supposed to have occurred, and that Bloxam had left the school prior to 1823 and so had not personally witnessed the

event casts serious doubt on the reliability of his testimony. Moreover, Webb Ellis was an individual of relatively low status, with little influence within the school and thus it is unlikely that, acting alone, he would have been able to invoke such a landmark change in the game. Most conclusively, however, there is no evidence, and indeed little reason to believe, that handling would have been either prohibited by custom, or enforced in any way, in 1823 or beforehand (**folk games**). The prohibition on the use of hands in football, Dunning and Sheard argue, arises from the **public school status rivalry** between Rugby and Eton in the 1840s.

Bloxam's Webb Ellis story was resurrected in a report of the Old Rugbeian Society in 1895, the year in which **commercialization** and professionalization processes led to a split between the union and league forms of the game. Dunning and Sheard argue that the search for the origins of the game stemmed from the threat that the northern professional game posed to the Rugbeian's dominance of the game. The Webb Ellis story (correctly) asserts Rugby School's proprietorship over the game's origins, and thus provides legitimacy to their claims to have authority over the administration of the game (**invented traditions**).

Finally, Dunning and Sheard note that reductionist origin myths such as this are common in contemporary societies in which common modes of thinking stress the power of the individual relative to social structures (**agency and structure**). Contrary to such 'Great Man' theories of history, they argue, social developments are more adequately understood in terms of the complex interweaving of many interdependent people, where unintended consequences are as prevalent as intended consequences (**figurational sociology**).

Key Reading

Dunning, E. and Sheard, K. (2005) *Barbarians, Gentlemen and Players: A Sociological Study of the Development of Rugby Football*, 2nd edn. London: Routledge.

Dunning, E., Malcolm, D. and Waddington, I. (2004) 'Conclusion: figurational sociology and the development of modern sport', in E. Dunning, D. Malcolm and I. Waddington (eds), *Sport Histories: Figurational Studies of the Development of Modern Sports*. London: Routledge. pp. 191–206.

WOODS, TIGER (1976–)

Eldrick 'Tiger' Woods rose to fame as a junior amateur golfer in the early 1990s, before turning professional in 1997 at the age of 21. He reached number 1 in the Official World Golf Rankings within 42 weeks of becoming a professional and in 2000 became the first golfer to simultaneously hold all four 'majors'. Commercially, Woods signed a deal with **Nike** in 1996 worth an estimated $40 million over five years (Nike claimed that its golf shoe sales doubled in that year) and is thought to have earned $65 million in 2000 alone (a year in which one individual reportedly paid £1.1 million to play a single round of golf with him).

Publicly, there has been considerable debate about the 'Tiger Woods effect'. Interest in the sport, ticket sales for events, and the viewing figures for golf events (even those in which Woods does not participate), have risen dramatically since his arrival, leading some to claim that Woods has had a unique transformative effect on the sport. Part of this democratizing of golf has involved Woods and his father (who died in the spring of 2006) running golf clinics for inner city children and, latterly, the establishment of a Tiger Woods Foundation to introduce golf to children who might not otherwise have the chance to play the game.

However, underpinning this democratization of the game, and of perhaps greater interest to sociologists of sport, has been the relationship between Woods and **race** relations **discourse** in America. Famously describing his multi-ethnicity as Cablinasian on the Oprah Winfrey show in 1997 (Ca,

Caucasian; bl, black; in, Indian; Asian – Cablinasian), Woods not only challenged the tradition of racism and virtual **apartheid**-like structure of American golf, but through his marketing by Nike, did so in a highly confrontational manner. His initial, 'Hello World' campaign with Nike linked the colour of his skin to limited playing opportunities in America. Nike were accused of playing a crude 'race card' but, nevertheless, Woods was established as incontrovertibly African-American, and highlighted the issue of race in American society as a whole. However, critics saw Woods as also representing something of the regression in race relations to the extent that he became seen as an exemplification of the American dream. This, authors noted, obscured the more common African-American experience of poverty and social exclusion (**social inclusion**). Woods, however, subsequently shied away from race issues, failing to support the campaigns of the National Association for the Advancement of Black People and was accused of having his potentially progressive force being 'effectively neutered' by corporate capital (Cole and Andrews, 2001).

Key Reading

Cole, C. and Andrews, D.L. (2001) 'America's new son: Tiger Woods and America's multi-culturalism', in D.L. Andrews and S.J. Jackson (eds), *Sport Stars: The Cultural Politics of Sporting Celebrity*. London: Routledge. pp. 70–86.

Smart, B. (2005) *The Sports Star: Modern Sport and the Cultural Economy of Sporting Celebrity*. London: Sage.

WORLD SYSTEM THEORY

Immanuel Wallerstein's world system theory is based on the division of the world capitalist economy into four sectors: the core (northwest Europe, North America, Japan); the semi-periphery (southern Europe and the Mediterranean region); the periphery (Eastern

Europe, north Africa, parts of Asia); and the external area (most of Africa, parts of Asia, the Indian subcontinent). A country's position within this world system is determined by a combination of colonial history and economic power (**imperialism**). The power of the core countries is based on their manufacturing and agricultural industries, their proletarianized labour forces, and their centralized governmental power structures. Core countries seize control of multinational organizations (e.g. the United Nations, but also **FIFA** and the **IOC**) and structure world trade and international relations (and sport) in their own interests. Non-core countries are enmeshed in a set of economic relations that enrich the core sector while reproducing the non-core's dependency on the powerful industrial nations. This, Wallerstein viewed, as the logic of the capitalist world economy. The central criticism of this model has been its tendency towards economic reductionism (**Marxism**).

World system theory has been used in the study of sport in three main ways. Predominantly Wallerstein's work has been used to understand **sport labour migration** (Magee and Sugden, 2002), and the idea that the world system entails an international division of labour, with core countries using their economic power to exploit the human resources of the periphery. George Sage (1994) has also used world system theory in his analysis of the global sporting goods industry, particularly with regard to the relocation strategies of corporations such as **Nike**, enabling them to exploit cheaper labour made possible through restricted workers' rights

legislation. Finally, Darby has tried to apply Wallerstein's ideas to a world system of football. His evidence suggests that while playing strength is partly determined by economic power (European nations dominate the top rankings for international football), the pattern is broken by the playing success of relatively economically weak nations such as Brazil and Nigeria, and the lack of playing success of Japan and the US. It is, however, apparent that FIFA's core European members have attempted to monopolize power and resources in the game by restricting the influence of periphery nations in decision-making structures.

Key Reading

Darby, P. (2000) 'Africa's place in FIFA's global order: a theoretical frame', *Soccer and Society*, 1 (2): 36–61.

Magee, J. and Sugden, J. (2002) '"The world at their feet": professional football and international labour migration', *Journal of Sport and Social Issues*, 26 (4): 421–37.

Sage, G. (1994) 'De-industrialization and the American sporting goods industry', in R.C. Wilcox (ed.), *Sport in the Global Village*. Morganstown, WV: Fitness Information Technology Inc. pp. 38–51.

WORLD WIDE WEB

(Internet, the)

X

X-GAMES

(lifestyle sports)

YOUTH SPORTS PARTICIPATION

There are two commonplace assumptions regarding sports participation amongst the young: (1) that participation rates are a 'problem'; and (2) that sport and physical activity are becoming less and less popular in direct proportion to the increasing popularity of sedentary leisure activities, such as TV and computer games. The participation of young people in sport is considered an important basis for **lifelong participation** and associated **health** benefits.

Notwithstanding the fact that the measures in studies of sports participation may be considered somewhat conservative and provide little evidence about the intensity and quality of the activity, the data reveal some relatively clear patterns. First and foremost among these patterns is the trend towards *increased* participation among young people and adults in the UK and, for that matter, a number of Western European countries (e.g. Belgium, Estonia, Finland, Germany, the Netherlands and Norway). While there remains a significant minority of young people doing relatively little or absolutely nothing in participatory terms, more young people in the UK are doing more sport and physical recreation than ever before. A Sport England report published in 2003 found that 80 per cent of secondary age youngsters spent more than one hour a week on sport and exercise outside PE lessons and 40 per cent spent as much as, or more than, five hours per week (Sport England, 2003).

Alongside an increase in levels of participation, there has been a marked decline in the drop-out rate during late adolescence and young people are much more likely to continue participating in sport and physical activities after completing their full-time education. In addition to the general increase in participation, young people in particular are nowadays involved in a broader and more diverse range of sports and physical activities. A feature of this trend has been a shift towards so-called 'lifestyle activities', characterized as being non- (or at least less-) competitive, more recreational, individual or small group activities (which can, in effect, be undertaken in the ways that people want, with whom they want and when they want), and often with a health and fitness orientation. Despite the fact that only a small minority play competitive sports in their adult life, the trends reflect a supplementation rather than a wholesale rejection of sport and physical activity per se. Increasingly, popular sports and physical activities among young people over recent decades include conventional sports (such as basketball, girls' football and golf), recreational forms of conventional sporting forms (for example, swimming, 5-a-side football) and 'lifestyle' activities (cycling, dance, **aerobics**, watersports and skateboarding, etc.; see also **lifestyle sports**).

The growth in youth sports participation in the UK in particular has been explained with reference to a combination of social processes: a broadening of PE curricula from the 1970s onwards alongside a substantial growth in sport and recreation centres. These have tended to coincide with developments in youth cultures towards more individualized youth lifestyles – in which young people prefer to do what they want with whom they want at times of their own choosing and in which **gender**, **class** and **race**/ethnic differences have become blurred but by no means eradicated (**postmodernism**).

Key Reading

Coalter, F. (1999) 'Sport and recreation in the United Kingdom: go with the flow or buck the trends?', *Managing Leisure*, 4: 24–39.

Roberts, K. (1997). 'Same activities, different meanings: British youth cultures in the 1990s', *Leisure Studies*, 16 (1): 1–15.

Roberts, K. and Brodie, D. (1992) *Inner-City Sport: Who Plays and What Are the Benefits?* Culemborg: Giordano Bruno.

Sport England (2003) *Young People and Sport in England. Trends in Participation 1994–2002.* London: Sport England.

Ken Green

Name Index

Subject Index

913008